D0571591

WORKS OF

HENRY DAVID THOREAU

Henry D. Thoreau.

WORKS OF
HENRY DAVID THOREAU

ILLUSTRATED

EDITED BY
LILY OWENS

AVENEL BOOKS
NEW YORK

Originally published in 1906 as *The Writings of Henry David Thoreau*. Included in this anthology are: *Volume II: Walden*, and selections from *Volume III: The Maine Woods; Volume IV: Cape Cod and Miscellanies;* and *Volume V: Excursions and Poems.*

This edition is published by Avenel Books, distributed by Crown Publishers, Inc.

b c d e f g h

1981 EDITION

Manufactured in the United States of America

Library of Congress Cataloging in Publication Data

Thoreau, Henry David, 1817-1862.
  Works of Henry David Thoreau.

  Selections from The writings of Henry David Thoreau originally published: Boston: Houghton Mifflin, 1906. 20 v.
  Consists of: Walden, selections from The Maine Woods, Cape Cod and Miscellanies, and Excursions and Poems.
  I. Owens, Lily. II. Title.
PS3042.094   818'.309   81-4652
ISBN 0-517-33630-8   AACR2

CONTENTS

INTRODUCTION

Time is but the stream I go a-fishing in. I drink at it;
but while I drink I see the sandy bottom and detect
how shallow it is. Its thin current slides away, but
eternity remains. I would drink deeper; fish in the
sky, whose bottom is pebbly with stars.

THUS speaks Thoreau in *Walden*, his most famous
work. The strength of idea and simplicity of expression reveal the man who has come, finally, to be
regarded as one of America's greatest writers. Thoreau was that unique individual, a man who lived his
ideals. He synthesized the strands of his life into a
harmonious whole, offering us a vision of life as it
could be lived: simply, freely, and well.

And yet, Thoreau was not wholly a moralist, but a
versatile and poetic writer. His nature essays are
among the most lyrical ever written. His light-
hearted travel books are entertaining and informa-
tive views of nineteenth century New England. The
humor, subtle or crackling, which threads through
all his writing, achieves a salty sophistication in
"The Wellfleet Oysterman" chapter of *Cape Cod*.
Impassioned political essays reveal his keen perception of social complexities.

Walden best incorporates his many talents. It is a
record of his experiment in living the simple life, a
marking of the days as they passed, and the journal
of a naturalist; a history of house-raising and gardening, and a guide to other would-be adventurers;

INTRODUCTION

an observation of wilderness and human relations; a summation of his life's philosophy and a critique of society.

Thoreau has influenced major political figures and movements from all hues of the political spectrum; Mahatma Gandhi, American presidents, early British labor partisans, the civil rights and freedom movements of the sixties, and the antinuclear movement have all drawn inspiration from his works. And yet, Thoreau was not a naturally political man. He was essentially an individualist and moralist. What he wanted most from government (and from most people) was to be left alone. Thus, few can embrace his philosophy whole. Slavery alone roused Thoreau to activism. The brutal disregard of human rights, worsened by a newly passed fugitive slave law, led him to join the abolitionists.

Included in this edition are "Civil Disobedience" and "Life Without Principle," Thoreau's renowned political essays; the complete *Walden*; selected chapters from the travel books, *Cape Cod* and *Maine Woods*; and four of his best-loved nature essays.

This volume is reprinted from the first complete edition of Thoreau's works, published in 1906. Illustrating the text are thirty of the photographs which graced the 1906 edition. Commissioned by Thoreau's publishers, photographer Herbert Wendell Gleason painstakingly followed Thoreau's path through Massachusetts and Maine, capturing the flavor as well as the fact of Thoreau's environment. An accomplished and adventuresome photographer,

INTRODUCTION

it is only appropriate that Gleason's strong, austere photographs should complement Thoreau's words.

Thoreau's writings have never been more timely than they are today. One hundred years ago, he showed us the debilitating effects of unbridled growth and complexity. He praised the life of simple pleasures, nonconformity, and contemplation, and unveiled to us the beauty and satisfactions of nature. Today, when society has grown only more confusingly complex and threatens to overwhelm the individual, the small community, and the natural world, we still have much to learn from Thoreau. A thorough thinker, he offers solutions as well as critiques, inspiration as well as observation.

> We hug the earth—how rarely we mount! Methinks we might elevate ourselves a little more. We might climb a tree, at least.

LILY OWENS

WORKS OF

HENRY DAVID THOREAU

WALDEN

Walden Pond, from site of Thoreau's hut

I

ECONOMY

W HEN I wrote the following pages, or rather the bulk of them, I lived alone, in the woods, a mile from any neighbor, in a house which I had built myself, on the shore of Walden Pond, in Concord, Massachusetts, and earned my living by the labor of my hands only. I lived there two years and two months. At present I am a sojourner in civilized life again.

I should not obtrude my affairs so much on the notice of my readers if very particular inquiries had not been made by my townsmen concerning my mode of life, which some would call impertinent, though they do not appear to me at all impertinent, but, considering the circumstances, very natural and pertinent. Some have asked what I got to eat; if I did not feel lonesome; if I was not afraid; and the like. Others have been curious to learn what portion of my income I devoted to charitable purposes; and some, who have large families, how many poor children I maintained. I will therefore ask those of my readers who feel no particular interest in me to pardon me if I undertake to answer some of these questions in this book. In most books, the *I*, or first person, is omitted; in this it will be retained; that, in respect to egotism, is the main difference. We commonly do not remember that it is, after all, always the first person that is speaking. I should not talk so much about myself if there were anybody else whom I knew as well. Unfortunately, I am confined to this theme by the narrowness of my experience. Moreover, I, on my side, require of every writer, first or last, a simple and sincere account of his own life, and not merely what he has heard of other men's lives; some such account as he would send to his kindred from a distant land; for if he has lived sincerely, it must have been in a distant land to me. Perhaps these pages are more particularly addressed to poor students. As for the rest of my readers, they will accept such portions as apply to them. I trust that none will stretch the seams in putting on the coat, for it may do good service to him whom it fits.

I would fain say something, not so much concerning the Chinese and Sandwich Islanders as you who read these pages, who are said to live in New England; something about your condition, especially your outward condition or circumstances in this world, in this town, what it is, whether it is necessary that it be as bad as it is, whether it cannot be improved as well as not. I have travelled a good deal in Concord; and everywhere, in shops, and offices, and fields, the inhabitants have appeared to me to be doing penance in a thousand remarkable ways. What I have heard of Bramins sitting exposed to four fires and looking in the face of the sun; or hanging suspended, with their heads downward, over flames; or looking at the heavens over their shoulders "until it becomes impossible for them to resume their natural position, while from the twist of the neck nothing but liquids can pass into the stomach;" or dwelling,

chained for life, at the foot of a tree; or measuring with
their bodies, like caterpillars, the breadth of vast empires; or standing on one leg on the tops of pillars, —
even these forms of conscious penance are hardly more
incredible and astonishing than the scenes which I daily
witness. The twelve labors of Hercules were trifling in
comparison with those which my neighbors have undertaken; for they were only twelve, and had an end; but
I could never see that these men slew or captured any
monster or finished any labor. They have no friend
Iolaus to burn with a hot iron the root of the hydra's
head, but as soon as one head is crushed, two spring
up.

I see young men, my townsmen, whose misfortune it
is to have inherited farms, houses, barns, cattle, and
farming tools; for these are more easily acquired than
got rid of. Better if they had been born in the open pasture and suckled by a wolf, that they might have seen
with clearer eyes what field they were called to labor in.
Who made them serfs of the soil? Why should they eat
their sixty acres, when man is condemned to eat only his
peck of dirt? Why should they begin digging their graves
as soon as they are born? They have got to live a man's
life, pushing all these things before them, and get on as
well as they can. How many a poor immortal soul have
I met well-nigh crushed and smothered under its load,
creeping down the road of life, pushing before it a barn
seventy-five feet by forty, its Augean stables never
cleansed, and one hundred acres of land, tillage, mowing, pasture, and wood-lot! The portionless, who struggle with no such unnecessary inherited encumbrances,

find it labor enough to subdue and cultivate a few cubic feet of flesh.

But men labor under a mistake. The better part of the man is soon plowed into the soil for compost. By a seeming fate, commonly called necessity, they are employed, as it says in an old book, laying up treasures which moth and rust will corrupt and thieves break through and steal. It is a fool's life, as they will find when they get to the end of it, if not before. It is said that Deucalion and Pyrrha created men by throwing stones over their heads behind them: —

> Inde genus durum sumus, experiensque laborum,
> Et documenta damus quâ simus origine nati.

Or, as Raleigh rhymes it in his sonorous way, —

> "From thence our kind hard-hearted is, enduring pain and care,
> Approving that our bodies of a stony nature are."

So much for a blind obedience to a blundering oracle, throwing the stones over their heads behind them, and not seeing where they fell.

Most men, even in this comparatively free country, through mere ignorance and mistake, are so occupied with the factitious cares and superfluously coarse labors of life that its finer fruits cannot be plucked by them. Their fingers, from excessive toil, are too clumsy and tremble too much for that. Actually, the laboring man has not leisure for a true integrity day by day; he cannot afford to sustain the manliest relations to men; his labor would be depreciated in the market. He has no time to be anything but a machine. How can he remember well his ignorance — which his growth requires —

who has so often to use his knowledge? We should feed
and clothe him gratuitously sometimes, and recruit him
with our cordials, before we judge of him. The finest
qualities of our nature, like the bloom on fruits, can be
preserved only by the most delicate handling. Yet we do
not treat ourselves nor one another thus tenderly.

Some of you, we all know, are poor, find it hard to
live, are sometimes, as it were, gasping for breath. I
have no doubt that some of you who read this book are
unable to pay for all the dinners which you have actually
eaten, or for the coats and shoes which are fast wearing
or are already worn out, and have come to this page to
spend borrowed or stolen time, robbing your creditors
of an hour. It is very evident what mean and sneaking
lives many of you live, for my sight has been whetted by
experience; always on the limits, trying to get into business and trying to get out of debt, a very ancient slough,
called by the Latins *aes alienum*, another's brass, for
some of their coins were made of brass; still living, and
dying, and buried by this other's brass; always promising to pay, promising to pay, to-morrow, and dying
to-day, insolvent; seeking to curry favor, to get custom,
by how many modes, only not state-prison offences;
lying, flattering, voting, contracting yourselves into a
nutshell of civility, or dilating into an atmosphere of
thin and vaporous generosity, that you may persuade
your neighbor to let you make his shoes, or his hat, or
his coat, or his carriage, or import his groceries for
him; making yourselves sick, that you may lay up
something against a sick day, something to be tucked
away in an old chest, or in a stocking behind the plas-

tering, or, more safely, in the brick bank; no matter where, no matter how much or how little.

I sometimes wonder that we can be so frivolous, I may almost say, as to attend to the gross but somewhat foreign form of servitude called Negro Slavery, there are so many keen and subtle masters that enslave both North and South. It is hard to have a Southern overseer; it is worse to have a Northern one; but worst of all when you are the slave-driver of yourself. Talk of a divinity in man! Look at the teamster on the highway, wending to market by day or night; does any divinity stir within him? His highest duty to fodder and water his horses! What is his destiny to him compared with the shipping interests? Does not he drive for Squire Make-a-stir? How godlike, how immortal, is he? See how he cowers and sneaks, how vaguely all the day he fears, not being immortal nor divine, but the slave and prisoner of his own opinion of himself, a fame won by his own deeds. Public opinion is a weak tyrant compared with our own private opinion. What a man thinks of himself, that it is which determines, or rather indicates, his fate. Self-emancipation even in the West Indian provinces of the fancy and imagination, — what Wilberforce is there to bring that about? Think, also, of the ladies of the land weaving toilet cushions against the last day, not to betray too green an interest in their fates! As if you could kill time without injuring eternity.

The mass of men lead lives of quiet desperation. What is called resignation is confirmed desperation. From the desperate city you go into the desperate country, and have to console yourself with the bravery of minks and muskrats. A stereotyped but unconscious despair is concealed even under what are called the games and amusements of mankind. There is no play in them, for this comes after work. But it is a characteristic of wisdom not to do desperate things.

When we consider what, to use the words of the catechism, is the chief end of man, and what are the true necessaries and means of life, it appears as if men had deliberately chosen the common mode of living because they preferred it to any other. Yet they honestly think there is no choice left. But alert and healthy natures remember that the sun rose clear. It is never too late to give up our prejudices. No way of thinking or doing, however ancient, can be trusted without proof. What everybody echoes or in silence passes by as true to-day may turn out to be falsehood to-morrow, mere smoke of opinion, which some had trusted for a cloud that would sprinkle fertilizing rain on their fields. What old people say you cannot do, you try and find that you can. Old deeds for old people, and new deeds for new. Old people did not know enough once, perchance, to fetch fresh fuel to keep the fire a-going; new people put a little dry wood under a pot, and are whirled round the globe with the speed of birds, in a way to kill old people, as the phrase is. Age is no better, hardly so well, qualified for an instructor as youth, for it has not profited so much as it has lost. One may almost doubt if the wisest man has learned anything of absolute value by living. Practically, the old have no very important advice to give the young, their own experience has been so partial, and their lives have been such miserable failures, for private reasons, as they must believe; and it may be that they have some faith left which belies that experience, and they are only less young than they were. I have lived some thirty years on this planet, and I have yet to hear the first syllable of valuable or even earnest advice from my seniors. They have told me nothing, and probably cannot tell me anything to the purpose. Here is life, an experiment to a great extent untried by me; but it does not avail me that they have tried it. If I have any experience which I think valuable, I am sure to reflect that this my Mentors said nothing about.

One farmer says to me, "You cannot live on vegetable food solely, for it furnishes nothing to make bones with;" and so he religiously devotes a part of his day to supplying his system with the raw material of bones; walking all the while he talks behind his oxen, which, with vegetable-made bones, jerk him and his lumbering plow along in spite of every obstacle. Some things are really necessaries of life in some circles, the most helpless and diseased, which in others are luxuries merely, and in others still are entirely unknown.

The whole ground of human life seems to some to have been gone over by their predecessors, both the heights and the valleys, and all things to have been cared for. According to Evelyn, "the wise Solomon prescribed ordinances for the very distances of trees; and the Roman prætors have decided how often you may go into your neighbor's land to gather the acorns which fall on it without trespass, and what share belongs to that neighbor." Hippocrates has even left directions how we should cut our nails; that is, even with the ends of the fingers, neither shorter nor longer. Undoubtedly the very tedium and ennui which presume to have exhausted the variety and the joys of life are as old as Adam. But man's capacities have never been measured; nor are we to judge of what he can do by any precedents, so little has been tried. Whatever have been thy failures hitherto, "be not afflicted, my child, for who shall assign to thee what thou hast left undone?"

We might try our lives by a thousand simple tests; as, for instance, that the same sun which ripens my beans illumines at once a system of earths like ours. If I had remembered this it would have prevented some mistakes. This was not the light in which I hoed them. The stars are the apexes of what wonderful triangles! What distant and different beings in the various mansions of the universe are contemplating the same one at the same moment! Nature and human life are as various as our several constitutions. Who shall say what prospect life offers to another? Could a greater miracle take place than for us to look through each other's eyes for an instant? We should live in all the ages of the world in an hour; ay, in all the worlds of the ages. History, Poetry, Mythology! — I know of no reading of another's experience so startling and informing as this would be.

The greater part of what my neighbors call good I believe in my soul to be bad, and if I repent of anything, it is very likely to be my good behavior. What demon possessed me that I behaved so well? You may say the wisest thing you can, old man, — you who have lived seventy years, not without honor of a kind, — I hear an irresistible voice which invites me away from all that.

One generation abandons the enterprises of another like stranded vessels.

I think that we may safely trust a good deal more than we do. We may waive just so much care of ourselves as we honestly bestow elsewhere. Nature is as well adapted to our weakness as to our strength. The incessant anxiety and strain of some is a well-nigh incurable form of disease. We are made to exaggerate the importance of what work we do; and yet how much is not done by us! or, what if we had been taken sick? How vigilant we are! determined not to live by faith if we can avoid it; all the day long on the alert, at night we unwillingly say our prayers and commit ourselves to uncertainties. So thoroughly and sincerely are we compelled to live, reverencing our life, and denying the possibility of change. This is the only way, we say; but there are as many ways as there can be drawn radii from one centre. All change is a miracle to contemplate; but it is a miracle which is taking place every instant. Confucius said, "To know that we know what we know, and that we do not know what we do not know, that is true knowledge." When one man has reduced a fact of the imagination to be a fact to his understanding, I foresee that all men will at length establish their lives on that basis.

Let us consider for a moment what most of the trouble and anxiety which I have referred to is about, and how much it is necessary that we be troubled, or at least careful. It would be some advantage to live a primitive and frontier life, though in the midst of an outward civilization, if only to learn what are the gross necessaries of life and what methods have been taken to obtain them;

or even to look over the old day-books of the merchants, to see what it was that men most commonly bought at the stores, what they stored, that is, what are the grossest groceries. For the improvements of ages have had but little influence on the essential laws of man's existence: as our skeletons, probably, are not to be distinguished from those of our ancestors.

By the words, *necessary of life*, I mean whatever, of all that man obtains by his own exertions, has been from the first, or from long use has become, so important to human life that few, if any, whether from savageness, or poverty, or philosophy, ever attempt to do without it. To many creatures there is in this sense but one necessary of life, Food. To the bison of the prairie it is a few inches of palatable grass, with water to drink; unless he seeks the Shelter of the forest or the mountain's shadow. None of the brute creation requires more than Food and Shelter. The necessaries of life for man in this climate may, accurately enough, be distributed under the several heads of Food, Shelter, Clothing, and Fuel; for not till we have secured these are we prepared to entertain the true problems of life with freedom and a prospect of success. Man has invented, not only houses, but clothes and cooked food; and possibly from the accidental discovery of the warmth of fire, and the consequent use of it, at first a luxury, arose the present necessity to sit by it. We observe cats and dogs acquiring the same second nature. By proper Shelter and Clothing we legitimately retain our own internal heat; but with an excess of these, or of Fuel, that is, with an external heat greater than our own internal, may not cookery properly be said to begin? Darwin, the naturalist, says of the inhabitants of Tierra del Fuego, that while his own party, who were well clothed and sitting close to a fire, were far from too warm, these naked savages, who were farther off, were observed, to his great surprise, "to be streaming with perspiration at undergoing such a roasting." So, we are told, the New Hollander goes naked with impunity, while the European shivers in his clothes. Is it impossible to combine the hardiness of these savages with the intellectualness of the civilized man? According to Liebig, man's body is a stove, and food the fuel which keeps up the internal combustion in the lungs. In cold weather we eat more, in warm less. The animal heat is the result of a slow combustion, and disease and death take place when this is too rapid; or for want of fuel, or from some defect in the draught, the fire goes out. Of course the vital heat is not to be confounded with fire; but so much for analogy. It appears, therefore, from the above list, that the expression, *animal life*, is nearly synonymous with the expression, *animal heat;* for while Food may be regarded as the Fuel which keeps up the fire within us, — and Fuel serves only to prepare that Food or to increase the warmth of our bodies by addition from without, — Shelter and Clothing also serve only to retain the *heat* thus generated and absorbed.

The grand necessity, then, for our bodies, is to keep warm, to keep the vital heat in us. What pains we accordingly take, not only with our Food, and Clothing, and Shelter, but with our beds, which are our night-clothes, robbing the nests and breasts of birds to prepare this shelter within a shelter, as the mole has its bed of grass and leaves at the end of its burrow! The poor man is wont to complain that this is a cold world; and to cold, no less physical than social, we refer directly a great part of our ails. The summer, in some climates, makes possible to man a sort of Elysian life. Fuel, except to cook his Food, is then unnecessary; the sun is his fire, and many of the fruits are sufficiently cooked by its rays; while Food generally is more various, and more easily obtained, and Clothing and Shelter are wholly or half unnecessary. At the present day, and in this country, as I find by my own experience, a few implements, a knife, an axe, a spade, a wheelbarrow, etc., and for the studious, lamplight, stationery, and access to a few books, rank next to necessaries, and can all be obtained at a trifling cost. Yet some, not wise, go to the other side of the globe, to barbarous and unhealthy regions, and devote themselves to trade for ten or twenty years, in order that they may live, — that is, keep comfortably warm, — and die in New England at last. The luxuriously rich are not simply kept comfortably warm, but unnaturally hot; as I implied before, they are cooked, of course à la mode.

Most of the luxuries, and many of the so-called comforts of life, are not only not indispensable, but positive hindrances to the elevation of mankind. With respect to luxuries and comforts, the wisest have ever lived a more simple and meagre life than the poor. The ancient philosophers, Chinese, Hindoo, Persian, and Greek, were a class than which none has been poorer in outward riches, none so rich in inward. We know not much about them. It is remarkable that *we* know so much of them as we do. The same is true of the more modern reformers and benefactors of their race. None can be an impartial or wise observer of human life but from the vantage ground of what *we* should call voluntary poverty. Of a life of luxury the fruit is luxury, whether in agriculture, or commerce, or literature, or art. There are nowadays professors of philosophy, but not philosophers. Yet it is admirable to profess because it was once admirable to live. To be a philosopher is not merely to have subtle thoughts, nor even to found a school, but so to love wisdom as to live according to its dictates, a life of simplicity, independence, magnanimity, and trust. It is to solve some of the problems of life, not only theoretically, but practically. The success of great scholars and thinkers is commonly a courtier-like success, not kingly, not manly. They make shift to live merely by conformity, practically as their fathers did, and are in no sense the progenitors of a nobler race of men. But why do men degenerate ever? What makes families run out? What is the nature of the luxury which enervates and destroys nations? Are we sure that there is none of it in our own lives? The philosopher is in advance of his age even in the outward form of his life. He is not fed, sheltered, clothed, warmed, like his contemporaries. How can a man be a philosopher and not maintain his vital heat by better methods than other men?

When a man is warmed by the several modes which I have described, what does he want next? Surely not more warmth of the same kind, as more and richer food, larger and more splendid houses, finer and more abundant clothing, more numerous, incessant and hotter fires, and the like. When he has obtained those things which are necessary to life, there is another alternative than to obtain the superfluities; and that is, to adventure on life now, his vacation from humbler toil having commenced. The soil, it appears, is suited to the seed, for it has sent its radicle downward, and it may now send its shoot upward also with confidence. Why has man rooted himself thus firmly in the earth, but that he may rise in the same proportion into the heavens above? — for the nobler plants are valued for the fruit they bear at last in the air and light, far from the ground, and are not treated like the humbler esculents, which, though they may be biennials, are cultivated only till they have perfected their root, and often cut down at top for this purpose, so that most would not know them in their flowering season.

I do not mean to prescribe rules to strong and valiant natures, who will mind their own affairs whether in heaven or hell, and perchance build more magnificently and spend more lavishly than the richest, without ever impoverishing themselves, not knowing how they live, — if, indeed, there are any such, as has been dreamed; nor to those who find their encouragement and inspiration in precisely the present condition of things, and cherish it with the fondness and enthusiasm of lovers, — and, to some extent, I reckon myself in this number; I do not speak to those who are well employed, in whatever circumstances, and they know whether they are well employed or not; — but mainly to the mass of men who are discontented, and idly complaining of the hard-

ness of their lot or of the times, when they might improve
them. There are some who complain most energetically
and inconsolably of any, because they are, as they say,
doing their duty. I also have in my mind that seemingly
wealthy, but most terribly impoverished class of all, who
have accumulated dross, but know not how to use it, or
get rid of it, and thus have forged their own golden or
silver fetters.

If I should attempt to tell how I have desired to spend
my life in years past, it would probably surprise those
of my readers who are somewhat acquainted with its
actual history; it would certainly astonish those who
know nothing about it. I will only hint at some of the
enterprises which I have cherished.

In any weather, at any hour of the day or night, I have
been anxious to improve the nick of time, and notch it
on my stick too; to stand on the meeting of two eternities, the past and future, which is precisely the present
moment; to toe that line. You will pardon some ob-
scurities, for there are more secrets in my trade than in
most men's, and yet not voluntarily kept, but insep-
arable from its very nature. I would gladly tell all that
I know about it, and never paint "No Admittance" on
my gate.

I long ago lost a hound, a bay horse, and a turtle-
dove, and am still on their trail. Many are the travellers
I have spoken concerning them, describing their tracks
and what calls they answered to. I have met one or two
who had heard the hound, and the tramp of the horse,
and even seen the dove disappear behind a cloud, and

they seemed as anxious to recover them as if they had lost them themselves.

To anticipate, not the sunrise and the dawn merely, but, if possible, Nature herself! How many mornings, summer and winter, before yet any neighbor was stirring about his business, have I been about mine! No doubt, many of my townsmen have met me returning from this enterprise, farmers starting for Boston in the twilight, or woodchoppers going to their work. It is true, I never assisted the sun materially in his rising, but, doubt not, it was of the last importance only to be present at it.

So many autumn, ay, and winter days, spent outside the town, trying to hear what was in the wind, to hear and carry it express! I well-nigh sunk all my capital in it, and lost my own breath into the bargain, running in the face of it. If it had concerned either of the political parties, depend upon it, it would have appeared in the Gazette with the earliest intelligence. At other times watching from the observatory of some cliff or tree, to telegraph any new arrival; or waiting at evening on the hill-tops for the sky to fall, that I might catch something, though I never caught much, and that, manna-wise, would dissolve again in the sun.

For a long time I was reporter to a journal, of no very wide circulation, whose editor has never yet seen fit to print the bulk of my contributions, and, as is too common with writers, I got only my labor for my pains. However, in this case my pains were their own reward.

For many years I was self-appointed inspector of snow-storms and rain-storms, and did my duty faithfully; surveyor, if not of highways, then of forest paths and all across-lot routes, keeping them open, and ravines bridged and passable at all seasons, where the public heel had testified to their utility.

I have looked after the wild stock of the town, which give a faithful herdsman a good deal of trouble by leaping fences; and I have had an eye to the unfrequented nooks and corners of the farm; though I did not always know whether Jonas or Solomon worked in a particular field to-day; that was none of my business. I have watered the red huckleberry, the sand cherry and the nettle-tree, the red pine and the black ash, the white grape and the yellow violet, which might have withered else in dry seasons.

In short, I went on thus for a long time (I may say it without boasting), faithfully minding my business, till it became more and more evident that my townsmen would not after all admit me into the list of town officers, nor make my place a sinecure with a moderate allowance. My accounts, which I can swear to have kept faithfully, I have, indeed, never got audited, still less accepted, still less paid and settled. However, I have not set my heart on that.

Not long since, a strolling Indian went to sell baskets at the house of a well-known lawyer in my neighborhood. "Do you wish to buy any baskets?" he asked. "No, we do not want any," was the reply. "What!" exclaimed the Indian as he went out the gate, "do you mean to starve us?" Having seen his industrious white neighbors so well off, — that the lawyer had only to weave arguments, and, by some magic, wealth and standing followed, — he had said to himself: I will go into business; I will weave baskets; it is a thing which I can do. Thinking that when he had made the baskets he would have done his part, and then it would be the white man's to buy them. He had not discovered that it was necessary for him to make it worth the other's while to buy them, or at least make him think that it was so, or to make something else which it would be worth his while to buy. I too had woven a kind of basket of a delicate texture, but I had not made it worth any one's while to buy them. Yet not the less, in my case, did I think it worth my while to weave them, and instead of studying how to make it worth men's while to buy my baskets, I studied rather how to avoid the necessity of selling them. The life which men praise and regard as successful is but one kind. Why should we exaggerate any one kind at the expense of the others?

Finding that my fellow-citizens were not likely to offer me any room in the court house, or any curacy or living anywhere else, but I must shift for myself, I turned my face more exclusively than ever to the woods, where I was better known. I determined to go into business at once, and not wait to acquire the usual capital, using such slender means as I had already got. My purpose in going to Walden Pond was not to live cheaply nor to live dearly there, but to transact some private business with the fewest obstacles; to be hindered from accomplishing which for want of a little common sense, a little enterprise and business talent, appeared not so sad as foolish.

I have always endeavored to acquire strict business

habits; they are indispensable to every man. If your
trade is with the Celestial Empire, then some small
counting house on the coast, in some Salem harbor, will
be fixture enough. You will export such articles as the
country affords, purely native products, much ice and
pine timber and a little granite, always in native bot-
toms. These will be good ventures. To oversee all the
details yourself in person; to be at once pilot and captain, and owner and underwriter; to buy and sell and
keep the accounts; to read every letter received, and
write or read every letter sent; to superintend the dis-
charge of imports night and day; to be upon many
parts of the coast almost at the same time, — often the
richest freight will be discharged upon a Jersey shore;
— to be your own telegraph, unweariedly sweeping the
horizon, speaking all passing vessels bound coastwise;
to keep up a steady despatch of commodities, for the
supply of such a distant and exorbitant market; to
keep yourself informed of the state of the markets, prospects of war and peace everywhere, and anticipate the
tendencies of trade and civilization, — taking advantage of the results of all exploring expeditions, using
new passages and all improvements in navigation; —
charts to be studied, the position of reefs and new lights
and buoys to be ascertained, and ever, and ever, the
logarithmic tables to be corrected, for by the error of
some calculator the vessel often splits upon a rock that
should have reached a friendly pier, — there is the un-
told fate of La Perouse; — universal science to be kept
pace with, studying the lives of all great discoverers and
navigators, great adventurers and merchants, from

Hanno and the Phœnicians down to our day; in fine, account of stock to be taken from time to time, to know how you stand. It is a labor to task the faculties of a man, — such problems of profit and loss, of interest, of tare and tret, and gauging of all kinds in it, as demand a universal knowledge.

I have thought that Walden Pond would be a good place for business, not solely on account of the railroad and the ice trade; it offers advantages which it may not be good policy to divulge; it is a good post and a good foundation. No Neva marshes to be filled; though you must everywhere build on piles of your own driving. It is said that a flood-tide, with a westerly wind, and ice in the Neva, would sweep St. Petersburg from the face of the earth.

As this business was to be entered into without the usual capital, it may not be easy to conjecture where those means, that will still be indispensable to every such undertaking, were to be obtained. As for Clothing, to come at once to the practical part of the question, perhaps we are led oftener by the love of novelty and a regard for the opinions of men, in procuring it, than by a true utility. Let him who has work to do recollect that the object of clothing is, first, to retain the vital heat, and secondly, in this state of society, to cover nakedness, and he may judge how much of any necessary or important work may be accomplished without adding to his wardrobe. Kings and queens who wear a suit but once, though made by some tailor or dressmaker to their majesties, cannot know the comfort of wearing a suit that fits. They are no better than wooden horses to hang the clean clothes on. Every day our garments become more assimilated to ourselves, receiving the impress of the wearer's character, until we hesitate to lay them aside without such delay and medical appliances and some such solemnity even as our bodies. No man ever stood the lower in my estimation for having a patch in his clothes; yet I am sure that there is greater anxiety, commonly, to have fashionable, or at least clean and unpatched clothes, than to have a sound conscience. But even if the rent is not mended, perhaps the worst vice betrayed is improvidence. I sometimes try my acquaintances by such tests as this, — Who could wear a patch, or two extra seams only, over the knee? Most behave as if they believed that their prospects for life would be ruined if they should do it. It would be easier for them to hobble to town with a broken leg than with a broken pantaloon. Often if an accident happens to a gentleman's legs, they can be mended; but if a similar accident happens to the legs of his pantaloons, there is no help for it; for he considers, not what is truly respectable, but what is respected. We know but few men, a great many coats and breeches. Dress a scarecrow in your last shift, you standing shiftless by, who would not soonest salute the scarecrow? Passing a cornfield the other day, close by a hat and coat on a stake, I recognized the owner of the farm. He was only a little more weather-beaten than when I saw him last. I have heard of a dog that barked at every stranger who approached his master's premises with clothes on, but was easily quieted by a naked thief. It is an interesting question how far men would retain their relative rank if they were divested of their clothes. Could you, in such a case, tell surely of any company of civilized men which belonged to the most respected class? When Madam Pfeiffer, in her adventurous travels round the world, from east to west, had got so near home as Asiatic Russia, she says that she felt the necessity of wearing other than a travelling dress, when she went to meet the authorities, for she "was now in a civilized country, where . . . people are judged of by their clothes." Even in our democratic New England towns the accidental possession of wealth, and its manifestation in dress and equipage alone, obtain for the possessor almost universal respect. But they who yield such respect, numerous as they are, are so far heathen, and need to have a missionary sent to them. Beside, clothes introduced sewing, a kind of work which you may call endless; a woman's dress, at least, is never done.

A man who has at length found something to do will not need to get a new suit to do it in; for him the old will do, that has lain dusty in the garret for an indeterminate period. Old shoes will serve a hero longer than they have served his valet, — if a hero ever has a valet, — bare feet are older than shoes, and he can make them do. Only they who go to soirées and legislative halls must have new coats, coats to change as often as the man changes in them. But if my jacket and trousers, my hat and shoes, are fit to worship God in, they will do; will they not? Who ever saw his old clothes, — his old coat, actually worn out, resolved into its primitive elements, so that it was not a deed of charity to bestow it on some poor boy, by him perchance to be bestowed on some poorer still, or shall we say richer, who could do with less? I say, beware of all enterprises that require new clothes, and not rather a new wearer of clothes. If there is not a new man, how can the new clothes be made to fit? If you have any enterprise before you, try it in your old clothes. All men want, not something to *do with*, but something to *do*, or rather something to *be*. Perhaps we should never procure a new suit, however ragged or dirty the old, until we have so conducted, so enterprised or sailed in some way, that we feel like new men in the old, and that to retain it would be like keeping new wine in old bottles. Our moulting season, like that of the fowls, must be a crisis in our lives. The loon retires to solitary ponds to spend it. Thus also the snake casts its slough, and the caterpillar its wormy coat, by an internal industry and expansion; for clothes are but our outmost cuticle and mortal coil. Otherwise we shall be found sailing under false colors, and be inevitably cashiered at last by our own opinion, as well as that of mankind.

We don garment after garment, as if we grew like exogenous plants by addition without. Our outside and often thin and fanciful clothes are our epidermis, or false skin, which partakes not of our life, and may be stripped off here and there without fatal injury; our thicker garments, constantly worn, are our cellular integument, or cortex; but our shirts are our liber, or true bark, which cannot be removed without girdling and so destroying the man. I believe that all races at some seasons wear something equivalent to the shirt. It is desirable that a man be clad so simply that he can lay his hands on himself in the dark, and that he live in all respects so compactly and preparedly that, if an enemy take the town, he can, like the old philosopher, walk out the gate empty-handed without anxiety. While one thick garment is, for most purposes, as good as three thin ones, and cheap clothing can be obtained at prices really to suit customers; while a thick coat can be bought for five dollars, which will last as many years, thick pantaloons for two dollars, cowhide boots for a dollar and a half a pair, a summer hat for a quarter of a dollar, and a winter cap for sixty-two and a half cents, or a better be made at home at a nominal cost, where is he so poor that, clad in such a suit, *of his own earning*, there will not be found wise men to do him reverence?

When I ask for a garment of a particular form, my tailoress tells me gravely, "They do not make them so now," not emphasizing the "They" at all, as if she quoted an authority as impersonal as the Fates, and I find it difficult to get made what I want, simply because she cannot believe that I mean what I say, that I am so rash. When I hear this oracular sentence, I am for a moment absorbed in thought, emphasizing to myself each word separately that I may come at the meaning of it, that I may find out by what degree of consanguinity *They* are related to *me*, and what authority they may have in an affair which affects me so nearly; and, finally, I am inclined to answer her with equal mystery, and without any more emphasis of the "they," — "It is true, they did not make them so recently, but they do now." Of what use this measuring of me if she does not measure my character, but only the breadth of my shoulders, as it were a peg to hang the coat on ? We worship not the Graces, nor the Parcæ, but Fashion. She spins and weaves and cuts with full authority. The head monkey at Paris puts on a traveller's cap, and all the monkeys in America do the same. I sometimes despair of getting anything quite simple and honest done in this world by the help of men. They would have to be passed through a powerful press first, to squeeze their old notions out of them, so that they would not soon get upon their legs again; and then there would be some one in the company with a maggot in his head, hatched from an egg deposited there nobody knows when, for not even fire kills these things, and you would have lost your labor. Nevertheless, we will not forget that some Egyptian wheat was handed down to us by a mummy.

On the whole, I think that it cannot be maintained that dressing has in this or any country risen to the dignity of an art. At present men make shift to wear what they can get. Like shipwrecked sailors, they put on what they can find on the beach, and at a little distance, whether of space or time, laugh at each other's masquerade. Every generation laughs at the old fashions, but follows religiously the new. We are amused at beholding the costume of Henry VIII., or Queen Elizabeth, as much as if it was that of the King and Queen of the Cannibal Islands. All costume off a man is pitiful or grotesque. It is only the serious eye peering from and the sincere life passed within it which restrain laughter and consecrate the costume of any people. Let Harlequin be taken with a fit of the colic and his trappings will have to serve that mood too. When the soldier is hit by a cannon-ball, rags are as becoming as purple.

The childish and savage taste of men and women for new patterns keeps how many shaking and squinting through kaleidoscopes that they may discover the particular figure which this generation requires to-day. The manufacturers have learned that this taste is merely whimsical. Of two patterns which differ only by a few threads more or less of a particular color, the one will be sold readily, the other lie on the shelf, though it frequently happens that after the lapse of a season the latter becomes the most fashionable. Comparatively, tattooing is not the hideous custom which it is called. It is not barbarous merely because the printing is skin-deep and unalterable.

I cannot believe that our factory system is the best mode by which men may get clothing. The condition of the operatives is becoming every day more like that of the English; and it cannot be wondered at, since, as far as I have heard or observed, the principal object is, not that mankind may be well and honestly clad, but, unquestionably, that the corporations may be enriched. In the long run men hit only what they aim at. Therefore, though they should fail immediately, they had better aim at something high.

As for a Shelter, I will not deny that this is now a necessary of life, though there are instances of men having done without it for long periods in colder countries than this. Samuel Laing says that "the Laplander in his skin dress, and in a skin bag which he puts over his head and shoulders, will sleep night after night on the

snow . . . in a degree of cold which would extinguish
the life of one exposed to it in any woollen clothing." He
had seen them asleep thus. Yet he adds, "They are not
hardier than other people." But, probably, man did not
live long on the earth without discovering the convenience which there is in a house, the domestic comforts,
which phrase may have originally signified the satisfactions of the house more than of the family; though these
must be extremely partial and occasional in those
climates where the house is associated in our thoughts
with winter or the rainy season chiefly, and two thirds
of the year, except for a parasol, is unnecessary. In our
climate, in the summer, it was formerly almost solely a
covering at night. In the Indian gazettes a wigwam was
the symbol of a day's march, and a row of them cut or
painted on the bark of a tree signified that so many
times they had camped. Man was not made so large
limbed and robust but that he must seek to narrow his
world, and wall in a space such as fitted him. He was
at first bare and out of doors; but though this was pleasant enough in serene and warm weather, by daylight,
the rainy season and the winter, to say nothing of the
torrid sun, would perhaps have nipped his race in the
bud if he had not made haste to clothe himself with
the shelter of a house. Adam and Eve, according to the
fable, wore the bower before other clothes. Man wanted
a home, a place of warmth, or comfort, first of physical
warmth, then the warmth of the affections.

We may imagine a time when, in the infancy of the
human race, some enterprising mortal crept into a hollow in a rock for shelter. Every child begins the world

again, to some extent, and loves to stay outdoors, even in wet and cold. It plays house, as well as horse, having an instinct for it. Who does not remember the interest with which, when young, he looked at shelving rocks, or any approach to a cave? It was the natural yearning of that portion of our most primitive ancestor which still survived in us. From the cave we have advanced to roofs of palm leaves, of bark and boughs, of linen woven and stretched, of grass and straw, of boards and shingles, of stones and tiles. At last, we know not what it is to live in the open air, and our lives are domestic in more senses than we think. From the hearth the field is a great distance. It would be well, perhaps, if we were to spend more of our days and nights without any obstruction between us and the celestial bodies, if the poet did not speak so much from under a roof, or the saint dwell there so long. Birds do not sing in caves, nor do doves cherish their innocence in dovecots.

However, if one designs to construct a dwelling-house, it behooves him to exercise a little Yankee shrewdness, lest after all he find himself in a workhouse, a labyrinth without a clue, a museum, an almshouse, a prison, or a splendid mausoleum instead. Consider first how slight a shelter is absolutely necessary. I have seen Penobscot Indians, in this town, living in tents of thin cotton cloth, while the snow was nearly a foot deep around them, and I thought that they would be glad to have it deeper to keep out the wind. Formerly, when how to get my living honestly, with freedom left for my proper pursuits, was a question which vexed me even more than it does now, for unfortunately I am become somewhat callous,

I used to see a large box by the railroad, six feet long by three wide, in which the laborers locked up their tools at night; and it suggested to me that every man who was hard pushed might get such a one for a dollar, and, having bored a few auger holes in it, to admit the air at least, get into it when it rained and at night, and hook down the lid, and so have freedom in his love, and in his soul be free. This did not appear the worst, nor by any means a despicable alternative. You could sit up as late as you pleased, and, whenever you got up, go abroad without any landlord or house-lord dogging you for rent. Many a man is harassed to death to pay the rent of a larger and more luxurious box who would not have frozen to death in such a box as this. I am far from jesting. Economy is a subject which admits of being treated with levity, but it cannot so be disposed of. A comfortable house for a rude and hardy race, that lived mostly out of doors, was once made here almost entirely of such materials as Nature furnished ready to their hands. Gookin, who was superintendent of the Indians subject to the Massachusetts Colony, writing in 1674, says, "The best of their houses are covered very neatly, tight and warm, with barks of trees, slipped from their bodies at those seasons when the sap is up, and made into great flakes, with pressure of weighty timber, when they are green. . . . The meaner sort are covered with mats which they make of a kind of bul-rush, and are also indifferently tight and warm, but not so good as the former. . . . Some I have seen, sixty or a hundred feet long and thirty feet broad. . . . I have often lodged in their wigwams, and found them as warm as the best English houses." He adds that they were commonly carpeted and lined within with well-wrought embroidered mats, and were furnished with various utensils. The Indians had advanced so far as to regulate the effect of the wind by a mat suspended over the hole in the roof and moved by a string. Such a lodge was in the first instance constructed in a day or two at most, and taken down and put up in a few hours; and every family owned one, or its apartment in one.

In the savage state every family owns a shelter as good as the best, and sufficient for its coarser and simpler wants; but I think that I speak within bounds when I say that, though the birds of the air have their nests, and the foxes their holes, and the savages their wigwams, in modern civilized society not more than one half the families own a shelter. In the large towns and cities, where civilization especially prevails, the number of those who own a shelter is a very small fraction of the whole. The rest pay an annual tax for this outside garment of all, become indispensable summer and winter, which would buy a village of Indian wigwams, but now helps to keep them poor as long as they live. I do not mean to insist here on the disadvantage of hiring compared with owning, but it is evident that the savage owns his shelter because it costs so little, while the civilized man hires his commonly because he cannot afford to own it; nor can he, in the long run, any better afford to hire. But, answers one, by merely paying this tax the poor civilized man secures an abode which is a palace compared with the savage's. An annual rent of from twenty-five to a hundred dollars (these are the

country rates) entitles him to the benefit of the improvements of centuries, spacious apartments, clean paint and
paper, Rumford fireplace, back plastering, Venetian
blinds, copper pump, spring lock, a commodious cellar,
and many other things. But how happens it that he who
is said to enjoy these things is so commonly a *poor* civilized man, while the savage, who has them not, is rich
as a savage? If it is asserted that civilization is a real
advance in the condition of man, — and I think that it
is, though only the wise improve their advantages, —
it must be shown that it has produced better dwellings
without making them more costly; and the cost of a
thing is the amount of what I will call life which is required to be exchanged for it, immediately or in the
long run. An average house in this neighborhood costs
perhaps eight hundred dollars, and to lay up this sum
will take from ten to fifteen years of the laborer's life,
even if he is not encumbered with a family, — estimat-
ing the pecuniary value of every man's labor at one
dollar a day, for if some receive more, others receive
less; — so that he must have spent more than half his
life commonly before *his* wigwam will be earned. If we
suppose him to pay a rent instead, this is but a doubtful
choice of evils. Would the savage have been wise to
exchange his wigwam for a palace on these terms?

It may be guessed that I reduce almost the whole advantage of holding this superfluous property as a fund
in store against the future, so far as the individual is
concerned, mainly to the defraying of funeral expenses.
But perhaps a man is not required to bury himself.
Nevertheless this points to an important distinction be-

tween the civilized man and the savage; and, no doubt,
they have designs on us for our benefit, in making the
life of a civilized people an *institution*, in which the life
of the individual is to a great extent absorbed, in order
to preserve and perfect that of the race. But I wish to
show at what a sacrifice this advantage is at present
obtained, and to suggest that we may possibly so live
as to secure all the advantage without suffering any of
the disadvantage. What mean ye by saying that the
poor ye have always with you, or that the fathers have
eaten sour grapes, and the children's teeth are set on
edge?

"As I live, saith the Lord God, ye shall not have occasion any more to use this proverb in Israel."

"Behold all souls are mine; as the soul of the father,
so also the soul of the son is mine: the soul that sinneth
it shall die."

When I consider my neighbors, the farmers of Concord, who are at least as well off as the other classes, I
find that for the most part they have been toiling twenty,
thirty, or forty years, that they may become the real
owners of their farms, which commonly they have inherited with encumbrances, or else bought with hired
money, — and we may regard one third of that toil as
the cost of their houses, — but commonly they have
not paid for them yet. It is true, the encumbrances
sometimes outweigh the value of the farm, so that the
farm itself becomes one great encumbrance, and still a
man is found to inherit it, being well acquainted with
it, as he says. On applying to the assessors, I am surprised to learn that they cannot at once name a dozen in

the town who own their farms free and clear. If you would know the history of these homesteads, inquire at the bank where they are mortgaged. The man who has actually paid for his farm with labor on it is so rare that every neighbor can point to him. I doubt if there are three such men in Concord. What has been said of the merchants, that a very large majority, even ninety-seven in a hundred, are sure to fail, is equally true of the farmers. With regard to the merchants, however, one of them says pertinently that a great part of their failures are not genuine pecuniary failures, but merely failures to fulfil their engagements, because it is inconvenient; that is, it is the moral character that breaks down. But this puts an infinitely worse face on the matter, and suggests, beside, that probably not even the other three succeed in saving their souls, but are perchance bankrupt in a worse sense than they who fail honestly. Bankruptcy and repudiation are the springboards from which much of our civilization vaults and turns its somersets, but the savage stands on the unelastic plank of famine. Yet the Middlesex Cattle Show goes off here with *éclat* annually, as if all the joints of the agricultural machine were suent.

The farmer is endeavoring to solve the problem of a livelihood by a formula more complicated than the problem itself. To get his shoestrings he speculates in herds of cattle. With consummate skill he has set his trap with a hair springe to catch comfort and independence, and then, as he turned away, got his own leg into it. This is the reason he is poor; and for a similar reason we are all poor in respect to a thousand savage

comforts, though surrounded by luxuries. As Chapman
sings, —

> " The false society of men —
> — for earthly greatness
> All heavenly comforts rarefies to air."

And when the farmer has got his house, he may not
be the richer but the poorer for it, and it be the house
that has got him. As I understand it, that was a valid
objection urged by Momus against the house which
Minerva made, that she "had not made it movable, by
which means a bad neighborhood might be avoided;"
and it may still be urged, for our houses are such unwieldy property that we are often imprisoned rather
than housed in them; and the bad neighborhood to be
avoided is our own scurvy selves. I know one or two
families, at least, in this town, who, for nearly a generation, have been wishing to sell their houses in the
outskirts and move into the village, but have not been
able to accomplish it, and only death will set them free.

Granted that the *majority* are able at last either to
own or hire the modern house with all its improvements.
While civilization has been improving our houses, it has
not equally improved the men who are to inhabit them.
It has created palaces, but it was not so easy to create
noblemen and kings. And *if the civilized man's pursuits
are no worthier than the savage's, if he is employed the
greater part of his life in obtaining gross necessaries and
comforts merely, why should he have a better dwelling
than the former ?*

But how do the poor *minority* fare ? Perhaps it will
be found that just in proportion as some have been

placed in outward circumstances above the savage, others have been degraded below him. The luxury of one class is counterbalanced by the indigence of another. On the one side is the palace, on the other are the almshouse and "silent poor." The myriads who built the pyramids to be the tombs of the Pharaohs were fed on garlic, and it may be were not decently buried themselves. The mason who finishes the cornice of the palace returns at night perchance to a hut not so good as a wigwam. It is a mistake to suppose that, in a country where the usual evidences of civilization exist, the condition of a very large body of the inhabitants may not be as degraded as that of savages. I refer to the degraded poor, not now to the degraded rich. To know this I should not need to look farther than to the shanties which everywhere border our railroads, that last improvement in civilization; where I see in my daily walks human beings living in sties, and all winter with an open door, for the sake of light, without any visible, often imaginable, wood-pile, and the forms of both old and young are permanently contracted by the long habit of shrinking from cold and misery, and the development of all their limbs and faculties is checked. It certainly is fair to look at that class by whose labor the works which distinguish this generation are accomplished. Such too, to a greater or less extent, is the condition of the operatives of every denomination in England, which is the great workhouse of the world. Or I could refer you to Ireland, which is marked as one of the white or enlightened spots on the map. Contrast the physical condition of the Irish with that of the North

American Indian, or the South Sea Islander, or any other savage race before it was degraded by contact with the civilized man. Yet I have no doubt that that people's rulers are as wise as the average of civilized rulers. Their condition only proves what squalidness may consist with civilization. I hardly need refer now to the laborers in our Southern States who produce the staple exports of this country, and are themselves a staple production of the South. But to confine myself to those who are said to be in *moderate* circumstances.

Most men appear never to have considered what a house is, and are actually though needlessly poor all their lives because they think that they must have such a one as their neighbors have. As if one were to wear any sort of coat which the tailor might cut out for him, or, gradually leaving off palm-leaf hat or cap of wood-chuck skin, complain of hard times because he could not afford to buy him a crown! It is possible to invent a house still more convenient and luxurious than we have, which yet all would admit that man could not afford to pay for. Shall we always study to obtain more of these things, and not sometimes to be content with less? Shall the respectable citizen thus gravely teach, by precept and example, the necessity of the young man's providing a certain number of superfluous glow-shoes, and umbrellas, and empty guest chambers for empty guests, before he dies? Why should not our furniture be as simple as the Arab's or the Indian's? When I think of the benefactors of the race, whom we have apotheosized as messengers from heaven, bearers of divine gifts to man, I do not see in my mind any retinue at their heels, any carload of fashionable furniture. Or what if I were to allow — would it not be a singular allowance? — that our furniture should be more complex than the Arab's, in proportion as we are morally and intellectually his superiors! At present our houses are cluttered and defiled with it, and a good housewife would sweep out the greater part into the dust hole, and not leave her morning's work undone. Morning work! By the blushes of Aurora and the music of Memnon, what should be man's *morning work* in this world? I had three pieces of limestone on my desk, but I was terrified to find that they required to be dusted daily, when the furniture of my mind was all undusted still, and I threw them out the window in disgust. How, then, could I have a furnished house? I would rather sit in the open air, for no dust gathers on the grass, unless where man has broken ground.

It is the luxurious and dissipated who set the fashions which the herd so diligently follow. The traveller who stops at the best houses, so called, soon discovers this, for the publicans presume him to be a Sardanapalus, and if he resigned himself to their tender mercies he would soon be completely emasculated. I think that in the railroad car we are inclined to spend more on luxury than on safety and convenience, and it threatens without attaining these to become no better than a modern drawing-room, with its divans, and ottomans, and sunshades, and a hundred other oriental things, which we are taking west with us, invented for the ladies of the harem and the effeminate natives of the Celestial Empire, which Jonathan should be ashamed to know the

names of. I would rather sit on a pumpkin and have it
all to myself than be crowded on a velvet cushion. I
would rather ride on earth in an ox cart, with a free
circulation, than go to heaven in the fancy car of an
excursion train and breathe a *malaria* all the way.

The very simplicity and nakedness of man's life in
the primitive ages imply this advantage, at least, that
they left him still but a sojourner in nature. When he
was refreshed with food and sleep, he contemplated his
journey again. He dwelt, as it were, in a tent in this
world, and was either threading the valleys, or crossing
the plains, or climbing the mountain-tops. But lo! men
have become the tools of their tools. The man who in-
dependently plucked the fruits when he was hungry is
become a farmer; and he who stood under a tree for
shelter, a housekeeper. We now no longer camp as for
a night, but have settled down on earth and forgotten
heaven. We have adopted Christianity merely as an
improved method of *agri*-culture. We have built for
this world a family mansion, and for the next a family
tomb. The best works of art are the expression of man's
struggle to free himself from this condition, but the
effect of our art is merely to make this low state comfortable and that higher state to be forgotten. There is
actually no place in this village for a work of *fine* art,
if any had come down to us, to stand, for our lives, our
houses and streets, furnish no proper pedestal for it.
There is not a nail to hang a picture on, nor a shelf to
receive the bust of a hero or a saint. When I consider
how our houses are built and paid for, or not paid for,
and their internal economy managed and sustained, I

wonder that the floor does not give way under the visitor
while he is admiring the gewgaws upon the mantel-
piece, and let him through into the cellar, to some solid
and honest though earthy foundation. I cannot but
perceive that this so-called rich and refined life is a
thing jumped at, and I do not get on in the enjoyment of the *fine* arts which adorn it, my attention being
wholly occupied with the jump; for I remember that
the greatest genuine leap, due to human muscles alone,
on record, is that of certain wandering Arabs, who are
said to have cleared twenty-five feet on level ground.
Without factitious support, man is sure to come to earth
again beyond that distance. The first question which
I am tempted to put to the proprietor of such great
impropriety is, Who bolsters you? Are you one of the
ninety-seven who fail, or the three who succeed? Answer me these questions, and then perhaps I may look
at your bawbles and find them ornamental. The cart
before the horse is neither beautiful nor useful. Before
we can adorn our houses with beautiful objects the
walls must be stripped, and our lives must be stripped,
and beautiful housekeeping and beautiful living be laid
for a foundation: now, a taste for the beautiful is most
cultivated out of doors, where there is no house and no
housekeeper.

Old Johnson, in his "Wonder-Working Providence,"
speaking of the first settlers of this town, with whom
he was contemporary, tells us that "they burrow themselves in the earth for their first shelter under some hillside, and, casting the soil aloft upon timber, they make
a smoky fire against the earth, at the highest side." They

did not "provide them houses," says he, "till the earth, by the Lord's blessing, brought forth bread to feed them," and the first year's crop was so light that "they were forced to cut their bread very thin for a long season." The secretary of the Province of New Netherland, writing in Dutch, in 1650, for the information of those who wished to take up land there, states more particularly that "those in New Netherland, and especially in New England, who have no means to build farmhouses at first according to their wishes, dig a square pit in the ground, cellar fashion, six or seven feet deep, as long and as broad as they think proper, case the earth inside with wood all round the wall, and line the wood with the bark of trees or something else to prevent the caving in of the earth; floor this cellar with plank, and wainscot it overhead for a ceiling, raise a roof of spars clear up, and cover the spars with bark or green sods, so that they can live dry and warm in these houses with their entire families for two, three, and four years, it being understood that partitions are run through those cellars which are adapted to the size of the family. The wealthy and principal men in New England, in the beginning of the colonies, commenced their first dwelling-houses in this fashion for two reasons: firstly, in order not to waste time in building, and not to want food the next season; secondly, in order not to discourage poor laboring people whom they brought over in numbers from Fatherland. In the course of three or four years, when the country became adapted to agriculture, they built themselves handsome houses, spending on them several thousands."

In this course which our ancestors took there was a show of prudence at least, as if their principle were to satisfy the more pressing wants first. But are the more pressing wants satisfied now? When I think of acquiring for myself one of our luxurious dwellings, I am deterred, for, so to speak, the country is not yet adapted to *human* culture, and we are still forced to cut our *spiritual* bread far thinner than our forefathers did their wheaten. Not that all architectural ornament is to be neglected even in the rudest periods; but let our houses first be lined with beauty, where they come in contact with our lives, like the tenement of the shellfish, and not overlaid with it. But, alas! I have been inside one or two of them, and know what they are lined with.

Though we are not so degenerate but that we might possibly live in a cave or a wigwam or wear skins to-day, it certainly is better to accept the advantages, though so dearly bought, which the invention and industry of mankind offer. In such a neighborhood as this, boards and shingles, lime and bricks, are cheaper and more easily obtained than suitable caves, or whole logs, or bark in sufficient quantities, or even well-tempered clay or flat stones. I speak understandingly on this subject, for I have made myself acquainted with it both theoretically and practically. With a little more wit we might use these materials so as to become richer than the richest now are, and make our civilization a blessing. The civilized man is a more experienced and wiser savage. But to make haste to my own experiment.

Near the end of March, 1845, I borrowed an axe and went down to the woods by Walden Pond, nearest to where I intended to build my house, and began to cut down some tall, arrowy white pines, still in their youth, for timber. It is difficult to begin without borrowing, but perhaps it is the most generous course thus to permit your fellow-men to have an interest in your enterprise. The owner of the axe, as he released his hold on it, said that it was the apple of his eye; but I returned it sharper than I received it. It was a pleasant hillside where I worked, covered with pine woods, through which I looked out on the pond, and a small open field in the woods where pines and hickories were springing up. The ice in the pond was not yet dissolved, though there were some open spaces, and it was all dark-colored and saturated with water. There were some slight flurries of snow during the days that I worked there; but for the most part when I came out on to the railroad, on my way home, its yellow sand-heap stretched away gleaming in the hazy atmosphere, and the rails shone in the spring sun, and I heard the lark and pewee and other birds already come to commence another year with us. They were pleasant spring days, in which the winter of man's discontent was thawing as well as the earth, and the life that had lain torpid begun to stretch itself. One day, when my axe had come off and I had cut a green hickory for a wedge, driving it with a stone, and had placed the whole to soak in a pond-hole in order to swell the wood, I saw a striped snake run into the water, and he lay on the bottom, apparently without inconvenience, as long as I stayed there, or more than a quarter of an hour; perhaps because he had not yet fairly come out of the torpid state. It appeared to me that for a like reason men remain in their present low and primitive condition; but if they should feel the influence of the spring of springs arousing them, they would of necessity rise to a higher and more ethereal life. I had previously seen the snakes in frosty mornings in my path with portions of their bodies still numb and inflexible, waiting for the sun to thaw them. On the 1st of April it rained and melted the ice, and in the early part of the day, which was very foggy, I heard a stray goose groping about over the pond and cackling as if lost, or like the spirit of the fog.

So I went on for some days cutting and hewing timber, and also studs and rafters, all with my narrow axe, not having many communicable or scholar-like thoughts, singing to myself, —

> Men say they know many things;
> But lo! they have taken wings, —
> The arts and sciences,
> And a thousand appliances;
> The wind that blows
> Is all that anybody knows.

I hewed the main timbers six inches square, most of the studs on two sides only, and the rafters and floor timbers on one side, leaving the rest of the bark on, so that they were just as straight and much stronger than sawed ones. Each stick was carefully mortised or tenoned by its stump, for I had borrowed other tools by this time. My days in the woods were not very long ones; yet I usually carried my dinner of bread and butter, and read the newspaper in which it was wrapped, at noon, sitting amid the green pine boughs which I had cut off, and to my bread was imparted some of their fragrance, for my hands were covered with a thick coat of pitch. Before I had done I was more the friend than the foe of the pine tree, though I had cut down some of them, having become better acquainted with it. Sometimes a rambler in the wood was attracted by the sound of my axe, and we chatted pleasantly over the chips which I had made.

By the middle of April, for I made no haste in my work, but rather made the most of it, my house was framed and ready for the raising. I had already bought the shanty of James Collins, an Irishman who worked on the Fitchburg Railroad, for boards. James Collins' shanty was considered an uncommonly fine one. When I called to see it he was not at home. I walked about the outside, at first unobserved from within, the window was so deep and high. It was of small dimensions, with a peaked cottage roof, and not much else to be seen, the dirt being raised five feet all around as if it were a compost heap. The roof was the soundest part, though a good deal warped and made brittle by the sun. Doorsill there was none, but a perennial passage for the hens under the door-board. Mrs. C. came to the door and asked me to view it from the inside. The hens were driven in by my approach. It was dark, and had a dirt floor for the most part, dank, clammy, and aguish, only here a board and there a board which would not bear removal. She lighted a lamp to show me the inside of the roof and the walls, and also that the board floor

extended under the bed, warning me not to step into
the cellar, a sort of dust hole two feet deep. In her own
words, they were "good boards overhead, good boards
all around, and a good window," — of two whole
squares originally, only the cat had passed out that way
lately. There was a stove, a bed, and a place to sit, an
infant in the house where it was born, a silk parasol,
gilt-framed looking-glass, and a patent new coffee-mill
nailed to an oak sapling, all told. The bargain was soon
concluded, for James had in the meanwhile returned.
I to pay four dollars and twenty-five cents to-night,
he to vacate at five to-morrow morning, selling to
nobody else meanwhile: I to take possession at six. It
were well, he said, to be there early, and anticipate certain indistinct but wholly unjust claims on the score of
ground rent and fuel. This he assured me was the only
encumbrance. At six I passed him and his family on
the road. One large bundle held their all, — bed, coffee-
mill, looking-glass, hens, — all but the cat; she took to
the woods and became a wild cat, and, as I learned afterward, trod in a trap set for woodchucks, and so became
a dead cat at last.

I took down this dwelling the same morning, drawing the nails, and removed it to the pond-side by small
cartloads, spreading the boards on the grass there to
bleach and warp back again in the sun. One early
thrush gave me a note or two as I drove along the woodland path. I was informed treacherously by a young
Patrick that neighbor Seeley, an Irishman, in the intervals of the carting, transferred the still tolerable, straight,
and drivable nails, staples, and spikes to his pocket, and

then stood when I came back to pass the time of day, and look freshly up, unconcerned, with spring thoughts, at the devastation; there being a dearth of work, as he said. He was there to represent spectatordom, and help make this seemingly insignificant event one with the removal of the gods of Troy.

I dug my cellar in the side of a hill sloping to the south, where a woodchuck had formerly dug his burrow, down through sumach and blackberry roots, and the lowest stain of vegetation, six feet square by seven deep, to a fine sand where potatoes would not freeze in any winter. The sides were left shelving, and not stoned; but the sun having never shone on them, the sand still keeps its place. It was but two hours' work. I took particular pleasure in this breaking of ground, for in almost all latitudes men dig into the earth for an equable temperature. Under the most splendid house in the city is still to be found the cellar where they store their roots as of old, and long after the superstructure has disappeared posterity remark its dent in the earth. The house is still but a sort of porch at the entrance of a burrow.

At length, in the beginning of May, with the help of some of my acquaintances, rather to improve so good an occasion for neighborliness than from any necessity, I set up the frame of my house. No man was ever more honored in the character of his raisers than I. They are destined, I trust, to assist at the raising of loftier structures one day. I began to occupy my house on the 4th of July, as soon as it was boarded and roofed, for the boards were carefully feather-edged and lapped, so that it was perfectly impervious to rain, but before boarding I laid the foundation of a chimney at one end, bringing two cartloads of stones up the hill from the pond in my arms. I built the chimney after my hoeing in the fall, before a fire became necessary for warmth, doing my cooking in the meanwhile out of doors on the ground, early in the morning: which mode I still think is in some respects more convenient and agreeable than the usual one. When it stormed before my bread was baked, I fixed a few boards over the fire, and sat under them to watch my loaf, and passed some pleasant hours in that way. In those days, when my hands were much employed, I read but little, but the least scraps of paper which lay on the ground, my holder, or tablecloth, afforded me as much entertainment, in fact answered the same purpose as the Iliad.

It would be worth the while to build still more deliberately than I did, considering, for instance, what foundation a door, a window, a cellar, a garret, have in the nature of man, and perchance never raising any superstructure until we found a better reason for it than our temporal necessities even. There is some of the same fitness in a man's building his own house that there is in a bird's building its own nest. Who knows but if men constructed their dwellings with their own hands, and provided food for themselves and families simply and honestly enough, the poetic faculty would be universally developed, as birds universally sing when they are so engaged? But alas! we do like cowbirds and cuckoos, which lay their eggs in nests which other birds have

built, and cheer no traveller with their chattering and
unmusical notes. Shall we forever resign the pleasure of
construction to the carpenter? What does architecture
amount to in the experience of the mass of men? I never
in all my walks came across a man engaged in so simple
and natural an occupation as building his house. We
belong to the community. It is not the tailor alone who
is the ninth part of a man; it is as much the preacher,
and the merchant, and the farmer. Where is this division of labor to end? and what object does it finally
serve? No doubt another *may* also think for me; but
it is not therefore desirable that he should do so to the
exclusion of my thinking for myself.

True, there are architects so called in this country,
and I have heard of one at least possessed with the idea
of making architectural ornaments have a core of truth,
a necessity, and hence a beauty, as if it were a revelation
to him. All very well perhaps from his point of view,
but only a little better than the common dilettantism.
A sentimental reformer in architecture, he began at the
cornice, not at the foundation. It was only how to put
a core of truth within the ornaments, that every sugar-
plum, in fact, might have an almond or caraway seed in
it, — though I hold that almonds are most wholesome
without the sugar, — and not how the inhabitant, the
indweller, might build truly within and without, and let
the ornaments take care of themselves. What reasonable man ever supposed that ornaments were something
outward and in the skin merely, — that the tortoise got
his spotted shell, or the shell-fish its mother-o'-pearl
tints, by such a contract as the inhabitants of Broad-

way their Trinity Church? But a man has no more to do
with the style of architecture of his house than a tortoise
with that of its shell: nor need the soldier be so idle as
to try to paint the precise *color* of his virtue on his standard. The enemy will find it out. He may turn pale
when the trial comes. This man seemed to me to lean
over the cornice, and timidly whisper his half truth to
the rude occupants who really knew it better than he.
What of architectural beauty I now see, I know has
gradually grown from within outward, out of the necessities and character of the indweller, who is the only
builder, — out of some unconscious truthfulness, and
nobleness, without ever a thought for the appearance;
and whatever additional beauty of this kind is destined
to be produced will be preceded by a like unconscious
beauty of life. The most interesting dwellings in this
country, as the painter knows, are the most unpretend-
ing, humble log huts and cottages of the poor commonly; it is the life of the inhabitants whose shells they
are, and not any peculiarity in their surfaces merely,
which makes them *picturesque;* and equally interesting
will be the citizen's suburban box, when his life shall be
as simple and as agreeable to the imagination, and there
is as little straining after effect in the style of his dwelling. A great proportion of architectural ornaments are
literally hollow, and a September gale would strip them
off, like borrowed plumes, without injury to the sub-
stantials. They can do without *architecture* who have
no olives nor wines in the cellar. What if an equal ado
were made about the ornaments of style in literature,
and the architects of our bibles spent as much time

about their cornices as the architects of our churches do? So are made the *belles-lettres* and the *beaux-arts* and their professors. Much it concerns a man, forsooth, how a few sticks are slanted over him or under him, and what colors are daubed upon his box. It would signify somewhat, if, in any earnest sense, *he* slanted them and daubed it; but the spirit having departed out of the tenant, it is of a piece with constructing his own coffin, — the architecture of the grave, and "carpenter" is but another name for "coffin-maker." One man says, in his despair or indifference to life, take up a handful of the earth at your feet, and paint your house that color. Is he thinking of his last and narrow house? Toss up a copper for it as well. What an abundance of leisure he must have! Why do you take up a handful of dirt? Better paint your house your own complexion; let it turn pale or blush for you. An enterprise to improve the style of cottage architecture! When you have got my ornaments ready, I will wear them.

Before winter I built a chimney, and shingled the sides of my house, which were already impervious to rain, with imperfect and sappy shingles made of the first slice of the log, whose edges I was obliged to straighten with a plane.

I have thus a tight shingled and plastered house, ten feet wide by fifteen long, and eight-feet posts, with a garret and a closet, a large window on each side, two trap-doors, one door at the end, and a brick fireplace opposite. The exact cost of my house, paying the usual price for such materials as I used, but not counting the work, all of which was done by myself, was as follows;

and I give the details because very few are able to tell
exactly what their houses cost, and fewer still, if any,
the separate cost of the various materials which com-
pose them: —

Boards	$8 03½,	mostly·shanty boards.
Refuse shingles for roof and		
sides	4 00	
Laths	1 25	
Two second-hand windows		
with glass	2 43	
One thousand old brick .	4 00	
Two casks of lime . . .	2 40	That was high.
Hair	0 31	More than I needed.
Mantle-tree iron	0 15	
Nails	3 90	
Hinges and screws . . .	0 14	
Latch	0 10	
Chalk	0 01	
Transportation	1 40	{ I carried a good part on my back.
In all	$28 12½	

These are all the materials, excepting the timber,
stones, and sand, which I claimed by squatter's right.
I have also a small woodshed adjoining, made chiefly
of the stuff which was left after building the house.

I intend to build me a house which will surpass any
on the main street in Concord in grandeur and luxury,
as soon as it pleases me as much and will cost me no
more than my present one.

I thus found that the student who wishes for a shelter
can obtain one for a lifetime at an expense not greater

than the rent which he now pays annually. If I seem to boast more than is becoming, my excuse is that I brag for humanity rather than for myself; and my short-comings and inconsistencies do not affect the truth of my statement. Notwithstanding much cant and hypoc-risy, — chaff which I find it difficult to separate from my wheat, but for which I am as sorry as any man, — I will breathe freely and stretch myself in this respect, it is such a relief to both the moral and physical sys-tem; and I am resolved that I will not through humility become the devil's attorney. I will endeavor to speak a good word for the truth. At Cambridge College the mere rent of a student's room, which is only a little larger than my own, is thirty dollars each year, though the corporation had the advantage of building thirty-two side by side and under one roof, and the occupant suffers the inconvenience of many and noisy neighbors, and perhaps a residence in the fourth story. I cannot but think that if we had more true wisdom in these respects, not only less education would be needed, be-cause, forsooth, more would already have been acquired, but the pecuniary expense of getting an education would in a great measure vanish. Those conveniences which the student requires at Cambridge or elsewhere cost him or somebody else ten times as great a sacrifice of life as they would with proper management on both sides. Those things for which the most money is de-manded are never the things which the student most wants. Tuition, for instance, is an important item in the term bill, while for the far more valuable education which he gets by associating with the most cultivated of his contemporaries no charge is made. The mode of founding a college is, commonly, to get up a subscription of dollars and cents, and then, following blindly the principles of a division of labor to its extreme, — a principle which should never be followed but with circumspection, — to call in a contractor who makes this a subject of speculation, and he employs Irishmen or other operatives actually to lay the foundations, while the students that are to be are said to be fitting themselves for it; and for these oversights successive generations have to pay. I think that it would be *better than this*, for the students, or those who desire to be benefited by it, even to lay the foundation themselves. The student who secures his coveted leisure and retirement by systematically shirking any labor necessary to man obtains but an ignoble and unprofitable leisure, defrauding himself of the experience which alone can make leisure fruitful. "But," says one, "you do not mean that the students should go to work with their hands instead of their heads?" I do not mean that exactly, but I mean something which he might think a good deal like that; I mean that they should not *play* life, or *study* it merely, while the community supports them at this expensive game, but earnestly *live* it from beginning to end. How could youths better learn to live than by at once trying the experiment of living? Methinks this would exercise their minds as much as mathematics. If I wished a boy to know something about the arts and sciences, for instance, I would not pursue the common course, which is merely to send him into the neighborhood of some professor, where anything is professed and practised

but the art of life; — to survey the world through a
telescope or a microscope, and never with his natural
eye; to study chemistry, and not learn how his bread is
made, or mechanics, and not learn how it is earned; to
discover new satellites to Neptune, and not detect the
motes in his eyes, or to what vagabond he is a satellite
himself; or to be devoured by the monsters that swarm
all around him, while contemplating the monsters in a
drop of vinegar. Which would have advanced the most
at the end of a month, — the boy who had made his
own jackknife from the ore which he had dug and
smelted, reading as much as would be necessary for
this — or the boy who had attended the lectures on
metallurgy at the Institute in the meanwhile, and had
received a Rogers penknife from his father? Which
would be most likely to cut his fingers? . . . To my
astonishment I was informed on leaving college that I
had studied navigation! — why, if I had taken one turn
down the harbor I should have known more about it.
Even the *poor* student studies and is taught only *political*
economy, while that economy of living which is synonymous with philosophy is not even sincerely professed
in our colleges. The consequence is, that while he is
reading Adam Smith, Ricardo, and Say, he runs his
father in debt irretrievably.

As with our colleges, so with a hundred "modern
improvements;" there is an illusion about them; there
is not always a positive advance. The devil goes on
exacting compound interest to the last for his early share
and numerous succeeding investments in them. Our
inventions are wont to be pretty toys, which distract

our attention from serious things. They are but improved means to an unimproved end, an end which
it was already but too easy to arrive at; as railroads lead
to Boston or New York. We are in great haste to construct a magnetic telegraph from Maine to Texas; but
Maine and Texas, it may be, have nothing important
to communicate. Either is in such a predicament as the
man who was earnest to be introduced to a distinguished
deaf woman, but when he was presented, and one end
of her ear trumpet was put into his hand, had nothing
to say. As if the main object were to talk fast and not
to talk sensibly. We are eager to tunnel under the Atlantic and bring the Old World some weeks nearer to the
New; but perchance the first news that will leak through
into the broad, flapping American ear will be that the
Princess Adelaide has the whooping cough. After all, the
man whose horse trots a mile in a minute does not carry
the most important messages; he is not an evangelist,
nor does he come round eating locusts and wild honey.
I doubt if Flying Childers ever carried a peck of corn
to mill.

One says to me, "I wonder that you do not lay up
money; you love to travel; you might take the cars and
go to Fitchburg to-day and see the country." But I am
wiser than that. I have learned that the swiftest traveller
is he that goes afoot. I say to my friend, Suppose we try
who will get there first. The distance is thirty miles; the
fare ninety cents. That is almost a day's wages. I remember when wages were sixty cents a day for laborers
on this very road. Well, I start now on foot, and get
there before night; I have travelled at that rate by the

week together. You will in the meanwhile have earned your fare, and arrive there some time to-morrow, or possibly this evening, if you are lucky enough to get a job in season. Instead of going to Fitchburg, you will be working here the greater part of the day. And so, if the railroad reached round the world, I think that I should keep ahead of you; and as for seeing the country and getting experience of that kind, I should have to cut your acquaintance altogether.

Such is the universal law, which no man can ever outwit, and with regard to the railroad even we may say it is as broad as it is long. To make a railroad round the world available to all mankind is equivalent to grading the whole surface of the planet. Men have an indistinct notion that if they keep up this activity of joint stocks and spades long enough all will at length ride somewhere, in next to no time, and for nothing; but though a crowd rushes to the depot, and the conductor shouts "All aboard!" when the smoke is blown away and the vapor condensed, it will be perceived that a few are riding, but the rest are run over, — and it will be called, and will be, "A melancholy accident." No doubt they can ride at last who shall have earned their fare, that is, if they survive so long, but they will probably have lost their elasticity and desire to travel by that time. This spending of the best part of one's life earning money in order to enjoy a questionable liberty during the least valuable part of it reminds me of the Englishman who went to India to make a fortune first, in order that he might return to England and live the life of a poet. He should have gone up garret at once. "What!"

exclaim a million Irishmen starting up from all the shanties in the land,"is not this railroad which we have built a good thing?" Yes, I answer, *comparatively* good, that is, you might have done worse; but I wish, as you are brothers of mine, that you could have spent your time better than digging in this dirt.

Before I finished my house, wishing to earn ten or twelve dollars by some honest and agreeable method, in order to meet my unusual expenses, I planted about two acres and a half of light and sandy soil near it chiefly with beans, but also a small part with potatoes, corn, peas, and turnips. The whole lot contains eleven acres, mostly growing up to pines and hickories, and was sold the preceding season for eight dollars and eight cents an acre. One farmer said that it was "good for nothing but to raise cheeping squirrels on." I put no manure whatever on this land, not being the owner, but merely a squatter, and not expecting to cultivate so much again, and I did not quite hoe it all once. I got out several cords of stumps in plowing, which supplied me with fuel for a long time, and left small circles of virgin mould, easily distinguishable through the summer by the greater luxuriance of the beans there. The dead and for the most part unmerchantable wood behind my house, and the driftwood from the pond, have supplied the remainder of my fuel. I was obliged to hire a team and a man for the plowing, though I held the plow myself. My farm outgoes for the first season were, for implements, seed, work, etc., $14.72½. The seed corn was given me. This never costs anything to

speak of, unless you plant more than enough. I got
twelve bushels of beans, and eighteen bushels of potatoes,
beside some peas and sweet corn. The yellow corn and
turnips were too late to come to anything. My whole
income from the farm was

$$\$23\ 44$$

Deducting the outgoes 14 72½

There are left $8 71½,

beside produce consumed and on hand at the time this
estimate was made of the value of $4.50, — the amount
on hand much more than balancing a little grass which
I did not raise. All things considered, that is, considering
the importance of a man's soul and of to-day, notwithstanding the short time occupied by my experiment,
nay, partly even because of its transient character, I
believe that that was doing better than any farmer in
Concord did that year.

The next year I did better still, for I spaded up all the
land which I required, about a third of an acre, and I
learned from the experience of both years, not being in
the least awed by many celebrated works on husbandry,
Arthur Young among the rest, that if one would live
simply and eat only the crop which he raised, and raise
no more than he ate, and not exchange it for an insufficient quantity of more luxurious and expensive things,
he would need to cultivate only a few rods of ground,
and that it would be cheaper to spade up that than to
use oxen to plow it, and to select a fresh spot from
time to time than to manure the old, and he could do all
his necessary farm work as it were with his left hand at

odd hours in the summer; and thus he would not be
tied to an ox, or horse, or cow, or pig, as at present. I
desire to speak impartially on this point, and as one not
interested in the success or failure of the present economical and social arrangements. I was more independent than any farmer in Concord, for I was not
anchored to a house or farm, but could follow the bent
of my genius, which is a very crooked one, every moment. Beside being better off than they already, if my
house had been burned or my crops had failed, I should
have been nearly as well off as before.

I am wont to think that men are not so much the
keepers of herds as herds are the keepers of men, the
former are so much the freer. Men and oxen exchange
work; but if we consider necessary work only, the oxen
will be seen to have greatly the advantage, their farm
is so much the larger. Man does some of his part of the
exchange work in his six weeks of haying, and it is no
boy's play. Certainly no nation that lived simply in all
respects, that is, no nation of philosophers, would commit so great a blunder as to use the labor of animals.
True, there never was and is not likely soon to be a nation of philosophers, nor am I certain it is desirable that
there should be. However, *I* should never have broken
a horse or bull and taken him to board for any work
he might do for me, for fear I should become a horse-
man or a herds-man merely; and if society seems to be
the gainer by so doing, are we certain that what is one
man's gain is not another's loss, and that the stable-boy
has equal cause with his master to be satisfied? Granted
that some public works would not have been constructed

without this aid, and let man share the glory of such with the ox and horse; does it follow that he could not have accomplished works yet more worthy of himself in that case? When men begin to do, not merely unnecessary or artistic, but luxurious and idle work, with their assistance, it is inevitable that a few do all the exchange work with the.oxen, or, in other words, become the slaves of the strongest. Man thus not only works for the animal within him, but, for a symbol of this, he works for the animal without him. Though we have many substantial houses of brick or stone, the prosperity of the farmer is still measured by the degree to which the barn overshadows the house. This town is said to have the largest houses for oxen, cows, and horses hereabouts, and it is not behindhand in its public buildings; but there are very few halls for free worship or free speech in this county. It should not be by their architecture, but why not even by their power of abstract thought, that nations should seek to commemorate themselves? How much more admirable the Bhagvat-Geeta than all the ruins of the East! Towers and temples are the luxury of princes. A simple and independent mind does not toil at the bidding of any prince. Genius is not a retainer to any emperor, nor is its material silver, or gold, or marble, except to a trifling extent. To what end, pray, is so much stone hammered? In Arcadia, when I was there, I did not see any hammering stone. Nations are possessed with an insane ambition to perpetuate the memory of themselves by the amount of hammered stone they leave. What if equal pains were taken to smooth and polish their manners?

One piece of good sense would be more memorable than
a monument as high as the moon. I love better to see
stones in place. The grandeur of Thebes was a vulgar
grandeur. More sensible is a rod of stone wall that
bounds an honest man's field than a hundred-gated
Thebes that has wandered farther from the true end of
life. The religion and civilization which are barbaric
and heathenish build splendid temples; but what you
might call Christianity does not. Most of the stone a
nation hammers goes toward its tomb only. It buries
itself alive. As for the Pyramids, there is nothing to
wonder at in them so much as the fact that so many
men could be found degraded enough to spend their
lives constructing a tomb for some ambitious booby,
whom it would have been wiser and manlier to have
drowned in the Nile, and then given his body to the
dogs. I might possibly invent some excuse for them and
him, but I have no time for it. As for the religion and
love of art of the builders, it is much the same all the
world over, whether the building be an Egyptian temple
or the United States Bank. It costs more than it comes
to. The mainspring is vanity, assisted by the love of
garlic and bread and butter. Mr. Balcom, a promising
young architect, designs it on the back of his Vitruvius,
with hard pencil and ruler, and the job is let out to
Dobson & Sons, stonecutters. When the thirty centuries
begin to look down on it, mankind begin to look up at
it. As for your high towers and monuments, there was
a crazy fellow once in this town who undertook to dig
through to China, and he got so far that, as he said, he
heard the Chinese pots and kettles rattle; but I think

that I shall not go out of my way to admire the hole which he made. Many are concerned about the monuments of the West and the East, — to know who built them. For my part, I should like to know who in those days did not build them, — who were above such trifling. But to proceed with my statistics.

By surveying, carpentry, and day-labor of various other kinds in the village in the meanwhile, for I have as many trades as fingers, I had earned $13.34. The expense of food for eight months, namely, from July 4th to March 1st, the time when these estimates were made, though I lived there more than two years, — not counting potatoes, a little green corn, and some peas, which I had raised, nor considering the value of what was on hand at the last date, — was

Rice	$1 73½	
Molasses	1 73	Cheapest form of the saccharine.
Rye meal	1 04¾	
Indian meal . . .	0 99¾	Cheaper than rye.
Pork	0 22	
Flour	0 88	{ Costs more than Indian meal, both money and trouble.
Sugar	0 80	
Lard	0 05	
Apples	0 25	
Dried apple . . .	0 22	
Sweet potatoes . .	0 10	
One pumpkin . . .	0 6	
One watermelon . .	0 2	
Salt	0 3	

All experiments which failed.

Yes, I did eat $8.74, all told; but I should not thus unblushingly publish my guilt, if I did not know that most of my readers were equally guilty with myself, and that their deeds would look no better in print. The next year I sometimes caught a mess of fish for my dinner, and once I went so far as to slaughter a woodchuck which ravaged my bean-field, — effect his transmigration, as a Tartar would say, — and devour him, partly for experiment's sake; but though it afforded me a momentary enjoyment, notwithstanding a musky flavor, I saw that the longest use would not make that a good practice, however it might seem to have your woodchucks ready dressed by the village butcher.

Clothing and some incidental expenses within the same dates, though little can be inferred from this item, amounted to

$$\$8 \ 40\tfrac{3}{4}$$

Oil and some household utensils . . 2 00

So that all the pecuniary outgoes, excepting for washing and mending, which for the most part were done out of the house, and their bills have not yet been received, — and these are all and more than all the ways by which money necessarily goes out in this part of the world, — were

House	$28 12½
Farm one year	14 72½
Food eight months	8 74
Clothing, etc., eight months	8 40¾
Oil, etc., eight months	2 00
In all	$61 99¾

I address myself now to those of my readers who have a living to get. And to meet this I have for farm produce sold

$23 44

Earned by day-labor 13 34

In all $36 78,

which subtracted from the sum of the outgoes leaves a balance of $25.21¾ on the one side, — this being very nearly the means with which I started, and the measure of expenses to be incurred, — and on the other, beside the leisure and independence and health thus secured, a comfortable house for me as long as I choose to occupy it.

These statistics, however accidental and therefore uninstructive they may appear, as they have a certain completeness, have a certain value also. Nothing was given me of which I have not rendered some account. It appears from the above estimate, that my food alone cost me in money about twenty-seven cents a week. It was, for nearly two years after this, rye and Indian meal without yeast, potatoes, rice, a very little salt pork, molasses, and salt; and my drink, water. It was fit that I should live on rice, mainly, who loved so well the philosophy of India. To meet the objections of some inveterate cavillers, I may as well state, that if I dined out occasionally, as I always had done, and I trust shall have opportunities to do again, it was frequently to the detriment of my domestic arrangements. But the dining out, being, as I have stated, a constant element, does not in the least affect a comparative statement like this.

I learned from my two years' experience that it would cost incredibly little trouble to obtain one's necessary food, even in this latitude; that a man may use as simple a diet as the animals, and yet retain health and strength. I have made a satisfactory dinner, satisfactory on several accounts, simply off a dish of purslane (*Portulaca oleracea*) which I gathered in my cornfield, boiled and salted. I give the Latin on account of the savoriness of the trivial name. And pray what more can a reasonable man desire, in peaceful times, in ordinary noons, than a sufficient number of ears of green sweet corn boiled, with the addition of salt? Even the little variety which I used was a yielding to the demands of appetite, and not of health. Yet men have come to such a pass that they frequently starve, not for want of necessaries, but for want of luxuries; and I know a good woman who thinks that her son lost his life because he took to drinking water only.

The reader will perceive that I am treating the subject rather from an economic than a dietetic point of view, and he will not venture to put my abstemiousness to the test unless he has a well-stocked larder.

Bread I at first made of pure Indian meal and salt, genuine hoe-cakes, which I baked before my fire out of doors on a shingle or the end of a stick of timber sawed off in building my house; but it was wont to get smoked and to have a piny flavor. I tried flour also; but have at last found a mixture of rye and Indian meal most convenient and agreeable. In cold weather it was no little amusement to bake several small loaves of this in succession, tending and turning them as carefully as an

Egyptian his hatching eggs. They were a real cereal fruit which I ripened, and they had to my senses a fragrance like that of other noble fruits, which I kept in as long as possible by wrapping them in cloths. I made a study of the ancient and indispensable art of bread-making, consulting such authorities as offered, going back to the primitive days and first invention of the unleavened kind, when from the wildness of nuts and meats men first reached the mildness and refinement of this diet, and travelling gradually down in my studies through that accidental souring of the dough which, it is supposed, taught the leavening process, and through the various fermentations thereafter, till I came to " good, sweet, wholesome bread," the staff of life. Leaven, which some deem the soul of bread, the *spiritus* which fills its cellular tissue, which is religiously preserved like the vestal fire, — some precious bottleful, I suppose, first brought over in the Mayflower, did the business for America, and its influence is still rising, swelling, spreading, in cerealian billows over the land, — this seed I regularly and faithfully procured from the village, till at length one morning I forgot the rules, and scalded my yeast; by which accident I discovered that even this was not indispensable, — for my discoveries were not by the synthetic but analytic process, — and I have gladly omitted it since, though most housewives earnestly assured me that safe and wholesome bread without yeast might not be, and elderly people prophesied a speedy decay of the vital forces. Yet I find it not to be an essential ingredient, and after going without it for a year am still in the land of the living; and I

am glad to escape the trivialness of carrying a bottleful in my pocket, which would sometimes pop and dis-
charge its contents to my discomfiture. It is simpler and
more respectable to omit it. Man is an animal who
more than any other can adapt himself to all climates
and circumstances. Neither did I put any sal-soda, or
other acid or alkali, into my bread. It would seem that I
made it according to the recipe which Marcus Porcius
Cato gave about two centuries before Christ. "Panem
depsticium sic facito. Manus mortariumque bene lavato.
Farinam in mortarium indito, aquae paulatim addito,
subigitoque pulchre. Ubi bene subegeris, defingito, co-
quitoque sub testu." Which I take to mean, "Make
kneaded bread thus. Wash your hands and trough well.
Put the meal into the trough, add water gradually, and
knead it thoroughly. When you have kneaded it
well, mould it, and bake it under a cover," that is, in a
baking-kettle. Not a word about leaven. But I did not
always use this staff of life. At one time, owing to the
emptiness of my purse, I saw none of it for more than a
month.

Every New Englander might easily raise all his own
breadstuffs in this land of rye and Indian corn, and not
depend on distant and fluctuating markets for them.
Yet so far are we from simplicity and independence
that, in Concord, fresh and sweet meal is rarely sold in
the shops, and hominy and corn in a still coarser form are
hardly used by any. For the most part the farmer gives
to his cattle and hogs the grain of his own producing,
and buys flour, which is at least no more wholesome, at
a greater cost, at the store. I saw that I could easily

raise my bushel or two of rye and Indian corn, for the former will grow on the poorest land, and the latter does not require the best, and grind them in a hand-mill, and so do without rice and pork; and if I must have some concentrated sweet, I found by experiment that I could make a very good molasses either of pumpkins or beets, and I knew that I needed only to set out a few maples to obtain it more easily still, and while these were growing I could use various substitutes beside those which I have named. "For," as the Forefathers sang, —

"we can make liquor to sweeten our lips
Of pumpkins and parsnips and walnut-tree chips."

Finally, as for salt, that grossest of groceries, to obtain this might be a fit occasion for a visit to the seashore, or, if I did without it altogether, I should probably drink the less water. I do not learn that the Indians ever troubled themselves to go after it.

Thus I could avoid all trade and barter, so far as my food was concerned, and having a shelter already, it would only remain to get clothing and fuel. The pantaloons which I now wear were woven in a farmer's family, — thank Heaven there is so much virtue still in man; for I think the fall from the farmer to the operative as great and memorable as that from the man to the farmer; — and in a new country, fuel is an encumbrance. As for a habitat, if I were not permitted still to squat, I might purchase one acre at the same price for which the land I cultivated was sold — namely, eight dollars and eight cents. But as it was, I considered that I enhanced the value of the land by squatting on it.

There is a certain class of unbelievers who sometimes ask me such questions as, if I think that I can live on vegetable food alone; and to strike at the root of the matter at once, — for the root is faith, — I am accustomed to answer such, that I can live on board nails. If they cannot understand that, they cannot understand much that I have to say. For my part, I am glad to hear of experiments of this kind being tried; as that a young man tried for a fortnight to live on hard, raw corn on the ear, using his teeth for all mortar. The squirrel tribe tried the same and succeeded. The human race is interested in these experiments, though a few old women who are incapacitated for them, or who own their thirds in mills, may be alarmed.

My furniture, part of which I made myself, — and the rest cost me nothing of which I have not rendered an account, — consisted of a bed, a table, a desk, three chairs, a looking-glass three inches in diameter, a pair of tongs and andirons, a kettle, a skillet, and a frying-pan, a dipper, a wash-bowl, two knives and forks, three plates, one cup, one spoon, a jug for oil, a jug for molasses, and a japanned lamp. None is so poor that he need sit on a pumpkin. That is shiftlessness. There is a plenty of such chairs as I like best in the village garrets to be had for taking them away. Furniture! Thank God, I can sit and I can stand without the aid of a furniture warehouse. What man but a philosopher would not be ashamed to see his furniture packed in a cart and going up country exposed to the light of heaven and the eyes of men, a beggarly account of empty boxes? That is Spaulding's furniture. I could never tell from inspecting such a load whether it belonged to a so-called rich man or a poor one; the owner always seemed poverty-stricken. Indeed, the more you have of such things the poorer you are. Each load looks as if it contained the contents of a dozen shanties; and if one shanty is poor, this is a dozen times as poor. Pray, for what do we *move* ever but to get rid of our furniture, our *exuviæ;* at last to go from this world to another newly furnished, and leave this to be burned? It is the same as if all these traps were buckled to a man's belt, and he could not move over the rough country where our lines are cast without dragging them, — dragging his trap. He was a lucky fox that left his tail in the trap. The muskrat will gnaw his third leg off to be free. No wonder man has lost his elasticity. How often he is at a dead set! "Sir, if I may be so bold, what do you mean by a dead set?" If you are a seer, whenever you meet a man you will see all that he owns, ay, and much that he pretends to disown, behind him, even to his kitchen furniture and all the trumpery which he saves and will not burn, and he will appear to be harnessed to it and making what headway he can. I think that the man is at a dead set who has got through a knot-hole or gateway where his sledge load of furniture cannot follow him. I cannot but feel compassion when I hear some trig, compact-looking man, seemingly free, all girded and ready, speak of his "furniture," as whether it is insured or not. "But what shall I do with my furniture?" My gay butterfly is entangled in a spider's web then. Even those who seem for a long while not to have any,

if you inquire more narrowly you will find have some
stored in somebody's barn. I look upon England to-
day as an old gentleman who is travelling with a great
deal of baggage, trumpery which has accumulated from
long housekeeping, which he has not the courage to
burn; great trunk, little trunk, bandbox and bundle.
Throw away the first three at least. It would surpass
the powers of a well man nowadays to take up his bed
and walk, and I should certainly advise a sick one to
lay down his bed and run. When I have met an immi-
grant tottering under a bundle which contained his all,
— looking like an enormous wen which had grown out
of the nape of his neck, — I have pitied him, not because
that was his all, but because he had all *that* to carry. If
I have got to drag my trap, I will take care that it be
a light one and do not nip me in a vital part. But
perchance it would be wisest never to put one's paw
into it.

I would observe, by the way, that it costs me nothing
for curtains, for I have no gazers to shut out but the
sun and moon, and I am willing that they should look
in. The moon will not sour milk nor taint meat of mine,
nor will the sun injure my furniture or fade my carpet;
and if he is sometimes too warm a friend, I find it still
better economy to retreat behind some curtain which
nature has provided, than to add a single item to the
details of housekeeping. A lady once offered me a mat,
but as I had no room to spare within the house, nor
time to spare within or without to shake it, I declined
it, preferring to wipe my feet on the sod before my door.
It is best to avoid the beginnings of evil.

Not long since I was present at the auction of a deacon's effects, for his life had not been ineffectual: —

"The evil that men do lives after them."

As usual, a great proportion was trumpery which had begun to accumulate in his father's day. Among the rest was a dried tapeworm. And now, after lying half a century in his garret and other dust holes, these things were not burned; instead of a *bonfire*, or purifying destruction of them, there was an *auction*, or increasing of them. The neighbors eagerly collected to view them, bought them all, and carefully transported them to their garrets and dust holes, to lie there till their estates are settled, when they will start again. When a man dies he kicks the dust.

The customs of some savage nations might, perchance, be profitably imitated by us, for they at least go through the semblance of casting their slough annually; they have the idea of the thing, whether they have the reality or not. Would it not be well if we were to celebrate such a "busk," or "feast of first fruits," as Bartram describes to have been the custom of the Mucclasse Indians? "When a town celebrates the busk," says he, "having previously provided themselves with new clothes, new pots, pans, and other household utensils and furniture, they collect all their worn out clothes and other despicable things, sweep and cleanse their houses, squares, and the whole town, of their filth, which with all the remaining grain and other old provisions they cast together into one common heap, and consume it with fire. After having taken medicine, and fasted for three days, all the fire in the town is extinguished. During this fast they abstain from the gratification of every appetite and passion whatever. A general amnesty is proclaimed; all malefactors may return to their town."

"On the fourth morning, the high priest, by rubbing dry wood together, produces new fire in the public square, from whence every habitation in the town is supplied with the new and pure flame."

They then feast on the new corn and fruits, and dance and sing for three days, "and the four following days they receive visits and rejoice with their friends from neighboring towns who have in like manner purified and prepared themselves."

The Mexicans also practised a similar purification at the end of every fifty-two years, in the belief that it was time for the world to come to an end.

I have scarcely heard of a truer sacrament, that is, as the dictionary defines it, "outward and visible sign of an inward and spiritual grace," than this, and I have no doubt that they were originally inspired directly from Heaven to do thus, though they have no Biblical record of the revelation.

For more than five years I maintained myself thus solely by the labor of my hands, and I found that, by working about six weeks in a year, I could meet all the expenses of living. The whole of my winters, as well as most of my summers, I had free and clear for study. I have thoroughly tried school-keeping, and found that my expenses were in proportion, or rather out of proportion, to my income, for I was obliged to dress and train, not to say think and believe, accordingly, and I lost my time into the bargain. As I did not teach for the good of my fellow-men, but simply for a livelihood, this was a failure. I have tried trade; but I found that it would take ten years to get under way in that, and that then I should probably be on my way to the devil. I was actually afraid that I might by that time be doing what is called a good business. When formerly I was looking about to see what I could do for a living, some sad experience in conforming to the wishes of friends being fresh in my mind to tax my ingenuity, I thought often and seriously of picking huckleberries; that surely I could do, and its small profits might suffice, — for my greatest skill has been to want but little, — so little capital it required, so little distraction from my wonted moods, I foolishly thought. While my acquaintances went unhesitatingly into trade or the professions, I contemplated this occupation as most like theirs; ranging the hills all summer to pick the berries which came in my way, and thereafter carelessly dispose of them; so, to keep the flocks of Admetus. I also dreamed that I might gather the wild herbs, or carry evergreens to such villagers as loved to be reminded of the woods, even to the city, by hay-cart loads. But I have since learned that trade curses everything it handles; and though you trade in messages from heaven, the whole curse of trade attaches to the business.

As I preferred some things to others, and especially valued my freedom, as I could fare hard and yet succeed well, I did not wish to spend my time in earning rich carpets or other fine furniture, or delicate cookery, or a house in the Grecian or the Gothic style just yet. If there are any to whom it is no interruption to acquire these things, and who know how to use them when acquired, I relinquish to them the pursuit. Some are "industrious," and appear to love labor for its own sake, or perhaps because it keeps them out of worse mischief; to such I have at present nothing to say. Those who would not know what to do with more leisure than they now enjoy, I might advise to work twice as hard as they do, — work till they pay for themselves, and get their free papers. For myself I found that the occupation of a day-laborer was the most independent of any, especially as it required only thirty or forty days in a year to support one. The laborer's day ends with the going down of the sun, and he is then free to devote himself to his chosen pursuit, independent of his labor; but his employer, who speculates from month to month, has no respite from one end of the year to the other.

In short, I am convinced, both by faith and experience, that to maintain one's self on this earth is not a hardship but a pastime, if we will live simply and wisely; as the pursuits of the simpler nations are still the sports of the more artificial. It is not necessary that a man should earn his living by the sweat of his brow, unless he sweats easier than I do.

One young man of my acquaintance, who has inherited some acres, told me that he thought he should live as I did, *if he had the means.* I would not have any one adopt *my* mode of living on any account; for, beside that before he has fairly learned it I may have found

out another for myself, I desire that there may be as
many different persons in the world as possible; but I
would have each one be very careful to find out and
pursue *his own* way, and not his father's or his mother's
or his neighbor's instead. The youth may build or plant
or sail, only let him not be hindered from doing that
which he tells me he would like to do. It is by a mathe-
matical point only that we are wise, as the sailor or the
fugitive slave keeps the polestar in his eye; but that is
sufficient guidance for all our life. We may not arrive
at our port within a calculable period, but we would
preserve the true course.

Undoubtedly, in this case, what is true for one is truer
still for a thousand, as a large house is not proportionally
more expensive than a small one, since one roof may
cover, one cellar underlie, and one wall separate several
apartments. But for my part, I preferred the solitary
dwelling. Moreover, it will commonly be cheaper to
build the whole yourself than to convince another of the
advantage of the common wall; and when you have
done this, the common partition, to be much cheaper,
must be a thin one, and that other may prove a bad
neighbor, and also not keep his side in repair. The only
coöperation which is commonly possible is exceedingly
partial and superficial; and what little true coöperation
there is, is as if it were not, being a harmony inaudible
to men. If a man has faith, he will coöperate with equal
faith everywhere; if he has not faith, he will continue to
live like the rest of the world, whatever company he is
joined to. To coöperate in the highest as well as the
lowest sense, means *to get our living together*. I heard it

proposed lately that two young men should travel together over the world, the one without money, earning his means as he went, before the mast and behind
the plow, the other carrying a bill of exchange in his
pocket. It was easy to see that they could not long be
companions or coöperate, since one would not *operate*
at all. They would part at the first interesting crisis in
their adventures. Above all, as I have implied, the man
who goes alone can start to-day; but he who travels
with another must wait till that other is ready, and it
may be a long time before they get off.

But all this is very selfish, I have heard some of my
townsmen say. I confess that I have hitherto indulged
very little in philanthropic enterprises. I have made
some sacrifices to a sense of duty, and among others have
sacrificed this pleasure also. There are those who have
used all their arts to persuade me to undertake the support of some poor family in the town; and if I had nothing to do — for the devil finds employment for the idle
— I might try my hand at some such pastime as that.
However, when I have thought to indulge myself in this
respect, and lay their Heaven under an obligation by
maintaining certain poor persons in all respects as comfortably as I maintain myself, and have even ventured
so far as to make them the offer, they have one and all
unhesitatingly preferred to remain poor. While my
townsmen and women are devoted in so many ways to
the good of their fellows, I trust that one at least may be
spared to other and less humane pursuits. You must
have a genius for charity as well as for anything else. As

for Doing-good, that is one of the professions which are full. Moreover, I have tried it fairly, and, strange as it may seem, am satisfied that it does not agree with my constitution. Probably I should not consciously and deliberately forsake my particular calling to do the good which society demands of me, to save the universe from annihilation; and I believe that a like but infinitely greater steadfastness elsewhere is all that now preserves it. But I would not stand between any man and his genius; and to him who does this work, which I decline, with his whole heart and soul and life, I would say, Persevere, even if the world call it doing evil, as it is most likely they will.

I am far from supposing that my case is a peculiar one; no doubt many of my readers would make a similar defence. At doing something, — I will not engage that my neighbors shall pronounce it good, — I do not hesitate to say that I should be a capital fellow to hire; but what that is, it is for my employer to find out. What *good* I do, in the common sense of that word, must be aside from my main path, and for the most part wholly unintended. Men say, practically, Begin where you are and such as you are, without aiming mainly to become of more worth, and with kindness aforethought go about doing good. If I were to preach at all in this strain, I should say rather, Set about being good. As if the sun should stop when he had kindled his fires up to the splendor of a moon or a star of the sixth magnitude, and go about like a Robin Goodfellow, peeping in at every cottage window, inspiring lunatics, and tainting meats, and making darkness visible, instead of steadily increasing his

genial heat and beneficence till he is of such brightness
that no mortal can look him in the face, and then, and
in the meanwhile too, going about the world in his own
orbit, doing it good, or rather, as a truer philosophy has
discovered, the world going about him getting good.
When Phaëton, wishing to prove his heavenly birth by
his beneficence, had the sun's chariot but one day, and
drove out of the beaten track, he burned several blocks
of houses in the lower streets of heaven, and scorched the
surface of the earth, and dried up every spring, and made
the great desert of Sahara, till at length Jupiter hurled
him headlong to the earth with a thunderbolt, and the
sun, through grief at his death, did not shine for a year.

There is no odor so bad as that which arises from goodness tainted. It is human, it is divine, carrion. If I knew
for a certainty that a man was coming to my house with
the conscious design of doing me good, I should run for
my life, as from that dry and parching wind of the African deserts called the simoom, which fills the mouth and
nose and ears and eyes with dust till you are suffocated,
for fear that I should get some of his good done to me,
— some of its virus mingled with my blood. No, — in
this case I would rather suffer evil the natural way. A
man is not a good *man* to me because he will feed me if
I should be starving, or warm me if I should be freezing,
or pull me out of a ditch if I should ever fall into one. I
can find you a Newfoundland dog that will do as much.
Philanthropy is not love for one's fellow-man in the
broadest sense. Howard was no doubt an exceedingly
kind and worthy man in his way, and has his reward;
but, comparatively speaking, what are a hundred How-

ards to *us*, if their philanthropy do not help *us* in our best estate, when we are most worthy to be helped? I never heard of a philanthropic meeting in which it was sincerely proposed to do any good to me, or the like of me.

The Jesuits were quite balked by those Indians who, being burned at the stake, suggested new modes of torture to their tormentors. Being superior to physical suffering, it sometimes chanced that they were superior to any consolation which the missionaries could offer; and the law to do as you would be done by fell with less persuasiveness on the ears of those who, for their part, did not care how they were done by, who loved their enemies after a new fashion, and came very near freely forgiving them all they did.

Be sure that you give the poor the aid they most need, though it be your example which leaves them far behind. If you give money, spend yourself with it, and do not merely abandon it to them. We make curious mistakes sometimes. Often the poor man is not so cold and hungry as he is dirty and ragged and gross. It is partly his taste, and not merely his misfortune. If you give him money, he will perhaps buy more rags with it. I was wont to pity the clumsy Irish laborers who cut ice on the pond, in such mean and ragged clothes, while I shivered in my more tidy and somewhat more fashionable garments, till, one bitter cold day, one who had slipped into the water came to my house to warm him, and I saw him strip off three pairs of pants and two pairs of stockings ere he got down to the skin, though they were dirty and ragged enough, it is true, and that he could afford to refuse the *extra* garments which I offered him, he had so many *intra* ones. This ducking was the very thing he needed. Then I began to pity myself, and I saw that it would be a greater charity to bestow on me a flannel shirt than a whole slop-shop on him. There are a thousand hacking at the branches of evil to one who is striking at the root, and it may be that he who bestows the largest amount of time and money on the needy is doing the most by his mode of life to produce that misery which he strives in vain to relieve. It is the pious slave-breeder devoting the proceeds of every tenth slave to buy a Sunday's liberty for the rest. Some show their kindness to the poor by employing them in their kitchens. Would they not be kinder if they employed themselves there? You boast of spending a tenth part of your income in charity; maybe you should spend the nine tenths so, and done with it. Society recovers only a tenth part of the property then. Is this owing to the generosity of him in whose possession it is found, or to the remissness of the officers of justice?

Philanthropy is almost the only virtue which is sufficiently appreciated by mankind. Nay, it is greatly overrated; and it is our selfishness which overrates it. A robust poor man, one sunny day here in Concord, praised a fellow-townsman to me, because, as he said, he was kind to the poor; meaning himself. The kind uncles and aunts of the race are more esteemed than its true spiritual fathers and mothers. I once heard a reverend lecturer on England, a man of learning and intelligence, after enumerating her scientific, literary, and political worthies, Shakespeare, Bacon, Crom-

well, Milton, Newton, and others, speak next of her
Christian heroes, whom, as if his profession required it
of him, he elevated to a place far above all the rest, as
the greatest of the great.   They were Penn, Howard,
and Mrs. Fry.   Every one must feel the falsehood and
cant of this.   The last were not England's best men and
women; only, perhaps, her best philanthropists.

I would not subtract anything from the praise that
is due to philanthropy, but merely demand justice for
all who by their lives and works are a blessing to mankind.   I do not value chiefly a man's uprightness and
benevolence, which are, as it were, his stem and leaves.
Those plants of whose greenness withered we make
herb tea for the sick serve but a humble use, and are
most employed by quacks.   I want the flower and fruit
of a man; that some fragrance be wafted over from him
to me, and some ripeness flavor our intercourse.   His
goodness must not be a partial and transitory act, but
a constant superfluity, which costs him nothing and of
which he is unconscious.   This is a charity that hides a
multitude of sins.   The philanthropist too often surrounds mankind with the remembrance of his own cast-
off griefs as an atmosphere, and calls it sympathy.   We
should impart our courage, and not our despair, our
health and ease, and not our disease, and take care that
this does not spread by contagion.   From what southern
plains comes up the voice of wailing?   Under what latitudes reside the heathen to whom we would send light?
Who is that intemperate and brutal man whom we would
redeem?   If anything ail a man, so that he does not perform his functions, if he have a pain in his bowels even,

— for that is the seat of sympathy, — he forthwith sets about reforming — the world. Being a microcosm himself, he discovers — and it is a true discovery, and he is the man to make it — that the world has been eating green apples; to his eyes, in fact, the globe itself is a great green apple, which there is danger awful to think of that the children of men will nibble before it is ripe; and straightway his drastic philanthropy seeks out the Esquimau and the Patagonian, and embraces the populous Indian and Chinese villages; and thus, by a few years of philanthropic activity, the powers in the meanwhile using him for their own ends, no doubt, he cures himself of his dyspepsia, the globe acquires a faint blush on one or both of its cheeks, as if it were beginning to be ripe, and life loses its crudity and is once more sweet and wholesome to live. I never dreamed of any enormity greater than I have committed. I never knew, and never shall know, a worse man than myself.

I believe that what so saddens the reformer is not his sympathy with his fellows in distress, but, though he be the holiest son of God, is his private ail. Let this be righted, let the spring come to him, the morning rise over his couch, and he will forsake his generous companions without apology. My excuse for not lecturing against the use of tobacco is, that I never chewed it, that is a penalty which reformed tobacco-chewers have to pay; though there are things enough I have chewed which I could lecture against. If you should ever be betrayed into any of these philanthropies, do not let your left hand know what your right hand does, for it is not worth knowing. Rescue the drowning and tie your shoestrings. Take your time, and set about some free labor.

Our manners have been corrupted by communication with the saints. Our hymn-books resound with a melodious cursing of God and enduring Him forever. One would say that even the prophets and redeemers had rather consoled the fears than confirmed the hopes of man. There is nowhere recorded a simple and irrepressible satisfaction with the gift of life, any memorable praise of God. All health and success does me good, however far off and withdrawn it may appear; all disease and failure helps to make me sad and does me evil, however much sympathy it may have with me or I with it. If, then, we would indeed restore mankind by truly Indian, botanic, magnetic, or natural means, let us first be as simple and well as Nature ourselves, dispel the clouds which hang over our own brows, and take up a little life into our pores. Do not stay to be an overseer of the poor, but endeavor to become one of the worthies of the world.

I read in the Gulistan, or Flower Garden, of Sheik Sadi of Shiraz, that "they asked a wise man, saying: Of the many celebrated trees which the Most High God has created lofty and umbrageous, they call none azad, or free, excepting the cypress, which bears no fruit; what mystery is there in this? He replied: Each has its appropriate produce, and appointed season, during the continuance of which it is fresh and blooming, and during their absence dry and withered; to neither of which states is the cypress exposed, being always flourishing; and of this nature are the azads, or religious independents. — Fix not thy heart on that which is transitory; for the Dijlah, or Tigris, will continue to flow through Bagdad after the race of caliphs is extinct: if thy hand has plenty, be liberal as the date tree; but if it affords nothing to give away, be an azad, or free man, like the cypress."

COMPLEMENTAL VERSES

THE PRETENSIONS OF POVERTY

Thou dost presume too much, poor needy wretch,
To claim a station in the firmament
Because thy humble cottage, or thy tub,
Nurses some lazy or pedantic virtue
In the cheap sunshine or by shady springs,
With roots and pot-herbs; where thy right hand,
Tearing those humane passions from the mind,
Upon whose stocks fair blooming virtues flourish,
Degradeth nature, and benumbeth sense,
And, Gorgon-like, turns active men to stone.
We not require the dull society
Of your necessitated temperance,
Or that unnatural stupidity
That knows nor joy nor sorrow; nor your forc'd
Falsely exalted passive fortitude
Above the active. This low abject brood,
That fix their seats in mediocrity,
Become your servile minds; but we advance
Such virtues only as admit excess,
Brave, bounteous acts, regal magnificence,
All-seeing prudence, magnanimity
That knows no bound, and that heroic virtue
For which antiquity hath left no name,
But patterns only, such as Hercules,
Achilles, Theseus. Back to thy loath'd cell;
And when thou seest the new enlightened sphere,
Study to know but what those worthies were.

                              T. CAREW.

II

WHERE I LIVED, AND WHAT I LIVED FOR

At a certain season of our life we are accustomed to consider every spot as the possible site of a house. I have thus surveyed the country on every side within a dozen miles of where I live. In imagination I have bought all the farms in succession, for all were to be bought, and I knew their price. I walked over each farmer's premises, tasted his wild apples, discoursed on husbandry with him, took his farm at his price, at any price, mortgaging it to him in my mind; even put a higher price on it, — took everything but a deed of it, — took his word for his deed, for I dearly love to talk, — cultivated it, and him too to some extent, I trust, and withdrew when I had enjoyed it long enough, leaving him to carry it on. This experience entitled me to be regarded as a sort of real-estate broker by my friends. Wherever I sat, there I might live, and the landscape radiated from me accordingly. What is a house but a *sedes*, a seat? — better if a country seat. I discovered many a site for a house not likely to be soon improved, which some might have thought too far from the village, but to my eyes the village was too far from it. Well, there I might live, I said; and there I did live, for an hour, a summer and a winter life; saw how I could let the years run off, buffet the winter through, and see the spring come in. The future inhabitants of this region, wherever they may place their houses, may be sure that they have been anticipated. An afternoon sufficed to lay out the land into orchard, wood-lot, and pasture, and to decide what fine oaks or pines should be left to stand before the door, and whence each blasted tree could be seen to the best advantage; and then I let it lie, fallow perchance, for a man is rich in proportion to the number of things which he can afford to let alone.

My imagination carried me so far that I even had the refusal of several farms, — the refusal was all I wanted, — but I never got my fingers burned by actual possession. The nearest that I came to actual possession was when I bought the Hollowell place, and had begun to sort my seeds, and collected materials with which to make a wheelbarrow to carry it on or off with; but before the owner gave me a deed of it, his wife — every man has such a wife — changed her mind and wished to keep it, and he offered me ten dollars to release him. Now, to speak the truth, I had but ten cents in the world, and it surpassed my arithmetic to tell, if I was that man who had ten cents, or who had a farm, or ten dollars, or all together. However, I let him keep the ten dollars and the farm too, for I had carried it far enough; or rather, to be generous, I sold him the farm for just what I gave for it, and, as he was not a rich man, made him a present of ten dollars, and still had my ten cents, and seeds, and materials for a wheelbarrow left. I found thus that I had been a rich man without any damage to my poverty. But I retained the landscape, and I have since annually carried off what it yielded without a wheelbarrow. With respect to landscapes, —

"I am monarch of all I *survey*,
My right there is none to dispute."

I have frequently seen a poet withdraw, having enjoyed the most valuable part of a farm, while the crusty farmer supposed that he had got a few wild apples only. Why, the owner does not know it for many years when a poet has put his farm in rhyme, the most admirable kind of invisible fence, has fairly impounded it, milked it, skimmed it, and got all the cream, and left the farmer only the skimmed milk.

The real attractions of the Hollowell farm, to me, were: its complete retirement, being about two miles from the village, half a mile from the nearest neighbor, and separated from the highway by a broad field; its bounding on the river, which the owner said protected it by its fogs from frosts in the spring, though that was nothing to me; the gray color and ruinous state of the house and barn, and the dilapidated fences, which put such an interval between me and the last occupant; the hollow and lichen-covered apple trees, gnawed by rabbits, showing what kind of neighbors I should have; but above all, the recollection I had of it from my earliest voyages up the river, when the house was concealed behind a dense grove of red maples, through which I heard the house-dog bark. I was in haste to buy it, before the proprietor finished getting out some rocks, cutting down the hollow apple trees, and grubbing up some young birches which had sprung up in the pasture, or, in short, had made any more of his improvements. To enjoy these advantages I was ready to carry it on; like Atlas, to take the world on my shoulders, — I never heard what compensation he received for that, — and do all those things which had no other motive or excuse but that I might pay for it and be unmolested in my possession of it; for I knew all the while that it would yield the most abundant crop of the kind I wanted, if I could only afford to let it alone. But it turned out as I have said.

All that I could say, then, with respect to farming on a large scale — I have always cultivated a garden — was, that I had had my seeds ready. Many think that seeds improve with age. I have no doubt that time discriminates between the good and the bad; and when at last I shall plant, I shall be less likely to be disappointed. But I would say to my fellows, once for all, As long as possible live free and uncommitted. It makes but little difference whether you are committed to a farm or the county jail.

Old Cato, whose " De Re Rusticâ " is my " Cultivator," says, — and the only translation I have seen makes sheer nonsense of the passage, — " When you think of getting a farm turn it thus in your mind, not to buy greedily; nor spare your pains to look at it, and do not think it enough to go round it once. The oftener you go there the more it will please you, if it is good." I think I shall not buy greedily, but go round and round it as long as I live, and be buried in it first, that it may please me the more at last.

The present was my next experiment of this kind, which I purpose to describe more at length, for convenience putting the experience of two years into one. As I have said, I do not propose to write an ode to dejection, but to brag as lustily as chanticleer in the morning, standing on his roost, if only to wake my neighbors up.

When first I took up my abode in the woods, that is, began to spend my nights as well as days there, which, by accident, was on Independence Day, or the Fourth of July, 1845, my house was not finished for winter, but was merely a defence against the rain, without plastering or chimney, the walls being of rough, weather-stained boards, with wide chinks, which made it cool at night. The upright white hewn studs and freshly planed door and window casings gave it a clean and airy look, especially in the morning, when its timbers were saturated with dew, so that I fancied that by noon some sweet gum would exude from them. To my imagination it retained throughout the day more or less of this auroral character, reminding me of a certain house on a mountain which I had visited a year before. This was an airy and unplastered cabin, fit to entertain a travelling god, and where a goddess might trail her garments. The winds which passed over my dwelling were such as sweep over the ridges of mountains, bearing the broken strains, or celestial parts only, of terrestrial music. The morning wind forever blows, the poem of creation is uninterrupted; but few are the ears that hear it. Olympus is but the outside of the earth everywhere.

The only house I had been the owner of before, if I except a boat, was a tent, which I used occasionally when making excursions in the summer, and this is still rolled up in my garret; but the boat, after passing from hand to hand, has gone down the stream of time. With this more substantial shelter about me, I had made some progress toward settling in the world. This frame, so slightly clad, was a sort of crystallization around me, and reacted on the builder. It was suggestive somewhat as a picture in outlines. I did not need to go outdoors to take the air, for the atmosphere within had lost none of its freshness. It was not so much within-doors as behind a door where I sat, even in the rainiest weather. The Harivansa says, "An abode without birds is like a meat without seasoning." Such was not my abode, for I found myself suddenly neighbor to the birds; not by having imprisoned one, but having caged myself near them. I was not only nearer to some of those which commonly frequent the garden and the orchard, but to those wilder and more thrilling songsters of the forest which never, or rarely, serenade a villager, — the wood thrush, the veery, the scarlet tanager, the field sparrow, the whip-poor-will, and many others.

I was seated by the shore of a small pond, about a mile and a half south of the village of Concord and somewhat higher than it, in the midst of an extensive wood between that town and Lincoln, and about two miles south of that our only field known to fame, Concord Battle Ground; but I was so low in the woods that the opposite shore, half a mile off, like the rest, covered with wood, was my most distant horizon. For the first week, whenever I looked out on the pond it impressed me like a tarn high up on the side of a mountain, its bottom far above the surface of other lakes, and, as the

sun arose, I saw it throwing off its nightly clothing of
mist, and here and there, by degrees, its soft ripples or
its smooth reflecting surface was revealed, while the
mists, like ghosts, were stealthily withdrawing in every
direction into the woods, as at the breaking up of some
nocturnal conventicle. The very dew seemed to hang
upon the trees later into the day than usual, as on the
sides of mountains.

This small lake was of most value as a neighbor in
the intervals of a gentle rain-storm in August, when,
both air and water being perfectly still, but the sky overcast, mid-afternoon had all the serenity of evening, and
the wood thrush sang around, and was heard from shore
to shore. A lake like this is never smoother than at such
a time; and the clear portion of the air above it being
shallow and darkened by clouds, the water, full of light
and reflections, becomes a lower heaven itself so much
the more important. From a hill-top near by, where the
wood had been recently cut off, there was a pleasing
vista southward across the pond, through a wide inden-
tation in the hills which form the shore there, where
their opposite sides sloping toward each other suggested
a stream flowing out in that direction through a wooded
valley, but stream there was none. That way I looked
between and over the near green hills to some distant
and higher ones in the horizon, tinged with blue. Indeed, by standing on tiptoe I could catch a glimpse
of some of the peaks of the still bluer and more distant mountain ranges in the northwest, those true-blue
coins from heaven's own mint, and also of some portion
of the village. But in other directions, even from this

point, I could not see over or beyond the woods which
surrounded me. It is well to have some water in your
neighborhood, to give buoyancy to and float the earth.
One value even of the smallest well is, that when you
look into it you see that earth is not continent but in-
sular. This is as important as that it keeps butter cool.
When I looked across the pond from this peak toward
the Sudbury meadows, which in time of flood I distinguished elevated perhaps by a mirage in their seeth-
ing valley, like a coin in a basin, all the earth beyond
the pond appeared like a thin crust insulated and floated
even by this small sheet of intervening water, and I was
reminded that this on which I dwelt was but *dry land*.

Though the view from my door was still more contracted, I did not feel crowded or confined in the least.
There was pasture enough for my imagination. The low
shrub oak plateau to which the opposite shore arose
stretched away toward the prairies of the West and the
steppes of Tartary, affording ample room for all the
roving families of men. "There are none happy in the
world but beings who enjoy freely a vast horizon," —
said Damodara, when his herds required new and
larger pastures.

Both place and time were changed, and I dwelt nearer
to those parts of the universe and to those eras in history which had most attracted me. Where I lived was
as far off as many a region viewed nightly by astronomers. We are wont to imagine rare and delectable
places in some remote and more celestial corner of the
system, behind the constellation of Cassiopeia's Chair,
far from noise and disturbance. I discovered that my

house actually had its site in such a withdrawn, but forever new and unprofaned, part of the universe. If it were worth the while to settle in those parts near to the Pleiades or the Hyades, to Aldebaran or Altair, then I was really there, or at an equal remoteness from the life which I had left behind, dwindled and twinkling with as fine a ray to my nearest neighbor, and to be seen only in moonless nights by him. Such was that part of creation where I had squatted; —

> "There was a shepherd that did live,
> And held his thoughts as high
> As were the mounts whereon his flocks
> Did hourly feed him by."

What should we think of the shepherd's life if his flocks always wandered to higher pastures than his thoughts?

Every morning was a cheerful invitation to make my life of equal simplicity, and I may say innocence, with Nature herself. I have been as sincere a worshipper of Aurora as the Greeks. I got up early and bathed in the pond; that was a religious exercise, and one of the best things which I did. They say that characters were engraven on the bathing tub of King Tching-thang to this effect: "Renew thyself completely each day; do it again, and again, and forever again." I can understand that. Morning brings back the heroic ages. I was as much affected by the faint hum of a mosquito making its invisible and unimaginable tour through my apartment at earliest dawn, when I was sitting with door and windows open, as I could be by any trumpet that ever sang of fame. It was Homer's requiem; itself an Iliad and Odyssey in the air, singing its own wrath and

Great Fringed Orchis

Blueberry blossoms

wanderings. There was something cosmical about it; a standing advertisement, till forbidden, of the everlasting vigor and fertility of the world. The morning, which is the most memorable season of the day, is the awakening hour. Then there is least somnolence in us; and for an hour, at least, some part of us awakes which slumbers all the rest of the day and night. Little is to be expected of that day, if it can be called a day, to which we are not awakened by our Genius, but by the mechanical nudgings of some servitor, are not awakened by our own newly acquired force and aspirations from within, accompanied by the undulations of celestial music, instead of factory bells, and a fragrance filling the air — to a higher life than we fell asleep from; and thus the darkness bear its fruit, and prove itself to be good, no less than the light. That man who does not believe that each day contains an earlier, more sacred, and auroral hour than he has yet profaned, has despaired of life, and is pursuing a descending and darkening way. After a partial cessation of his sensuous life, the soul of man, or its organs rather, are reinvigorated each day, and his Genius tries again what noble life it can make. All memorable events, I should say, transpire in morning time and in a morning atmosphere. The Vedas say, "All intelligences awake with the morning." Poetry and art, and the fairest and most memorable of the actions of men, date from such an hour. All poets and heroes, like Memnon, are the children of Aurora, and emit their music at sunrise. To him whose elastic and vigorous thought keeps pace with the sun, the day is a perpetual morning. It matters not what the clocks say or the attitudes and labors of men. Morning is when I am awake and there is a dawn in me. Moral reform is the effort to throw off sleep. Why is it that men give so poor an account of their day if they have not been slumbering? They are not such poor calculators. If they had not been overcome with drowsiness, they would have performed something. The millions are awake enough for physical labor; but only one in a million is awake enough for effective intellectual exertion, only one in a hundred millions to a poetic or divine life. To be awake is to be alive. I have never yet met a man who was quite awake. How could I have looked him in the face?

We must learn to reawaken and keep ourselves awake, not by mechanical aids, but by an infinite expectation of the dawn, which does not forsake us in our soundest sleep. I know of no more encouraging fact than the unquestionable ability of man to elevate his life by a conscious endeavor. It is something to be able to paint a particular picture, or to carve a statue, and so to make a few objects beautiful; but it is far more glorious to carve and paint the very atmosphere and medium through which we look, which morally we can do. To affect the quality of the day, that is the highest of arts. Every man is tasked to make his life, even in its details, worthy of the contemplation of his most elevated and critical hour. If we refused, or rather used up, such paltry information as we get, the oracles would distinctly inform us how this might be done.

I went to the woods because I wished to live deliberately, to front only the essential facts of life, and see if I could not learn what it had to teach, and not, when I came to die, discover that I had not lived. I did not wish to live what was not life, living is so dear; nor did I wish to practise resignation, unless it was quite necessary. I wanted to live deep and suck out all the marrow of life, to live so sturdily and Spartan-like as to put to rout all that was not life, to cut a broad swath and shave close, to drive life into a corner, and reduce it to its lowest terms, and, if it proved to be mean, why then to get the whole and genuine meanness of it, and publish its meanness to the world; or if it were sublime, to know it by experience, and be able to give a true account of it in my next excursion. For most men, it appears to me, are in a strange uncertainty about it, whether it is of the devil or of God, and have *somewhat hastily* concluded that it is the chief end of man here to "glorify God and enjoy him forever."

Still we live meanly, like ants; though the fable tells us that we were long ago changed into men; like pygmies we fight with cranes; it is error upon error, and clout upon clout, and our best virtue has for its occasion a superfluous and evitable wretchedness. Our life is frittered away by detail. An honest man has hardly need to count more than his ten fingers, or in extreme cases he may add his ten toes, and lump the rest. Simplicity, simplicity, simplicity! I say, let your affairs be as two or three, and not a hundred or a thousand; instead of a million count half a dozen, and keep your accounts on your thumb-nail. In the midst of this chopping sea of civilized life, such are the clouds and storms and quicksands and thousand-and-one items to be al-

lowed for, that a man has to live, if he would not founder
and go to the bottom and not make his port at all, by
dead reckoning, and he must be a great calculator indeed
who succeeds. Simplify, simplify. Instead of three
meals a day, if it be necessary eat but one; instead of a
hundred dishes, five; and reduce other things in proportion. Our life is like a German Confederacy, made
up of petty states, with its boundary forever fluctuating,
so that even a German cannot tell you how it is bounded
at any moment. The nation itself, with all its so-called
internal improvements, which, by the way are all external and superficial, is just such an unwieldy and
overgrown establishment, cluttered with furniture and
tripped up by its own traps, ruined by luxury and heed-
less expense, by want of calculation and a worthy aim,
as the million households in the land; and the only cure
for it, as for them, is in a rigid economy, a stern and more
than Spartan simplicity of life and elevation of purpose.
It lives too fast. Men think that it is essential that the
Nation have commerce, and export ice, and talk through
a telegraph, and ride thirty miles an hour, without a
doubt, whether *they* do or not; but whether we should
live like baboons or like men, is a little uncertain. If we
do not get out sleepers, and forge rails, and devote days
and nights to the work, but go to tinkering upon our
lives to improve *them*, who will build railroads? And
if railroads are not built, how shall we get to heaven in
season? But if we stay at home and mind our business,
who will want railroads? We do not ride on the railroad;
it rides upon us. Did you ever think what those sleepers
are that underlie the railroad? Each one is a man, an

Irishman, or a Yankee man. The rails are laid on them, and they are covered with sand, and the cars run smoothly over them. They are sound sleepers, I assure you. And every few years a new lot is laid down and run over; so that, if some have the pleasure of riding on a rail, others have the misfortune to be ridden upon. And when they run over a man that is walking in his sleep, a supernumerary sleeper in the wrong position, and wake him up, they suddenly stop the cars, and make a hue and cry about it, as if this were an exception. I am glad to know that it takes a gang of men for every five miles to keep the sleepers down and level in their beds as it is, for this is a sign that they may some-time get up again.

Why should we live with such hurry and waste of life? We are determined to be starved before we are hungry. Men say that a stitch in time saves nine, and so they take a thousand stitches to-day to save nine to-morrow. As for *work*, we have n't any of any consequence. We have the Saint Vitus' dance, and cannot possibly keep our heads still. If I should only give a few pulls at the parish bell-rope, as for a fire, that is, without setting the bell, there is hardly a man on his farm in the outskirts of Concord, notwithstanding that press of engagements which was his excuse so many times this morning, nor a boy, nor a woman, I might almost say, but would for-sake all and follow that sound, not mainly to save pro-perty from the flames, but, if we will confess the truth, much more to see it burn, since burn it must, and we, be it known, did not set it on fire, — or to see it put out, and have a hand in it, if that is done as handsomely;

yes, even if it were the parish church itself. Hardly a man takes a half-hour's nap after dinner, but when he wakes he holds up his head and asks, "What's the news?" as if the rest of mankind had stood his sentinels. Some give directions to be waked every half-hour, doubtless for no other purpose; and then, to pay for it, they tell what they have dreamed. After a night's sleep the news is as indispensable as the breakfast. "Pray tell me anything new that has happened to a man anywhere on this globe," — and he reads it over his coffee and rolls, that a man has had his eyes gouged out this morning on the Wachito River; never dreaming the while that he lives in the dark unfathomed mammoth cave of this world, and has but the rudiment of an eye himself.

For my part, I could easily do without the post-office. I think that there are very few important communications made through it. To speak critically, I never received more than one or two letters in my life — I wrote this some years ago — that were worth the postage. The penny-post is, commonly, an institution through which you seriously offer a man that penny for his thoughts which is so often safely offered in jest. And I am sure that I never read any memorable news in a newspaper. If we read of one man robbed, or murdered, or killed by accident, or one house burned, or one vessel wrecked, or one steamboat blown up, or one cow run over on the Western Railroad, or one mad dog killed, or one lot of grasshoppers in the winter, — we never need read of another. One is enough. If you are acquainted with the principle, what do you care for a myriad instances and applications? To a philosopher all *news*, as it is called, is gossip, and they who edit and read it are old women over their tea. Yet not a few are greedy after this gossip. There was such a rush, as I hear, the other day at one of the offices to learn the foreign news by the last arrival, that several large squares of plate glass belonging to the establishment were broken by the pressure, — news which I seriously think a ready wit might write a twelvemonth, or twelve years, beforehand with sufficient accuracy. As for Spain, for instance, if you know how to throw in Don Carlos and the Infanta, and Don Pedro and Seville and Granada, from time to time in the right proportions, — they may have changed the names a little since I saw the papers, — and serve up a bull-fight when other entertainments fail, it will be true to the letter, and give us as good an idea of the exact state or ruin of things in Spain as the most succinct and lucid reports under this head in the newspapers: and as for England, almost the last significant scrap of news from that quarter was the revolution of 1649; and if you have learned the history of her crops for an average year, you never need attend to that thing again, unless your speculations are of a merely pecuniary character. If one may judge who rarely looks into the newspapers, nothing new does ever happen in foreign parts, a French revolution not excepted.

What news! how much more important to know what that is which was never old! "Kieou-he-yu (great dignitary of the state of Wei) sent a man to Khoung-tseu to know his news. Khoung-tseu caused the messenger to be seated near him, and questioned him in these terms:

What is your master doing? The messenger answered
with respect: My master desires to diminish the number of his faults, but he cannot come to the end of them.
The messenger being gone, the philosopher remarked:
What a worthy messenger! What a worthy messenger!" The preacher, instead of vexing the ears of
drowsy farmers on their day of rest at the end of the
week, — for Sunday is the fit conclusion of an ill-spent
week, and not the fresh and brave beginning of a new
one, — with this one other draggle-tail of a sermon,
should shout with thundering voice, "Pause! Avast!
Why so seeming fast, but deadly slow?"

Shams and delusions are esteemed for soundest
truths, while reality is fabulous. If men would steadily
observe realities only, and not allow themselves to be
deluded, life, to compare it with such things as we
know, would be like a fairy tale and the Arabian Nights'
Entertainments. If we respected only what is inevitable and has a right to be, music and poetry would resound along the streets. When we are unhurried and
wise, we perceive that only great and worthy things
have any permanent and absolute existence, that
petty fears and petty pleasures are but the shadow of
the reality. This is always exhilarating and sublime.
By closing the eyes and slumbering, and consenting to
be deceived by shows, men establish and confirm their
daily life of routine and habit everywhere, which still
is built on purely illusory foundations. Children, who
play life, discern its true law and relations more clearly
than men, who fail to live it worthily, but who think
that they are wiser by experience, that is, by failure. I

have read in a Hindoo book, that "there was a king's
son, who, being expelled in infancy from his native
city, was brought up by a forester, and, growing up to
maturity in that state, imagined himself to belong to
the barbarous race with which he lived. One of his
father's ministers having discovered him, revealed to
him what he was, and the misconception of his character
was removed, and he knew himself to be a prince. So
soul," continues the Hindoo philosopher, "from the
circumstances in which it is placed, mistakes its own
character, until the truth is revealed to it by some holy
teacher, and then it knows itself to be *Brahme.*" I perceive that we inhabitants of New England live this
mean life that we do because our vision does not penetrate the surface of things. We think that that *is* which
appears to be. If a man should walk through this town
and see only the reality, where, think you, would the
" Mill-dam " go to? If he should give us an account of
the realities he beheld there, we should not recognize
the place in his description. Look at a meeting-house, or
a court-house, or a jail, or a shop, or a dwelling-house,
and say what that thing really is before a true gaze, and
they would all go to pieces in your account of them.
Men esteem truth remote, in the outskirts of the system, behind the farthest star, before Adam and after
the last man. In eternity there is indeed something true
and sublime. But all these times and places and occasions are now and here. God himself culminates in the
present moment, and will never be more divine in the
lapse of all the ages. And we are enabled to apprehend
at all what is sublime and noble only by the perpetual

instilling and drenching of the reality that surrounds us. The universe constantly and obediently answers to our conceptions; whether we travel fast or slow, the track is laid for us. Let us spend our lives in conceiving then. The poet or the artist never yet had so fair and noble a design but some of his posterity at least could accomplish it.

Let us spend one day as deliberately as Nature, and not be thrown off the track by every nutshell and mosquito's wing that falls on the rails. Let us rise early and fast, or break fast, gently and without perturbation; let company come and let company go, let the bells ring and the children cry, — determined to make a day of it. Why should we knock under and go with the stream? Let us not be upset and overwhelmed in that terrible rapid and whirlpool called a dinner, situated in the meridian shallows. Weather this danger and you are safe, for the rest of the way is down hill. With unrelaxed nerves, with morning vigor, sail by it, looking another way, tied to the mast like Ulysses. If the engine whistles, let it whistle till it is hoarse for its pains. If the bell rings, why should we run? We will consider what kind of music they are like. Let us settle ourselves, and work and wedge our feet downward through the mud and slush of opinion, and prejudice, and tradition, and delusion, and appearance, that alluvion which covers the globe, through Paris and London, through New York and Boston and Concord, through Church and State, through poetry and philosophy and religion, till we come to a hard bottom and rocks in place, which we can call *reality*, and say, This is, and no mistake; and then begin, having a *point d'appui*, below freshet and frost and fire, a place where you might found a wall or a state, or set a lamp-post safely, or perhaps a gauge, not a Nilometer, but a Realometer, that future ages might know how deep a freshet of shams and appearances had gathered from time to time. If you stand right fronting and face to face to a fact, you will see the sun glimmer on both its surfaces, as if it were a cimeter, and feel its sweet edge dividing you through the heart and marrow, and so you will happily conclude your mortal career. Be it life or death, we crave only reality. If we are really dying, let us hear the rattle in our throats and feel cold in the extremities; if we are alive, let us go about our business.

Time is but the stream I go a-fishing in. I drink at it; but while I drink I see the sandy bottom and detect how shallow it is. Its thin current slides away, but eternity remains. I would drink deeper; fish in the sky, whose bottom is pebbly with stars. I cannot count one. I know not the first letter of the alphabet. I have always been regretting that I was not as wise as the day I was born. The intellect is a cleaver; it discerns and rifts its way into the secret of things. I do not wish to be any more busy with my hands than is necessary. My head is hands and feet. I feel all my best faculties concentrated in it. My instinct tells me that my head is an organ for burrowing, as some creatures use their snout and fore paws, and with it I would mine and burrow my way through these hills. I think that the richest vein is somewhere hereabouts; so by the divining-rod and thin rising vapors I judge; and here I will begin to mine.

III

READING

With a little more deliberation in the choice of their pursuits, all men would perhaps become essentially students and observers, for certainly their nature and destiny are interesting to all alike. In accumulating property for ourselves or our posterity, in founding a family or a state, or acquiring fame even, we are mortal; but in dealing with truth we are immortal, and need fear no change nor accident. The oldest Egyptian or Hindoo philosopher raised a corner of the veil from the statue of the divinity; and still the trembling robe remains raised, and I gaze upon as fresh a glory as he did, since it was I in him that was then so bold, and it is he in me that now reviews the vision. No dust has settled on that robe; no time has elapsed since that divinity was revealed. That time which we really improve, or which is improvable, is neither past, present, nor future.

My residence was more favorable, not only to thought, but to serious reading, than a university; and though I was beyond the range of the ordinary circulating library, I had more than ever come within the influence of those books which circulate round the world, whose sentences were first written on bark, and are now merely copied from time to time on to linen paper. Says the poet Mîr

Camar Uddîn Mast, "Being seated to run through the region of the spiritual world; I have had this advantage in books. To be intoxicated by a single glass of wine; I have experienced this pleasure when I have drunk the liquor of the esoteric doctrines." I kept Homer's Iliad on my table through the summer, though I looked at his page only now and then. Incessant labor with my hands, at first, for I had my house to finish and my beans to hoe at the same time, made more study impossible. Yet I sustained myself by the prospect of such reading in future. I read one or two shallow books of travel in the intervals of my work, till that employment made me ashamed of myself, and I asked where it was then that *I* lived.

The student may read Homer or Æschylus in the Greek without danger of dissipation or luxuriousness, for it implies that he in some measure emulate their heroes, and consecrate morning hours to their pages. The heroic books, even if printed in the character of our mother tongue, will always be in a language dead to degenerate times; and we must laboriously seek the meaning of each word and line, conjecturing a larger sense than common use permits out of what wisdom and valor and generosity we have. The modern cheap and fertile press, with all its translations, has done little to bring us nearer to the heroic writers of antiquity. They seem as solitary, and the letter in which they are printed as rare and curious, as ever. It is worth the expense of youthful days and costly hours, if you learn only some words of an ancient language, which are raised out of the trivialness of the street, to be perpetual suggestions and provocations. It is not in vain that the farmer remembers and repeats the few Latin words which he has heard. Men sometimes speak as if the study of the classics would at length make way for more modern and practical studies; but the adventurous student will always study classics, in whatever language they may be written and however ancient they may be. For what are the classics but the noblest recorded thoughts of man? They are the only oracles which are not decayed, and there are such answers to the most modern inquiry in them as Delphi and Dodona never gave. We might as well omit to study Nature because she is old. To read well, that is, to read true books in a true spirit, is a noble exercise, and one that will task the reader more than any exercise which the customs of the day esteem. It requires a training such as the athletes underwent, the steady intention almost of the whole life to this object. Books must be read as deliberately and reservedly as they were written. It is not enough even to be able to speak the language of that nation by which they are written, for there is a memorable interval between the spoken and the written language, the language heard and the language read. The one is commonly transitory, a sound, a tongue, a dialect merely, almost brutish, and we learn it unconsciously, like the brutes, of our mothers. The other is the maturity and experience of that; if that is our mother tongue, this is our father tongue, a reserved and select expression, too significant to be heard by the ear, which we must be born again in order to speak. The crowds of men who merely *spoke* the Greek and Latin tongues in the Middle Ages were not entitled by the accident of birth to *read* the works of genius written in those languages; for these were not written in that Greek or Latin which they knew, but in the select language of literature. They had not learned the nobler dialects of Greece and Rome, but the very materials on which they were written were waste paper to them, and they prized instead a cheap contemporary literature. But when the several nations of Europe had acquired distinct though rude written languages of their own, sufficient for the purposes of their rising literatures, then first learning revived, and scholars were enabled to discern from that remoteness the treasures of antiquity. What the Roman and Grecian multitude could not *hear*, after the lapse of ages a few scholars *read*, and a few scholars only are still reading it.

However much we may admire the orator's occasional bursts of eloquence, the noblest written words are commonly as far behind or above the fleeting spoken language as the firmament with its stars is behind the clouds. *There* are the stars, and they who can may read them. The astronomers forever comment on and observe them. They are not exhalations like our daily colloquies and vaporous breath. What is called eloquence in the forum is commonly found to be rhetoric in the study. The orator yields to the inspiration of a transient occasion, and speaks to the mob before him, to those who can *hear* him; but the writer, whose more equable life is his occasion, and who would be distracted by the event and the crowd which inspire the orator, speaks to the intellect and heart of mankind, to all in any age who can *understand* him.

No wonder that Alexander carried the Iliad with him
on his expeditions in a precious casket. A written word
is the choicest of relics. It is something at once more
intimate with us and more universal than any other
work of art. It is the work of art nearest to life itself. It
may be translated into every language, and not only be
read but actually breathed from all human lips; — not
be represented on canvas or in marble only, but be
carved out of the breath of life itself. The symbol of an
ancient man's thought becomes a modern man's speech.
Two thousand summers have imparted to the monuments of Grecian literature, as to her marbles, only a
maturer golden and autumnal tint, for they have carried their own serene and celestial atmosphere into all
lands to protect them against the corrosion of time.
Books are the treasured wealth of the world and the fit
inheritance of generations and nations. Books, the oldest and the best, stand naturally and rightfully on the
shelves of every cottage. They have no cause of their
own to plead, but while they enlighten and sustain the
reader his common sense will not refuse them. Their
authors are a natural and irresistible aristocracy in
every society, and, more than kings or emperors, exert
an influence on mankind. When the illiterate and perhaps scornful trader has earned by enterprise and industry his coveted leisure and independence, and is
admitted to the circles of wealth and fashion, he turns
inevitably at last to those still higher but yet inaccessible circles of intellect and genius, and is sensible only of
the imperfection of his culture and the vanity and insufficiency of all his riches, and further proves his good

sen'se by the pains which he takes to secure for his children that intellectual culture whose want he so keenly
feels; and thus it is that he becomes the founder of a
family.

Those who have not learned to read the ancient
classics in the language in which they were written must
have a very imperfect knowledge of the history of the
human race; for it is remarkable that no transcript of
them has ever been made into any modern tongue,
unless our civilization itself may be regarded as such a
transcript. Homer has never yet been printed in English, nor Æschylus, nor Virgil even, — works as refined,
as solidly done, and as beautiful almost as the morning
itself; for later writers, say what we will of their genius,
have rarely, if ever, equalled the elaborate beauty and
finish and the lifelong and heroic literary labors of the
ancients. They only talk of forgetting them who never
knew them. It will be soon enough to forget them when
we have the learning and the genius which will enable
us to attend to and appreciate them. That age will be
rich indeed when those relics which we call Classics,
and the still older and more than classic but even less
known Scriptures of the nations, shall have still further
accumulated, when the Vaticans shall be filled with
Vedas and Zendavestas and Bibles, with Homers and
Dantes and Shakespeares, and all the centuries to come
shall have successively deposited their trophies in the
forum of the world. By such a pile we may hope to
scale heaven at last.

The works of the great poets have never yet been
read by mankind, for only great poets can read them.

They have only been read as the multitude read the stars, at most astrologically, not astronomically. Most men have learned to read to serve a paltry convenience, as they have learned to cipher in order to keep accounts and not be cheated in trade; but of reading as a noble intellectual exercise they know little or nothing; yet this only is reading, in a high sense, not that which lulls us as a luxury and suffers the nobler faculties to sleep the while, but what we have to stand on tip-toe to read and devote our most alert and wakeful hours to.

I think that having learned our letters we should read the best that is in literature, and not be forever repeating our a-b-abs, and words of one syllable, in the fourth or fifth classes, sitting on the lowest and foremost form all our lives. Most men are satisfied if they read or hear read, and perchance have been convicted by the wisdom of one good book, the Bible, and for the rest of their lives vegetate and dissipate their faculties in what is called easy reading. There is a work in several volumes in our Circulating Library entitled "Little Reading," which I thought referred to a town of that name which I had not been to. There are those who, like cormorants and ostriches, can digest all sorts of this, even after the fullest dinner of meats and vegetables, for they suffer nothing to be wasted. If others are the machines to provide this provender, they are the machines to read it. They read the nine thousandth tale about Zebulon and Sephronia, and how they loved as none had ever loved before, and neither did the course of their true love run smooth,— at any rate, how it did run and stumble, and get up again and go on! how some poor unfortunate

got up on to a steeple, who had better never have gone
up as far as the belfry; and then, having needlessly got
him up there, the happy novelist rings the bell for all the
world to come together and hear, O dear! how he did
get down again! For my part, I think that they had better metamorphose all such aspiring heroes of universal
noveldom into man weather-cocks, as they used to put
heroes among the constellations, and let them swing
round there till they are rusty, and not come down at
all to bother honest men with their pranks. The next
time the novelist rings the bell I will not stir though the
meeting-house burn down. "The Skip of the Tip-Toe-
Hop, a Romance of the Middle Ages, by the celebrated
author of 'Tittle-Tol-Tan,' to appear in monthly parts;
a great rush; don't all come together." All this they
read with saucer eyes, and erect and primitive curiosity,
and with unwearied gizzard, whose corrugations even
yet need no sharpening, just as some little four-year-old
bencher his two-cent gilt-covered edition of Cinderella,
— without any improvement, that I can see, in the pro-
nunciation, or accent, or emphasis, or any more skill
in extracting or inserting the moral. The result is dulness of sight, a stagnation of the vital circulations, and
a general deliquium and sloughing off of all the intellectual faculties. This sort of gingerbread is baked
daily and more sedulously than pure wheat or rye-and-
Indian in almost every oven, and finds a surer market.

The best books are not read even by those who are
called good readers. What does our Concord culture
amount to? There is in this town, with a very few exceptions, no taste for the best or for very good books

even in English literature, whose words all can read and spell. Even the college-bred and so-called liberally educated men here and elsewhere have really little or no acquaintance with the English classics; and as for the recorded wisdom of mankind, the ancient classics and Bibles, which are accessible to all who will know of them, there are the feeblest efforts anywhere made to become acquainted with them. I know a woodchopper, of middle age, who takes a French paper, not for news as he says, for he is above that, but to "keep himself in practice," he being a Canadian by birth; and when I ask him what he considers the best thing he can do in this world, he says, beside this, to keep up and add to his English. This is about as much as the college-bred generally do or aspire to do, and they take an English paper for the purpose. One who has just come from reading perhaps one of the best English books will find how many with whom he can converse about it ? Or suppose he comes from reading a Greek or Latin classic in the original, whose praises are familiar even to the so-called illiterate; he will find nobody at all to speak to, but must keep silence about it. Indeed, there is hardly the professor in our colleges, who, if he has mastered the difficulties of the language, has proportionally mastered the difficulties of the wit and poetry of a Greek poet, and has any sympathy to impart to the alert and heroic reader; and as for the sacred Scriptures, or Bibles of mankind, who in this town can tell me even their titles ? Most men do not know that any nation but the Hebrews have had a scripture. A man, any man, will go considerably out of his way to pick up a silver dollar; but here are golden words, which the wisest men of antiquity have uttered, and whose worth the wise of every succeeding age have assured us of; — and yet we learn to read only as far as Easy Reading, the primers and class-books, and when we leave school, the " Little Reading," and story-books, which are for boys and beginners; and our reading, our conversation and thinking, are all on a very low level, worthy only of pygmies and manikins.

I aspire to be acquainted with wiser men than this our Concord soil has produced, whose names are hardly known here. Or shall I hear the name of Plato and never read his book? As if Plato were my townsman and I never saw him, — my next neighbor and I never heard him speak or attended to the wisdom of his words. But how actually is it? His Dialogues, which contain what was immortal in him, lie on the next shelf, and yet I never read them. We are underbred and low-lived and illiterate; and in this respect I confess I do not make any very broad distinction between the illiterateness of my townsman who cannot read at all and the illiterateness of him who has learned to read only what is for children and feeble intellects. We should be as good as the worthies of antiquity, but partly by first knowing how good they were. We are a race of tit-men, and soar but little higher in our intellectual flights than the columns of the daily paper.

It is not all books that are as dull as their readers. There are probably words addressed to our condition exactly, which, if we could really hear and understand, would be more salutary than the morning or the spring to our lives, and possibly put a new aspect on the face of things for us. How many a man has dated a new era in his life from the reading of a book. The book exists for us, perchance, which will explain our miracles and reveal new ones. The at present unutterable things we may find somewhere uttered. These same questions that disturb and puzzle and confound us have in their turn occurred to all the wise men; not one has been omitted; and each has answered them, according to his ability, by his words and his life. Moreover, with wisdom we shall learn liberality. The solitary hired man on a farm in the outskirts of Concord, who has had his second birth and peculiar religious experience, and is driven as he believes into silent gravity and exclusiveness by his faith, may think it is not true; but Zoroaster, thousands of years ago, travelled the same road and had the same experience; but he, being wise, knew it to be universal, and treated his neighbors accordingly, and is even said to have invented and established worship among men. Let him humbly commune with Zoroaster then, and through the liberalizing influence of all the worthies, with Jesus Christ himself, and let "our church" go by the board.

We boast that we belong to the Nineteenth Century and are making the most rapid strides of any nation. But consider how little this village does for its own culture. I do not wish to flatter my townsmen, nor to be flattered by them, for that will not advance either of us. We need to be provoked, — goaded like oxen, as we are, into a trot. We have a comparatively decent system of common schools, schools for infants only; but excepting the half-starved Lyceum in the winter, and latterly the puny beginning of a library suggested by the State, no school for ourselves. We spend more on almost any article of bodily aliment or ailment than on our mental aliment. It is time that we had uncommon schools, that we did not leave off our education when we begin to be men and women. It is time that villages were universities, and their elder inhabitants the fellows of universities, with leisure — if they are, indeed, so well off — to pursue liberal studies the rest of their lives. Shall the world be confined to one Paris or one Oxford forever? Cannot students be boarded here and get a liberal education under the skies of Concord? Can we not hire some Abélard to lecture to us? Alas! what with foddering the cattle and tending the store, we are kept from school too long, and our education is sadly neglected. In this country, the village should in some respects take the place of the nobleman of Europe. It should be the patron of the fine arts. It is rich enough. It wants only the magnanimity and refinement. It can spend money enough on such things as farmers and traders value, but it is thought Utopian to propose spending money for things which more intelligent men know to be of far more worth. This town has spent seventeen thousand dollars on a town-house, thank fortune or politics, but probably it will not spend so much on living wit, the true meat to put into that shell, in a hundred years. The one hundred and twenty-five dollars annually subscribed for a Lyceum in the winter is better spent than any other equal sum raised in the town. If we live in the Nineteenth Century, why should we not enjoy the advantages which the Nineteenth Century offers? Why should our life be in any respect provincial? If we will read newspapers, why not skip the gossip of Boston and take the best newspaper in the world at once? — not be sucking the pap of "neutral family" papers, or browsing "Olive-Branches" here in New England. Let the reports of all the learned societies come to us, and we will see if they know anything. Why should we leave it to Harper & Brothers and Redding & Co. to select our reading? As the nobleman of cultivated taste surrounds himself with whatever conduces to his culture, — genius — learning — wit — books — paintings — statuary — music — philosophical instruments, and the like; so let the village do, — not stop short at a pedagogue, a parson, a sexton, a parish library, and three selectmen, because our Pilgrim forefathers got through a cold winter once on a bleak rock with these. To act collectively is according to the spirit of our institutions; and I am confident that, as our circumstances are more flourishing, our means are greater than the nobleman's. New England can hire all the wise men in the world to come and teach her, and board them round the while, and not be provincial at all. That is the *uncommon* school we want. Instead of noblemen, let us have noble villages of men. If it is necessary, omit one bridge over the river, go round a little there, and throw one arch at least over the darker gulf of ignorance which surrounds us.

IV

SOUNDS

But while we are confined to books, though the most select and classic, and read only particular written languages, which are themselves but dialects and provincial, we are in danger of forgetting the language which all things and events speak without metaphor, which alone is copious and standard. Much is published, but little printed. The rays which stream through the shutter will be no longer remembered when the shutter is wholly removed. No method nor discipline can supersede the necessity of being forever on the alert. What is a course of history or philosophy, or poetry, no matter how well selected, or the best society, or the most admirable routine of life, compared with the discipline of looking always at what is to be seen? Will you be a reader, a student merely, or a seer? Read your fate, see what is before you, and walk on into futurity.

I did not read books the first summer; I hoed beans. Nay, I often did better than this. There were times when I could not afford to sacrifice the bloom of the present moment to any work, whether of the head or hands. I love a broad margin to my life. Sometimes, in a summer morning, having taken my accustomed bath, I sat in my sunny doorway from sunrise till noon, rapt in a revery, amidst the pines and hickories and sumachs, in undisturbed solitude and stillness, while the birds sang around or flitted noiseless through the house, until by the sun falling in at my west window, or the noise of some traveller's wagon on the distant highway, I was reminded of the lapse of time. I grew in those seasons like corn in the night, and they were far better than any work of the hands would have been. They were not time subtracted from my life, but so much over and above my usual allowance. I realized what the Orientals mean by contemplation and the forsaking of works. For the most part, I minded not how the hours went. The day advanced as if to light some work of mine; it was morning, and lo, now it is evening, and nothing memorable is accomplished. Instead of singing like the birds, I silently smiled at my incessant good fortune. As the sparrow had its trill, sitting on the hickory before my door, so had I my chuckle or suppressed warble which he might hear out of my nest. My days were not days of the week, bearing the stamp of any heathen deity, nor were they minced into hours and fretted by the ticking of a clock; for I lived like the Puri Indians, of whom it is said that "for yesterday, to-day, and to-morrow they have only one word, and they express the variety of meaning by pointing backward for yesterday, forward for to-morrow, and overhead for the passing day." This was sheer idleness to my fellow-townsmen, no doubt; but if the birds and flowers had tried me by their standard, I should not have been found wanting. A man must find his occasions in himself, it is true. The natural day is very calm, and will hardly reprove his indolence.

I had this advantage, at least, in my mode of life, over those who were obliged to look abroad for amusement, to society and the theatre, that my life itself was become my amusement and never ceased to be novel. It was a drama of many scenes and without an end. If we were always, indeed, getting our living, and regulating our lives according to the last and best mode we had learned, we should never be troubled with ennui. Follow your genius closely enough, and it will not fail to show you a fresh prospect every hour. Housework was a pleasant pastime. When my floor was dirty, I rose early, and, setting all my furniture out of doors on the grass, bed and bedstead making but one budget, dashed water on the floor, and sprinkled white sand from the pond on it, and then with a broom scrubbed it clean and white; and by the time the villagers had broken their fast the morning sun had dried my house sufficiently to allow me to move in again, and my meditations were almost uninterrupted. It was pleasant to see my whole household effects out on the grass, making a little pile like a gypsy's pack, and my three-legged table, from which I did not remove the books and pen and ink, standing amid the pines and hickories. They seemed glad to get out themselves, and as if unwilling to be brought in. I was sometimes tempted to stretch an awning over them and take my seat there. It was worth the while to see the sun shine on these things, and hear the free wind blow on them; so much more interesting most familiar objects look out of doors than in the house. A bird sits on the next bough, life-everlasting grows under the table, and blackberry vines run round its legs; pine cones, chestnut burs, and strawberry leaves are strewn about. It looked as if this was the way these forms came to be transferred to our furniture, to tables, chairs, and bedsteads, — because they once stood in their midst.

My house was on the side of a hill, immediately on the edge of the larger wood, in the midst of a young forest of pitch pines and hickories, and half a dozen rods from the pond, to which a narrow footpath led down the hill. In my front yard grew the strawberry, blackberry, and life-everlasting, johnswort and golden-rod, shrub oaks and sand cherry, blueberry and ground-nut. Near the end of May, the sand cherry (*Cerasus pumila*) adorned the sides of the path with its delicate flowers arranged in umbels cylindrically about its short stems, which last, in the fall, weighed down with good-sized and handsome cherries, fell over in wreaths like rays on every side. I tasted them out of compliment to Nature, though they were scarcely palatable. The sumach (*Rhus glabra*) grew luxuriantly about the house, pushing up through the embankment which I had made, and growing five or six feet the first season. Its broad pinnate tropical leaf was pleasant though strange to look on. The large buds, suddenly pushing out late in the spring from dry sticks which had seemed to be dead, developed themselves as by magic into graceful green and tender boughs, an inch in diameter; and sometimes, as I sat at my window, so heedlessly did they grow and tax their weak joints, I heard a fresh and tender bough suddenly fall like a fan to the ground, when there was not a breath of air stirring, broken off by its own weight. In August, the large masses of berries, which, when in flower, had attracted many wild bees, gradually assumed their bright velvety crimson hue, and by their weight again bent down and broke the tender limbs.

As I sit at my window this summer afternoon, hawks are circling about my clearing; the tantivy of wild pigeons, flying by twos and threes athwart my view, or perching restless on the white pine boughs behind my house, gives a voice to the air; a fish hawk dimples the glassy surface of the pond and brings up a fish; a mink steals out of the marsh before my door and seizes a frog by the shore; the sedge is bending under the weight of the reed-birds flitting hither and thither; and for the last half-hour I have heard the rattle of railroad cars, now dying away and then reviving like the beat of a partridge, conveying travellers from Boston to the country. For I did not live so out of the world as that boy who, as I hear, was put out to a farmer in the east part of the town, but ere long ran away and came home again, quite down at the heel and homesick. He had never seen such a dull and out-of-the-way place; the folks were all gone off; why, you could n't even hear the whistle! I doubt if there is such a place in Massachusetts now: —

> "In truth, our village has become a butt
> For one of those fleet railroad shafts, and o'er
> Our peaceful plain its soothing sound is — Concord."

The Fitchburg Railroad touches the pond about a hundred rods south of where I dwell. I usually go to the

village along its causeway, and am, as it were, related to
society by this link. The men on the freight trains, who
go over the whole length of the road, bow to me as to an
old acquaintance, they pass me so often, and apparently
they take me for an employee; and so I am. I too would
fain be a track-repairer somewhere in the orbit of the
earth.

The whistle of the locomotive penetrates my woods
summer and winter, sounding like the scream of a hawk
sailing over some farmer's yard, informing me that many
restless city merchants are arriving within the circle of
the town, or adventurous country traders from the other
side. As they come under one horizon, they shout their
warning to get off the track to the other, heard sometimes through the circles of two towns. Here come your
groceries, country; your rations, countrymen! Nor is
there any man so independent on his farm that he can
say them nay. And here's your pay for them! screams
the countryman's whistle; timber like long battering-
rams going twenty miles an hour against the city's walls,
and chairs enough to seat all the weary and heavy-laden
that dwell within them. With such huge and lumbering
civility the country hands a chair to the city. All the Indian huckleberry hills are stripped, all the cranberry
meadows are raked into the city. Up comes the cotton,
down goes the woven cloth; up comes the silk, down
goes the woollen; up come the books, but down goes
the wit that writes them.

When I meet the engine with its train of cars moving
off with planetary motion, — or, rather, like a comet, for
the beholder knows not if with that velocity and with that

direction it will ever revisit this system, since its orbit
does not look like a returning curve, — with its steam
cloud like a banner streaming behind in golden and
silver wreaths, like many a downy cloud which I have
seen, high in the heavens, unfolding its masses to the
light, — as if this travelling demigod, this cloud-com-
peller, would ere long take the sunset sky for the livery
of his train; when I hear the iron horse make the hills
echo with his snort like thunder, shaking the earth with
his feet, and breathing fire and smoke from his nostrils
(what kind of winged horse or fiery dragon they will put
into the new Mythology I don't know), it seems as if
the earth had got a race now worthy to inhabit it. If all
were as it seems, and men made the elements their
servants for noble ends! If the cloud that hangs over
the engine were the perspiration of heroic deeds, or as
beneficent as that which floats over the farmer's fields,
then the elements and Nature herself would cheerfully
accompany men on their errands and be their escort.

I watch the passage of the morning cars with the same
feeling that I do the rising of the sun, which is hardly
more regular. Their train of clouds stretching far behind and rising higher and higher, going to heaven while
the cars are going to Boston, conceals the sun for a
minute and casts my distant field into the shade, a celestial train beside which the petty train of cars which
hugs the earth is but the barb of the spear. The stabler
of the iron horse was up early this winter morning by the
light of the stars amid the mountains, to fodder and harness his steed. Fire, too, was awakened thus early to
put the vital heat in him and get him off. If the enter-

prise were as innocent as it is early! If the snow lies deep, they strap on his snowshoes, and, with the giant plow, plow a furrow from the mountains to the sea-board, in which the cars, like a following drill-barrow, sprinkle all the restless men and floating merchandise in the country for seed. All day the fire-steed flies over the country, stopping only that his master may rest, and I am awakened by his tramp and defiant snort at mid-night, when in some remote glen in the woods he fronts the elements incased in ice and snow; and he will reach his stall only with the morning star, to start once more on his travels without rest or slumber. Or perchance, at evening, I hear him in his stable blowing off the super-fluous energy of the day, that he may calm his nerves and cool his liver and brain for a few hours of iron slum-ber. If the enterprise were as heroic and commanding as it is protracted and unwearied!

Far through unfrequented woods on the confines of towns, where once only the hunter penetrated by day, in the darkest night dart these bright saloons without the knowledge of their inhabitants; this moment stop-ping at some brilliant station-house in town or city, where a social crowd is gathered, the next in the Dismal Swamp, scaring the owl and fox. The startings and ar-rivals of the cars are now the epochs in the village day. They go and come with such regularity and precision, and their whistle can be heard so far, that the farmers set their clocks by them, and thus one well-conducted institution regulates a whole country. Have not men improved somewhat in punctuality since the railroad was invented? Do they not talk and think faster in the

depot than they did in the stage-office? There is something electrifying in the atmosphere of the former place.
I have been astonished at the miracles it has wrought;
that some of my neighbors, who, I should have prophesied, once for all, would never get to Boston by so prompt
a conveyance, are on hand when the bell rings. To do
things "railroad fashion" is now the byword; and it is
worth the while to be warned so often and so sincerely
by any power to get off its track. There is no stopping
to read the riot act, no firing over the heads of the mob,
in this case. We have constructed a fate, an *Atropos*,
that never turns aside. (Let that be the name of your
engine.) Men are advertised that at a certain hour and
minute these bolts will be shot toward particular points
of the compass; yet it interferes with no man's business,
and the children go to school on the other track. We live
the steadier for it. We are all educated thus to be sons
of Tell. The air is full of invisible bolts. Every path but
your own is the path of fate. Keep on your own track,
then.

What recommends commerce to me is its enterprise
and bravery. It does not clasp its hands and pray to
Jupiter. I see these men every day go about their business with more or less courage and content, doing more
even than they suspect, and perchance better employed
than they could have consciously devised. I am less
affected by their heroism who stood up for half an hour
in the front line at Buena Vista, than by the steady and
cheerful valor of the men who inhabit the snow-plow
for their winter quarters; who have not merely the
three-o'-clock-in-the-morning courage, which Bonaparte

thought was the rarest, but whose courage does not go to rest so early, who go to sleep only when the storm sleeps or the sinews of their iron steed are frozen. On this morning of the Great Snow, perchance, which is still raging and chilling men's blood, I hear the muffled tone of their engine bell from out the fog bank of their chilled breath, which announces that the cars *are coming*, without long delay, notwithstanding the veto of a New England northeast snow-storm, and I behold the plowmen covered with snow and rime, their heads peering above the mould-board which is turning down other than daisies and the nests of field mice, like bowlders of the Sierra Nevada, that occupy an outside place in the universe.

Commerce is unexpectedly confident and serene, alert, adventurous, and unwearied. It is very natural in its methods withal, far more so than many fantastic enterprises and sentimental experiments, and hence its singular success. I am refreshed and expanded when the freight train rattles past me, and I smell the stores which go dispensing their odors all the way from Long Wharf to Lake Champlain, reminding me of foreign parts, of coral reefs, and Indian oceans, and tropical climes, and the extent of the globe. I feel more like a citizen of the world at the sight of the palm-leaf which will cover so many flaxen New England heads the next summer, the Manilla hemp and cocoanut husks, the old junk, gunny bags, scrap iron, and rusty nails. This carload of torn sails is more legible and interesting now than if they should be wrought into paper and printed books. Who can write so graphically the history of the storms they

have weathered as these rents have done? They are
proof-sheets which need no correction. Here goes lumber from the Maine woods, which did not go out to sea
in the last freshet, risen four dollars on the thousand because of what did go out or was split up; pine, spruce,
cedar, — first, second, third and fourth qualities, so
lately all of one quality, to wave over the bear, and
moose, and caribou. Next rolls Thomaston lime, a
prime lot, which will get far among the hills before it
gets slacked. These rags in bales, of all hues and qualities, the lowest condition to which cotton and linen descend, the final result of dress, — of patterns which are
now no longer cried up, unless it be in Milwaukee, as
those splendid articles, English, French, or American
prints, ginghams, muslins, etc., gathered from all quarters both of fashion and poverty, going to become paper
of one color or a few shades only, on which, forsooth, will
be written tales of real life, high and low, and founded
on fact! This closed car smells of salt fish, the strong
New England and commercial scent, reminding me of
the Grand Banks and the fisheries. Who has not seen
a salt fish, thoroughly cured for this world, so that nothing can spoil it, and putting the perseverance of the
saints to the blush? with which you may sweep or pave
the streets, and split your kindlings, and the teamster
shelter himself and his lading against sun, wind, and
rain behind it, — and the trader, as a Concord trader
once did, hang it up by his door for a sign when he commences business, until at last his oldest customer cannot
tell surely whether it be animal, vegetable, or mineral,
and yet it shall be as pure as a snowflake, and if it be

put into a pot and boiled, will come out an excellent dun
fish for a Saturday's dinner. Next Spanish hides, with
the tails still preserving their twist and the angle of elevation they had when the oxen that wore them were
careering over the pampas of the Spanish main, — a type
of all obstinacy, and evincing how almost hopeless and
incurable are all constitutional vices. I confess, that
practically speaking, when I have learned a man's real
disposition, I have no hopes of changing it for the better
or worse in this state of existence. As the Orientals say,
"A cur's tail may be warmed, and pressed, and bound
round with ligatures, and after a twelve years' labor bestowed upon it, still it will retain its natural form." The
only effectual cure for such inveteracies as these tails
exhibit is to make glue of them, which I believe is what is
usually done with them, and then they will stay put and
stick. Here is a hogshead of molasses or of brandy directed to John Smith, Cuttingsville, Vermont, some trader
among the Green Mountains, who imports for the farmers
near his clearing, and now perchance stands over his
bulkhead and thinks of the last arrivals on the coast, how
they may affect the price for him, telling his customers
this moment, as he has told them twenty times before
this morning, that he expects some by the next train of
prime quality. It is advertised in the Cuttingsville
Times.

While these things go up other things come down.
Warned by the whizzing sound, I look up from my book
and see some tall pine, hewn on far northern hills, which
has winged its way over the Green Mountains and the
Connecticut, shot like an arrow through the township

within ten minutes, and scarce another eye beholds it;
going

> "to be the mast
> Of some great ammiral."

And hark! here comes the cattle-train bearing the cattle
of a thousand hills, sheepcots, stables, and cow-yards in
the air, drovers with their sticks, and shepherd boys in
the midst of their flocks, all but the mountain pastures,
whirled along like leaves blown from the mountains by
the September gales. The air is filled with the bleating
of calves and sheep, and the hustling of oxen, as if a pastoral valley were going by. When the old bell-wether at
the head rattles his bell, the mountains do indeed skip
like rams and the little hills like lambs. A carload of
drovers, too, in the midst, on a level with their droves
now, their vocation gone, but still clinging to their useless sticks as their badge of office. But their dogs, where
are they? It is a stampede to them; they are quite
thrown out; they have lost the scent. Methinks I hear
them barking behind the Peterboro' Hills, or panting up
the western slope of the Green Mountains. They will not
be in at the death. Their vocation, too, is gone. Their
fidelity and sagacity are below par now. They will slink
back to their kennels in disgrace, or perchance run wild
and strike a league with the wolf and the fox. So is
your pastoral life whirled past and away. But the bell
rings, and I must get off the track and let the cars go
by; —

> What's the railroad to me?
> I never go to see
> Where it ends.

It fills a few hollows,
And makes banks for the swallows,
It sets the sand a-blowing,
And the blackberries a-growing,

but I cross it like a cart-path in the woods. I will not have my eyes put out and my ears spoiled by its smoke and steam and hissing.

Now that the cars are gone by and all the restless world with them, and the fishes in the pond no longer feel their rumbling, I am more alone than ever. For the rest of the long afternoon, perhaps, my meditations are interrupted only by the faint rattle of a carriage or team along the distant highway.

Sometimes, on Sundays, I heard the bells, the Lincoln, Acton, Bedford, or Concord bell, when the wind was favorable, a faint, sweet, and, as it were, natural melody, worth importing into the wilderness. At a sufficient distance over the woods this sound acquires a certain vibratory hum, as if the pine needles in the horizon were the strings of a harp which it swept. All sound heard at the greatest possible distance produces one and the same effect, a vibration of the universal lyre, just as the intervening atmosphere makes a distant ridge of earth interesting to our eyes by the azure tint it imparts to it. There came to me in this case a melody which the air had strained, and which had conversed with every leaf and needle of the wood, that portion of the sound which the elements had taken up and modulated and echoed from vale to vale. The echo is, to some extent, an original sound, and therein is the magic and charm of it. It is not merely a repetition of what was worth repeating in the bell, but partly the voice of the wood; the same trivial words and notes sung by a wood-nymph.

At evening, the distant lowing of some cow in the horizon beyond the woods sounded sweet and melodious, and at first I would mistake it for the voices of certain minstrels by whom I was sometimes serenaded, who might be straying over hill and dale; but soon I was not unpleasantly disappointed when it was prolonged into the cheap and natural music of the cow. I do not mean to be satirical, but to express my appreciation of those youths' singing, when I state that I perceived clearly that it was akin to the music of the cow, and they were at length one articulation of Nature.

Regularly at half-past seven, in one part of the summer, after the evening train had gone by, the whip-poor-wills chanted their vespers for half an hour, sitting on a stump by my door, or upon the ridge-pole of the house. They would begin to sing almost with as much precision as a clock, within five minutes of a particular time, referred to the setting of the sun, every evening. I had a rare opportunity to become acquainted with their habits. Sometimes I heard four or five at once in different parts of the wood, by accident one a bar behind another, and so near me that I distinguished not only the cluck after each note, but often that singular buzzing sound like a fly in a spider's web, only proportionally louder. Sometimes one would circle round and round me in the woods a few feet distant as if tethered by a string, when probably I was near its eggs. They sang at intervals throughout the night, and were again as musical as ever just before and about dawn.

When other birds are still, the screech owls take up the strain, like mourning women their ancient u-lu-lu. Their dismal scream is truly Ben Jonsonian. Wise midnight hags! It is no honest and blunt tu-whit tu-who of the poets, but, without jesting, a most solemn graveyard ditty, the mutual consolations of suicide lovers remembering the pangs and the delights of supernal love in the infernal groves. Yet I love to hear their wailing, their doleful responses, trilled along the woodside; reminding me sometimes of music and singing birds; as if it were the dark and tearful side of music, the regrets and sighs that would fain be sung. They are the spirits, the low spirits and melancholy forebodings, of fallen souls that once in human shape night-walked the earth and did the deeds of darkness, now expiating their sins with their wailing hymns or threnodies in the scenery of their transgressions. They give me a new sense of the variety and capacity of that nature which is our common dwelling. *Oh-o-o-o-o that I never had been bor-r-r-r-n!* sighs one on this side of the pond, and circles with the restlessness of despair to some new perch on the gray oaks. Then — *that I never had been bor-r-r-r-n!* echoes another on the farther side with tremulous sincerity, and — *bor-r-r-r-n!* comes faintly from far in the Lincoln woods.

I was also serenaded by a hooting owl. Near at hand you could fancy it the most melancholy sound in Nature, as if she meant by this to stereotype and make permanent in her choir the dying moans of a human being, — some poor weak relic of mortality who has left hope behind, and howls like an animal, yet with human sobs, on entering the dark valley, made more awful by a certain gurgling melodiousness, — I find myself beginning with the letters *gl* when I try to imitate it, — expressive of a mind which has reached the gelatinous, mildewy stage in the mortification of all healthy and courageous thought. It reminded me of ghouls and idiots and insane howlings. But now one answers from far woods in a strain made really melodious by distance, — *Hoo hoo hoo, hoorer hoo;* and indeed for the most part it suggested only pleasing associations, whether heard by day or night, summer or winter.

I rejoice that there are owls. Let them do the idiotic and maniacal hooting for men. It is a sound admirably suited to swamps and twilight woods which no day illustrates, suggesting a vast and undeveloped nature which men have not recognized. They represent the stark twilight and unsatisfied thoughts which all have. All day the sun has shone on the surface of some savage swamp, where the single spruce stands hung with usnea lichens, and small hawks circulate above, and the chickadee lisps amid the evergreens, and the partridge and rabbit skulk beneath; but now a more dismal and fitting day dawns, and a different race of creatures awakes to express the meaning of Nature there.

Late in the evening I heard the distant rumbling of wagons over bridges, — a sound heard farther than almost any other at night, — the baying of dogs, and sometimes again the lowing of some disconsolate cow in a distant barn-yard. In the meanwhile all the shore rang with the trump of bullfrogs, the sturdy spirits of

ancient wine-bibbers and wassailers, still unrepentant,
trying to sing a catch in their Stygian lake, — if the
Walden nymphs will pardon the comparison, for
though there are almost no weeds, there are frogs there,
— who would fain keep up the hilarious rules of their
old festal tables, though their voices have waxed hoarse
and solemnly grave, mocking at mirth, and the wine
has lost its flavor, and become only liquor to distend
their paunches, and sweet intoxication never comes to
drown the memory of the past, but mere saturation and
waterloggedness and distention. The most aldermanic,
with his chin upon a heart-leaf, which serves for a napkin to his drooling chaps, under this northern shore
quaffs a deep draught of the once scorned water, and
passes round the cup with the ejaculation *tr-r-r-oonk*,
tr-r-r-oonk, tr-r-r-oonk ! and straightway comes over the
water from some distant cove the same password repeated, where the next in seniority and girth has gulped
down to his mark; and when this observance has made
the circuit of the shores, then ejaculates the master of
ceremonies, with satisfaction, *tr-r-r-oonk !* and each in
his turn repeats the same down to the least distended,
leakiest, and flabbiest paunched, that there be no mistake; and then the bowl goes round again and again,
until the sun disperses the morning mist, and only the
patriarch is not under the pond, but vainly bellowing
troonk from time to time, and pausing for a reply.

I am not sure that I ever heard the sound of cock-
crowing from my clearing, and I thought that it might be
worth the while to keep a cockerel for his music merely,
as a singing bird. The note of this once wild Indian

pheasant is certainly the most remarkable of any bird's, and if they could be naturalized without being domesticated, it would soon become the most famous sound in our woods, surpassing the clangor of the goose and the hooting of the owl; and then imagine the cackling of the hens to fill the pauses when their lords' clarions rested! No wonder that man added this bird to his tame stock, — to say nothing of the eggs and drumsticks. To walk in a winter morning in a wood where these birds abounded, their native woods, and hear the wild cockerels crow on the trees, clear and shrill for miles over the resounding earth, drowning the feebler notes of other birds, — think of it! It would put nations on the alert. Who would not be early to rise, and rise earlier and earlier every successive day of his life, till he became unspeakably healthy, wealthy, and wise? This foreign bird's note is celebrated by the poets of all countries along with the notes of their native songsters. All climates agree with brave Chanticleer. He is more indigenous even than the natives. His health is ever good, his lungs are sound, his spirits never flag. Even the sailor on the Atlantic and Pacific is awakened by his voice; but its shrill sound never roused me from my slumbers. I kept neither dog, cat, cow, pig, nor hens, so that you would have said there was a deficiency of domestic sounds; neither the churn, nor the spinning-wheel, nor even the singing of the kettle, nor the hissing of the urn, nor children crying, to comfort one. An old-fashioned man would have lost his senses or died of ennui before this. Not even rats in the wall, for they were starved out, or rather were never baited in, — only squirrels on the roof and under the floor, a whip-poor-will on the ridge-pole, a blue jay screaming beneath the window, a hare or woodchuck under the house, a screech owl or a cat owl behind it, a flock of wild geese or a laughing loon on the pond, and a fox to bark in the night. Not even a lark or an oriole, those mild plantation birds, ever visited my clearing. No cockerels to crow nor hens to cackle in the yard. No yard! but unfenced nature reaching up to your very sills. A young forest growing up under your windows, and wild sumachs and blackberry vines breaking through into your cellar; sturdy pitch pines rubbing and creaking against the shingles for want of room, their roots reaching quite under the house. Instead of a scuttle or a blind blown off in the gale, — a pine tree snapped off or torn up by the roots behind your house for fuel. Instead of no path to the front-yard gate in the Great Snow, — no gate — no front-yard, — and no path to the civilized world.

V

SOLITUDE

This is a delicious evening, when the whole body is one sense, and imbibes delight through every pore. I go and come with a strange liberty in Nature, a part of herself. As I walk along the stony shore of the pond in my shirt-sleeves, though it is cool as well as cloudy and windy, and I see nothing special to attract me, all the elements are unusually congenial to me. The bullfrogs trump to usher in the night, and the note of the whip-poor-will is borne on the rippling wind from over the water. Sympathy with the fluttering alder and poplar leaves almost takes away my breath; yet, like the lake, my serenity is rippled but not ruffled. These small waves raised by the evening wind are as remote from storm as the smooth reflecting surface. Though it is now dark, the wind still blows and roars in the wood, the waves still dash, and some creatures lull the rest with their notes. The repose is never complete. The wildest animals do not repose, but seek their prey now; the fox, and skunk, and rabbit, now roam the fields and woods without fear. They are Nature's watchmen, — links which connect the days of animated life.

When I return to my house I find that visitors have been there and left their cards, either a bunch of flowers, or a wreath of evergreen, or a name in pencil on a yellow walnut leaf or a chip. They who come rarely to the woods take some little piece of the forest into their hands to play with by the way, which they leave, either intentionally or accidentally. One has peeled a willow wand, woven it into a ring, and dropped it on my table. I could always tell if visitors had called in my absence, either by the bended twigs or grass, or the print of their shoes, and generally of what sex or age or quality they were by some slight trace left, as a flower dropped, or a bunch of grass plucked and thrown away, even as far off as the railroad, half a mile distant, or by the lingering odor of a cigar or pipe. Nay, I was frequently notified of the passage of a traveller along the highway sixty rods off by the scent of his pipe.

There is commonly sufficient space about us. Our horizon is never quite at our elbows. The thick wood is not just at our door, nor the pond, but somewhat is always clearing, familiar and worn by us, appropriated and fenced in some way, and reclaimed from Nature. For what reason have I this vast range and circuit, some square miles of unfrequented forest, for my privacy, abandoned to me by men? My nearest neighbor is a mile distant, and no house is visible from any place but the hill-tops within half a mile of my own. I have my horizon bounded by woods all to myself; a distant view of the railroad where it touches the pond on the one hand, and of the fence which skirts the woodland road on the other. But for the most part it is as solitary where I live as on the prairies. It is as much Asia or Africa as New England. I have, as it were, my own sun and moon and stars, and a little world all to myself. At night there was never a traveller passed my house, or knocked at my door, more than if I were the first or last man; unless it were in the spring, when at long intervals some came from the village to fish for pouts, — they plainly fished much more in the Walden Pond of their own natures, and baited their hooks with darkness, — but they soon retreated, usually with light baskets, and left "the world to darkness and to me," and the black kernel of the night was never profaned by any human neighborhood. I believe that men are generally still a little afraid of the dark, though the witches are all hung, and Christianity and candles have been introduced.

Yet I experienced sometimes that the most sweet and tender, the most innocent and encouraging society may be found in any natural object, even for the poor misanthrope and most melancholy man. There can be no very black melancholy to him who lives in the midst of nature and has his senses still. There was never yet such a storm but it was Æolian music to a healthy and innocent ear. Nothing can rightly compel a simple and brave man to a vulgar sadness. While I enjoy the friendship of the seasons I trust that nothing can make life a burden to me. The gentle rain which waters my beans and keeps me in the house to-day is not drear and melancholy, but good for me too. Though it prevents my hoeing them, it is of far more worth than my hoeing. If it should continue so long as to cause the seeds to rot in the ground and destroy the potatoes in the low lands, it would still be good for the grass on the uplands, and, being good for the grass, it would be good for me. Sometimes, when I compare myself with other men, it seems as if I were more favored by the gods than they, beyond any deserts that I am conscious of; as if I had a warrant and surety at their hands which my fellows have not, and were especially guided and guarded. I do not flatter myself, but if it be possible they flatter me. I have never felt lonesome, or in the least oppressed by a sense of solitude, but once, and that was a few weeks after I came to the woods, when, for an hour, I doubted if the near neighborhood of man was not essential to a serene and healthy life. To be alone was something unpleasant. But I was at the same time conscious of a slight insanity in my mood, and seemed to foresee my recovery. In the midst of a gentle rain while these thoughts prevailed, I was suddenly sensible of such sweet and beneficent society in Nature, in the very pattering of the drops, and in every sound and sight around my house, an infinite and unaccountable friendliness all at once like an atmosphere sustaining me, as made the fancied advantages of human neighborhood insignificant, and I have never thought of them since. Every little pine needle expanded and swelled with sympathy and befriended me. I was so distinctly made aware of the presence of something kindred to me, even in scenes which we are accustomed to call wild and dreary, and also that the nearest of blood to me and humanest was not a person nor a villager, that I thought no place could ever be strange to me again. —

> "Mourning untimely consumes the sad;
> Few are their days in the land of the living,
> Beautiful daughter of Toscar."

Some of my pleasantest hours were during the long

rain-storms in the spring or fall, which confined me to the house for the afternoon as well as the forenoon, soothed by their ceaseless roar and pelting; when an early twilight ushered in a long evening in which many thoughts had time to take root and unfold themselves. In those driving northeast rains which tried the village houses so, when the maids stood ready with mop and pail in front entries to keep the deluge out, I sat behind my door in my little house, which was all entry, and thoroughly enjoyed its protection. In one heavy thunder-shower the lightning struck a large pitch pine across the pond, making a very conspicuous and perfectly regular spiral groove from top to bottom, an inch or more deep, and four or five inches wide, as you would groove a walking-stick. I passed it again the other day, and was struck with awe on looking up and beholding that mark, now more distinct than ever, where a terrific and resist-less bolt came down out of the harmless sky eight years ago. Men frequently say to me, "I should think you would feel lonesome down there, and want to be nearer to folks, rainy and snowy days and nights especially." I am tempted to reply to such, — This whole earth which we inhabit is but a point in space. How far apart, think you, dwell the two most distant inhabitants of yonder star, the breadth of whose disk cannot be appreciated by our instruments? Why should I feel lonely? is not our planet in the Milky Way? This which you put seems to me not to be the most important question. What sort of space is that which separates a man from his fellows and makes him solitary? I have found that no exertion of the legs can bring two minds much nearer to one another. What do we want most to dwell near to? Not to many men surely, the depot, the post-office, the bar-room, the meeting-house, the school-house, the grocery, Beacon Hill, or the Five Points, where men most congregate, but to the perennial source of our life, whence in all our experience we have found that to issue, as the willow stands near the water and sends out its roots in that direction. This will vary with different natures, but this is the place where a wise man will dig his cellar. . . . I one evening overtook one of my townsmen, who has accumulated what is called "a handsome property," — though I never got a *fair* view of it, — on the Walden road, driving a pair of cattle to market, who inquired of me how I could bring my mind to give up so many of the comforts of life. I answered that I was very sure I liked it passably well; I was not joking. And so I went home to my bed, and left him to pick his way through the darkness and the mud to Brighton, — or Bright-town, — which place he would reach some time in the morning.

Any prospect of awakening or coming to life to a dead man makes indifferent all times and places. The place where that may occur is always the same, and indescribably pleasant to all our senses. For the most part we allow only outlying and transient circumstances to make our occasions. They are, in fact, the cause of our distraction. Nearest to all things is that power which fashions their being. *Next* to us the grandest laws are continually being executed. *Next* to us is not the workman whom we have hired, with whom we love so well to talk, but the workman whose work we are.

"How vast and profound is the influence of the subtile powers of Heaven and of Earth!"

"We seek to perceive them, and we do not see them; we seek to hear them, and we do not hear them; identified with the substance of things, they cannot be separated from them."

"They cause that in all the universe men purify and sanctify their hearts, and clothe themselves in their holiday garments to offer sacrifices and oblations to their ancestors. It is an ocean of subtile intelligences. They are everywhere, above us, on our left, on our right; they environ us on all sides."

We are the subjects of an experiment which is not a little interesting to me. Can we not do without the society of our gossips a little while under these circumstances, — have our own thoughts to cheer us? Confucius says truly, "Virtue does not remain as an abandoned orphan; it must of necessity have neighbors."

With thinking we may be beside ourselves in a sane sense. By a conscious effort of the mind we can stand aloof from actions and their consequences; and all things, good and bad, go by us like a torrent. We are not wholly involved in Nature. I may be either the driftwood in the stream, or Indra in the sky looking down on it. I *may* be affected by a theatrical exhibition; on the other hand, I *may not* be affected by an actual event which appears to concern me much more. I only know myself as a human entity; the scene, so to speak, of thoughts and affections; and am sensible of a certain doubleness by which I can stand as remote from myself as from another. However intense my experience, I am conscious of the presence and criticism of a part of me, which, as it were, is not a part of me, but spectator, sharing no experience, but taking note of it; and that is no more I than it is you. When the play, it may be the tragedy, of life is over, the spectator goes his way. It was a kind of fiction, a work of the imagination only, so far as he was concerned. This doubleness may easily make us poor neighbors and friends sometimes.

I find it wholesome to be alone the greater part of the time. To be in company, even with the best, is soon wearisome and dissipating. I love to be alone. I never found the companion that was so companionable as solitude. We are for the most part more lonely when we go abroad among men than when we stay in our chambers. A man thinking or working is always alone, let him be where he will. Solitude is not measured by the miles of space that intervene between a man and his fellows. The really diligent student in one of the crowded hives of Cambridge College is as solitary as a dervis in the desert. The farmer can work alone in the field or the woods all day, hoeing or chopping, and not feel lonesome, because he is employed; but when he comes home at night he cannot sit down in a room alone, at the mercy of his thoughts, but must be where he can "see the folks," and recreate, and, as he thinks, remunerate himself for his day's solitude; and hence he wonders how the student can sit alone in the house all night and most of the day without ennui and "the blues;" but he does not realize that the student, though in the house, is still at work in *his* field, and chopping in *his* woods, as the farmer in his, and in turn seeks the same recreation and society that the latter does, though it may be a more condensed form of it.

Society is commonly too cheap. We meet at very short intervals, not having had time to acquire any new value for each other. We meet at meals three times a day, and give each other a new taste of that old musty cheese that we are. We have had to agree on a certain set of rules, called etiquette and politeness, to make this frequent meeting tolerable and that we need not come to open war. We meet at the post-office, and at the sociable, and about the fireside every night; we live thick and are in each other's way, and stumble over one another, and I think that we thus lose some respect for one another. Certainly less frequency would suffice for all important and hearty communications. Consider the girls in a factory, — never alone, hardly in their dreams. It would be better if there were but one inhabitant to a square mile, as where I live. The value of a man is not in his skin, that we should touch him.

I have heard of a man lost in the woods and dying of famine and exhaustion at the foot of a tree, whose loneliness was relieved by the grotesque visions with which, owing to bodily weakness, his diseased imagination surrounded him, and which he believed to be real. So also, owing to bodily and mental health and strength, we may be continually cheered by a like but more normal and natural society, and come to know that we are never alone.

I have a great deal of company in my house; especially in the morning, when nobody calls. Let me suggest a few comparisons, that some one may convey an idea

of my situation. I am no more lonely than the loon in
the pond that laughs so loud, or than Walden Pond
itself. What company has that lonely lake, I pray?
And yet it has not the blue devils, but the blue angels
in it, in the azure tint of its waters. The sun is alone,
except in thick weather, when there sometimes appear
to be two, but one is a mock sun. God is alone,—but
the devil, he is far from being alone; he sees a great
deal of company; he is legion. I am no more lonely
than a single mullein or dandelion in a pasture, or a bean
leaf, or sorrel, or a horse-fly, or a humblebee. I am no
more lonely than the Mill Brook, or a weathercock,
or the north star, or the south wind, or an April shower,
or a January thaw, or the first spider in a new house.

I have occasional visits in the long winter evenings,
when the snow falls fast and the wind howls in the
wood, from an old settler and original proprietor, who
is reported to have dug Walden Pond, and stoned it,
and fringed it with pine woods; who tells me stories of
old time and of new eternity; and between us we manage to pass a cheerful evening with social mirth and
pleasant views of things, even without apples or cider, —
a most wise and humorous friend, whom I love much,
who keeps himself more secret than ever did Goffe or
Whalley; and though he is thought to be dead, none
can show where he is buried. An elderly dame, too,
dwells in my neighborhood, invisible to most persons,
in whose odorous herb garden I love to stroll sometimes, gathering simples and listening to her fables;
for she has a genius of unequalled fertility, and her
memory runs back farther than mythology, and she can

tell me the original of every fable, and on what fact every one is founded, for the incidents occurred when she was young. A ruddy and lusty old dame, who delights in all weathers and seasons, and is likely to outlive all her children yet.

The indescribable innocence and beneficence of Nature, — of sun and wind and rain, of summer and winter, — such health, such cheer, they afford forever! and such sympathy have they ever with our race, that all Nature would be affected, and the sun's brightness fade, and the winds would sigh humanely, and the clouds rain tears, and the woods shed their leaves and put on mourning in midsummer, if any man should ever for a just cause grieve. Shall I not have intelligence with the earth? Am I not partly leaves and vegetable mould myself?

What is the pill which will keep us well, serene, contented? Not my or thy great-grandfather's, but our great-grandmother Nature's universal, vegetable, botanic medicines, by which she has kept herself young always, outlived so many old Parrs in her day, and fed her health with their decaying fatness. For my panacea, instead of one of those quack vials of a mixture dipped from Acheron and the Dead Sea, which come out of those long shallow black-schooner looking wagons which we sometimes see made to carry bottles, let me have a draught of undiluted morning air. Morning air! If men will not drink of this at the fountain-head of the day, why, then, we must even bottle up some and sell it in the shops, for the benefit of those who have lost their subscription ticket to morning time in this world. But remember, it will not keep quite till noonday even in the coolest cellar, but drive out the stopples long ere that and follow westward the steps of Aurora. I am no worshipper of Hygeia, who was the daughter of that old herb-doctor Æsculapius, and who is represented on monuments holding a serpent in one hand, and in the other a cup out of which the serpent sometimes drinks; but rather of Hebe, cup-bearer to Jupiter, who was the daughter of Juno and wild lettuce, and who had the power of restoring gods and men to the vigor of youth. She was probably the only thoroughly sound-conditioned, healthy, and robust young lady that ever walked the globe, and wherever she came it was spring.

VI

VISITORS

I THINK that I love society as much as most, and am
ready enough to fasten myself like a bloodsucker for
the time to any full-blooded man that comes in my way.
I am naturally no hermit, but might possibly sit out the
sturdiest frequenter of the bar-room, if my business
called me thither.

I had three chairs in my house; one for solitude, two
for friendship, three for society. When visitors came in
larger and unexpected numbers there was but the third
chair for them all, but they generally economized the
room by standing up. It is surprising how many great
men and women a small house will contain. I have had
twenty-five or thirty souls, with their bodies, at once under my roof, and yet we often parted without being aware
that we had come very near to one another. Many of
our houses, both public and private, with their almost
innumerable apartments, their huge halls and their
cellars for the storage of wines and other munitions of
peace, appear to me extravagantly large for their inhabitants. They are so vast and magnificent that the
latter seem to be only vermin which infest them. I am
surprised when the herald blows his summons before
some Tremont or Astor or Middlesex House, to see
come creeping out over the piazza for all inhabitants a

ridiculous mouse, which soon again slinks into some hole in the pavement.

One inconvenience I sometimes experienced in so small a house, the difficulty of getting to a sufficient distance from my guest when we began to utter the big thoughts in big words. You want room for your thoughts to get into sailing trim and run a course or two before they make their port. The bullet of your thought must have overcome its lateral and ricochet motion and fallen into its last and steady course before it reaches the ear of the hearer, else it may plow out again through the side of his head. Also, our sentences wanted room to unfold and form their columns in the interval. Individuals, like nations, must have suitable broad and natural boundaries, even a considerable neutral ground, between them. I have found it a singular luxury to talk across the pond to a companion on the opposite side. In my house we were so near that we could not begin to hear, — we could not speak low enough to be heard; as when you throw two stones into calm water so near that they break each other's undulations. If we are merely loquacious and loud talkers, then we can afford to stand very near together, cheek by jowl, and feel each other's breath; but if we speak reservedly and thoughtfully, we want to be farther apart, that all animal heat and moisture may have a chance to evaporate. If we would enjoy the most intimate society with that in each of us which is without, or above, being spoken to, we must not only be silent, but commonly so far apart bodily that we cannot possibly hear each other's voice in any case. Referred to this standard, speech is for the convenience of those who are

hard of hearing; but there are many fine things which
we cannot say if we have to shout. As the conversation
began to assume a loftier and grander tone, we gradually
shoved our chairs farther apart till they touched the wall
in opposite 'corners, and then commonly there was not
room enough.

My "best" room, however, my withdrawing room,
always ready for company, on whose carpet the sun
rarely fell, was the pine wood behind my house. Thither
in summer days, when distinguished guests came, I
took them, and a priceless domestic swept the floor and
dusted the furniture and kept the things in order.

If one guest came he sometimes partook of my frugal
meal, and it was no interruption to conversation to be
stirring a hasty-pudding, or watching the rising and ma-
turing of a loaf of bread in the ashes, in the meanwhile.
But if twenty came and sat in my house there was nothing said about dinner, though there might be bread
enough for two, more than if eating were a forsaken
habit; but we naturally practised abstinence; and this
was never felt to be an offence against hospitality, but
the most proper and considerate course. The waste and
decay of physical life, which so often needs repair,
seemed miraculously retarded in such a case, and the
vital vigor stood its ground. I could entertain thus a
thousand as well as twenty; and if any ever went away
disappointed or hungry from my house when they found
me at home, they may depend upon it that I sympathized
with them at least. So easy is it, though many housekeepers doubt it, to establish new and better customs
in the place of the old. You need not rest your reputa-

tion on the dinners you give. For my own part, I was never so effectually deterred from frequenting a man's house, by any kind of Cerberus whatever, as by the parade one made about dining me, which I took to be a very polite and roundabout hint never to trouble him so again. I think I shall never revisit those scenes. I should be proud to have for the motto of my cabin those lines of Spenser which one of my visitors inscribed on a yellow walnut leaf for a card: —

"Arrivèd there, the little house they fill,
  Ne looke for entertainment where none was;
Rest is their feast, and all things at their will:
  The noblest mind the best contentment has."

When Winslow, afterward governor of the Plymouth Colony, went with a companion on a visit of ceremony to Massasoit on foot through the woods, and arrived tired and hungry at his lodge, they were well received by the king, but nothing was said about eating that day. When the night arrived, to quote their own words,— "He laid us on the bed with himself and his wife, they at the one end and we at the other, it being only plank, laid a foot from the ground, and a thin mat upon them. Two more of his chief men, for want of room, pressed by and upon us; so that we were worse weary of our lodging than of our journey." At one o'clock the next day Massasoit "brought two fishes that he had shot," about thrice as big as a bream; "these being boiled, there were at least forty looked for a share in them. The most ate of them. This meal only we had in two nights and a day; and had not one of us bought a partridge, we had taken our journey fasting." Fearing that they would be light-headed for want of food and also sleep, owing to "the savages' barbarous singing, (for they used to sing themselves asleep,)" and that they might get home while they had strength to travel, they departed. As for lodging, it is true they were but poorly entertained, though what they found an inconvenience was no doubt intended for an honor; but as far as eating was concerned, I do not see how the Indians could have done better. They had nothing to eat themselves, and they were wiser than to think that apologies could supply the place of food to their guests; so they drew their belts tighter and said nothing about it. Another time when Winslow visited them, it being a season of plenty with them, there was no deficiency in this respect.

As for men, they will hardly fail one anywhere. I had more visitors while I lived in the woods than at any other period of my life; I mean that I had some. I met several there under more favorable circumstances than I could anywhere else. But fewer came to see me on trivial business. In this respect, my company was winnowed by my mere distance from town. I had withdrawn so far within the great ocean of solitude, into which the rivers of society empty, that for the most part, so far as my needs were concerned, only the finest sediment was deposited around me. Beside, there were wafted to me evidences of unexplored and uncultivated continents on the other side.

Who should come to my lodge this morning but a true Homeric or Paphlagonian man, — he had so suitable and poetic a name that I am sorry I cannot print it here, — a Canadian, a woodchopper and post-maker, who

can hole fifty posts in a day, who made his last supper
on a woodchuck which his dog caught. He, too, has
heard of Homer, and, "if it were not for books," would
"not know what to do rainy days," though perhaps he
has not read one wholly through for many rainy seasons.
Some priest who could pronounce the Greek itself taught
him to read his verse in the Testament in his native parish far away; and now I must translate to him, while
he holds the book, Achilles' reproof to Patroclus for his
sad countenance. — "Why are you in tears, Patroclus,
like a young girl?" —

> "Or have you alone heard some news from Phthia?
> They say that Menœtius lives yet, son of Actor,
> And Peleus lives, son of Æacus, among the Myrmidons,
> Either of whom having died, we should greatly grieve."

He says, "That's good." He has a great bundle of white
oak bark under his arm for a sick man, gathered this
Sunday morning. "I suppose there's no harm in going
after such a thing to-day," says he. To him Homer was
a great writer, though what his writing was about he did
not know. A more simple and natural man it would be
hard to find. Vice and disease, which cast such a sombre moral hue over the world, seemed to have hardly
any existence for him. He was about twenty-eight years
old, and had left Canada and his father's house a dozen
years before to work in the States, and earn money to
buy a farm with at last, perhaps in his native country.
He was cast in the coarsest mould; a stout but sluggish
body, yet gracefully carried, with a thick sunburnt neck,
dark bushy hair, and dull sleepy blue eyes, which were
occasionally lit up with expression. He wore a flat gray

cloth cap, a dingy wool-colored greatcoat, and cow-hide boots. He was a great consumer of meat, usually carrying his dinner to his work a couple of miles past my house, — for he chopped all summer, — in a tin pail; cold meats, often cold woodchucks, and coffee in a stone bottle which dangled by a string from his belt; and sometimes he offered me a drink. He came along early, crossing my bean-field, though without anxiety or haste to get to his work, such as Yankees exhibit. He was n't a-going to hurt himself. He did n't care if he only earned his board. Frequently he would leave his dinner in the bushes, when his dog had caught a wood-chuck by the way, and go back a mile and a half to dress it and leave it in the cellar of the house where he boarded, after deliberating first for half an hour whether he could not sink it in the pond safely till nightfall, — loving to dwell long upon these themes. He would say, as he went by in the morning, "How thick the pigeons are! If work-ing every day were not my trade, I could get all the meat I should want by hunting, — pigeons, woodchucks, rab-bits, partridges, — by gosh! I could get all I should want for a week in one day."

He was a skilful chopper, and indulged in some flour-ishes and ornaments in his art. He cut his trees level and close to the ground, that the sprouts which came up afterward might be more vigorous and a sled might slide over the stumps; and instead of leaving a whole tree to support his corded wood, he would pare it away to a slender stake or splinter which you could break off with your hand at last.

He interested me because he was so quiet and solitary

and so happy withal; a well of good humor and contentment which overflowed at his eyes. His mirth was
without alloy. Sometimes I saw him at his work in the
woods, felling trees, and he would greet me with a laugh
of inexpressible satisfaction, and a salutation in Canadian French, though he spoke English as well. When I
approached him he would suspend his work, and with
half-suppressed mirth lie along the trunk of a pine which
he had felled, and, peeling off the inner bark, roll it up
into a ball and chew it while he laughed and talked.
Such an exuberance of animal spirits had he that he
sometimes tumbled down and rolled on the ground with
laughter at anything which made him think and tickled
him. Looking round upon the trees he would exclaim,
— "By George! I can enjoy myself well enough here
chopping; I want no better sport." Sometimes, when
at leisure, he amused himself all day in the woods with
a pocket pistol, firing salutes to himself at regular intervals as he walked. In the winter he had a fire by which
at noon he warmed his coffee in a kettle; and as he sat
on a log to eat his dinner the chickadees would sometimes come round and alight on his arm and peck at
the potato in his fingers; and he said that he "liked to
have the little *fellers* about him."

In him the animal man chiefly was developed. In
physical endurance and contentment he was cousin to
the pine and the rock. I asked him once if he was not
sometimes tired at night, after working all day; and he
answered, with a sincere and serious look, " Gorrappit, I
never was tired in my life." But the intellectual and what
is called spiritual man in him were slumbering as in an

infant. He had been instructed only in that innocent and ineffectual way in which the Catholic priests teach the aborigines, by which the pupil is never educated to the degree of consciousness, but only to the degree of trust and reverence, and a child is not made a man, but kept a child. When Nature made him, she gave him a strong body and contentment for his portion, and propped him on every side with reverence and reliance, that he might live out his threescore years and ten a child. He was so genuine and unsophisticated that no introduction would serve to introduce him, more than if you introduced a woodchuck to your neighbor. He had got to find him out as you did. He would not play any part. Men paid him wages for work, and so helped to feed and clothe him; but he never exchanged opinions with them. He was so simply and naturally humble — if he can be called humble who never aspires — that humility was no distinct quality in him, nor could he conceive of it. Wiser men were demigods to him. If you told him that such a one was coming, he did as if he thought that anything so grand would expect nothing of himself, but take all the responsibility on itself, and let him be forgotten still. He never heard the sound of praise. He particularly reverenced the writer and the preacher. Their performances were miracles. When I told him that I wrote considerably, he thought for a long time that it was merely the handwriting which I meant, for he could write a remarkably good hand himself. I sometimes found the name of his native parish handsomely written in the snow by the highway, with the proper French accent, and knew that he had passed. I asked him if he

ever wished to write his thoughts. He said that he had
read and written letters for those who could not, but he
never tried to write thoughts, — no, he could not, he
could not tell what to put first, it would kill him, and
then there was spelling to be attended to at the same
time!

I heard that a distinguished wise man and reformer
asked him if he did not want the world to be changed;
but he answered with a chuckle of surprise in his Canadian accent, not knowing that the question had ever
been entertained before, "No, I like it well enough."
It would have suggested many things to a philosopher
to have dealings with him. To a stranger he appeared
to know nothing of things in general; yet I sometimes
saw in him a man whom I had not seen before, and I
did not know whether he was as wise as Shakespeare or
as simply ignorant as a child, whether to suspect him
of a fine poetic consciousness or of stupidity. A townsman told me that when he met him sauntering through
the village in his small close-fitting cap, and whistling to
himself, he reminded him of a prince in disguise.

His only books were an almanac and an arithmetic,
in which last he was considerably expert. The former
was a sort of cyclopædia to him, which he supposed to
contain an abstract of human knowledge, as indeed it
does to a considerable extent. I loved to sound him on
the various reforms of the day, and he never failed to
look at them in the most simple and practical light. He
had never heard of such things before. Could he do
without factories? I asked. He had worn the home-
made Vermont gray, he said, and that was good. Could

he dispense with tea and coffee? Did this country afford any beverage beside water? He had soaked hemlock leaves in water and drank it, and thought that was better than water in warm weather. When I asked him if he could do without money, he showed the convenience of money in such a way as to suggest and coincide with the most philosophical accounts of the origin of this institution, and the very derivation of the word *pecunia*. If an ox were his property, and he wished to get needles and thread at the store, he thought it would be inconvenient and impossible soon to go on mortgaging some portion of the creature each time to that amount. He could defend many institutions better than any philosopher, because, in describing them as they concerned him, he gave the true reason for their prevalence, and speculation had not suggested to him any other. At another time, hearing Plato's definition of a man, — a biped without feathers, — and that one exhibited a cock plucked and called it Plato's man, he thought it an important difference that the *knees* bent the wrong way. He would sometimes exclaim, "How I love to talk! By George, I could talk all day!" I asked him once, when I had not seen him for many months, if he had got a new idea this summer. "Good Lord," said he, "a man that has to work as I do, if he does not forget the ideas he has had, he will do well. May be the man you hoe with is inclined to race; then, by gorry, your mind must be there; you think of weeds." He would sometimes ask me first on such occasions, if I had made any improvement. One winter day I asked him if he was always satisfied with himself, wishing to suggest a substitute within him for the priest without, and some higher motive for living. "Satisfied!" said he; "some men are satisfied with one thing, and some with another. One man, perhaps, if he has got enough, will be satisfied to sit all day with his back to the fire and his belly to the table, by George!" Yet I never, by any manœuvring, could get him to take the spiritual view of things; the highest that he appeared to conceive of was a simple expediency, such as you might expect an animal to appreciate; and this, practically, is true of most men. If I suggested any improvement in his mode of life, he merely answered, without expressing any regret, that it was too late. Yet he thoroughly believed in honesty and the like virtues.

There was a certain positive originality, however slight, to be detected in him, and I occasionally observed that he was thinking for himself and expressing his own opinion, a phenomenon so rare that I would any day walk ten miles to observe it, and it amounted to the re-origination of many of the institutions of society. Though he hesitated, and perhaps failed to express himself distinctly, he always had a presentable thought behind. Yet his thinking was so primitive and immersed in his animal life, that, though more promising than a merely learned man's, it rarely ripened to anything which can be reported. He suggested that there might be men of genius in the lowest grades of life, however permanently humble and illiterate, who take their own view always, or do not pretend to see at all; who are as bottomless even as Walden Pond was thought to be, though they may be dark and muddy.

Many a traveller came out of his way to see me and the inside of my house, and, as an excuse for calling, asked for a glass of water. I told them that I drank at the pond, and pointed thither, offering to lend them a dipper. Far off as I lived, I was not exempted from that annual visitation which occurs, methinks, about the first of April, when everybody is on the move; and I had my share of good luck, though there were some curious specimens among my visitors. Half-witted men from the almshouse and elsewhere came to see me; but I endeavored to make them exercise all the wit they had, and make their confessions to me; in such cases making wit the theme of our conversation; and so was compensated. Indeed, I found some of them to be wiser than the so-called *overseers* of the poor and select-men of the town, and thought it was time that the tables were turned. With respect to wit, I learned that there was not much difference between the half and the whole. One day, in particular, an inoffensive, simple-minded pauper, whom with others I had often seen used as fencing stuff, standing or sitting on a bushel in the fields to keep cattle and himself from straying, visited me, and expressed a wish to live as I did. He told me, with the utmost simplicity and truth, quite superior, or rather *inferior*, to anything that is called humility, that he was "deficient in intellect." These were his words. The Lord had made him so, yet he supposed the Lord cared as much for him as for an-other. "I have always been so," said he, "from my child-hood; I never had much mind; I was not like other children; I am weak in the head. It was the Lord's

will, I suppose." And there he was to prove the truth
of his words. He was a metaphysical puzzle to me. I
have rarely met a fellow-man on such promising ground,
— it was so simple and sincere and so true all that he
said. And, true enough, in proportion as he appeared
to humble himself was he exalted. I did not know at
first but it was the result of a wise policy. It seemed that
from such a basis of truth and frankness as the poor
weak-headed pauper had laid, our intercourse might
go forward to something better than the intercourse of
sages.

I had some guests from those not reckoned commonly
among the town's poor, but who should be; who are
among the world's poor, at any rate; guests who ap-
pcal, not to your hospitality, but to your *hospitalality ;*
who earnestly wish to be helped, and preface their appeal with the information that they are resolved, for one
thing, never to help themselves. I require of a visitor
that he be not actually starving, though he may have
the very best appetite in the world, however he got it.
Objects of charity are not guests. Men who did not
know when their visit had terminated, though I went
about my business again, answering them from greater
and greater remoteness. Men of almost every degree
of wit called on me in the migrating season. Some who
had more wits than they knew what to do with; runaway slaves with plantation manners, who listened
from time to time, like the fox in the fable, as if they
heard the hounds a-baying on their track, and looked
at me beseechingly, as much as to say, —

"O Christian, will you send me back?"

One real runaway slave, among the rest, whom I helped to forward toward the north star. Men of one idea, like a hen with one chicken, and that a duckling; men of a thousand ideas, and unkempt heads, like those hens which are made to take charge of a hundred chickens, all in pursuit of one bug, a score of them lost in every morning's dew, — and become frizzled and mangy in consequence; men of ideas instead of legs, a sort of intellectual centipede that made you crawl all over. One man proposed a book in which visitors should write their names, as at the White Mountains; but, alas! I have too good a memory to make that necessary.

I could not but notice some of the peculiarities of my visitors. Girls and boys and young women generally seemed glad to be in the woods. They looked in the pond and at the flowers, and improved their time. Men of business, even farmers, thought only of solitude and employment, and of the great distance at which I dwelt from something or other; and though they said that they loved a ramble in the woods occasionally, it was obvious that they did not. Restless committed men, whose time was all taken up in getting a living or keeping it; ministers who spoke of God as if they enjoyed a monopoly of the subject, who could not bear all kinds of opinions; doctors, lawyers, uneasy housekeepers who pried into my cupboard and bed when I was out, — how came Mrs. —— to know that my sheets were not as clean as hers? — young men who had ceased to be young, and had concluded that it was safest to follow the beaten track of the professions, — all these generally said that it was not possible to do so much good in my position. Ay! there was the rub. The old and infirm and the timid, of whatever age or sex, thought most of sickness, and sudden accident and death; to them life seemed full of danger, — what danger is there if you don't think of any? — and they thought that a prudent man would carefully select the safest position, where Dr. B. might be on hand at a moment's warning. To them the village was literally a *com-munity*, a league for mutual defence, and you would suppose that they would not go a-huckleberrying without a medicine chest. The amount of it is, if a man is alive, there is always *danger* that he may die, though the danger must be allowed to be less in proportion as he is dead-and-alive to begin with. A man sits as many risks as he runs. Finally, there were the self-styled reformers, the greatest bores of all, who thought that I was forever singing, —

> This is the house that I built;
> This is the man that lives in the house that I built;

but they did not know that the third line was, —

> These are the folks that worry the man
> That lives in the house that I built.

I did not fear the hen-harriers, for I kept no chickens; but I feared the men-harriers rather.

I had more cheering visitors than the last. Children come a-berrying, railroad men taking a Sunday morning walk in clean shirts, fishermen and hunters, poets and philosophers; in short, all honest pilgrims, who came out to the woods for freedom's sake, and really left the village behind, I was ready to greet with, — "Welcome, Englishmen! welcome, Englishmen!" for I had had communication with that race.

VII

THE BEAN-FIELD

Meanwhile my beans, the length of whose rows, added together, was seven miles already planted, were impatient to be hoed, for the earliest had grown considerably before the latest were in the ground; indeed they were not easily to be put off. What was the meaning of this so steady and self-respecting, this small Herculean labor, I knew not. I came to love my rows, my beans, though so many more than I wanted. They attached me to the earth, and so I got strength like Antæus. But why should I raise them? Only Heaven knows. This was my curious labor all summer, — to make this portion of the earth's surface, which had yielded only cinquefoil, blackberries, johnswort, and the like, before, sweet wild fruits and pleasant flowers, produce instead this pulse. What shall I learn of beans or beans of me? I cherish them, I hoe them, early and late I have an eye to them; and this is my day's work. It is a fine broad leaf to look on. My auxiliaries are the dews and rains which water this dry soil, and what fertility is in the soil itself, which for the most part is lean and effete. My enemies are worms, cool days, and most of all woodchucks. The last have nibbled for me a quarter of an acre clean. But what right had I to oust johnswort and the rest, and break up their ancient herb garden? Soon, however, the remaining beans will be too tough for them, and go forward to meet new foes.

When I was four years old, as I well remember, I was brought from Boston to this my native town, through these very woods and this field, to the pond. It is one of the oldest scenes stamped on my memory. And now to-night my flute has waked the echoes over that very water. The pines still stand here older than I; or, if some have fallen, I have cooked my supper with their stumps, and a new growth is rising all around, preparing another aspect for new infant eyes. Almost the same johnswort springs from the same perennial root in this pasture, and even I have at length helped to clothe that fabulous landscape of my infant dreams, and one of the results of my presence and influence is seen in these bean leaves, corn blades, and potato vines.

I planted about two acres and a half of upland; and as it was only about fifteen years since the land was cleared, and I myself had got out two or three cords of stumps, I did not give it any manure; but in the course of the summer it appeared by the arrowheads which I turned up in hoeing, that an extinct nation had anciently dwelt here and planted corn and beans ere white men came to clear the land, and so, to some extent, had exhausted the soil for this very crop.

Before yet any woodchuck or squirrel had run across the road, or the sun had got above the shrub oaks, while all the dew was on, though the farmers warned me against it, — I would advise you to do all your work if possible while the dew is on, — I began to level the ranks of haughty weeds in my bean-field and throw

dust upon their heads. Early in the morning I worked
barefooted, dabbling like a plastic artist in the dewy
and crumbling sand, but later in the day the sun blis-
tered my feet. There the sun lighted me to hoe beans,
pacing slowly backward and forward over that yellow
gravelly upland, between the long green rows, fifteen
rods, the one end terminating in a shrub oak copse
where I could rest in the shade, the other in a blackberry field where the green berries deepened their tints
by the time I had made another bout. Removing the
weeds, putting fresh soil about the bean stems, and
encouraging this weed which I had sown, making the
yellow soil express its summer thought in bean leaves
and blossoms rather than in wormwood and piper and
millet grass, making the earth say beans instead of
grass, — this was my daily work. As I had little aid
from horses or cattle, or hired men or boys, or improved
implements of husbandry, I was much slower, and became much more intimate with my beans than usual.
But labor of the hands, even when pursued to the verge
of drudgery, is perhaps never the worst form of idleness.
It has a constant and imperishable moral, and to the
scholar it yields a classic result. A very *agricola labori-
osus* was I to travellers bound westward through Lincoln and Wayland to nobody knows where; they sitting
at their ease in gigs, with elbows on knees, and reins
loosely hanging in festoons; I the home-staying, laborious native of the soil. But soon my homestead was out
of their sight and thought. It was the only open and
cultivated field for a great distance on either side of the
road, so they made the most of it; and sometimes the

man in the field heard more of travellers' gossip and comment than was meant for his ear: "Beans so late! peas so late!" — for I continued to plant when others had begun to hoe, — the ministerial husbandman had not suspected it. "Corn, my boy, for fodder; corn for fodder." "Does he *live* there?" asks the black bonnet of the gray coat; and the hard-featured farmer reins up his grateful dobbin to inquire what you are doing where he sees no manure in the furrow, and recommends a little chip dirt, or any little waste stuff, or it may be ashes or plaster. But here were two acres and a half of furrows, and only a hoe for cart and two hands to draw it, — there being an aversion to other carts and horses, — and chip dirt far away. Fellow-travellers as they rattled by compared it aloud with the fields which they had passed, so that I came to know how I stood in the agricultural world. This was one field not in Mr. Coleman's report. And, by the way, who estimates the value of the crop which nature yields in the still wilder fields unimproved by man? The crop of *English* hay is carefully weighed, the moisture calculated, the silicates and the potash; but in all dells and pond-holes in the woods and pastures and swamps grows a rich and various crop only unreaped by man. Mine was, as it were, the connecting link between wild and cultivated fields; as some states are civilized, and others half-civilized, and others savage or barbarous, so my field was, though not in a bad sense, a half-cultivated field. They were beans cheerfully returning to their wild and primitive state that I cultivated, and my hoe played the *Ranz des Vaches* for them.

Near at hand, upon the topmost spray of a birch, sings the brown thrasher — or red mavis, as some love to call him — all the morning, glad of your society, that would find out another farmer's field if yours were not here. While you are planting the seed, he cries, — "Drop it, drop it, — cover it up, cover it up, — pull it up, pull it up, pull it up." But this was not corn, and so it was safe from such enemies as he. You may wonder what his rigmarole, his amateur Paganini performances on one string or on twenty, have to do with your planting, and yet prefer it to leached ashes or plaster. It was a cheap sort of top dressing in which I had entire faith.

As I drew a still fresher soil about the rows with my hoe, I disturbed the ashes of unchronicled nations who in primeval years lived under these heavens, and their small implements of war and hunting were brought to the light of this modern day. They lay mingled with other natural stones, some of which bore the marks of having been burned by Indian fires, and some by the sun, and also bits of pottery and glass brought hither by the recent cultivators of the soil. When my hoe tinkled against the stones, that music echoed to the woods and the sky, and was an accompaniment to my labor which yielded an instant and immeasurable crop. It was no longer beans that I hoed, nor I that hoed beans; and I remembered with as much pity as pride, if I remembered at all, my acquaintances who had gone to the city to attend the oratorios. The nighthawk circled overhead in the sunny afternoons — for I sometimes made a day of it — like a mote in the eye, or in heaven's eye, falling from time to time with a swoop and a sound as if the heavens were rent, torn at last to very rags and tatters, and yet a seamless cope remained; small imps that fill the air and lay their eggs on the ground on bare sand or rocks on the tops of hills, where few have found them; graceful and slender like ripples caught up from the pond, as leaves are raised by the wind to float in the heavens; such kindredship is in nature. The hawk is aerial brother of the wave which he sails over and surveys, those his perfect air-inflated wings answering to the elemental unfledged pinions of the sea. Or sometimes I watched a pair of hen-hawks circling high in the sky, alternately soaring and descending, approaching and leaving one another, as if they were the embodiment of my own thoughts. Or I was attracted by the passage of wild pigeons from this wood to that, with a slight quivering winnowing sound and carrier haste; or from under a rotten stump my hoe turned up a sluggish portentous and outlandish spotted salamander, a trace of Egypt and the Nile, yet our contemporary. When I paused to lean on my hoe, these sounds and sights I heard and saw anywhere in the row, a part of the inexhaustible entertainment which the country offers.

On gala days the town fires its great guns, which echo like popguns to these woods, and some waifs of martial music occasionally penetrate thus far. To me, away there in my bean-field at the other end of the town, the big guns sounded as if a puffball had burst; and when there was a military turnout of which I was ignorant, I have sometimes had a vague sense all the day of some sort of itching and disease in the horizon, as if some eruption would break out there soon, either scarlatina or canker-rash, until at length some more favorable puff of wind, making haste over the fields and up the Way-land road, brought me information of the "trainers." It seemed by the distant hum as if somebody's bees had swarmed, and that the neighbors, according to Virgil's advice, by a faint *tintinnabulum* upon the most sonorous of their domestic utensils, were endeavoring to call them down into the hive again. And when the sound died quite away, and the hum had ceased, and the most fa-vorable breezes told no tale, I knew that they had got the last drone of them all safely into the Middlesex hive, and that now their minds were bent on the honey with which it was smeared.

I felt proud to know that the liberties of Massachusetts and of our fatherland were in such safe keeping; and as I turned to my hoeing again I was filled with an inex-pressible confidence, and pursued my labor cheerfully with a calm trust in the future.

When there were several bands of musicians, it sounded as if all the village was a vast bellows, and all the buildings expanded and collapsed alternately with a din. But sometimes it was a really noble and inspir-ing strain that reached these woods, and the trumpet that sings of fame, and I felt as if I could spit a Mexican with a good relish, — for why should we always stand for trifles ? — and looked round for a woodchuck or a skunk to exercise my chivalry upon. These martial strains seemed as far away as Palestine, and reminded me of a march of crusaders in the horizon, with a slight tantivy and tremulous motion of the elm tree tops which overhang the village. This was one of the *great* days; though the sky had from my clearing only the same everlastingly great look that it wears daily, and I saw no difference in it.

It was a singular experience that long acquaintance which I cultivated with beans, what with planting, and hoeing, and harvesting, and threshing, and picking over and selling them, — the last was the hardest of all, — I might add eating, for I did taste. I was determined to know beans. When they were growing, I used to hoe from five o'clock in the morning till noon, and commonly spent the rest of the day about other affairs. Consider the intimate and curious acquaintance one makes with various kinds of weeds, — it will bear some iteration in the account, for there was no little iteration in the labor, — disturbing their delicate organizations so ruthlessly, and making such invidious distinctions with his hoe, levelling whole ranks of one species, and sedulously cultivating another. That's Roman wormwood, — that's pigweed, — that's sorrel, — that's piper-grass, — have at him, chop him up, turn his roots upward to the sun, don't let him have a fibre in the shade, if you do he'll turn himself t'other side up and be as green as a leek in two days. A long war, not with cranes, but with weeds, those Trojans who had sun and rain and dews on their side. Daily the beans saw me come to their rescue armed with a hoe, and thin the ranks of their enemies, filling up the trenches with weedy dead. Many a lusty crest-waving Hector, that towered a whole foot above his crowding comrades, fell before my weapon and rolled in the dust.

Those summer days which some of my contemporaries devoted to the fine arts in Boston or Rome, and others to contemplation in India, and others to trade in London or New York, I thus, with the other farmers of New England, devoted to husbandry. Not that I wanted beans to eat, for I am by nature a Pythagorean, so far as beans are concerned, whether they mean porridge or voting, and exchanged them for rice; but, perchance, as some must work in fields if only for the sake of tropes and expression, to serve a parable-maker one day. It was on the whole a rare amusement, which, continued too long, might have become a dissipation. Though I gave them no manure, and did not hoe them all once, I hoed them unusually well as far as I went, and was paid for it in the end, "there being in truth," as Evelyn says, "no compost or lætation whatsoever comparable to this continual motion, repastination, and turning of the mould with the spade." "The earth," he adds elsewhere, "especially if fresh, has a certain magnetism in it, by which it attracts the salt, power, or virtue (call it either) which gives it life, and is the logic of all the labor and stir we keep about it, to sustain us; all dungings and other sordid temperings being but the vicars succedaneous to this improvement." Moreover, this being one of those "worn-out and exhausted lay fields which enjoy their sabbath," had perchance, as Sir Kenelm Digby thinks likely, attracted "vital spirits" from the air. I harvested twelve bushels of beans.

But to be more particular, for it is complained that Mr. Coleman has reported chiefly the expensive experiments of gentlemen farmers, my outgoes were, —

For a hoe	$0 54	
Plowing, harrowing, and furrowing .	7 50	Too much.
Beans for seed	3 12½	
Potatoes "	1 33	
Peas "	0 40	
Turnip seed	0 06	
White line for crow fence	0 02	
Horse cultivator and boy three hours .	1 00	
Horse and cart to get crop	0 75	

In all $14 72½

My income was (patrem familias vendacem, non emacem esse oportet), from

Nine bushels and twelve quarts of beans sold .	$16 94
Five " large potatoes	2 50
Nine " small	2 25
Grass	1 00
Stalks	0 75

In all $23 44

Leaving a pecuniary profit, as I have elsewhere
said, of $8 71½

This is the result of my experience in raising beans. Plant the common small white bush bean about the first of June, in rows three feet by eighteen inches apart, being careful to select fresh round and unmixed seed. First look out for worms, and supply vacancies by planting anew. Then look out for woodchucks, if it is an exposed place, for they will nibble off the earliest tender leaves almost clean as they go; and again, when the young tendrils make their appearance, they have notice of it, and will shear them off with both buds and young pods, sitting erect like a squirrel. But above all harvest as early as possible, if you would escape frosts and have a fair and salable crop; you may save much loss by this means.

This further experience also I gained. I said to myself, I will not plant beans and corn with so much industry another summer, but such seeds, if the seed is not lost, as sincerity, truth, simplicity, faith, innocence, and the like, and see if they will not grow in this soil, even with less toil and manurance, and sustain me, for surely it has not been exhausted for these crops. Alas! I said this to myself; but now another summer is gone, and another, and another, and I am obliged to say to you, Reader, that the seeds which I planted, if indeed they *were* the seeds of those virtues, were wormeaten or had lost their vitality, and so did not come up. Commonly men will only be brave as their fathers were brave, or timid. This generation is very sure to plant corn and beans each new year precisely as the Indians did centuries ago and taught the first settlers to do, as if there were a fate in it. I saw an old man the other day, to my astonishment, making the holes with a hoe for the seventieth time at least, and not for himself to lie down in! But why should not the New Englander try new adventures, and not lay so much stress on his grain, his potato and grass crop, and his orchards, — raise other crops than these? Why concern ourselves so much about our beans for seed, and not be concerned at all about a new generation of men? We should really be fed and cheered if when we met a man we were sure to see that some of the qualities which I have named, which we all prize more than those other productions, but which are for the most part broadcast and floating in the air, had taken root and grown in him. Here comes such a subtle and ineffable quality, for instance, as truth or justice, though the slightest amount or new variety of it, along the road. Our ambassadors should be instructed to send home such seeds as these, and Congress help to distribute them over all the land. We should never stand upon ceremony with sincerity. We should never cheat and insult and banish one another by our meanness, if there were present the kernel of worth and friendliness. We should not meet thus in haste. Most men I do not meet at all, for they seem not to have time; they are busy about their beans. We would not deal with a man thus plodding ever, leaning on a hoe or a spade as a staff between his work, not as a mushroom, but partially risen out of the earth, something more than erect, like swallows alighted and walking on the ground: —

> "And as he spake, his wings would now and then
> Spread, as he meant to fly, then close again, —"

so that we should suspect that we might be conversing with an angel. Bread may not always nourish us; but it always does us good, it even takes stiffness out of our joints, and makes us supple and buoyant, when we knew not what ailed us, to recognize any generosity in man or Nature, to share any unmixed and heroic joy.

Ancient poetry and mythology suggest, at least, that husbandry was once a sacred art; but it is pursued with irreverent haste and heedlessness by us, our object being to have large farms and large crops merely. We have no festival, nor procession, nor ceremony, not excepting our cattle-shows and so-called Thanksgivings, by which the farmer expresses a sense of the sacredness of his calling, or is reminded of its sacred origin. It is the premium and the feast which tempt him. He sacrifices not to Ceres and the Terrestrial Jove, but to the infernal Plutus rather. By avarice and selfishness, and a grovelling habit, from which none of us is free, of regarding the soil as property, or the means of acquiring property chiefly, the landscape is deformed, husbandry is degraded with us, and the farmer leads the meanest of lives. He knows Nature but as a robber. Cato says that the profits of agriculture are particularly pious or just (*maximeque pius quaestus*), and according to Varro the old Romans "called the same earth Mother and Ceres, and thought that they who cultivated it led a pious and useful life, and that they alone were left of the race of King Saturn."

We are wont to forget that the sun looks on our cultivated fields and on the prairies and forests without distinction. They all reflect and absorb his rays alike, and the former make but a small part of the glorious picture which he beholds in his daily course. In his view the earth is all equally cultivated like a garden. Therefore we should receive the benefit of his light and heat with a corresponding trust and magnanimity. What though I value the seed of these beans, and harvest that in the fall of the year? This broad field which I have looked at so long looks not to me as the principal cultivator, but away from me to influences more genial to it, which water and make it green. These beans have results which are not harvested by me. Do they not grow for woodchucks partly? The ear of wheat (in Latin *spica*, obsoletely *speca*, from *spe*, hope) should not be the only hope of the husbandman; its kernel or grain (*granum*, from *gerendo*, bearing) is not all that it bears. How, then, can our harvest fail? Shall I not rejoice also at the abundance of the weeds whose seeds are the granary of the birds? It matters little comparatively whether the fields fill the farmer's barns. The true husbandman will cease from anxiety, as the squirrels manifest no concern whether the woods will bear chestnuts this year or not, and finish his labor with every day, relinquishing all claim to the produce of his fields, and sacrificing in his mind not only his first but his last fruits also.

Pines planted by Thoreau on his bean-field

Thoreau's cove, Walden Pond, showing Indian Path

VIII

THE VILLAGE

AFTER hoeing, or perhaps reading and writing, in the forenoon, I usually bathed again in the pond, swimming across one of its coves for a stint, and washed the dust of labor from my person, or smoothed out the last wrinkle which study had made, and for the afternoon was absolutely free. Every day or two I strolled to the village to hear some of the gossip which is incessantly going on there, circulating either from mouth to mouth, or from newspaper to newspaper, and which, taken in homœopathic doses, was really as refreshing in its way as the rustle of leaves and the peeping of frogs. As I walked in the woods to see the birds and squirrels, so I walked in the village to see the men and boys; instead of the wind among the pines I heard the carts rattle. In one direction from my house there was a colony of muskrats in the river meadows; under the grove of elms and buttonwoods in the other horizon was a village of busy men, as curious to me as if they had been prairie-dogs, each sitting at the mouth of its burrow, or running over to a neighbor's to gossip. I went there frequently to observe their habits. The village appeared to me a great news room; and on one side, to support it, as once at Redding & Company's on State Street, they kept nuts and raisins, or salt and meal and other groceries. Some

have such a vast appetite for the former commodity,
that is, the news, and such sound digestive organs, that
they can sit forever in public avenues without stirring,
and let it simmer and whisper through them like the
Etesian winds, or as if inhaling ether, it only producing
numbness and insensibility to pain, — otherwise it
would often be painful to hear, — without affecting the
consciousness. I hardly ever failed, when I rambled
through the village, to see a row of such worthies, either
sitting on a ladder sunning themselves, with their bodies
inclined forward and their eyes glancing along the line
this way and that, from time to time, with a voluptuous
expression, or else leaning against a barn with their
hands in their pockets, like caryatides, as if to prop it up.
They, being commonly out of doors, heard whatever
was in the wind. These are the coarsest mills, in which
all gossip is first rudely digested or cracked up before it
is emptied into finer and more delicate hoppers within
doors. I observed that the vitals of the village were the
grocery, the bar-room, the post-office, and the bank;
and, as a necessary part of the machinery, they kept a
bell, a big gun, and a fire-engine, at convenient places;
and the houses were so arranged as to make the most of
mankind, in lanes and fronting one another, so that
every traveller had to run the gauntlet, and every man,
woman, and child might get a lick at him. Of course,
those who were stationed nearest to the head of the line,
where they could most see and be seen, and have the first
blow at him, paid the highest prices for their places;
and the few straggling inhabitants in the outskirts, where
long gaps in the line began to occur, and the traveller

could get over walls or turn aside into cow-paths, and so escape, paid a very slight ground or window tax. Signs were hung out on all sides to allure him; some to catch him by the appetite, as the tavern and victualling cellar; some by the fancy, as the dry goods store and the jeweller's; and others by the hair or the feet or the skirts, as the barber, the shoemaker, or the tailor. Besides, there was a still more terrible standing invitation to call at every one of these houses, and company expected about these times. For the most part I escaped wonderfully from these dangers, either by proceeding at once boldly and without deliberation to the goal, as is recommended to those who run the gauntlet, or by keeping my thoughts on high things, like Orpheus, who, "loudly singing the praises of the gods to his lyre, drowned the voices of the Sirens, and kept out of danger." Sometimes I bolted suddenly, and nobody could tell my whereabouts, for I did not stand much about gracefulness, and never hesitated at a gap in a fence. I was even accustomed to make an irruption into some houses, where I was well entertained, and after learning the kernels and very last sieveful of news, — what had subsided, the prospects of war and peace, and whether the world was likely to hold together much longer, — I was let out through the rear avenues, and so escaped to the woods again.

It was very pleasant, when I stayed late in town, to launch myself into the night, especially if it was dark and tempestuous, and set sail from some bright village parlor or lecture room, with a bag of rye or Indian meal upon my shoulder, for my snug harbor in the woods, having made all tight without and withdrawn under hatches with a merry crew of thoughts, leaving only my outer man at the helm, or even tying up the helm when it was plain sailing. I had many a genial thought by the cabin fire "as I sailed." I was never cast away nor distressed in any weather, though I encountered some severe storms. It is darker in the woods, even in common nights, than most suppose. I frequently had to look up at the opening between the trees above the path in order to learn my route, and, where there was no cart-path, to feel with my feet the faint track which I had worn, or steer by the known relation of particular trees which I felt with my hands, passing between two pines for instance, not more than eighteen inches apart, in the midst of the woods, invariably in the darkest night. Sometimes, after coming home thus late in a dark and muggy night, when my feet felt the path which my eyes could not see, dreaming and absent-minded all the way, until I was aroused by having to raise my hand to lift the latch, I have not been able to recall a single step of my walk, and I have thought that perhaps my body would find its way home if its master should forsake it, as the hand finds its way to the mouth without assistance. Several times, when a visitor chanced to stay into evening, and it proved a dark night, I was obliged to conduct him to the cart-path in the rear of the house, and then point out to him the direction he was to pursue, and in keeping which he was to be guided rather by his feet than his eyes. One very dark night I directed thus on their way two young men who had been fishing in the pond. They lived about a mile off through the woods, and were quite used to the route. A day or two after one

of them told me that they wandered about the greater
part of the night, close by their own premises, and did
not get home till toward morning, by which time, as
there had been several heavy showers in the meanwhile,
and the leaves were very wet, they were drenched to
their skins. I have heard of many going astray even in
the village streets, when the darkness was so thick that
you could cut it with a knife, as the saying is. Some who
live in the outskirts, having come to town a-shopping
in their wagons, have been obliged to put up for the
night; and gentlemen and ladies making a call have
gone half a mile out of their way, feeling the sidewalk
only with their feet, and not knowing when they turned.
It is a surprising and memorable, as well as valuable experience, to be lost in the woods any time. Often in a
snow-storm, even by day, one will come out upon a well-
known road and yet find it impossible to tell which way
leads to the village. Though he knows that he has travelled it a thousand times, he cannot recognize a feature
in it, but it is as strange to him as if it were a road in
Siberia. By night, of course, the perplexity is infinitely
greater. In our most trivial walks, we are constantly,
though unconsciously, steering like pilots by certain
well-known beacons and headlands, and if we go beyond our usual course we still carry in our minds the
bearing of some neighboring cape; and not till we are
completely lost, or turned round, — for a man needs
only to be turned round once with his eyes shut in this
world to be lost, — do we appreciate the vastness and
strangeness of nature. Every man has to learn the
points of compass again as often as he awakes, whether

from sleep or any abstraction. Not till we are lost, in other words, not till we have lost the world, do we begin to find ourselves, and realize where we are and the infinite extent of our relations.

One afternoon, near the end of the first summer, when I went to the village to get a shoe from the cobbler's, I was seized and put into jail, because, as I have elsewhere related, I did not pay a tax to, or recognize the authority of, the State which buys and sells men, women, and children, like cattle at the door of its senate-house. I had gone down to the woods for other purposes. But, wherever a man goes, men will pursue and paw him with their dirty institutions, and, if they can, constrain him to belong to their desperate odd-fellow society. It is true, I might have resisted forcibly with more or less effect, might have run "amok" against society; but I preferred that society should run "amok" against me, it being the desperate party. However, I was released the next day, obtained my mended shoe, and returned to the woods in season to get my dinner of huckleberries on Fair Haven Hill. I was never molested by any person but those who represented the State. I had no lock nor bolt but for the desk which held my papers, not even a nail to put over my latch or windows. I never fastened my door night or day, though I was to be absent several days; not even when the next fall I spent a fortnight in the woods of Maine. And yet my house was more respected than if it had been surrounded by a file of soldiers. The tired rambler could rest and warm himself by my fire, the literary amuse himself with the few books on my table, or the curious, by opening my closet door, see what was left of my dinner, and what prospect I had of a supper. Yet, though many people of every class came this way to the pond, I suffered no serious inconvenience from these sources, and I never missed anything but one small book, a volume of Homer, which perhaps was improperly gilded, and this I trust a soldier of our camp has found by this time. I am convinced, that if all men were to live as simply as I then did, thieving and robbery would be unknown. These take place only in communities where some have got more than is sufficient while others have not enough. The Pope's Homers would soon get properly distributed.

> "Nec bella fuerunt,
> Faginus astabat dum scyphus ante dapes."

> "Nor wars did men molest,
> When only beechen bowls were in request."

"You who govern public affairs, what need have you to employ punishments? Love virtue, and the people will be virtuous. The virtues of a superior man are like the wind; the virtues of a common man are like the grass; the grass, when the wind passes over it, bends."

IX

THE PONDS

SOMETIMES, having had a surfeit of human society and gossip, and worn out all my village friends, I rambled still farther westward than I habitually dwell, into yet more unfrequented parts of the town, "to fresh woods and pastures new," or, while the sun was setting, made my supper of huckleberries and blueberries on Fair Haven Hill, and laid up a store for several days. The fruits do not yield their true flavor to the purchaser of them, nor to him who raises them for the market. There is but one way to obtain it, yet few take that way. If you would know the flavor of huckleberries, ask the cow-boy or the partridge. It is a vulgar error to suppose that you have tasted huckleberries who never plucked them. A huckleberry never reaches Boston; they have not been known there since they grew on her three hills. The ambrosial and essential part of the fruit is lost with the bloom which is rubbed off in the market cart, and they become mere provender. As long as Eternal Justice reigns, not one innocent huckleberry can be transported thither from the country's hills.

Occasionally, after my hoeing was done for the day, I joined some impatient companion who had been fishing on the pond since morning, as silent and motionless as a duck or a floating leaf, and, after practising various kinds of philosophy, had concluded commonly, by the time I arrived, that he belonged to the ancient sect of Cœnobites. There was one older man, an excellent fisher and skilled in all kinds of woodcraft, who was pleased to look upon my house as a building erected for the convenience of fishermen; and I was equally pleased when he sat in my doorway to arrange his lines. Once in a while we sat together on the pond, he at one end of the boat, and I at the other; but not many words passed between us, for he had grown deaf in his later years, but he occasionally hummed a psalm, which harmonized well enough with my philosophy. Our intercourse was thus altogether one of unbroken harmony, far more pleasing to remember than if it had been carried on by speech. When, as was commonly the case, I had none to commune with, I used to raise the echoes by striking with a paddle on the side of my boat, filling the surrounding woods with circling and dilating sound, stirring them up as the keeper of a menagerie his wild beasts, until I elicited a growl from every wooded vale and hillside.

In warm evenings I frequently sat in the boat playing the flute, and saw the perch, which I seem to have charmed, hovering around me, and the moon travelling over the ribbed bottom, which was strewed with the wrecks of the forest. Formerly I had come to this pond adventurously, from time to time, in dark summer nights, with a companion, and, making a fire close to the water's edge, which we thought attracted the fishes, we caught pouts with a bunch of worms strung on a thread, and when we had done, far in the night, threw the burn-

ing brands high into the air like skyrockets, which, coming down into the pond, were quenched with a loud
hissing, and we were suddenly groping in total darkness. Through this, whistling a tune, we took our way
to the haunts of men again. But now I had made my
home by the shore.

Sometimes, after staying in a village parlor till the
family had all retired, I have returned to the woods,
and, partly with a view to the next day's dinner, spent
the hours of midnight fishing from a boat by moonlight,
serenaded by owls and foxes, and hearing, from time to
time, the creaking note of some unknown bird close at
hand. These experiences were very memorable and
valuable to me, — anchored in forty feet of water, and
twenty or thirty rods from the shore, surrounded sometimes by thousands of small perch and shiners, dimpling the surface with their tails in the moonlight, and
communicating by a long flaxen line with mysterious
nocturnal fishes which had their dwelling forty feet below, or sometimes dragging sixty feet of line about the
pond as I drifted in the gentle night breeze, now and
then feeling a slight vibration along it, indicative of
some life prowling about its extremity, of dull uncertain
blundering purpose there, and slow to make up its
mind. At length you slowly raise, pulling hand over
hand, some horned pout squeaking and squirming to
the upper air. It was very queer, especially in dark
nights, when your thoughts had wandered to vast and
cosmogonal themes in other spheres, to feel this faint
jerk, which came to interrupt your dreams and link
you to Nature again. It seemed as if I might next cast

my line upward into the air, as well as downward into this element, which was scarcely more dense. Thus I caught two fishes as it were with one hook.

The scenery of Walden is on a humble scale, and, though very beautiful, does not approach to grandeur, nor can it much concern one who has not long frequented it or lived by its shore; yet this pond is so remarkable for its depth and purity as to merit a particular description. It is a clear and deep green well, half a mile long and a mile and three quarters in circumference, and contains about sixty-one and a half acres; a perennial spring in the midst of pine and oak woods, without any visible inlet or outlet except by the clouds and evaporation. The surrounding hills rise abruptly from the water to the height of forty to eighty feet, though on the southeast and east they attain to about one hundred and one hundred and fifty feet respectively, within a quarter and a third of a mile. They are exclusively woodland. All our Concord waters have two colors at least; one when viewed at a distance, and another, more proper, close at hand. The first depends more on the light, and follows the sky. In clear weather, in summer, they appear blue at a little distance, especially if agitated, and at a great distance all appear alike. In stormy weather they are sometimes of a dark slate-color. The sea, however, is said to be blue one day and green another without any perceptible change in the atmosphere. I have seen our river, when, the landscape being covered with snow, both water and ice were almost as green as grass. Some consider blue "to be the color of pure

water, whether liquid or solid." But, looking directly
down into our waters from a boat, they are seen to be
of very different colors. Walden is blue at one time and
green at another, even from the same point of view.
Lying between the earth and the heavens, it partakes of
the color of both. Viewed from a hilltop it reflects the
color of the sky; but near at hand it is of a yellowish
tint next the shore where you can see the sand, then a
light green, which gradually deepens to a uniform dark
green in the body of the pond. In some lights, viewed
even from a hilltop, it is of a vivid green next the shore.
Some have referred this to the reflection of the verdure;
but it is equally green there against the railroad sand-
bank, and in the spring, before the leaves are expanded,
and it may be simply the result of the prevailing blue
mixed with the yellow of the sand. Such is the color of
its iris. This is that portion, also, where in the spring,
the ice being warmed by the heat of the sun reflected
from the bottom, and also transmitted through the
earth, melts first and forms a narrow canal about the
still frozen middle. Like the rest of our waters, when
much agitated, in clear weather, so that the surface of
the waves may reflect the sky at the right angle, or because there is more light mixed with it, it appears at a
little distance of a darker blue than the sky itself; and
at such a time, being on its surface, and looking with
divided vision, so as to see the reflection, I have discerned a matchless and indescribable light blue, such as
watered or changeable silks and sword blades suggest,
more cerulean than the sky itself, alternating with the original dark green on the opposite sides of the waves, which

last appeared but muddy in comparison. It is a vitreous greenish blue, as I remember it, like those patches of the winter sky seen through cloud vistas in the west before sundown. Yet a single glass of its water held up to the light is as colorless as an equal quantity of air. It is well known that a large plate of glass will have a green tint, owing, as the makers say, to its "body," but a small piece of the same will be colorless. How large a body of Walden water would be required to reflect a green tint I have never proved. The water of our river is black or a very dark brown to one looking directly down on it, and, like that of most ponds, imparts to the body of one bathing in it a yellowish tinge; but this water is of such crystalline purity that the body of the bather appears of an alabaster whiteness, still more unnatural, which, as the limbs are magnified and distorted withal, produces a monstrous effect, making fit studies for a Michael Angelo.

The water is so transparent that the bottom can easily be discerned at the depth of twenty-five or thirty feet. Paddling over it, you may see, many feet beneath the surface, the schools of perch and shiners, perhaps only an inch long, yet the former easily distinguished by their transverse bars, and you think that they must be ascetic fish that find a subsistence there. Once, in the winter, many years ago, when I had been cutting holes through the ice in order to catch pickerel, as I stepped ashore I tossed my axe back on to the ice, but, as if some evil genius had directed it, it slid four or five rods directly into one of the holes, where the water was twenty-five feet deep. Out of curiosity, I lay down on the ice and looked through the hole, until I saw the axe a little on one side, standing on its head, with its helve erect and gently swaying to and fro with the pulse of the pond; and there it might have stood erect and swaying till in the course of time the handle rotted off, if I had not disturbed it. Making another hole directly over it with an ice chisel which I had, and cutting down the longest birch which I could find in the neighborhood with my knife, I made a slip-noose, which I attached to its end, and, letting it down carefully, passed it over the knob of the handle, and drew it by a line along the birch, and so pulled the axe out again.

The shore is composed of a belt of smooth rounded white stones like paving-stones, excepting one or two short sand beaches, and is so steep that in many places a single leap will carry you into water over your head; and were it not for its remarkable transparency, that would be the last to be seen of its bottom till it rose on the opposite side. Some think it is bottomless. It is nowhere muddy, and a casual observer would say that there were no weeds at all in it; and of noticeable plants, except in the little meadows recently overflowed, which do not properly belong to it, a closer scrutiny does not detect a flag nor a bulrush, nor even a lily, yellow or white, but only a few small heart-leaves and potamogetons, and perhaps a water-target or two; all which however a bather might not perceive; and these plants are clean and bright like the element they grow in. The stones extend a rod or two into the water, and then the bottom is pure sand, except in the deepest parts, where there is usually a little sediment, probably from the decay of the leaves which have been wafted on to it so many successive falls, and a bright green weed is brought up on anchors even in midwinter.

We have one other pond just like this, White Pond, in Nine Acre Corner, about two and a half miles westerly; but, though I am acquainted with most of the ponds within a dozen miles of this centre, I do not know a third of this pure and well-like character. Successive nations perchance have drank at, admired, and fathomed it, and passed away, and still its water is green and pellucid as ever. Not an intermitting spring! Perhaps on that spring morning when Adam and Eve were driven out of Eden Walden Pond was already in existence, and even then breaking up in a gentle spring rain accompanied with mist and a southerly wind, and covered with myriads of ducks and geese, which had not heard of the fall, when still such pure lakes sufficed them. Even then it had commenced to rise and fall, and had clarified its waters and colored them of the hue they now wear, and obtained a patent of Heaven to be the only Walden Pond in the world and distiller of celestial dews. Who knows in how many unremembered nations' literatures this has been the Castalian Fountain? or what nymphs presided over it in the Golden Age? It is a gem of the first water which Concord wears in her coronet.

Yet perchance the first who came to this well have left some trace of their footsteps. I have been surprised to detect encircling the pond, even where a thick wood has just been cut down on the shore, a narrow shelf-like path in the steep hillside, alternately rising and falling, approaching and receding from the water's edge, as old probably as the race of man here, worn by the feet of aboriginal hunters, and still from time to time unwittingly trodden by the present occupants of the land. This is particularly distinct to one standing on the middle of the pond in winter, just after a light snow has fallen, appearing as a clear undulating white line, unobscured by weeds and twigs, and very obvious a quarter of a mile off in many places where in summer it is hardly distinguishable close at hand. The snow reprints it, as it were, in clear white type alto-relievo. The ornamented grounds of villas which will one day be built here may still preserve some trace of this.

The pond rises and falls, but whether regularly or not, and within what period, nobody knows, though, as usual, many pretend to know. It is commonly higher in the winter and lower in the summer, though not corresponding to the general wet and dryness. I can remember when it was a foot or two lower, and also when it was at least five feet higher, than when I lived by it. There is a narrow sand-bar running into it, with very deep water on one side, on which I helped boil a kettle of chowder, some six rods from the main shore, about the year 1824, which it has not been possible to do for twenty-five years; and, on the other hand, my friends used to listen with incredulity when I told them, that a few years later I was accustomed to fish from a boat in a secluded cove in the woods, fifteen rods from the only shore they knew, which place was long since converted into a meadow. But the pond has risen steadily for two years, and now, in the summer of '52, is just

five feet higher than when I lived there, or as high as it
was thirty years ago, and fishing goes on again in the
meadow. This makes a difference of level, at the outside, of six or seven feet; and yet the water shed by the
surrounding hills is insignificant in amount, and this
overflow must be referred to causes which affect the
deep springs. This same summer the pond has begun
to fall again. It is remarkable that this fluctuation,
whether periodical or not, appears thus to require many
years for its accomplishment. I have observed one rise
and a part of two falls, and I expect that a dozen or
fifteen years hence the water will again be as low as I
have ever known it. Flint's Pond, a mile eastward,
allowing for the disturbance occasioned by its inlets and
outlets, and the smaller intermediate ponds also, sympathize with Walden, and recently attained their greatest height at the same time with the latter. The same
is true, as far as my observation goes, of White Pond.

This rise and fall of Walden at long intervals serves
this use at least; the water standing at this great height
for a year or more, though it makes it difficult to walk
round it, kills the shrubs and trees which have sprung
up about its edge since the last rise, — pitch pines,
birches, alders, aspens, and others, — and, falling again,
leaves an unobstructed shore; for, unlike many ponds
and all waters which are subject to a daily tide, its shore
is cleanest when the water is lowest. On the side of the
pond next my house a row of pitch pines, fifteen feet
high, has been killed and tipped over as if by a lever,
and thus a stop put to their encroachments; and their
size indicates how many years have elapsed since the

last rise to this height. By this fluctuation the pond
asserts its title to a shore, and thus the *shore* is *shorn*,
and the trees cannot hold it by right of possession.
These are the lips of the lake, on which no beard grows.
It licks its chaps from time to time. When the water
is at its height, the alders, willows, and maples send
forth a mass of fibrous red roots several feet long from
all sides of their stems in the water, and to the height
of three or four feet from the ground, in the effort to
maintain themselves; and I have known the high blueberry bushes about the shore, which commonly produce
no fruit, bear an abundant crop under these circumstances.

Some have been puzzled to tell how the shore became
so regularly paved. My townsmen have all heard the
tradition — the oldest people tell me that they heard it
in their youth — that anciently the Indians were holding
a pow-wow upon a hill here, which rose as high into the
heavens as the pond now sinks deep into the earth, and
they used much profanity, as the story goes, though this
vice is one of which the Indians were never guilty, and
while they were thus engaged the hill shook and suddenly sank, and only one old squaw, named Walden,
escaped, and from her the pond was named. It has been
conjectured that when the hill shook these stones rolled
down its side and became the present shore. It is very
certain, at any rate, that once there was no pond here,
and now there is one; and this Indian fable does not
in any respect conflict with the account of that ancient
settler whom I have mentioned, who remembers so well
when he first came here with his divining-rod, saw a

thin vapor rising from the sward, and the hazel pointed steadily downward, and he concluded to dig a well here. As for the stones, many still think that they are hardly to be accounted for by the action of the waves on these hills; but I observe that the surrounding hills are remarkably full of the same kind of stones, so that they have been obliged to pile them up in walls on both sides of the railroad cut nearest the pond; and, moreover, there are most stones where the shore is most abrupt; so that, unfortunately, it is no longer a mystery to me. I detect the paver. If the name was not derived from that of some English locality, — Saffron Walden, for instance, — one might suppose that it was called originally *Walled-in* Pond.

The pond was my well ready dug. For four months in the year its water is as cold as it is pure at all times; and I think that it is then as good as any, if not the best, in the town. In the winter, all water which is exposed to the air is colder than springs and wells which are protected from it. The temperature of the pond water which had stood in the room where I sat from five o'clock in the afternoon till noon the next day, the sixth of March, 1846, the thermometer having been up to 65° or 70° some of the time, owing partly to the sun on the roof, was 42°, or one degree colder than the water of one of the coldest wells in the village just drawn. The temperature of the Boiling Spring the same day was 45°, or the warmest of any water tried, though it is the coldest that I know of in summer, when, beside, shallow and stagnant surface water is not mingled with it. Moreover, in summer, Walden never becomes so warm as most water which is exposed to the sun, on account of its depth. In the warmest weather I usually placed a pailful in my cellar, where it became cool in the night, and remained so during the day; though I also resorted to a spring in the neighborhood. It was as good when a week old as the day it was dipped, and had no taste of the pump. Whoever camps for a week in summer by the shore of a pond, needs only bury a pail of water a few feet deep in the shade of his camp to be independent of the luxury of ice.

There have been caught in Walden pickerel, one weighing seven pounds, — to say nothing of another which carried off a reel with great velocity, which the fisherman safely set down at eight pounds because he did not see him, — perch and pouts, some of each weighing over two pounds, shiners, chivins or roach (*Leuciscus pulchellus*), a very few breams, and a couple of eels, one weighing four pounds, — I am thus particular because the weight of a fish is commonly its only title to fame, and these are the only eels I have heard of here; — also, I have a faint recollection of a little fish some five inches long, with silvery sides and a greenish back, somewhat dace-like in its character, which I mention here chiefly to link my facts to fable. Nevertheless, this pond is not very fertile in fish. Its pickerel, though not abundant, are its chief boast. I have seen at one time lying on the ice pickerel of at least three different kinds: a long and shallow one, steel-colored, most like those caught in the river; a bright golden kind, with greenish reflections and remarkably deep, which is the most common here; and another, golden-colored, and

shaped like the last, but peppered on the sides with
small dark brown or black spots, intermixed with a
few faint blood-red ones, very much like a trout. The
specific name *reticulaius* would not apply to this; it
should be *guttatus* rather. These are all very firm fish,
and weigh more than their size promises. The shiners,
pouts, and perch also, and indeed all the fishes which
inhabit this pond, are much cleaner, handsomer, and
firmer-fleshed than those in the river and most other
ponds, as the water is purer, and they can easily be distinguished from them. Probably many ichthyologists
would make new varieties of some of them. There are
also a clean race of frogs and tortoises, and a few mus-
sels in it; muskrats and minks leave their traces about
it, and occasionally a travelling mud-turtle visits it.
Sometimes, when I pushed off my boat in the morning,
I disturbed a great mud-turtle which had secreted himself under the boat in the night. Ducks and geese
frequent it in the spring and fall, the white-bellied swallows (*Hirundo bicolor*) skim over it, and the peetweets
(*Totanus macularius*) "teeter" along its stony shores all
summer. I have sometimes disturbed a fish hawk sitting
on a white pine over the water; but I doubt if it is ever
profaned by the wing of a gull, like Fair Haven. At
most, it tolerates one annual loon. These are all the
animals of consequence which frequent it now.

You may see from a boat, in calm weather, near the
sandy eastern shore, where the water is eight or ten
feet deep, and also in some other parts of the pond,
some circular heaps half a dozen feet in diameter by a
foot in height, consisting of small stones less than a

hen's egg in size, where all around is bare sand. At first you wonder if the Indians could have formed them on the ice for any purpose, and so, when the ice melted, they sank to the bottom; but they are too regular and some of them plainly too fresh for that. They are similar to those found in rivers; but as there are no suckers nor lampreys here, I know not by what fish they could be made. Perhaps they are the nests of the chivin. These lend a pleasing mystery to the bottom.

The shore is irregular enough not to be monotonous. I have in my mind's eye the western, indented with deep bays, the bolder northern, and the beautifully scalloped southern shore, where successive capes overlap each other and suggest unexplored coves between. The forest has never so good a setting, nor is so distinctly beautiful, as when seen from the middle of a small lake amid hills which rise from the water's edge; for the water in which it is reflected not only makes the best foreground in such a case, but, with its winding shore, the most natural and agreeable boundary to it. There is no rawness nor imperfection in its edge there, as where the axe has cleared a part, or a cultivated field abuts on it. The trees have ample room to expand on the water side, and each sends forth its most vigorous branch in that direction. There Nature has woven a natural selvage, and the eye rises by just gradations from the low shrubs of the shore to the highest trees. There are few traces of man's hand to be seen. The water laves the shore as it did a thousand years ago.

A lake is the landscape's most beautiful and expressive feature. It is earth's eye; looking into which the beholder measures the depth of his own nature. The fluviatile trees next the shore are the slender eyelashes which fringe it, and the wooded hills and cliffs around are its overhanging brows.

Standing on the smooth sandy beach at the east end of the pond, in a calm September afternoon, when a slight haze makes the opposite shore-line indistinct, I have seen whence came the expression, "the glassy surface of a lake." When you invert your head, it looks like a thread of finest gossamer stretched across the valley, and gleaming against the distant pine woods, separating one stratum of the atmosphere from another. You would think that you could walk dry under it to the opposite hills, and that the swallows which skim over might perch on it. Indeed, they sometimes dive below the line, as it were by mistake, and are undeceived. As you look over the pond westward you are obliged to employ both your hands to defend your eyes against the reflected as well as the true sun, for they are equally bright; and if, between the two, you survey its surface critically, it is literally as smooth as glass, except where the skater insects, at equal intervals scattered over its whole extent, by their motions in the sun produce the finest imaginable sparkle on it, or, perchance, a duck plumes itself, or, as I have said, a swallow skims so low as to touch it. It may be that in the distance a fish describes an arc of three or four feet in the air, and there is one bright flash where it emerges, and another where it strikes the water; sometimes the whole silvery arc is revealed; or here and there, perhaps, is a thistle-down floating on its surface, which the fishes dart at and so dimple it again. It is like molten glass cooled but not congealed, and the few motes in it are pure and beautiful like the imperfections in glass. You may often detect a yet smoother and darker water, separated from the rest as if by an invisible cobweb, boom of the water nymphs, resting on it. From a hilltop you can see a fish leap in almost any part; for not a pickerel or shiner picks an insect from this smooth surface but it manifestly disturbs the equilibrium of the whole lake. It is wonderful with what elaborateness this simple fact is advertised, — this piscine murder will out, — and from my distant perch I distinguish the circling undulations when they are half a dozen rods in diameter. You can even detect a water-bug (*Gyrinus*) ceaselessly progressing over the smooth surface a quarter of a mile off; for they furrow the water slightly, making a conspicuous ripple bounded by two diverging lines, but the skaters glide over it without rippling it perceptibly. When the surface is considerably agitated there are no skaters nor waterbugs on it, but apparently, in calm days, they leave their havens and adventurously glide forth from the shore by short impulses till they completely cover it. It is a soothing employment, on one of those fine days in the fall when all the warmth of the sun is fully appreciated, to sit on a stump on such a height as this, overlooking the pond, and study the dimpling circles which are incessantly inscribed on its otherwise invisible surface amid the reflected skies and trees. Over this great expanse there is no disturbance but it is thus at once gently smoothed away and assuaged, as, when a vase of water is jarred, the trembling circles seek the shore and all is

smooth again. Not a fish can leap or an insect fall on
the pond but it is thus reported in circling dimples, in
lines of beauty, as it were the constant welling up of
its fountain, the gentle pulsing of its life, the heaving of
its breast. The thrills of joy and thrills of pain are
undistinguishable. How peaceful the phenomena of the
lake! Again the works of man shine as in the spring.
Ay, every leaf and twig and stone and cobweb sparkles
now at mid-afternoon as when covered with dew in a
spring morning. Every motion of an oar or an insect
produces a flash of light; and if an oar falls, how sweet
the echo!

In such a day, in September or October, Walden is
a perfect forest mirror, set round with stones as precious
to my eye as if fewer or rarer. Nothing so fair, so pure,
and at the same time so large, as a lake, perchance,
lies on the surface of the earth. Sky water. It needs
no fence. Nations come and go without defiling it. It is
a mirror which no stone can crack, whose quicksilver
will never wear off, whose gilding Nature continually
repairs; no storms, no dust, can dim its surface ever
fresh; — a mirror in which all impurity presented to
it sinks, swept and dusted by the sun's hazy brush, —
this the light dust-cloth, — which retains no breath
that is breathed on it, but sends its own to float as
clouds high above its surface, and be reflected in its
bosom still.

A field of water betrays the spirit that is in the air.
It is continually receiving new life and motion from
above. It is intermediate in its nature between land and
sky. On land only the grass and trees wave, but the

water itself is rippled by the wind. I see where the breeze dashes across it by the streaks or flakes of light. It is remarkable that we can look down on its surface. We shall, perhaps, look down thus on the surface of air at length, and mark where a still subtler spirit sweeps over it.

The skaters and water-bugs finally disappear in the latter part of October, when the severe frosts have come; and then and in November, usually, in a calm day, there is absolutely nothing to ripple the surface. One November afternoon, in the calm at the end of a rain-storm of several days' duration, when the sky was still completely overcast and the air was full of mist, I observed that the pond was remarkably smooth, so that it was difficult to distinguish its surface; though it no longer reflected the bright tints of October, but the sombre November colors of the surrounding hills. Though I passed over it as gently as possible, the slight undulations produced by my boat extended almost as far as I could see, and gave a ribbed appearance to the reflections. But, as I was looking over the surface, I saw here and there at a distance a faint glimmer, as if some skater insects which had escaped the frosts might be collected there, or, perchance, the surface, being so smooth, betrayed where a spring welled up from the bottom. Paddling gently to one of these places, I was surprised to find myself surrounded by myriads of small perch, about five inches long, of a rich bronze color in the green water, sporting there, and constantly rising to the surface and dimpling it, sometimes leaving bubbles on it. In such transparent and seemingly bottomless water, reflecting the clouds, I seemed to be floating through the air as in a balloon, and their swimming impressed me as a kind of flight or hovering, as if they were a compact flock of birds passing just beneath my level on the right or left, their fins, like sails, set all around them. There were many such schools in the pond, apparently improving the short season before winter would draw an icy shutter over their broad skylight, sometimes giving to the surface an appearance as if a slight breeze struck it, or a few rain-drops fell there. When I approached carelessly and alarmed them, they made a sudden plash and rippling with their tails, as if one had struck the water with a brushy bough, and instantly took refuge in the depths. At length the wind rose, the mist increased, and the waves began to run, and the perch leaped much higher than before, half out of water, a hundred black points, three inches long, at once above the surface. Even as late as the fifth of December, one year, I saw some dimples on the surface, and thinking it was going to rain hard immediately, the air being full of mist, I made haste to take my place at the oars and row homeward; already the rain seemed rapidly increasing, though I felt none on my cheek, and I anticipated a thorough soaking. But suddenly the dimples ceased, for they were produced by the perch, which the noise of my oars had scared into the depths, and I saw their schools dimly disappearing; so I spent a dry afternoon after all.

An old man who used to frequent this pond nearly sixty years ago, when it was dark with surrounding forests, tells me that in those days he sometimes saw it all alive with ducks and other water-fowl, and that there were many eagles about it. He came here a-fishing, and used an old log canoe which he found on the shore. It was made of two white pine logs dug out and pinned together, and was cut off square at the ends. It was very clumsy, but lasted a great many years before it became water-logged and perhaps sank to the bottom. He did not know whose it was; it belonged to the pond. He used to make a cable for his anchor of strips of hickory bark tied together. An old man, a potter, who lived by the pond before the Revolution, told him once that there was an iron chest at the bottom, and that he had seen it. Sometimes it would come floating up to the shore; but when you went toward it, it would go back into deep water and disappear. I was pleased to hear of the old log canoe, which took the place of an Indian one of the same material but more graceful construction, which perchance had first been a tree on the bank, and then, as it were, fell into the water, to float there for a generation, the most proper vessel for the lake. I remember that when I first looked into these depths there were many large trunks to be seen indistinctly lying on the bottom, which had either been blown over formerly, or left on the ice at the last cutting, when wood was cheaper; but now they have mostly disappeared.

When I first paddled a boat on Walden, it was completely surrounded by thick and lofty pine and oak woods, and in some of its coves grape-vines had run over the trees next the water and formed bowers under which a boat could pass. The hills which form its shores are so steep, and the woods on them were then so high, that, as you looked down from the west end, it had the appearance of an amphitheatre for some kind of sylvan spectacle. I have spent many an hour, when I was younger, floating over its surface as the zephyr willed, having paddled my boat to the middle, and lying on my back across the seats, in a summer forenoon, dreaming awake, until I was aroused by the boat touching the sand, and I arose to see what shore my fates had impelled me to; days when idleness was the most attractive and productive industry. Many a forenoon have I stolen away, preferring to spend thus the most valued part of the day; for I was rich, if not in money, in sunny hours and summer days, and spent them lavishly; nor do I regret that I did not waste more of them in the workshop or the teacher's desk. But since I left those shores the woodchoppers have still further laid them waste, and now for many a year there will be no more rambling through the aisles of the wood, with occasional vistas through which you see the water. My Muse may be excused if she is silent henceforth. How can you expect the birds to sing when their groves are cut down?

Now the trunks of trees on the bottom, and the old log canoe, and the dark surrounding woods, are gone, and the villagers, who scarcely know where it lies, instead of going to the pond to bathe or drink, are thinking to bring its water, which should be as sacred as the Ganges at least, to the village in a pipe, to wash their dishes with! — to earn their Walden by the turning of a cock or drawing of a plug! That devilish Iron Horse, whose

ear-rending neigh is heard throughout the town, has
muddied the Boiling Spring with his foot, and he it is
that has browsed off all the woods on Walden shore,
that Trojan horse, with a thousand men in his belly,
introduced by mercenary Greeks! Where is the country's champion, the Moore of Moore Hall, to meet him
at the Deep Cut and thrust an avenging lance between
the ribs of the bloated pest?

Nevertheless, of all the characters I have known,
perhaps Walden wears best, and best preserves its
purity. Many men have been likened to it, but few deserve that honor. Though the woodchoppers have laid
bare first this shore and then that, and the Irish have
built their sties by it, and the railroad has infringed on
its border, and the ice-men have skimmed it once, it is
itself unchanged, the same water which my youthful
eyes fell on; all the change is in me. It has not acquired
one permanent wrinkle after all its ripples. It is perennially young, and I may stand and see a swallow dip
apparently to pick an insect from its surface as of yore.
It struck me again to-night, as if I had not seen it almost
daily for more than twenty years, — Why, here is Walden, the same woodland lake that I discovered so many
years ago; where a forest was cut down last winter
another is springing up by its shore as lustily as ever;
the same thought is welling up to its surface that was
then; it is the same liquid joy and happiness to itself
and its Maker, ay, and it *may* be to me. It is the work
of a brave man surely, in whom there was no guile! He
rounded this water with his hand, deepened and clarified
it in his thought, and in his will bequeathed it to Con-

cord. I see by its face that it is visited by the same reflection; and I can almost say, Walden, is it you?

> It is no dream of mine,
> To ornament a line;
> I cannot come nearer to God and Heaven
> Than I live to Walden even.
> I am its stony shore,
> And the breeze that passes o'er;
> In the hollow of my hand
> Are its water and its sand,
> And its deepest resort
> Lies high in my thought.

The cars never pause to look at it; yet I fancy that
the engineers and firemen and brakemen, and those
passengers who have a season ticket and see it often,
are better men for the sight. The engineer does not forget at night, or his nature does not, that he has beheld
this vision of serenity and purity once at least during the
day. Though seen but once, it helps to wash out State
Street and the engine's soot. One proposes that it be
called "God's Drop."

I have said that Walden has no visible inlet nor outlet,
but it is on the one hand distantly and indirectly related
to Flint's Pond, which is more elevated, by a chain of
small ponds coming from that quarter, and on the other
directly and manifestly to Concord River, which is
lower, by a similar chain of ponds through which in
some other geological period it may have flowed, and
by a little digging, which God forbid, it can be made to
flow thither again. If by living thus reserved and austere,
like a hermit in the woods, so long, it has acquired such

wonderful purity, who would not regret that the comparatively impure waters of Flint's Pond should be
mingled with it, or itself should ever go to waste its
sweetness in the ocean wave?

Flint's, or Sandy Pond, in Lincoln, our greatest lake
and inland sea, lies about a mile east of Walden. It is
much larger, being said to contain one hundred and
ninety-seven acres, and is more fertile in fish; but it is
comparatively shallow, and not remarkably pure. A
walk through the woods thither was often my recreation. It was worth the while, if only to feel the wind
blow on your cheek freely, and see the waves run, and
remember the life of mariners. I went a-chestnutting
there in the fall, on windy days, when the nuts were
dropping into the water and were washed to my feet;
and one day, as I crept along its sedgy shore, the fresh
spray blowing in my face, I came upon the mouldering
wreck of a boat, the sides gone, and hardly more than
the impression of its flat bottom left amid the rushes;
yet its model was sharply defined, as if it were a large
decayed pad, with its veins. It was as impressive a wreck
as one could imagine on the seashore, and had as
good a moral. It is by this time mere vegetable mould
and undistinguishable pond shore, through which
rushes and flags have pushed up. I used to admire the
ripple marks on the sandy bottom, at the north end of
this pond, made firm and hard to the feet of the wader
by the pressure of the water, and the rushes which
grew in Indian file, in waving lines, corresponding to
these marks, rank behind rank, as if the waves had

planted them. There also I have found, in considerable quantities, curious balls, composed apparently of fine grass or roots, of pipewort perhaps, from half an inch to four inches in diameter, and perfectly spherical. These wash back and forth in shallow water on a sandy bottom, and are sometimes cast on the shore. They are either solid grass, or have a little sand in the middle. At first you would say that they were formed by the action of the waves, like a pebble; yet the smallest are made of equally coarse materials, half an inch long, and they are produced only at one season of the year. Moreover, the waves, I suspect, do not so much construct as wear down a material which has already acquired consistency. They preserve their form when dry for an indefinite period.

Flint's Pond! Such is the poverty of our nomenclature. What right had the unclean and stupid farmer, whose farm abutted on this sky water, whose shores he has ruthlessly laid bare, to give his name to it? Some skin-flint, who loved better the reflecting surface of a dollar, or a bright cent, in which he could see his own brazen face; who regarded even the wild ducks which settled in it as trespassers; his fingers grown into crooked and horny talons from the long habit of grasping harpy-like; — so it is not named for me. I go not there to see him nor to hear of him; who never *saw* it, who never bathed in it, who never loved it, who never protected it, who never spoke a good word for it, nor thanked God that He had made it. Rather let it be named from the fishes that swim in it, the wild fowl or quadrupeds which frequent it, the wild flowers which grow by its shores, or some wild man or child the thread of whose history is interwoven with its own; not from him who could show no title to it but the deed which a like-minded neighbor or legislature gave him, — him who thought only of its money value; whose presence perchance cursed all the shores; who exhausted the land around it, and would fain have exhausted the waters within it; who regretted only that it was not English hay or cranberry meadow, — there was nothing to redeem it, forsooth, in his eyes, — and would have drained and sold it for the mud at its bottom. It did not turn his mill, and it was no *privilege* to him to behold it. I respect not his labors, his farm where everything has its price, who would carry the landscape, who would carry his God, to market, if he could get anything for him; who goes to market *for* his god as it is; on whose farm nothing grows free, whose fields bear no crops, whose meadows no flowers, whose trees no fruits, but dollars; who loves not the beauty of his fruits, whose fruits are not ripe for him till they are turned to dollars. Give me the poverty that enjoys true wealth. Farmers are respectable and interesting to me in proportion as they are poor, — poor farmers. A model farm! where the house stands like a fungus in a muckheap, chambers for men, horses, oxen, and swine, cleansed and uncleansed, all contiguous to one another! Stocked with men! A great grease-spot, redolent of manures and buttermilk! Under a high state of cultivation, being manured with the hearts and brains of men! As if you were to raise your potatoes in the churchyard! Such is a model farm.

No, no; if the fairest features of the landscape are to

be named after men, let them be the noblest and worthiest men alone. Let our lakes receive as true names at least as the Icarian Sea, where "still the shore" a "brave attempt resounds."

Goose Pond, of small extent, is on my way to Flint's; Fair Haven, an expansion of Concord River, said to contain some seventy acres, is a mile southwest; and White Pond, of about forty acres, is a mile and a half beyond Fair Haven. This is my lake country. These, with Concord River, are my water privileges; and night and day, year in year out, they grind such grist as I carry to them.

Since the wood-cutters, and the railroad, and I myself have profaned Walden, perhaps the most attractive, if not the most beautiful, of all our lakes, the gem of the woods, is White Pond; — a poor name from its commonness, whether derived from the remarkable purity of its waters or the color of its sands. In these as in other respects, however, it is a lesser twin of Walden. They are so much alike that you would say they must be connected under ground. It has the same stony shore, and its waters are of the same hue. As at Walden, in sultry dog-day weather, looking down through the woods on some of its bays which are not so deep but that the reflection from the bottom tinges them, its waters are of a misty bluish-green or glaucous color. Many years since I used to go there to collect the sand by cartloads, to make sandpaper with, and I have continued to visit it ever since. One who frequents it proposes to call it Virid Lake. Perhaps it might be called Yellow Pine Lake, from the following circumstance. About fifteen years ago you could see the top of a pitch pine, of the kind called yellow pine hereabouts, though it is not a distinct species, projecting above the surface in deep water, many rods from the shore. It was even supposed by some that the pond had sunk, and this was one of the primitive forest that formerly stood there. I find that even so long ago as 1792, in a "Topographical Description of the Town of Concord," by one of its citizens, in the Collections of the Massachusetts Historical Society, the author, after speaking of Walden and White Ponds, adds, "In the middle of the latter may be seen, when the water is very low, a tree which appears as if it grew in the place where it now stands, although the roots are fifty feet below the surface of the water; the top of this tree is broken off, and at that place measures fourteen inches in diameter." In the spring of '49 I talked with the man who lives nearest the pond in Sudbury, who told me that it was he who got out this tree ten or fifteen years before. As near as he could remember, it stood twelve or fifteen rods from the shore, where the water was thirty or forty feet deep. It was in the winter, and he had been getting out ice in the forenoon, and had resolved that in the afternoon, with the aid of his neighbors, he would take out the old yellow pine. He sawed a channel in the ice toward the shore, and hauled it over and along and out on to the ice with oxen; but, before he had gone far in his work, he was surprised to find that it was wrong end upward, with the stumps of the branches pointing down, and the small end firmly fastened in the sandy bottom. It was about a foot in diameter at the big end, and he had expected to get a good saw-log, but it was so rotten as to be fit only for fuel, if for that. He had some of it in his shed then. There were marks of an axe and of woodpeckers on the butt. He thought that it might have been a dead tree on the shore, but was finally blown over into the pond, and after the top had become water-logged, while the butt-end was still dry and light, had drifted out and sunk wrong end up. His father, eighty years old, could not remember when it was not there. Several pretty large logs may still be seen lying on the bottom, where, owing to the undulation of the surface, they look like huge water snakes in motion.

This pond has rarely been profaned by a boat, for there is little in it to tempt a fisherman. Instead of the white lily, which requires mud, or the common sweet flag, the blue flag (*Iris versicolor*) grows thinly in the pure water, rising from the stony bottom all around the shore, where it is visited by hummingbirds in June; and the color both of its bluish blades and its flowers and especially their reflections, are in singular harmony with the glaucous water.

White Pond and Walden are great crystals on the surface of the earth, Lakes of Light. If they were permanently congealed, and small enough to be clutched, they would, perchance, be carried off by slaves, like precious stones, to adorn the heads of emperors; but being liquid, and ample, and secured to us and our successors forever, we disregard them, and run after the diamond of Kohinoor. They are too pure to have a market value; they contain no muck. How much more beautiful than our lives, how much more transparent than our characters, are they! We never learned meanness of them. How

much fairer than the pool before the farmer's door, in
which his ducks swim! Hither the clean wild ducks
come. Nature has no human inhabitant who appreciates
her. The birds with their plumage and their notes are
in harmony with the flowers, but what youth or maiden
conspires with the wild luxuriant beauty of Nature?
She flourishes most alone, far from the towns where they
reside. Talk of heaven! ye disgrace earth.

X

BAKER FARM

SOMETIMES I rambled to pine groves, standing like
temples, or like fleets at sea, full-rigged, with wavy
boughs, and rippling with light, so soft and green and
shady that the Druids would have forsaken their oaks
to worship in them; or to the cedar wood beyond Flint's
Pond, where the trees, covered with hoary blue berries,
spiring higher and higher, are fit to stand before Valhalla,
and the creeping juniper covers the ground with wreaths
full of fruit; or to swamps where the usnea lichen hangs
in festoons from the white spruce trees, and toadstools,
round tables of the swamp gods, cover the ground, and
more beautiful fungi adorn the stumps, like butterflies
or shells, vegetable winkles; where the swamp-pink and
dogwood grow, the red alder berry glows like eyes of
imps, the waxwork grooves and crushes the hardest
woods in its folds, and the wild holly berries make the
beholder forget his home with their beauty, and he is
dazzled and tempted by nameless other wild forbidden
fruits, too fair for mortal taste. Instead of calling on
some scholar, I paid many a visit to particular trees, of
kinds which are rare in this neighborhood, standing far
away in the middle of some pasture, or in the depths of
a wood or swamp, or on a hilltop; such as the black
birch, of which we have some handsome specimens two

feet in diameter; its cousin, the yellow birch, with its
loose golden vest, perfumed like the first; the beech,
which has so neat a bole and beautifully lichen-painted,
perfect in all its details, of which, excepting scattered
specimens, I know but one small grove of sizable trees
left in the township, supposed by some to have been
planted by the pigeons that were once baited with beech-
nuts near by; it is worth the while to see the silver grain
sparkle when you split this wood; the bass; the horn-
beam; the *Celtis occidentalis*, or false elm, of which we
have but one well-grown; some taller mast of a pine, a
shingle tree, or a more perfect hemlock than usual, standing like a pagoda in the midst of the woods; and many
others I could mention. These were the shrines I visited
both summer and winter.

Once it chanced that I stood in the very abutment of
a rainbow's arch, which filled the lower stratum of the
atmosphere, tinging the grass and leaves around, and
dazzling me as if I looked through colored crystal. It
was a lake of rainbow light, in which, for a short while,
I lived like a dolphin. If it had lasted longer it might
have tinged my employments and life. As I walked on
the railroad causeway, I used to wonder at the halo of
light around my shadow, and would fain fancy myself
one of the elect. One who visited me declared that the
shadows of some Irishmen before him had no halo about
them, that it was only natives that were so distinguished.
Benvenuto Cellini tells us in his memoirs, that, after a
certain terrible dream or vision which he had during his
confinement in the castle of St. Angelo a resplendent
light appeared over the shadow of his head at morning

and evening, whether he was in Italy or France, and it
was particularly conspicuous when the grass was moist
with dew. This was probably the same phenomenon to
which I have referred, which is especially observed in
the morning, but also at other times, and even by moonlight. Though a constant one, it is not commonly noticed, and, in the case of an excitable imagination like
Cellini's, it would be basis enough for superstition. Beside, he tells us that he showed it to very few. But are
they not indeed distinguished who are conscious that
they are regarded at all?

I set out one afternoon to go a-fishing to Fair Haven,
through the woods, to eke out my scanty fare of vegetables. My way led through Pleasant Meadow, an ad-
junct of the Baker Farm, that retreat of which a poet
has since sung, beginning, —

> " Thy entry is a pleasant field,
> Which some mossy fruit trees yield
> Partly to a ruddy brook,
> By gliding musquash undertook,
> And mercurial trout,
> Darting about."

I thought of living there before I went to Walden. I
" hooked " the apples, leaped the brook, and scared the
musquash and the trout. It was one of those afternoons
which seem indefinitely long before one, in which many
events may happen, a large portion of our natural life,
though it was already half spent when I started. By the
way there came up a shower, which compelled me to
stand half an hour under a pine, piling boughs over my

head, and wearing my handkerchief for a shed; and when at length I had made one cast over the pickerel-weed, standing up to my middle in water, I found myself suddenly in the shadow of a cloud, and the thunder began to rumble with such emphasis that I could do no more than listen to it. The gods must be proud, thought I, with such forked flashes to rout a poor unarmed fisherman. So I made haste for shelter to the nearest hut, which stood half a mile from any road, but so much the nearer to the pond, and had long been uninhabited: —

> "And here a poet builded,
> In the completed years,
> For behold a trivial cabin
> That to destruction steers."

So the Muse fables. But therein, as I found, dwelt now John Field, an Irishman, and his wife, and several children, from the broad-faced boy who assisted his father at his work, and now came running by his side from the bog to escape the rain, to the wrinkled, sibyl-like, cone-headed infant that sat upon its father's knee as in the palaces of nobles, and looked out from its home in the midst of wet and hunger inquisitively upon the stranger, with the privilege of infancy, not knowing but it was the last of a noble line, and the hope and cynosure of the world, instead of John Field's poor starveling brat. There we sat together under that part of the roof which leaked the least, while it showered and thundered without. I had sat there many times of old before the ship was built that floated this family to America. An honest, hard-working, but shiftless man plainly was John Field; and his wife, she too was brave to cook so many successive dinners in the recesses of that lofty stove; with round greasy face and bare breast, still thinking to improve her condition one day; with the never absent mop in one hand, and yet no effects of it visible anywhere. The chickens, which had also taken shelter here from the rain, stalked about the room like members of the family, too humanized, methought, to roast well. They stood and looked in my eye or pecked at my shoe significantly. Meanwhile my host told me his story, how hard he worked "bogging" for a neighboring farmer, turning up a meadow with a spade or bog hoe at the rate of ten dollars an acre and the use of the land with manure for one year, and his little broad-faced son worked cheerfully at his father's side the while, not knowing how poor a bargain the latter had made. I tried to help him with my experience, telling him that he was one of my nearest neighbors, and that I too, who came a-fishing here, and looked like a loafer, was getting my living like himself; that I lived in a tight, light, and clean house, which hardly cost more than the annual rent of such a ruin as his commonly amounts to; and how, if he chose, he might in a month or two build himself a palace of his own; that I did not use tea, nor coffee, nor butter, nor milk, nor fresh meat, and so did not have to work to get them; again, as I did not work hard, I did not have to eat hard, and it cost me but a trifle for my food; but as he began with tea, and coffee, and butter, and milk, and beef, he had to work hard to pay for them, and when he had worked hard he had to eat hard again to repair the waste of his system, — and so it was as broad as it was long, indeed it was broader than it was long, for he was discontented and wasted his life into the bargain; and yet he had rated it as a gain in coming to America, that here you could get tea, and coffee, and meat every day. But the only true America is that country where you are at liberty to pursue such a mode of life as may enable you to do without these, and where the state does not endeavor to compel you to sustain the slavery and war and other superfluous expenses which directly or indirectly result from the use of such things. For I purposely talked to him as if he were a philosopher, or desired to be one. I should be glad if all the meadows on the earth were left in a wild state, if that were the consequence of men's beginning to redeem themselves. A man will not need to study history to find out what is best for his own culture. But alas! the culture of an Irishman is an enterprise to be undertaken with a sort of moral bog hoe. I told him, that as he worked so hard at bogging, he required thick boots and stout clothing, which yet were soon soiled and worn out, but I wore light shoes and thin clothing, which cost not half so much, though he might think that I was dressed like a gentleman (which, however, was not the case), and in an hour or two, without labor, but as a recreation, I could, if I wished, catch as many fish as I should want for two days, or earn enough money to support me a week. If he and his family would live simply, they might all go a-huckleberrying in the summer for their amusement. John heaved a sigh at this, and his wife stared with arms a-kimbo, and both appeared to be wondering if they had capital enough to begin such a course with, or arithmetic enough to carry it through. It was sailing by dead reckoning to them, and they saw not clearly how to make their port so; therefore I suppose they still take life bravely, after their fashion, face to face, giving it tooth and nail, not having skill to split its massive columns with any fine entering wedge, and rout it in detail; — thinking to deal with it roughly, as one should handle a thistle. But they fight at an overwhelming disadvantage, — living, John Field, alas! without arithmetic, and failing so.

"Do you ever fish?" I asked. "Oh yes, I catch a mess now and then when I am lying by; good perch I catch." "What's your bait?" "I catch shiners with fishworms, and bait the perch with them." "You'd better go now, John," said his wife, with glistening and hopeful face; but John demurred.

The shower was now over, and a rainbow above the eastern woods promised a fair evening; so I took my departure. When I had got without I asked for a dish, hoping to get a sight of the well bottom, to complete my survey of the premises; but there, alas! are shallows and quicksands, and rope broken withal, and bucket irrecoverable. Meanwhile the right culinary vessel was selected, water was seemingly distilled, and after consultation and long delay passed out to the thirsty one, — not yet suffered to cool, not yet to settle. Such gruel sustains life here, I thought; so, shutting my eyes, and excluding the motes by a skilfully directed undercurrent, I drank to genuine hospitality the heartiest draught I could. I am not squeamish in such cases when manners are concerned.

As I was leaving the Irishman's roof after the rain,

bending my steps again to the pond, my haste to catch
pickerel, wading in retired meadows, in sloughs and bog-
holes, in forlorn and savage places, appeared for an
instant trivial to me who had been sent to school and
college; but as I ran down the hill toward the reddening
west, with the rainbow over my shoulder, and some faint
tinkling sounds borne to my ear through the cleansed
air, from I know not what quarter, my Good Genius
seemed to say, — Go fish and hunt far and wide day by
day, — farther and wider, — and rest thee by many
brooks and hearth-sides without misgiving. Remember
thy Creator in the days of thy youth. Rise free from care
before the dawn, and seek adventures. Let the noon find
thee by other lakes, and the night overtake thee everywhere at home. There are no larger fields than these, no
worthier games than may here be played. Grow wild
according to thy nature, like these sedges and brakes,
which will never become English hay. Let the thunder
rumble; what if it threaten ruin to farmers' crops? that
is not its errand to thee. Take shelter under the cloud,
while they flee to carts and sheds. Let not to get a living
be thy trade, but thy sport. Enjoy the land, but own it
not. Through want of enterprise and faith men are
where they are, buying and selling, and spending their
lives like serfs.

O Baker Farm!

" Landscape where the richest element
   Is a little sunshine innocent." . . .

" No one runs to revel
   On thy rail-fenced lea." . . .

" Debate with no man hast thou,
    With questions art never perplexed,
As tame at the first sight as now,
    In thy plain russet gabardine dressed." . . .

" Come ye who love,
    And ye who hate,
Children of the Holy Dove,
    And Guy Faux of the state,
And hang conspiracies
From the tough rafters of the trees!"

Men come tamely home at night only from the next
field or street, where their household echoes haunt, and
their life pines because it breathes its own breath over
again; their shadows, morning and evening, reach farther than their daily steps. We should come home from
far, from adventures, and perils, and discoveries every
day, with new experience and character.

Before I had reached the pond some fresh impulse
had brought out John Field, with altered mind, letting
go "bogging" ere this sunset. But he, poor man, disturbed only a couple of fins while I was catching a fair
string, and he said it was his luck; but when we changed
seats in the boat luck changed seats too. Poor John
Field! — I trust he does not read this, unless he will
improve by it, — thinking to live by some derivative old
country mode in this primitive new country, — to catch
perch with shiners. It is good bait sometimes, I allow.
With his horizon all his own, yet he a poor man, born
to be poor, with his inherited Irish poverty or poor life,
his Adam's grandmother and boggy ways, not to rise in
this world, he nor his posterity, till their wading webbed
bog-trotting feet get *talaria* to their heels.

XI

HIGHER LAWS

As I came home through the woods with my string of fish, trailing my pole, it being now quite dark, I caught a glimpse of a woodchuck stealing across my path, and felt a strange thrill of savage delight, and was strongly tempted to seize and devour him raw; not that I was hungry then, except for that wildness which he represented. Once or twice, however, while I lived at the pond, I found myself ranging the woods, like a half-starved hound, with a strange abandonment, seeking some kind of venison which I might devour, and no morsel could have been too savage for me. The wildest scenes had become unaccountably familiar. I found in myself, and still find, an instinct toward a higher, or, as it is named, spiritual life, as do most men, and another toward a primitive rank and savage one, and I reverence them both. I love the wild not less than the good. The wildness and adventure that are in fishing still recommended it to me. I like sometimes to take rank hold on life and spend my day more as the animals do. Perhaps I have owed to this employment and to hunting, when quite young, my closest acquaintance with Nature. They early introduce us to and detain us in scenery with which otherwise, at that age, we should have little acquaintance. Fishermen, hunters, woodchoppers, and others, spending their lives in the fields and woods, in a peculiar sense a part of Nature themselves, are often in a more favorable mood for observing her, in the intervals of their pursuits, than philosophers or poets even, who approach her with expectation. She is not afraid to exhibit herself to them. The traveller on the prairie is naturally a hunter, on the head waters of the Missouri and Columbia a trapper, and at the Falls of St. Mary a fisherman. He who is only a traveller learns things at second-hand and by the halves, and is poor authority. We are most interested when science reports what those men already know practically or instinctively, for that alone is a true *humanity*, or account of human experience.

They mistake who assert that the Yankee has few amusements, because he has not so many public holidays, and men and boys do not play so many games as they do in England, for here the more primitive but solitary amusements of hunting, fishing, and the like have not yet given place to the former. Almost every New England boy among my contemporaries shouldered a fowling-piece between the ages of ten and fourteen; and his hunting and fishing grounds were not limited, like the preserves of an English nobleman, but were more boundless even than those of a savage. No wonder, then, that he did not oftener stay to play on the common. But already a change is taking place, owing, not to an increased humanity, but to an increased scarcity of game, for perhaps the hunter is the greatest friend of the animals hunted, not excepting the Humane Society.

Moreover, when at the pond, I wished sometimes to add fish to my fare for variety. I have actually fished from the same kind of necessity that the first fishers did. Whatever humanity I might conjure up against it was all factitious, and concerned my philosophy more than my feelings. I speak of fishing only now, for I had long felt differently about fowling, and sold my gun before I went to the woods. Not that I am less humane than others, but I did not perceive that my feelings were much affected. I did not pity the fishes nor the worms. This was habit. As for fowling, during the last years that I carried a gun my excuse was that I was studying ornithology, and sought only new or rare birds. But I confess that I am now inclined to think that there is a finer way of studying ornithology than this. It requires so much closer attention to the habits of the birds, that, if for that reason only, I have been willing to omit the gun. Yet notwithstanding the objection on the score of humanity, I am compelled to doubt if equally valuable sports are ever substituted for these; and when some of my friends have asked me anxiously about their boys, whether they should let them hunt, I have answered, yes, — remembering that it was one of the best parts of my education, — *make* them hunters, though sportsmen only at first, if possible, mighty hunters at last, so that they shall not find game large enough for them in this or any vegetable wilderness, — hunters as well as fishers of men. Thus far I am of the opinion of Chaucer's nun, who

"yave not of the text a pulled hen
That saith that hunters ben not holy men."

There is a period in the history of the individual, as of
the race, when the hunters are the "best men," as the
Algonquins called them. We cannot but pity the boy
who has never fired a gun; he is no more humane, while
his education has been sadly neglected. This was my
answer with respect to those youths who were bent on
this pursuit, trusting that they would soon outgrow it.
No humane being, past the thoughtless age of boyhood,
will wantonly murder any creature which holds its
life by the same tenure that he does. The hare in its
extremity cries like a child. I warn you, mothers,
that my sympathies do not always make the usual phil-
anthropic distinctions.

Such is oftenest the young man's introduction to the
forest, and the most original part of himself. He goes
thither at first as a hunter and fisher, until at last, if he
has the seeds of a better life in him, he distinguishes his
proper objects, as a poet or naturalist it may be, and
leaves the gun and fish-pole behind. The mass of men
are still and always young in this respect. In some
countries a hunting parson is no uncommon sight. Such
a one might make a good shepherd's dog, but is far
from being the Good Shepherd. I have been surprised
to consider that the only obvious employment, except
wood-chopping, ice-cutting, or the like business, which
ever to my knowledge detained at Walden Pond for a
whole half-day any of my fellow-citizens, whether fathers or children of the town, with just one exception,
was fishing. Commonly they did not think that they
were lucky, or well paid for their time, unless they got
a long string of fish, though they had the opportunity

of seeing the pond all the while. They might go there a thousand times before the sediment of fishing would sink to the bottom and leave their purpose pure; but no doubt such a clarifying process would be going on all the while. The Governor and his Council faintly remember the pond, for they went a-fishing there when they were boys; but now they are too old and dignified to go a-fishing, and so they know it no more forever. Yet even they expect to go to heaven at last. If the legislature regards it, it is chiefly to regulate the number of hooks to be used there; but they know nothing about the hook of hooks with which to angle for the pond itself, impaling the legislature for a bait. Thus, even in civilized communities, the embryo man passes through the hunter stage of development.

I have found repeatedly, of late years, that I cannot fish without falling a little in self-respect. I have tried it again and again. I have skill at it, and, like many of my fellows, a certain instinct for it, which revives from time to time, but always when I have done I feel that it would have been better if I had not fished. I think that I do not mistake. It is a faint intimation, yet so are the first streaks of morning. There is unquestionably this instinct in me which belongs to the lower orders of creation; yet with every year I am less a fisherman, though without more humanity or even wisdom; at present I am no fisherman at all. But I see that if I were to live in a wilderness I should again be tempted to become a fisher and hunter in earnest. Beside, there is something essentially unclean about this diet and all flesh, and I began to see where housework commences, and whence the endeavor, which costs so much, to wear a tidy and respectable appearance each day, to keep the house sweet and free from all ill odors and sights. Having been my own butcher and scullion and cook, as well as the gentleman for whom the dishes were served up, I can speak from an unusually complete experience. The practical objection to animal food in my case was its uncleanness; and besides, when I had caught and cleaned and cooked and eaten my fish, they seemed not to have fed me essentially. It was insignificant and unnecessary, and cost more than it came to. A little bread or a few potatoes would have done as well, with less trouble and filth. Like many of my contemporaries, I had rarely for many years used animal food, or tea, or coffee, etc.; not so much because of any ill effects which I had traced to them, as because they were not agreeable to my imagination. The repugnance to animal food is not the effect of experience, but is an instinct. It appeared more beautiful to live low and fare hard in many respects; and though I never did so, I went far enough to please my imagination. I believe that every man who has ever been earnest to preserve his higher or poetic faculties in the best condition has been particularly inclined to abstain from animal food, and from much food of any kind. It is a significant fact, stated by entomologists, — I find it in Kirby and Spence, — that " some insects in their perfect state, though furnished with organs of feeding, make no use of them;" and they lay it down as "a general rule, that almost all insects in this state eat much less than in that of larvæ. The voracious caterpillar when

transformed into a butterfly . . . and the gluttonous
maggot when become a fly " content themselves with
a drop or two of honey or some other sweet liquid.
The abdomen under the wings of the butterfly still
represents the larva. This is the tidbit which tempts
his insectivorous fate. The gross feeder is a man in
the larva state; and there are whole nations in that
condition, nations without fancy or imagination, whose
vast abdomens betray them.

It is hard to provide and cook so simple and clean a
diet as will not offend the imagination; but this, I think,
is to be fed when we feed the body; they should both
sit down at the same table. Yet perhaps this may be
done. The fruits eaten temperately need not make us
ashamed of our appetites, nor interrupt the worthiest
pursuits. But put an extra condiment into your dish, and
it will poison you. It is not worth the while to live by
rich cookery. Most men would feel shame if caught
preparing with their own hands precisely such a dinner,
whether of animal or vegetable food, as is every day
prepared for them by others. Yet till this is otherwise
we are not civilized, and, if gentlemen and ladies, are
not true men and women. This certainly suggests what
change is to be made. It may be vain to ask why the
imagination will not be reconciled to flesh and fat. I
am satisfied that it is not. Is it not a reproach that man
is a carnivorous animal? True, he can and does live,
in a great measure, by preying on other animals; but
this is a miserable way, — as any one who will go to
snaring rabbits, or slaughtering lambs, may learn, —
and he will be regarded as a benefactor of his race who

shall teach man to confine himself to a more innocent and wholesome diet. Whatever my own practice may be, I have no doubt that it is a part of the destiny of the human race, in its gradual improvement, to leave off eating animals, as surely as the savage tribes have left off eating each other when they came in contact with the more civilized.

If one listens to the faintest but constant suggestions of his genius, which are certainly true, he sees not to what extremes, or even insanity, it may lead him; and yet that way, as he grows more resolute and faithful, his road lies. The faintest assured objection which one healthy man feels will at length prevail over the arguments and customs of mankind. No man ever followed his genius till it misled him. Though the result were bodily weakness, yet perhaps no one can say that the consequences were to be regretted, for these were a life in conformity to higher principles. If the day and the night are such that you greet them with joy, and life emits a fragrance like flowers and sweet-scented herbs, is more elastic, more starry, more immortal, — that is your success. All nature is your congratulation, and you have cause momentarily to bless yourself. The greatest gains and values are farthest from being appreciated. We easily come to doubt if they exist. We soon forget them. They are the highest reality. Perhaps the facts most astounding and most real are never communicated by man to man. The true harvest of my daily life is somewhat as intangible and indescribable as the tints of morning or evening. It is a little star-dust caught, a segment of the rainbow which I have clutched.

Yet, for my part, I was never unusually squeamish; I could sometimes eat a fried rat with a good relish, if it were necessary. I am glad to have drunk water so long, for the same reason that I prefer the natural sky to an opium-eater's heaven. I would fain keep sober always; and there are infinite degrees of drunkenness. I believe that water is the only drink for a wise man; wine is not so noble a liquor; and think of dashing the hopes of a morning with a cup of warm coffee, or of an evening with a dish of tea! Ah, how low I fall when I am tempted by them! Even music may be intoxicating. Such apparently slight causes destroyed Greece and Rome, and will destroy England and America. Of all ebriosity, who does not prefer to be intoxicated by the air he breathes? I have found it to be the most serious objection to coarse labors long continued, that they compelled me to eat and drink coarsely also. But to tell the truth, I find myself at present somewhat less particular in these respects. I carry less religion to the table, ask no blessing; not because I am wiser than I was, but, I am obliged to confess, because, however much it is to be regretted, with years I have grown more coarse and indifferent. Perhaps these questions are entertained only in youth, as most believe of poetry. My practice is "nowhere," my opinion is here. Nevertheless I am far from regarding myself as one of those privileged ones to whom the Ved refers when it says, that "he who has true faith in the Omnipresent Supreme Being may eat all that exists," that is, is not bound to inquire what is his food, or who prepares it; and even in their case it is to be observed, as a Hindoo commen-

tator has remarked, that the Vedant limits this privilege
to "the time of distress."

Who has not sometimes derived an inexpressible
satisfaction from his food in which appetite had no
share? I have been thrilled to think that I owed a mental perception to the commonly gross sense of taste, that
I have been inspired through the palate, that some
berries which I had eaten on a hillside had fed my
genius. "The soul not being mistress of herself," says
Thseng-tseu, "one looks, and one does not see; one
listens, and one does not hear; one eats, and one does
not know the savor of food." He who distinguishes the
true savor of his food can never be a glutton; he who
does not cannot be otherwise. A puritan may go to his
brown-bread crust with as gross an appetite as ever
an alderman to his turtle. Not that food which entereth
into the mouth defileth a man, but the appetite with
which it is eaten. It is neither the quality nor the
quantity, but the devotion to sensual savors; when
that which is eaten is not a viand to sustain our animal,
or inspire our spiritual life, but food for the worms that
possess us. If the hunter has a taste for mud-turtles,
muskrats, and other such savage tidbits, the fine lady
indulges a taste for jelly made of a calf's foot, or for
sardines from over the sea, and they are even. He goes
to the mill-pond, she to her preserve-pot. The wonder
is how they, how you and I, can live this slimy, beastly
life, eating and drinking.

Our whole life is startlingly moral. There is never
an instant's truce between virtue and vice. Goodness
is the only investment that never fails. In the music

of the harp which trembles round the world it is the insisting on this which thrills us. The harp is the travelling patterer for the Universe's Insurance Company, recommending its laws, and our little goodness is all the assessment that we pay. Though the youth at last grows indifferent, the laws of the universe are not indifferent, but are forever on the side of the most sensitive. Listen to every zephyr for some reproof, for it is surely there, and he is unfortunate who does not hear it. We cannot touch a string or move a stop but the charming moral transfixes us. Many an irksome noise, go a long way off, is heard as music, a proud, sweet satire on the meanness of our lives.

We are conscious of an animal in us, which awakens in proportion as our higher nature slumbers. It is reptile and sensual, and perhaps cannot be wholly expelled; like the worms which, even in life and health, occupy our bodies. Possibly we may withdraw from it, but never change its nature. I fear that it may enjoy a certain health of its own; that we may be well, yet not pure. The other day I picked up the lower jaw of a hog, with white and sound teeth and tusks, which suggested that there was an animal health and vigor distinct from the spiritual. This creature succeeded by other means than temperance and purity. "That in which men differ from brute beasts," says Mencius, "is a thing very inconsiderable; the common herd lose it very soon; superior men preserve it carefully." Who knows what sort of life would result if we had attained to purity? If I knew so wise a man as could teach me purity I would go to seek him forthwith. "A command over our passions, and over the external senses of the body, and good acts, are declared by the Ved to be indispensable in the mind's approximation to God." Yet the spirit can for the time pervade and control every member and function of the body, and transmute what in form is the grossest sensuality into purity and devotion. The generative energy, which, when we are loose, dissipates and makes us unclean, when we are continent invigorates and inspires us. Chastity is the flowering of man; and what are called Genius, Heroism, Holiness, and the like, are but various fruits which succeed it. Man flows at once to God when the channel of purity is open. By turns our purity inspires and our impurity casts us down. He is blessed who is assured that the animal is dying out in him day by day, and the divine being established. Perhaps there is none but has cause for shame on account of the inferior and brutish nature to which he is allied. I fear that we are such gods or demigods only as fauns and satyrs, the divine allied to beasts, the creatures of appetite, and that, to some extent, our very life is our disgrace. —

> "How happy 's he who hath due place assigned
> To his beasts and disafforested his mind!
> .   .   .   .
> Can use his horse, goat, wolf, and ev'ry beast,
> And is not ass himself to all the rest!
> Else man not only is the herd of swine,
> But he 's those devils too which did incline
> Them to a headlong rage, and made them worse."

All sensuality is one, though it takes many forms; all purity is one. It is the same whether a man eat, or drink, or cohabit, or sleep sensually. They are but one appetite, and we only need to see a person do any one of these things to know how great a sensualist he is. The impure can neither stand nor sit with purity. When the reptile is attacked at one mouth of his burrow, he shows himself at another. If you would be chaste, you must be temperate. What is chastity? How shall a man know if he is chaste? He shall not know it. We have heard of this virtue, but we know not what it is. We speak conformably to the rumor which we have heard. From exertion come wisdom and purity; from sloth ignorance and sensuality. In the student sensuality is a sluggish habit of mind. An unclean person is universally a slothful one, one who sits by a stove, whom the sun shines on prostrate, who reposes without being fatigued. If you would avoid uncleanness, and all the sins, work earnestly, though it be at cleaning a stable. Nature is hard to be overcome, but she must be overcome. What avails it that you are Christian, if you are not purer than the heathen, if you deny yourself no more, if you are not more religious? I know of many systems of religion esteemed heathenish whose precepts fill the reader with shame, and provoke him to new endeavors, though it be to the performance of rites merely.

I hesitate to say these things, but it is not because of the subject, — I care not how obscene my *words* are, — but because I cannot speak of them without betraying my impurity. We discourse freely without shame of one form of sensuality, and are silent about another. We are so degraded that we cannot speak simply of the necessary functions of human nature. In earlier ages, in some countries, every function was reverently spoken of and regulated by law. Nothing was too trivial for the Hindoo lawgiver, however offensive it may be to modern taste. He teaches how to eat, drink, cohabit, void excrement and urine, and the like, elevating what is mean, and does not falsely excuse himself by calling these things trifles.

Every man is the builder of a temple, called his body, to the god he worships, after a style purely his own, nor can he get off by hammering marble instead. We are all sculptors and painters, and our material is our own flesh and blood and bones. Any nobleness begins at once to refine a man's features, any meanness or sensuality to imbrute them.

John Farmer sat at his door one September evening, after a hard day's work, his mind still running on his labor more or less. Having bathed, he sat down to recreate his intellectual man. It was a rather cool evening, and some of his neighbors were apprehending a frost. He had not attended to the train of his thoughts long when he heard some one playing on a flute, and that sound harmonized with his mood. Still he thought of his work; but the burden of his thought was, that though this kept running in his head, and he found himself planning and contriving it against his will, yet it concerned him very little. It was no more than the scurf of his skin, which was constantly shuffled off. But the notes of the flute came home to his ears out of a different sphere from that he worked in, and suggested work for certain faculties which slumbered in him. They gently did away with the street, and the village, and the state in which he lived. A voice said to him, — Why do you stay here and live this mean moiling life, when a glorious existence is possible for you? Those same stars twinkle over other fields than these. — But how to come out of this condition and actually migrate thither? All that he could think of was to practise some new austerity, to let his mind descend into his body and redeem it, and treat himself with ever increasing respect.

XII

BRUTE NEIGHBORS

SOMETIMES I had a companion in my fishing, who
came through the village to my house from the other
side of the town, and the catching of the dinner was as
much a social exercise as the eating of it.

Hermit. I wonder what the world is doing now. I
have not heard so much as a locust over the sweet-fern
these three hours. The pigeons are all asleep upon their
roosts, — no flutter from them. Was that a farmer's
noon horn which sounded from beyond the woods just
now? The hands are coming in to boiled salt beef and
cider and Indian bread. Why will men worry themselves so? He that does not eat need not work. I wonder how much they have reaped. Who would live there
where a body can never think for the barking of Bose?
And oh, the housekeeping! to keep bright the devil's
door-knobs, and scour his tubs this bright day! Better
not keep a house. Say, some hollow tree; and then for
morning calls and dinner-parties! Only a woodpecker
tapping. Oh, they swarm; the sun is too warm there;
they are born too far into life for me. I have water from
the spring, and a loaf of brown bread on the shelf. —
Hark! I hear a rustling of the leaves. Is it some ill-fed
village hound yielding to the instinct of the chase? or
the lost pig which is said to be in these woods, whose

tracks I saw after the rain? It comes on apace; my sumachs and sweetbriers tremble. — Eh, Mr. Poet, is it you? How do you like the world to-day?

Poet. See those clouds; how they hang! That's the greatest thing I have seen to-day. There's nothing like it in old paintings, nothing like it in foreign lands, — unless when we were off the coast of Spain. That's a true Mediterranean sky. I thought, as I have my living to get, and have not eaten to-day, that I might go a-fishing. That's the true industry for poets. It is the only trade I have learned. Come, let's along.

Hermit. I cannot resist. My brown bread will soon be gone. I will go with you gladly soon, but I am just concluding a serious meditation. I think that I am near the end of it. Leave me alone, then, for a while. But that we may not be delayed, you shall be digging the bait meanwhile. Angleworms are rarely to be met with in these parts, where the soil was never fattened with manure; the race is nearly extinct. The sport of digging the bait is nearly equal to that of catching the fish, when one's appetite is not too keen; and this you may have all to yourself to-day. I would advise you to set in the spade down yonder among the ground-nuts, where you see the johnswort waving. I think that I may warrant you one worm to every three sods you turn up, if you look well in among the roots of the grass, as if you were weeding. Or, if you choose to go farther, it will not be unwise, for I have found the increase of fair bait to be very nearly as the squares of the distances.

Hermit alone. Let me see; where was I? Methinks I was nearly in this frame of mind; the world lay about at this angle. Shall I go to heaven or a-fishing? If I should soon bring this meditation to an end, would another so sweet occasion be likely to offer? I was as near being resolved into the essence of things as ever I was in my life. I fear my thoughts will not come back to me. If it would do any good, I would whistle for them. When they make us an offer, is it wise to say, We will think of it? My thoughts have left no track, and I cannot find the path again. What was it that I was thinking of? It was a very hazy day. I will just try these three sentences of Confut-see; they may fetch that state about again. I know not whether it was the dumps or a budding ecstasy. Mem. There never is but one opportunity of a kind.

Poet. How now, Hermit, is it too soon? I have got just thirteen whole ones, beside several which are imperfect or undersized; but they will do for the smaller fry; they do not cover up the hook so much. Those village worms are quite too large; a shiner may make a meal off one without finding the skewer.

Hermit. Well, then, let's be off. Shall we to the Concord? There's good sport there if the water be not too high.

Why do precisely these objects which we behold make a world? Why has man just these species of animals for his neighbors; as if nothing but a mouse could have filled this crevice? I suspect that Pilpay & Co. have put animals to their best use, for they are all beasts of burden, in a sense, made to carry some portion of our thoughts.

The mice which haunted my house were not the common ones, which are said to have been introduced into the country, but a wild native kind not found in the village. I sent one to a distinguished naturalist, and it interested him much. When I was building, one of these had its nest underneath the house, and before I had laid the second floor, and swept out the shavings, would come out regularly at lunch time and pick up the crumbs at my feet. It probably had never seen a man before; and it soon became quite familiar, and would run over my shoes and up my clothes. It could readily ascend the sides of the room by short impulses, like a squirrel, which it resembled in its motions. At length, as I leaned with my elbow on the bench one day, it ran up my clothes, and along my sleeve, and round and round the paper which held my dinner, while I kept the latter close, and dodged and played at bopeep with it; and when at last I held still a piece of cheese between my thumb and finger, it came and nibbled it, sitting in my hand, and afterward cleaned its face and paws, like a fly, and walked away.

A phœbe soon built in my shed, and a robin for protection in a pine which grew against the house. In June the partridge (*Tetrao umbellus*), which is so shy a bird, led her brood past my windows, from the woods in the rear to the front of my house, clucking and calling to them like a hen, and in all her behavior proving herself the hen of the woods. The young suddenly disperse on your approach, at a signal from the mother, as if a whirlwind had swept them away, and they so exactly resemble the dried leaves and twigs that many a traveller has placed his foot in the midst of a brood, and heard the whir of the old bird as she flew off, and her anxious calls and mewing, or seen her trail her wings to attract his attention, without suspecting their neighborhood. The parent will sometimes roll and spin round before you in such a dishabille, that you cannot, for a few moments, detect what kind of creature it is. The young squat still and flat, often running their heads under a leaf, and mind only their mother's directions given from a distance, nor will your approach make them run again and betray themselves. You may even tread on them, or have your eyes on them for a minute, without discovering them. I have held them in my open hand at such a time, and still their only care, obedient to their mother and their instinct, was to squat there without fear or trembling. So perfect is this instinct, that once, when I had laid them on the leaves again, and one accidentally fell on its side, it was found with the rest in exactly the same position ten minutes afterward. They are not callow like the young of most birds, but more perfectly developed and precocious even than chickens. The remarkably adult yet innocent expression of their open and serene eyes is very memorable. All intelligence seems reflected in them. They suggest not merely the purity of infancy, but a wisdom clarified by experience. Such an eye was not born when the bird was, but is coeval with the sky it reflects. The woods do not yield another such a gem. The traveller does not often look into such a limpid well. The ignorant or reckless sportsman often shoots the parent at such a time, and leaves these innocents to fall a prey to some prowling beast or bird, or gradually mingle with the decaying leaves which they so much resemble. It is said that when hatched by a hen they will directly disperse on some alarm, and so are lost, for they never hear the mother's call which gathers them again. These were my hens and chickens.

It is remarkable how many creatures live wild and free though secret in the woods, and still sustain themselves in the neighborhood of towns, suspected by hunters only. How retired the otter manages to live here! He grows to be four feet long, as big as a small boy, perhaps without any human being getting a glimpse of him. I formerly saw the raccoon in the woods behind where my house is built, and probably still heard their whinnering at night. Commonly I rested an hour or two in the shade at noon, after planting, and ate my lunch, and read a little by a spring which was the source of a swamp and of a brook, oozing from under Brister's Hill, half a mile from my field. The approach to this was through a succession of descending grassy hollows, full of young pitch pines, into a larger wood about the swamp. There, in a very secluded and shaded spot, under a spreading white pine, there was yet a clean, firm sward to sit on. I had dug out the spring and made a well of clear gray water, where I could dip up a pailful without roiling it, and thither I went for this purpose almost every day in midsummer, when the pond was warmest. Thither, too, the woodcock led her brood, to probe the mud for worms, flying but a foot above them down the bank, while they ran in a troop beneath; but at last, spying me, she would leave her young and circle round and round me, nearer

and nearer till within four or five feet, pretending broken
wings and legs, to attract my attention, and get off her
young, who would already have taken up their march,
with faint, wiry peep, single file through the swamp, as
she directed. Or I heard the peep of the young when I
could not see the parent bird. There too the turtle doves
sat over the spring, or fluttered from bough to bough
of the soft white pines over my head; or the red squirrel, coursing down the nearest bough, was particularly
familiar and inquisitive. You only need sit still long
enough in some attractive spot in the woods that all its
inhabitants may exhibit themselves to you by turns.

I was witness to events of a less peaceful character.
One day when I went out to my wood-pile, or rather my
pile of stumps, I observed two large ants, the one red,
the other much larger, nearly half an inch long, and
black, fiercely contending with one another. Having
once got hold they never let go, but struggled and wres-
tled and rolled on the chips incessantly. Looking farther, I was surprised to find that the chips were covered
with such combatants, that it was not a *duellum*, but a
bellum, a war between two races of ants, the red always
pitted against the black, and frequently two red ones to
one black. The legions of these Myrmidons covered all
the hills and vales in my wood-yard, and the ground was
already strewn with the dead and dying, both red and
black. It was the only battle which I have ever witnessed,
the only battle-field I ever trod while the battle was
raging; internecine war; the red republicans on the one
hand, and the black imperialists on the other. On every
side they were engaged in deadly combat, yet without

any noise that I could hear, and human soldiers never fought so resolutely. I watched a couple that were fast locked in each other's embraces, in a little sunny valley amid the chips, now at noonday prepared to fight till the sun went down, or life went out. The smaller red champion had fastened himself like a vice to his adversary's front, and through all the tumblings on that field never for an instant ceased to gnaw at one of his feelers near the root, having already caused the other to go by the board; while the stronger black one dashed him from side to side, and, as I saw on looking nearer, had already divested him of several of his members. They fought with more pertinacity than bulldogs. Neither manifested the least disposition to retreat. It was evident that their battle-cry was "Conquer or die." In the meanwhile there camc along a single red ant on the hillside of this valley, evidently full of excitement, who either had despatched his foe, or had not yet taken part in the battle; probably the latter, for he had lost none of his limbs; whose mother had charged him to return with his shield or upon it. Or perchance he was some Achilles, who had nourished his wrath apart, and had now come to avenge or rescue his Patroclus. He saw this unequal combat from afar, — for the blacks were nearly twice the size of the red, — he drew near with rapid pace till he stood on his guard within half an inch of the combatants; then, watching his opportunity, he sprang upon the black warrior, and commenced his operations near the root of his right fore leg, leaving the foe to select among his own members; and so there were three united for life, as if a new kind of attraction had been

invented which put all other locks and cements to shame.
I should not have wondered by this time to find that they
had their respective musical bands stationed on some
eminent chip, and playing their national airs the while,
to excite the slow and cheer the dying combatants. I
was myself excited somewhat even as if they had been
men. The more you think of it, the less the difference.
And certainly there is not the fight recorded in Concord
history, at least, if in the history of America, that will
bear a moment's comparison with this, whether for the
numbers engaged in it, or for the patriotism and heroism displayed. For numbers and for carnage it was an
Austerlitz or Dresden. Concord Fight! Two killed on
the patriots' side, and Luther Blanchard wounded!
Why here every ant was a Buttrick, — "Fire! for God's
sake fire!" — and thousands shared the fate of Davis
and Hosmer. There was not one hireling there. I have
no doubt that it was a principle they fought for, as much
as our ancestors, and not to avoid a three-penny tax on
their tea; and the results of this battle will be as important and memorable to those whom it concerns as those
of the battle of Bunker Hill, at least.

I took up the chip on which the three I have particularly described were struggling, carried it into my house,
and placed it under a tumbler on my window-sill, in
order to see the issue. Holding a microscope to the first-
mentioned red ant, I saw that, though he was assidu-
ously gnawing at the near fore leg of his enemy, having
severed his remaining feeler, his own breast was all torn
away, exposing what vitals he had there to the jaws
of the black warrior, whose breastplate was apparently

too thick for him to pierce; and the dark carbuncles of the sufferer's eyes shone with ferocity such as war only could excite. They struggled half an hour longer under the tumbler, and when I looked again the black soldier had severed the heads of his foes from their bodies, and the still living heads were hanging on either side of him like ghastly trophies at his saddle-bow, still apparently as firmly fastened as ever, and he was endeavoring with feeble struggles, being without feelers and with only the remnant of a leg, and I know not how many other wounds, to divest himself of them; which at length, after half an hour more, he accomplished. I raised the glass, and he went off over the window-sill in that crippled state. Whether he finally survived that combat, and spent the remainder of his days in some Hôtel des Invalides, I do not know; but I thought that his industry would not be worth much thereafter. I never learned which party was victorious, nor the cause of the war; but I felt for the rest of that day as if I had had my feelings excited and harrowed by witnessing the struggle, the ferocity and carnage, of a human battle before my door.

Kirby and Spence tell us that the battles of ants have long been celebrated and the date of them recorded, though they say that Huber is the only modern author who appears to have witnessed them. "Æneas Sylvius," say they, "after giving a very circumstantial account of one contested with great obstinacy by a great and small species on the trunk of a pear tree," adds that "'this action was fought in the pontificate of Eugenius the Fourth, in the presence of Nicholas Pistoriensis, an eminent lawyer, who related the whole history of the battle with the greatest fidelity.' A similar engagement between great and small ants is recorded by Olaus Magnus, in which the small ones, being victorious, are said to have buried the bodies of their own soldiers, but left those of their giant enemies a prey to the birds. This event happened previous to the expulsion of the tyrant Christiern the Second from Sweden." The battle which I witnessed took place in the Presidency of Polk, five years before the passage of Webster's Fugitive-Slave Bill.

Many a village Bose, fit only to course a mud-turtle in a victualling cellar, sported his heavy quarters in the woods, without the knowledge of his master, and ineffectually smelled at old fox burrows and woodchucks' holes; led perchance by some slight cur which nimbly threaded the wood, and might still inspire a natural terror in its denizens; — now far behind his guide, barking like a canine bull toward some small squirrel which had treed itself for scrutiny, then, cantering off, bending the bushes with his weight, imagining that he is on the track of some stray member of the jerbilla family. Once I was surprised to see a cat walking along the stony shore of the pond, for they rarely wander so far from home. The surprise was mutual. Nevertheless the most domestic cat, which has lain on a rug all her days, appears quite at home in the woods, and, by her sly and stealthy behavior, proves herself more native there than the regular inhabitants. Once, when berrying, I met with a cat with young kittens in the woods, quite wild, and they all, like their mother, had their backs up and were fiercely spitting at me. A few years before I lived in the woods there was what was called a "winged cat" in one of the farm-houses in Lincoln nearest the pond, Mr. Gilian Baker's. When I called to see her in June, 1842, she was gone a-hunting in the woods, as was her wont (I am not sure whether it was a male or female, and so use the more common pronoun), but her mistress told me that she came into the neighborhood a little more than a year before, in April, and was finally taken into their house; that she was of a dark brownish-gray color, with a white spot on her throat, and white feet, and had a large bushy tail like a fox; that in the winter the fur grew thick and flatted out along her sides, forming strips ten or twelve inches long by two and a half wide, and under her chin like a muff, the upper side loose, the under matted like felt, and in the spring these appendages dropped off. They gave me a pair of her "wings," which I keep still. There is no appearance of a membrane about them. Some thought it was part flying squirrel or some other wild animal, which is not impossible, for, according to naturalists, prolific hybrids have been produced by the union of the marten and domestic cat. This would have been the right kind of cat for me to keep, if I had kept any; for why should not a poet's cat be winged as well as his horse?

In the fall the loon (*Colymbus glacialis*) came, as usual, to moult and bathe in the pond, making the woods ring with his wild laughter before I had risen. At rumor of his arrival all the Mill-dam sportsmen are on the alert, in gigs and on foot, two by two and three by three, with patent rifles and conical balls and spy-glasses. They come rustling through the woods like autumn leaves, at

least ten men to one loon. Some station themselves on
this side of the pond, some on that, for the poor bird
cannot be omnipresent; if he dive here he must come up
there. But now the kind October wind rises, rustling
the leaves and rippling the surface of the water, so that
no loon can be heard or seen, though his foes sweep the
pond with spy-glasses, and make the woods resound with
their discharges. The waves generously rise and dash
angrily, taking sides with all water-fowl, and our sportsmen must beat a retreat to town and shop and unfinished
jobs. But they were too often successful. When I went
to get a pail of water early in the morning I frequently
saw this stately bird sailing out of my cove within a few
rods. If I endeavored to overtake him in a boat, in order
to see how he would manœuvre, he would dive and be
completely lost, so that I did not discover him again,
sometimes, till the latter part of the day. But I was
more than a match for him on the surface. He commonly went off in a rain.

As I was paddling along the north shore one very
calm October afternoon, for such days especially they
settle on to the lakes, like the milkweed down, having
looked in vain over the pond for a loon, suddenly one,
sailing out from the shore toward the middle a few rods
in front of me, set up his wild laugh and betrayed himself. I pursued with a paddle and he dived, but when
he came up I was nearer than before. He dived again,
but I miscalculated the direction he would take, and we
were fifty rods apart when he came to the surface this
time, for I had helped to widen the interval; and again
he laughed long and loud, and with more reason than

before. He manœuvred so cunningly that I could not
get within half a dozen rods of him. Each time, when he
came to the surface, turning his head this way and that,
he coolly surveyed the water and the land, and apparently
chose his course so that he might come up where there
was the widest expanse of water and at the greatest distance from the boat. It was surprising how quickly he
made up his mind and put his resolve into execution.
He led me at once to the widest part of the pond, and
could not be driven from it. While he was thinking one
thing in his brain, I was endeavoring to divine his thought
in mine. It was a pretty game, played on the smooth
surface of the pond, a man against a loon. Suddenly
your adversary's checker disappears beneath the board,
and the problem is to place yours nearest to where his
will appear again. Sometimes he would come up unexpectedly on the opposite side of me, having apparently
passed directly under the boat. So long-winded was he
and so unweariable, that when he had swum farthest he
would immediately plunge again, nevertheless; and then
no wit could divine where in the deep pond, beneath the
smooth surface, he might be speeding his way like a fish,
for he had time and ability to visit the bottom of the
pond in its deepest part. It is said that loons have been
caught in the New York lakes eighty feet beneath the
surface, with hooks set for trout, — though Walden is
deeper than that. How surprised must the fishes be to
see this ungainly visitor from another sphere speeding
his way amid their schools! Yet he appeared to know
his course as surely under water as on the surface, and
swam much faster there. Once or twice I saw a ripple

where he approached the surface, just put his head out to reconnoitre, and instantly dived again. I found that it was as well for me to rest on my oars and wait his reappearing as to endeavor to calculate where he would rise; for again and again, when I was straining my eyes over the surface one way, I would suddenly be startled by his unearthly laugh behind me. But why, after displaying so much cunning, did he invariably betray himself the moment he came up by that loud laugh? Did not his white breast enough betray him? He was indeed a silly loon, I thought. I could commonly hear the plash of the water when he came up, and so also detected him. But after an hour he seemed as fresh as ever, dived as willingly, and swam yet farther than at first. It was surprising to see how serenely he sailed off with unruffled breast when he came to the surface, doing all the work with his webbed feet beneath. His usual note was this demoniac laughter, yet somewhat like that of a water-fowl; but occasionally, when he had balked me most successfully and come up a long way off, he uttered a long-drawn unearthly howl, probably more like that of a wolf than any bird; as when a beast puts his muzzle to the ground and deliberately howls. This was his looning, — perhaps the wildest sound that is ever heard here, making the woods ring far and wide. I concluded that he laughed in derision of my efforts, confident of his own resources. Though the sky was by this time overcast, the pond was so smooth that I could see where he broke the surface when I did not hear him. His white breast, the stillness of the air, and the smoothness of the water were all against him. At length, having come up fifty rods off, he uttered one of those prolonged howls, as if calling on the god of loons to aid him, and immediately there came a wind from the east and rippled the surface, and filled the whole air with misty rain, and I was impressed as if it were the prayer of the loon answered, and his god was angry with me; and so I left him disappearing far away on the tumultuous surface.

For hours, in fall days, I watched the ducks cunningly tack and veer and hold the middle of the pond, far from the sportsman; tricks which they will have less need to practise in Louisiana bayous. When compelled to rise they would sometimes circle round and round and over the pond at a considerable height, from which they could easily see to other ponds and the river, like black motes in the sky; and, when I thought they had gone off thither long since, they would settle down by a slanting flight of a quarter of a mile on to a distant part which was left free; but what beside safety they got by sailing in the middle of Walden I do not know, unless they love its water for the same reason that I do.

XIII

HOUSE-WARMING

In October I went a-graping to the river meadows, and loaded myself with clusters more precious for their beauty and fragrance than for food. There, too, I admired, though I did not gather, the cranberries, small waxen gems, pendants of the meadow grass, pearly and red, which the farmer plucks with an ugly rake, leaving the smooth meadow in a snarl, heedlessly measuring them by the bushel and the dollar only, and sells the spoils of the meads to Boston and New York; destined to be *jammed*, to satisfy the tastes of lovers of Nature there. So butchers rake the tongues of bison out of the prairie grass, regardless of the torn and drooping plant. The barberry's brilliant fruit was likewise food for my eyes merely; but I collected a small store of wild apples for coddling, which the proprietor and travellers had overlooked. When chestnuts were ripe I laid up half a bushel for winter. It was very exciting at that season to roam the then boundless chestnut woods of Lincoln, — they now sleep their long sleep under the railroad, — with a bag on my shoulder, and a stick to open burs with in my hand, for I did not always wait for the frost, amid the rustling of leaves and the loud reproofs of the red squirrels and the jays, whose half-consumed nuts I sometimes stole, for the burs which they had selected

were sure to contain sound ones. Occasionally I climbed
and shook the trees. They grew also behind my house,
and one large tree, which almost overshadowed it, was,
when in flower, a bouquet which scented the whole
neighborhood, but the squirrels and the jays got most
of its fruit; the last coming in flocks early in the morning and picking the nuts out of the burs before they fell.
I relinquished these trees to them and visited the more
distant woods composed wholly of chestnut. These
nuts, as far as they went, were a good substitute for
bread. Many other substitutes might, perhaps, be found.
Digging one day for fishworms, I discovered the ground-
nut (*Apios tuberosa*) on its string, the potato of the aborigines, a sort of fabulous fruit, which I had begun to
doubt if I had ever dug and eaten in childhood, as I had
told, and had not dreamed it. I had often since seen its
crimpled red velvety blossom supported by the stems of
other plants without knowing it to be the same. Cultivation has well-nigh exterminated it. It has a sweetish
taste, much like that of a frost-bitten potato, and I found
it better boiled than roasted. This tuber seemed like a
faint promise of Nature to rear her own children and
feed them simply here at some future period. In these
days of fatted cattle and waving grain-fields this humble
root, which was once the *totem* of an Indian tribe, is
quite forgotten, or known only by its flowering vine; but
let wild Nature reign here once more, and the tender and
luxurious English grains will probably disappear before
a myriad of foes, and without the care of man the crow
may carry back even the last seed of corn to the great
cornfield of the Indian's God in the southwest, whence

he is said to have brought it; but the now almost exterminated ground-nut will perhaps revive and flourish in spite of frosts and wildness, prove itself indigenous, and resume its ancient importance and dignity as the diet of the hunter tribe. Some Indian Ceres or Minerva must have been the inventor and bestower of it; and when the reign of poetry commences here, its leaves and string of nuts may be represented on our works of art.

Already, by the first of September, I had seen two or three small maples turned scarlet across the pond, beneath where the white stems of three aspens diverged, at the point of a promontory, next the water. Ah, many a tale their color told! And gradually from week to week the character of each tree came out, and it admired itself reflected in the smooth mirror of the lake. Each morning the manager of this gallery substituted some new picture, distinguished by more brilliant or harmonious coloring, for the old upon the walls.

The wasps came by thousands to my lodge in October, as to winter quarters, and settled on my windows within and on the walls overhead, sometimes deterring visitors from entering. Each morning, when they were numbed with cold, I swept some of them out, but I did not trouble myself much to get rid of them; I even felt complimented by their regarding my house as a desirable shelter. They never molested me seriously, though they bedded with me; and they gradually disappeared, into what crevices I do not know, avoiding winter and unspeakable cold.

Like the wasps, before I finally went into winter quarters in November, I used to resort to the northeast side of Walden, which the sun, reflected from the pitch pine woods and the stony shore, made the fireside of the pond; it is so much pleasanter and wholesomer to be warmed by the sun while you can be, than by an artificial fire. I thus warmed myself by the still glowing embers which the summer, like a departed hunter, had left.

When I came to build my chimney I studied masonry. My bricks, being second-hand ones, required to be cleaned with a trowel, so that I learned more than usual of the qualities of bricks and trowels. The mortar on them was fifty years old, and was said to be still growing harder; but this is one of those sayings which men love to repeat whether they are true or not. Such sayings themselves grow harder and adhere more firmly with age, and it would take many blows with a trowel to clean an old wiseacre of them. Many of the villages of Mesopotamia are built of second-hand bricks of a very good quality, obtained from the ruins of Babylon, and the cement on them is older and probably harder still. However that may be, I was struck by the peculiar toughness of the steel which bore so many violent blows without being worn out. As my bricks had been in a chimney before, though I did not read the name of Nebuchadnezzar on them, I picked out as many fireplace bricks as I could find, to save work and waste, and I filled the spaces between the bricks about the fireplace with stones from the pond shore, and also made my mortar with the white sand from the same place. I lingered most about the fireplace, as the most vital part of the house. Indeed, I worked so deliberately, that though I commenced at the ground in the morning, a course of bricks raised a few inches above the floor served for my pillow at night; yet I did not get a stiff neck for it that I remember; my stiff neck is of older date. I took a poet to board for a fortnight about those times, which caused me to be put to it for room. He brought his own knife, though I had two, and we used to scour them by thrusting them into the earth. He shared with me the labors of cooking. I was pleased to see my work rising so square and solid by degrees, and reflected, that, if it proceeded slowly, it was calculated to endure a long time. The chimney is to some extent an independent structure, standing on the ground, and rising through the house to the heavens; even after the house is burned it still stands sometimes, and its importance and independence are apparent. This was toward the end of summer. It was now November.

The north wind had already begun to cool the pond, though it took many weeks of steady blowing to accomplish it, it is so deep. When I began to have a fire at evening, before I plastered my house, the chimney carried smoke particularly well, because of the numerous chinks between the boards. Yet I passed some cheerful evenings in that cool and airy apartment, surrounded by the rough brown boards full of knots, and rafters with the bark on high overhead. My house never pleased my eye so much after it was plastered, though I was obliged to confess that it was more comfortable. Should not every apartment in which man dwells be lofty

enough to create some obscurity overhead, where flickering shadows may play at evening about the rafters?
These forms are more agreeable to the fancy and imagination than fresco paintings or other the most expensive
furniture. I now first began to inhabit my house, I may
say, when I began to use it for warmth as well as shelter.
I had got a couple of old fire-dogs to keep the wood
from the hearth, and it did me good to see the soot
form on the back of the chimney which I had built, and
I poked the fire with more right and more satisfaction
than usual. My dwelling was small, and I could hardly
entertain an echo in it; but it seemed larger for being
a single apartment and remote from neighbors. All
the attractions of a house were concentrated in one
room; it was kitchen, chamber, parlor, and keeping-
room; and whatever satisfaction parent or child, master or servant, derive from living in a house, I enjoyed
it all. Cato says, the master of a family (*patremfa-
milias*) must have in his rustic villa "cellam oleariam,
vinariam, dolia multa, uti lubeat caritatem expectare,
et rei, et virtuti, et gloriae erit," that is, "an oil and
wine cellar, many casks, so that it may be pleasant to
expect hard times; it will be for his advantage, and
virtue, and glory." I had in my cellar a firkin of potatoes,
about two quarts of peas with the weevil in them, and
on my shelf a little rice, a jug of molasses, and of rye
and Indian meal a peck each.

I sometimes dream of a larger and more populous
house, standing in a golden age, of enduring materials,
and without gingerbread work, which shall still consist
of only one room, a vast, rude, substantial, primitive

hall, without ceiling or plastering, with bare rafters and purlins supporting a sort of lower heaven over one's head, — useful to keep off rain and snow, where the king and queen posts stand out to receive your homage, when you have done reverence to the prostrate Saturn of an older dynasty on stepping over the sill; a cavernous house, wherein you must reach up a torch upon a pole to see the roof; where some may live in the fireplace, some in the recess of a window, and some on settles, some at one end of the hall, some at another, and some aloft on rafters with the spiders, if they choose; a house which you have got into when you have opened the outside door, and the ceremony is over; where the weary traveller may wash, and eat, and converse, and sleep, without further journey; such a shelter as you would be glad to reach in a tempestuous night, containing all the essentials of a house, and nothing for house-keeping; where you can see all the treasures of the house at one view, and everything hangs upon its peg that a man should use; at once kitchen, pantry, parlor, chamber, storehouse, and garret; where you can see so necessary a thing as a barrel or a ladder, so convenient a thing as a cupboard, and hear the pot boil, and pay your respects to the fire that cooks your dinner, and the oven that bakes your bread, and the necessary furniture and utensils are the chief ornaments; where the washing is not put out, nor the fire, nor the mistress, and perhaps you are sometimes requested to move from off the trap-door, when the cook would descend into the cellar, and so learn whether the ground is solid or hollow beneath you without stamping. A house whose inside is as open and manifest as a bird's nest, and you cannot go in at the front door and out at the back without seeing some of its inhabitants; where to be a guest is to be presented with the freedom of the house, and not to be carefully excluded from seven eighths of it, shut up in a particular cell, and told to make yourself at home there, — in solitary confinement. Nowadays the host does not admit you to *his* hearth, but has got the mason to build one for yourself somewhere in his alley, and hospitality is the art of *keeping* you at the greatest distance. There is as much secrecy about the cooking as if he had a design to poison you. I am aware that I have been on many a man's premises, and might have been legally ordered off, but I am not aware that I have been in many men's houses. I might visit in my old clothes a king and queen who lived simply in such a house as I have described, if I were going their way; but backing out of a modern palace will be all that I shall desire to learn, if ever I am caught in one.

It would seem as if the very language of our parlors would lose all its nerve and degenerate into *palaver* wholly, our lives pass at such remoteness from its symbols, and its metaphors and tropes are necessarily so far fetched, through slides and dumb-waiters, as it were; in other words, the parlor is so far from the kitchen and workshop. The dinner even is only the parable of a dinner, commonly. As if only the savage dwelt near enough to Nature and Truth to borrow a trope from them. How can the scholar, who dwells away in the North West Territory or the Isle of Man, tell what is parliamentary in the kitchen?

However, only one or two of my guests were ever bold enough to stay and eat a hasty-pudding with me; but when they saw that crisis approaching they beat a hasty retreat rather, as if it would shake the house to its foundations. Nevertheless, it stood through a great many hasty-puddings.

I did not plaster till it was freezing weather. I brought over some whiter and cleaner sand for this purpose from the opposite shore of the pond in a boat, a sort of conveyance which would have tempted me to go much farther if necessary. My house had in the meanwhile been shingled down to the ground on every side. In lathing I was pleased to be able to send home each nail with a single blow of the hammer, and it was my ambition to transfer the plaster from the board to the wall neatly and rapidly. I remembered the story of a conceited fellow, who, in fine clothes, was wont to lounge about the village once, giving advice to workmen. Venturing one day to substitute deeds for words, he turned up his cuffs, seized a plasterer's board, and having loaded his trowel without mishap, with a complacent look toward the lathing overhead, made a bold gesture thitherward; and straightway, to his complete discomfiture, received the whole contents in his ruffled bosom. I admired anew the economy and convenience of plastering, which so effectually shuts out the cold and takes a handsome finish, and I learned the various casualties to which the plasterer is liable. I was surprised to see how thirsty the bricks were which drank up all the moisture in my plaster before I had smoothed it, and how many pailfuls of water it takes to christen a new hearth. I had the previous winter made

a small quantity of lime by burning the shells of the
Unio fluviatilis, which our river affords, for the sake of
the experiment; so that I knew where my materials
came from. I might have got good limestone within a
mile or two and burned it myself, if I had cared to
do so.

The pond had in the meanwhile skimmed over in the
shadiest and shallowest coves, some days or even weeks
before the general freezing. The first ice is especially
interesting and perfect, being hard, dark, and transparent, and affords the best opportunity that ever offers
for examining the bottom where it is shallow; for you
can lie at your length on ice only an inch thick, like a
skater insect on the surface of the water, and study the
bottom at your leisure, only two or three inches distant,
like a picture behind a glass, and the water is necessarily
always smooth then. There are many furrows in the sand
where some creature has travelled about and doubled
on its tracks; and, for wrecks, it is strewn with the cases
of caddis-worms made of minute grains of white quartz.
Perhaps these have creased it, for you find some of their
cases in the furrows, though they are deep and broad for
them to make. But the ice itself is the object of most interest, though you must improve the earliest opportunity
to study it. If you examine it closely the morning after
it freezes, you find that the greater part of the bubbles,
which at first appeared to be within it, are against its
under surface, and that more are continually rising from
the bottom; while the ice is as yet comparatively solid
and dark, that is, you see the water through it. These

bubbles are from an eightieth to an eighth of an inch in
diameter, very clear and beautiful, and you see your face
reflected in them through the ice. There may be thirty
or forty of them to a square inch. There are also already
within the ice narrow oblong perpendicular bubbles
about half an inch long, sharp cones with the apex upward; or oftener, if the ice is quite fresh, minute spherical bubbles one directly above another, like a string of
beads. But these within the ice are not so numerous nor
obvious as those beneath. I sometimes used to cast on
stones to try the strength of the ice, and those which
broke through carried in air with them, which formed
very large and conspicuous white bubbles beneath. One
day when I came to the same place forty-eight hours
afterward, I found that those large bubbles were still
perfect, though an inch more of ice had formed, as I
could see distinctly by the seam in the edge of a cake.
But as the last two days had been very warm, like an
Indian summer, the ice was not now transparent, showing the dark green color of the water, and the bottom,
but opaque and whitish or gray, and though twice as
thick was hardly stronger than before, for the air bubbles
had greatly expanded under this heat and run together,
and lost their regularity; they were no longer one directly over another, but often like silvery coins poured
from a bag, one overlapping another, or in thin flakes,
as if occupying slight cleavages. The beauty of the ice
was gone, and it was too late to study the bottom. Being
curious to know what position my great bubbles occupied with regard to the new ice, I broke out a cake
containing a middling sized one, and turned it bottom

upward. The new ice had formed around and under the
bubble, so that it was included between the two ices. It
was wholly in the lower ice, but close against the upper,
and was flattish, or perhaps slightly lenticular, with a
rounded edge, a quarter of an inch deep by four inches
in diameter; and I was surprised to find that directly
under the bubble the ice was melted with great regularity in the form of a saucer reversed, to the height of
five eighths of an inch in the middle, leaving a thin
partition there between the water and the bubble, hardly
an eighth of an inch thick; and in many places the small
bubbles in this partition had burst out downward, and
probably there was no ice at all under the largest bubbles,
which were a foot in diameter. I inferred that the infinite number of minute bubbles which I had first seen
against the under surface of the ice were now frozen in
likewise, and that each, in its degree, had operated like
a burning-glass on the ice beneath to melt and rot it.
These are the little air-guns which contribute to make
the ice crack and whoop.

At length the winter set in in good earnest, just as I
had finished plastering, and the wind began to howl
around the house as if it had not had permission to do so
till then. Night after night the geese came lumbering in
in the dark with a clangor and a whistling of wings, even
after the ground was covered with snow, some to alight
in Walden, and some flying low over the woods toward
Fair Haven, bound for Mexico. Several times, when returning from the village at ten or eleven o'clock at night,
I heard the tread of a flock of geese, or else ducks, on

the dry leaves in the woods by a pond-hole behind my
dwelling, where they had come up to feed, and the faint
honk or quack of their leader as they hurried off. In
1845 Walden froze entirely over for the first time on the
night of the 22d of December, Flint's and other shallower
ponds and the river having been frozen ten days or
more; in '46, the 16th; in '49, about the 31st; and in
'50, about the 27th of December; in '52, the 5th of January; in '53, the 31st of December. The snow had already covered the ground since the 25th of November,
and surrounded me suddenly with the scenery of winter.
I withdrew yet farther into my shell, and endeavored to
keep a bright fire both within my house and within my
breast. My employment out of doors now was to collect
the dead wood in the forest, bringing it in my hands or
on my shoulders, or sometimes trailing a dead pine tree
under each arm to my shed. An old forest fence which
had seen its best days was a great haul for me. I sacrificed it to Vulcan, for it was past serving the god Ter-
minus. How much more interesting an event is that
man's supper who has just been forth in the snow to
hunt, nay, you might say, steal, the fuel to cook it with!
His bread and meat are sweet. There are enough fagots
and waste wood of all kinds in the forests of most of our
towns to support many fires, but which at present warm
none, and, some think, hinder the growth of the young
wood. There was also the driftwood of the pond. In the
course of the summer I had discovered a raft of pitch
pine logs with the bark on, pinned together by the Irish
when the railroad was built. This I hauled up partly
on the shore. After soaking two years and then lying

high six months it was perfectly sound, though water-
logged past drying. I amused myself one winter day
with sliding this piecemeal across the pond, nearly half
a mile, skating behind with one end of a log fifteen feet
long on my shoulder, and the other on the ice; or I tied
several logs together with a birch withe, and then, with
a longer birch or alder which had a hook at the end,
dragged them across. Though completely waterlogged
and almost as heavy as lead, they not only burned long,
but made a very hot fire; nay, I thought that they burned
better for the soaking, as if the pitch, being confined by
the water, burned longer, as in a lamp.

Gilpin, in his account of the forest borderers of England, says that "the encroachments of trespassers, and
the houses and fences thus raised on the borders of the
forest," were "considered as great nuisances by the old
forest law, and were severely punished under the name
of *purprestures*, as tending *ad terrorem ferarum — ad
nocumentum forestae*, etc.," to the frightening of the game
and the detriment of the forest. But I was interested in
the preservation of the venison and the vert more than
the hunters or woodchoppers, and as much as though I
had been the Lord Warden himself; and if any part was
burned, though I burned it myself by accident, I grieved
with a grief that lasted longer and was more inconsol-
able than that of the proprietors; nay, I grieved when it
was cut down by the proprietors themselves. I would
that our farmers when they cut down a forest felt some
of that awe which the old Romans did when they came
to thin, or let in the light to, a consecrated grove (*lucum
conlucare*), that is, would believe that it is sacred to

some god. The Roman made an expiatory offering, and prayed, Whatever god or goddess thou art to whom this grove is sacred, be propitious to me, my family, and children, etc.

It is remarkable what a value is still put upon wood even in this age and in this new country, a value more permanent and universal than that of gold. After all our discoveries and inventions no man will go by a pile of wood. It is as precious to us as it was to our Saxon and Norman ancestors. If they made their bows of it, we make our gun-stocks of it. Michaux, more than thirty years ago, says that the price of wood for fuel in New York and Philadelphia "nearly equals, and sometimes exceeds, that of the best wood in Paris, though this immense capital annually requires more than three hundred thousand cords, and is surrounded to the distance of three hundred miles by cultivated plains." In this town the price of wood rises almost steadily, and the only question is, how much higher it is to be this year than it was the last. Mechanics and tradesmen who come in person to the forest on no other errand, are sure to attend the wood auction, and even pay a high price for the privilege of gleaning after the woodchopper. It is now many years that men have resorted to the forest for fuel and the materials of the arts: the New Englander and the New Hollander, the Parisian and the Celt, the farmer and Robin Hood, Goody Blake and Harry Gill; in most parts of the world the prince and the peasant, the scholar and the savage, equally require still a few sticks from the forest to warm them and cook their food. Neither could I do without them.

Every man looks at his wood-pile with a kind of affection. I loved to have mine before my window, and the more chips the better to remind me of my pleasing work. I had an old axe which nobody claimed, with which by spells in winter days, on the sunny side of the house, I played about the stumps which I had got out of my bean-field. As my driver prophesied when I was plowing, they warmed me twice, — once while I was splitting them, and again when they were on the fire, so that no fuel could give out more heat. As for the axe, I was advised to get the village blacksmith to "jump" it; but I jumped him, and, putting a hickory helve from the woods into it, made it do. If it was dull, it was at least hung true.

A few pieces of fat pine were a great treasure. It is interesting to remember how much of this food for fire is still concealed in the bowels of the earth. In previous years I had often gone "prospecting" over some bare hillside, where a pitch pine wood had formerly stood, and got out the fat pine roots. They are almost indestructible. Stumps thirty or forty years old, at least, will still be sound at the core, though the sapwood has all become vegetable mould, as appears by the scales of the thick bark forming a ring level with the earth four or five inches distant from the heart. With axe and shovel you explore this mine, and follow the marrowy store, yellow as beef tallow, or as if you had struck on a vein of gold, deep into the earth. But commonly I kindled my fire with the dry leaves of the forest, which I had stored up in my shed before the snow came. Green hickory finely split makes the woodchopper's kindlings, when he has a camp in the woods. Once in a while I got

a little of this. When the villagers were lighting their
fires beyond the horizon, I too gave notice to the various
wild inhabitants of Walden vale, by a smoky streamer
from my chimney, that I was awake. —

> Light-winged Smoke, Icarian bird,
> Melting thy pinions in thy upward flight,
> Lark without song, and messenger of dawn,
> Circling above the hamlets as thy nest;
> Or else, departing dream, and shadowy form
> Of midnight vision, gathering up thy skirts;
> By night star-veiling, and by day
> Darkening the light and blotting out the sun;
> Go thou my incense upward from this hearth,
> And ask the gods to pardon this clear flame.

Hard green wood just cut, though I used but little of
that, answered my purpose better than any other. I
sometimes left a good fire when I went to take a walk in
a winter afternoon; and when I returned, three or four
hours afterward, it would be still alive and glowing.
My house was not empty though I was gone. It was as
if I had left a cheerful housekeeper behind. It was I
and Fire that lived there; and commonly my housekeeper proved trustworthy. One day, however, as I was
splitting wood, I thought that I would just look in at the
window and see if the house was not on fire; it was the
only time I remember to have been particularly anxious
on this score; so I looked and saw that a spark had
caught my bed, and I went in and extinguished it when
it had burned a place as big as my hand. But my house
occupied so sunny and sheltered a position, and its roof
was so low, that I could afford to let the fire go out in
the middle of almost any winter day.

The moles nested in my cellar, nibbling every third potato, and making a snug bed even there of some hair left after plastering and of brown paper; for even the wildest animals love comfort and warmth as well as man, and they survive the winter only because they are so careful to secure them. Some of my friends spoke as if I was coming to the woods on purpose to freeze myself. The animal merely makes a bed, which he warms with his body, in a sheltered place; but man, having discovered fire, boxes up some air in a spacious apartment, and warms that, instead of robbing himself, makes that his bed, in which he can move about divested of more cumbrous clothing, maintain a kind of summer in the midst of winter, and by means of windows even admit the light, and with a lamp lengthen out the day. Thus he goes a step or two beyond instinct, and saves a little time for the fine arts. Though, when I had been exposed to the rudest blasts a long time, my whole body began to grow torpid, when I reached the genial atmosphere of my house I soon recovered my faculties and prolonged my life. But the most luxuriously housed has little to boast of in this respect, nor need we trouble ourselves to speculate how the human race may be at last destroyed. It would be easy to cut their threads any time with a little sharper blast from the north. We go on dating from Cold Fridays and Great Snows; but a little colder Friday, or greater snow would put a period to man's existence on the globe.

The next winter I used a small cooking-stove for economy, since I did not own the forest; but it did not keep fire so well as the open fireplace. Cooking was then, for the most part, no longer a poetic, but merely a chemic process. It will soon be forgotten, in these days of stoves, that we used to roast potatoes in the ashes, after the Indian fashion. The stove not only took up room and scented the house, but it concealed the fire, and I felt as if I had lost a companion. You can always see a face in the fire. The laborer, looking into it at evening, purifies his thoughts of the dross and earthiness which they have accumulated during the day. But I could no longer sit and look into the fire, and the pertinent words of a poet recurred to me with new force. —

" Never, bright flame, may be denied to me
  Thy dear, life imaging, close sympathy.
  What but my hopes shot upward e'er so bright?
  What but my fortunes sunk so low in night?
  Why art thou banished from our hearth and hall,
  Thou who art welcomed and beloved by all?
  Was thy existence then too fanciful
  For our life's common light, who are so dull?
  Did thy bright gleam mysterious converse hold
  With our congenial souls? secrets too bold?

  Well, we are safe and strong, for now we sit
  Beside a hearth where no dim shadows flit,
  Where nothing cheers nor saddens, but a fire
  Warms feet and hands — nor does to more aspire;
  By whose compact utilitarian heap
  The present may sit down and go to sleep,
  Nor fear the ghosts who from the dim past walked,
  And with us by the unequal light of the old wood fire talked."

XIV

FORMER INHABITANTS; AND WINTER VISITORS

I WEATHERED some merry snow-storms, and spent some cheerful winter evenings by my fireside, while the snow whirled wildly without, and even the hooting of the owl was hushed. For many weeks I met no one in my walks but those who came occasionally to cut wood and sled it to the village. The elements, however, abetted me in making a path through the deepest snow in the woods, for when I had once gone through the wind blew the oak leaves into my tracks, where they lodged, and by absorbing the rays of the sun melted the snow, and so not only made a dry bed for my feet, but in the night their dark line was my guide. For human society I was obliged to conjure up the former occupants of these woods. Within the memory of many of my townsmen the road near which my house stands resounded with the laugh and gossip of inhabitants, and the woods which border it were notched and dotted here and there with their little gardens and dwellings, though it was then much more shut in by the forest than now. In some places, within my own remembrance, the pines would scrape both sides of a chaise at once, and women and children who were compelled to go this way to Lincoln alone and on foot did it with fear, and often ran a good part

The leaning hemlocks

Concord elms

of the distance. Though mainly but a humble route to neighboring villages, or for the woodman's team, it once amused the traveller more than now by its variety, and lingered longer in his memory. Where now firm open fields stretch from the village to the woods, it then ran through a maple swamp on a foundation of logs, the remnants of which, doubtless, still underlie the present dusty highway, from the Stratten, now the Alms-House, Farm, to Brister's Hill.

East of my bean-field, across the road, lived Cato Ingraham, slave of Duncan Ingraham, Esquire, gentleman, of Concord village, who built his slave a house, and gave him permission to live in Walden Woods; — Cato, not Uticensis, but Concordiensis. Some say that he was a Guinea Negro. There are a few who remember his little patch among the walnuts, which he let grow up till he should be old and need them; but a younger and whiter speculator got them at last. He too, however, occupies an equally narrow house at present. Cato's half-obliterated cellar-hole still remains, though known to few, being concealed from the traveller by a fringe of pines. It is now filled with the smooth sumach (*Rhus glabra*), and one of the earliest species of goldenrod (*Solidago stricta*) grows there luxuriantly.

Here, by the very corner of my field, still nearer to town, Zilpha, a colored woman, had her little house, where she spun linen for the townsfolk, making the Walden Woods ring with her shrill singing, for she had a loud and notable voice. At length, in the war of 1812, her dwelling was set on fire by English soldiers, prisoners on parole, when she was away, and her cat and dog and

hens were all burned up together. She led a hard life,
and somewhat inhumane. One old frequenter of these
woods remembers, that as he passed her house one
noon he heard her muttering to herself over her gurgling pot, — "Ye are all bones, bones!" I have seen
bricks amid the oak copse there.

Down the road, on the right hand, on Brister's Hill,
lived Brister Freeman, "a handy Negro," slave of Squire
Cummings once, — there where grow still the apple
trees which Brister planted and tended; large old trees
now, but their fruit still wild and ciderish to my taste.
Not long since I read his epitaph in the old Lincoln
burying-ground, a little on one side, near the unmarked
graves of some British grenadiers who fell in the retreat
from Concord, — where he is styled "Sippio Brister,"
— Scipio Africanus he had some title to be called, —
"a man of color," as if he were discolored. It also
told me, with staring emphasis, when he died; which
was but an indirect way of informing me that he ever
lived. With him dwelt Fenda, his hospitable wife,
who told fortunes, yet pleasantly, — large, round, and
black, blacker than any of the children of night, such
a dusky orb as never rose on Concord before or since.

Farther down the hill, on the left, on the old road
in the woods, are marks of some homestead of the
Stratten family; whose orchard once covered all the
slope of Brister's Hill, but was long since killed out by
pitch pines, excepting a few stumps, whose old roots
furnish still the wild stocks of many a thrifty village
tree.

Nearer yet to town, you come to Breed's location, on

the other side of the way, just on the edge of the wood; ground famous for the pranks of a demon not distinctly named in old mythology, who has acted a prominent and astounding part in our New England life, and deserves, as much as any mythological character, to have his biography written one day; who first comes in the guise of a friend or hired man, and then robs and murders the whole family, — New-England Rum. But history must not yet tell the tragedies enacted here; let time intervene in some measure to assuage and lend an azure tint to them. Here the most indistinct and dubious tradition says that once a tavern stood; the well the same, which tempered the traveller's beverage and refreshed his steed. Here then men saluted one another, and heard and told the news, and went their ways again.

Breed's hut was standing only a dozen years ago, though it had long been unoccupied. It was about the size of mine. It was set on fire by mischievous boys, one Election night, if I do not mistake. I lived on the edge of the village then, and had just lost myself over Davenant's "Gondibert," that winter that I labored with a lethargy, — which, by the way, I never knew whether to regard as a family complaint, having an uncle who goes to sleep shaving himself, and is obliged to sprout potatoes in a cellar Sundays, in order to keep awake and keep the Sabbath, or as the consequence of my attempt to read Chalmers' collection of English poetry without skipping. It fairly overcame my Nervii. I had just sunk my head on this when the bells rung fire, and in hot haste the engines rolled that way, led by a straggling troop of men and boys, and I among the foremost, for I had leaped the brook. We thought it was far south over the woods, — we who had run to fires before, — barn, shop, or dwelling-house, or all together. "It's Baker's barn," cried one. "It is the Codman place," affirmed another. And then fresh sparks went up above the wood, as if the roof fell in, and we all shouted "Concord to the rescue!" Wagons shot past with furious speed and crushing loads, bearing, perchance, among the rest, the agent of the Insurance Company, who was bound to go however far; and ever and anon the engine bell tinkled behind, more slow and sure; and rearmost of all, as it was afterward whispered, came they who set the fire and gave the alarm. Thus we kept on like true idealists, rejecting the evidence of our senses, until at a turn in the road we heard the crackling and actually felt the heat of the fire from over the wall, and realized, alas! that we were there. The very nearness of the fire but cooled our ardor. At first we thought to throw a frog-pond on to it; but concluded to let it burn, it was so far gone and so worthless. So we stood round our engine, jostled one another, expressed our sentiments through speaking-trumpets, or in lower tone referred to the great conflagrations which the world has witnessed, including Bascom's shop, and, between ourselves, we thought that, were we there in season with our "tub," and a full frog-pond by, we could turn that threatened last and universal one into another flood. We finally retreated without doing any mischief, — returned to sleep and "Gondibert." But as for "Gondibert," I would except that passage in the preface about wit being the soul's powder, — "but most of mankind are strangers to wit, as Indians are to powder."

It chanced that I walked that way across the fields the following night, about the same hour, and hearing a low moaning at this spot, I drew near in the dark, and discovered the only survivor of the family that I know, the heir of both its virtues and its vices, who alone was interested in this burning, lying on his stomach and looking over the cellar wall at the still smouldering cinders beneath, muttering to himself, as is his wont. He had been working far off in the river meadows all day, and had improved the first moments that he could call his own to visit the home of his fathers and his youth. He gazed into the cellar from all sides and points of view by turns, always lying down to it, as if there was some treasure, which he remembered, concealed between the stones, where there was absolutely nothing but a heap of bricks and ashes. The house being gone, he looked at what there was left. He was soothed by the sympathy which my mere presence implied, and showed me, as well as the darkness permitted, where the well was covered up; which, thank Heaven, could never be burned; and he groped long about the wall to find the well-sweep which his father had cut and mounted, feeling for the iron hook or staple by which a burden had been fastened to the heavy end, — all that he could now cling to, — to convince me that it was no common "rider." I felt it, and still remark it almost daily in my walks, for by it hangs the history of a family.

Once more, on the left, where are seen the well and

lilac bushes by the wall, in the now open field, lived Nutting and Le Grosse. But to return toward Lincoln.

Farther in the woods than any of these, where the road approaches nearest to the pond, Wyman the potter squatted, and furnished his townsmen with earthenware, and left descendants to succeed him. Neither were they rich in worldly goods, holding the land by sufferance while they lived; and there often the sheriff came in vain to collect the taxes, and "attached a chip," for form's sake, as I have read in his accounts, there being nothing else that he could lay his hands on. One day in midsummer, when I was hoeing, a man who was carrying a load of pottery to market stopped his horse against my field and inquired concerning Wyman the younger. He had long ago bought a potter's wheel of him, and wished to know what had become of him. I had read of the potter's clay and wheel in Scripture, but it had never occurred to me that the pots we use were not such as had come down unbroken from those days, or grown on trees like gourds somewhere, and I was pleased to hear that so fictile an art was ever practiced in my neighborhood.

The last inhabitant of these woods before me was an Irishman, Hugh Quoil (if I have spelt his name with coil enough), who occupied Wyman's tenement, — Col. Quoil, he was called. Rumor said that he had been a soldier at Waterloo. If he had lived I should have made him fight his battles over again. His trade here was that of a ditcher. Napoleon went to St. Helena; Quoil came to Walden Woods. All I know of him is tragic. He was a man of manners, like one who had

seen the world, and was capable of more civil speech
than you could well attend to. He wore a greatcoat in
midsummer, being affected with the trembling delirium,
and his face was the color of carmine. He died in the
road at the foot of Brister's Hill shortly after I came to
the woods, so that I have not remembered him as a
neighbor. Before his house was pulled down, when his
comrades avoided it as "an unlucky castle," I visited
it. There lay his old clothes curled up by use, as if they
were himself, upon his raised plank bed. His pipe lay
broken on the hearth, instead of a bowl broken at the
fountain. The last could never have been the symbol
of his death, for he confessed to me that, though he had
heard of Brister's Spring, he had never seen it; and
soiled cards, kings of diamonds, spades, and hearts,
were scattered over the floor. One black chicken which
the administrator could not catch, black as night and
as silent, not even croaking, awaiting Reynard, still
went to roost in the next apartment. In the rear there
was the dim outline of a garden, which had been planted
but had never received its first hoeing, owing to those
terrible shaking fits, though it was now harvest time. It
was overrun with Roman wormwood and beggar-ticks,
which last stuck to my clothes for all fruit. The skin of
a woodchuck was freshly stretched upon the back of
the house, a trophy of his last Waterloo; but no warm
cap or mittens would he want more.

Now only a dent in the earth marks the site of
these dwellings, with buried cellar stones, and straw-
berries, raspberries, thimble-berries, hazel-bushes, and
sumachs growing in the sunny sward there; some pitch

pine or gnarled oak occupies what was the chimney nook, and a sweet-scented black birch, perhaps, waves where the door-stone was. Sometimes the well dent is visible, where once a spring oozed; now dry and tearless grass; or it was covered deep, — not to be discovered till some late day, — with a flat stone under the sod, when the last of the race departed. What a sorrowful act must that be, — the covering up of wells! coincident with the opening of wells of tears. These cellar dents, like deserted fox burrows, old holes, are all that is left where once were the stir and bustle of human life, and "fate, free-will, foreknowledge absolute," in some form and dialect or other were by turns discussed. But all I can learn of their conclusions amounts to just this, that "Cato and Brister pulled wool;" which is about as edifying as the history of more famous schools of philosophy.

Still grows the vivacious lilac a generation after the door and lintel and the sill are gone, unfolding its sweet-scented flowers each spring, to be plucked by the musing traveller; planted and tended once by children's hands, in front-yard plots, — now standing by wall-sides in retired pastures, and giving place to new-rising forests; — the last of that stirp, sole survivor of that family. Little did the dusky children think that the puny slip with its two eyes only, which they stuck in the ground in the shadow of the house and daily watered, would root itself so, and outlive them, and house itself in the rear that shaded it, and grown man's garden and orchard, and tell their story faintly to the lone wanderer a half-century after they had grown up and died. —

blossoming as fair, and smelling as sweet, as in that first spring. I mark its still tender, civil, cheerful, lilac colors.

But this small village, germ of something more, why did it fail while Concord keeps its ground? Were there no natural advantages, — no water privileges, forsooth? Ay, the deep Walden Pond and cool Brister's Spring, — privilege to drink long and healthy draughts at these, all unimproved by these men but to dilute their glass. They were universally a thirsty race. Might not the basket, stable-broom, mat-making, corn-parching, linen-spinning, and pottery business have thrived here, making the wilderness to blossom like the rose, and a numerous posterity have inherited the land of their fathers? The sterile soil would at least have been proof against a lowland degeneracy. Alas! how little does the memory of these human inhabitants enhance the beauty of the landscape! Again, perhaps, Nature will try, with me for a first settler, and my house raised last spring to be the oldest in the hamlet.

I am not aware that any man has ever built on the spot which I occupy. Deliver me from a city built on the site of a more ancient city, whose materials are ruins, whose gardens cemeteries. The soil is blanched and accursed there, and before that becomes necessary the earth itself will be destroyed. With such reminiscences I repeopled the woods and lulled myself asleep.

At this season I seldom had a visitor. When the snow lay deepest no wanderer ventured near my house for a week or fortnight at a time, but there I lived as snug as a meadow mouse, or as cattle and poultry which are said to have survived for a long time buried in drifts, even without food; or like that early settler's family in the town of Sutton, in this State, whose cottage was completely covered by the great snow of 1717 when he was absent, and an Indian found it only by the hole which the chimney's breath made in the drift, and so relieved the family. But no friendly Indian concerned himself about me; nor needed he, for the master of the house was at home. The Great Snow! How cheerful it is to hear of! When the farmers could not get to the woods and swamps with their teams, and were obliged to cut down the shade trees before their houses, and, when the crust was harder, cut off the trees in the swamps, ten feet from the ground, as it appeared the next spring.

In the deepest snows, the path which I used from the highway to my house, about half a mile long, might have been represented by a meandering dotted line, with wide intervals between the dots. For a week of even weather I took exactly the same number of steps, and of the same length, coming and going, stepping deliberately and with the precision of a pair of dividers in my own deep tracks, — to such routine the winter reduces us, — yet often they were filled with heaven's own blue. But no weather interfered fatally with my walks, or rather my going abroad, for I frequently tramped eight or ten miles through the deepest snow to keep an appointment with a beech tree, or a yellow birch, or an old acquaintance among the pines; when the ice and snow causing their limbs to droop, and so

sharpening their tops, had changed the pines into fir
trees; wading to the tops of the highest hills when the
snow was nearly two feet deep on a level, and shaking
down another snow-storm on my head at every step; or
sometimes creeping and floundering thither on my hands
and knees, when the hunters had gone into winter
quarters. One afternoon I amused myself by watching
a barred owl (*Strix nebulosa*) sitting on one of the
lower dead limbs of a white pine, close to the trunk,
in broad daylight, I standing within a rod of him. He
could hear me when I moved and cronched the snow
with my feet, but could not plainly see me. When I
made most noise he would stretch out his neck, and
erect his neck feathers, and open his eyes wide; but
their lids soon fell again, and he began to nod. I too
felt a slumberous influence after watching him half an
hour, as he sat thus with his eyes half open, like a cat,
winged brother of the cat. There was only a narrow
slit left between their lids, by which he preserved a
peninsular relation to me; thus, with half-shut eyes,
looking out from the land of dreams, and endeavoring
to realize me, vague object or mote that interrupted his
visions. At length, on some louder noise or my nearer
approach, he would grow uneasy and sluggishly turn
about on his perch, as if impatient at having his dreams
disturbed; and when he launched himself off and flapped
through the pines, spreading his wings to unexpected
breadth, I could not hear the slightest sound from
them. Thus, guided amid the pine boughs rather by a
delicate sense of their neighborhood than by sight,
feeling his twilight way, as it were, with his sensitive pin-

ions, he found a new perch, where he might in peace await the dawning of his day.

As I walked over the long causeway made for the railroad through the meadows, I encountered many a blustering and nipping wind, for nowhere has it freer play; and when the frost had smitten me on one cheek, heathen as I was, I turned to it the other also. Nor was it much better by the carriage road from Brister's Hill. For I came to town still, like a friendly Indian, when the contents of the broad open fields were all piled up between the walls of the Walden road, and half an hour sufficed to obliterate the tracks of the last traveller. And when I returned new drifts would have formed, through which I floundered, where the busy northwest wind had been depositing the powdery snow round a sharp angle in the road, and not a rabbit's track, nor even the fine print, the small type, of a meadow mouse was to be seen. Yet I rarely failed to find, even in midwinter, some warm and springy swamp where the grass and the skunk-cabbage still put forth with perennial verdure, and some hardier bird occasionally awaited the return of spring.

Sometimes, notwithstanding the snow, when I returned from my walk at evening I crossed the deep tracks of a woodchopper leading from my door, and found his pile of whittlings on the hearth, and my house filled with the odor of his pipe. Or on a Sunday afternoon, if I chanced to be at home, I heard the cronching of the snow made by the step of a long-headed farmer, who from far through the woods sought my house, to have a social "crack;" one of the few of his vocation who are "men on their farms;" who donned a frock instead of a professor's gown, and is as ready to extract the moral out of church or state as to haul a load of manure from his barn-yard. We talked of rude and simple times, when men sat about large fires in cold, bracing weather, with clear heads; and when other dessert failed, we tried our teeth on many a nut which wise squirrels have long since abandoned, for those which have the thickest shells are commonly empty.

The one who came from farthest to my lodge, through deepest snows and most dismal tempests, was a poet. A farmer, a hunter, a soldier, a reporter, even a philosopher, may be daunted; but nothing can deter a poet, for he is actuated by pure love. Who can predict his comings and goings? His business calls him out at all hours, even when doctors sleep. We made that small house ring with boisterous mirth and resound with the murmur of much sober talk, making amends then to Walden vale for the long silences. Broadway was still and deserted in comparison. At suitable intervals there were regular salutes of laughter, which might have been referred indifferently to the last-uttered or the forth-coming jest. We made many a "bran new" theory of life over a thin dish of gruel, which combined the advantages of conviviality with the clear-headedness which philosophy requires.

I should not forget that during my last winter at the pond there was another welcome visitor, who at one time came through the village, through snow and rain and darkness, till he saw my lamp through the trees, and shared with me some long winter evenings. One of the last of the philosophers, — Connecticut gave him to the world, — he peddled first her wares, afterwards, as he declares, his brains. These he peddles still, prompting God and disgracing man, bearing for fruit his brain only, like the nut its kernel. I think that he must be the man of the most faith of any alive. His words and attitude always suppose a better state of things than other men are acquainted with, and he will be the last man to be disappointed as the ages revolve. He has no venture in the present. But though comparatively disregarded now, when his day comes, laws unsuspected by most will take effect, and masters of families and rulers will come to him for advice. —

"How blind that cannot see serenity!"

A true friend of man; almost the only friend of human progress. An Old Mortality, say rather an Immortality, with unwearied patience and faith making plain the image engraven in men's bodies, the God of whom they are but defaced and leaning monuments. With his hospitable intellect he embraces children, beggars, insane, and scholars, and entertains the thought of all, adding to it commonly some breadth and elegance. I think that he should keep a caravansary on the world's highway, where philosophers of all nations might put up, and on his sign should be printed, "Entertainment for man, but not for his beast. Enter ye that have leisure and a quiet mind, who earnestly seek the right road." He is perhaps the sanest man and has the fewest crotchets of any I chance to know; the same yesterday and to-morrow. Of yore we had sauntered and talked, and effect-

ually put the world behind us; for he was pledged to
no institution in it, freeborn, *ingenuus*. Whichever way
we turned, it seemed that the heavens and the earth
had met together, since he enhanced the beauty of the
landscape. A blue-robed man, whose fittest roof is the
overarching sky which reflects his serenity. I do not
see how he can ever die; Nature cannot spare him.

Having each some shingles of thought well dried, we
sat and whittled them, trying our knives, and admiring
the clear yellowish grain of the pumpkin pine. We
waded so gently and reverently, or we pulled together
so smoothly, that the fishes of thought were not scared
from the stream, nor feared any angler on the bank, but
came and went grandly, like the clouds which float
through the western sky, and the mother-o'-pearl flocks
which sometimes form and dissolve there. There we
worked, revising mythology, rounding a fable here and
there, and building castles in the air for which earth
offered no worthy foundation. Great Looker! Great
Expecter! to converse with whom was a New England
Night's Entertainment. Ah! such discourse we had,
hermit and philosopher, and the old settler I have
spoken of, — we three, — it expanded and racked my
little house; I should not dare to say how many pounds'
weight there was above the atmospheric pressure on
every circular inch; it opened its seams so that they had
to be calked with much dulness thereafter to stop the
consequent leak; — but I had enough of that kind of
oakum already picked.

There was one other with whom I had "solid seasons," long to be remembered, at his house in the vil-

lage, and who looked in upon me from time to time; but I had no more for society there.

There too, as everywhere, I sometimes expected the Visitor who never comes. The Vishnu Purana says, "The house-holder is to remain at eventide in his court-yard as long as it takes to milk a cow, or longer if he pleases, to await the arrival of a guest." I often performed this duty of hospitality, waited long enough to milk a whole herd of cows, but did not see the man approaching from the town.

XV

WINTER ANIMALS

WHEN the ponds were firmly frozen, they afforded not only new and shorter routes to many points, but new views from their surfaces of the familiar landscape around them. When I crossed Flint's Pond, after it was covered with snow, though I had often paddled about and skated over it, it was so unexpectedly wide and so strange that I could think of nothing but Baffin's Bay. The Lincoln hills rose up around me at the extremity of a snowy plain, in which I did not remember to have stood before; and the fishermen, at an indeterminable distance over the ice, moving slowly about with their wolfish dogs, passed for sealers or Esquimaux, or in misty weather loomed like fabulous creatures, and I did not know whether they were giants or pygmies. I took this course when I went to lecture in Lincoln in the evening, travelling in no road and passing no house between my own hut and the lecture room. In Goose Pond, which lay in my way, a colony of muskrats dwelt, and raised their cabins high above the ice, though none could be seen abroad when I crossed it. Walden, being like the rest usually bare of snow, or with only shallow and interrupted drifts on it, was my yard where I could walk freely when the snow was nearly two feet deep on a level elsewhere and the villagers were confined to their streets. There, far from the village street, and except at very long intervals, from the jingle of sleigh-bells, I slid and skated, as in a vast moose-yard well trodden, overhung by oak woods and solemn pines bent down with snow or bristling with icicles.

For sounds in winter nights, and often in winter days, I heard the forlorn but melodious note of a hooting owl indefinitely far; such a sound as the frozen earth would yield if struck with a suitable plectrum, the very *lingua vernacula* of Walden Wood, and quite familiar to me at last, though I never saw the bird while it was making it. I seldom opened my door in a winter evening without hearing it; *Hoo hoo hoo, hoorer hoo,* sounded sonorously, and the first three syllables accented somewhat like *how der do;* or sometimes *hoo hoo* only. One night in the beginning of winter, before the pond froze over, about nine o'clock, I was startled by the loud honking of a goose, and, stepping to the door, heard the sound of their wings like a tempest in the woods as they flew low over my house. They passed over the pond toward Fair Haven, seemingly deterred from settling by my light, their commodore honking all the while with a regular beat. Suddenly an unmistakable cat owl from very near me, with the most harsh and tremendous voice I ever heard from any inhabitant of the woods, responded at regular intervals to the goose, as if determined to expose and disgrace this intruder from Hudson's Bay by exhibiting a greater compass and volume of voice in a native, and *boo-hoo* him out of Concord horizon. What do you mean by alarming the citadel at this time of night consecrated to me? Do you

think I am ever caught napping at such an hour, and
that I have not got lungs and a larynx as well as yourself? *Boo-hoo, boo-hoo, boo-hoo!* It was one of the most
thrilling discords I ever heard. And yet, if you had a
discriminating ear, there were in it the elements of a
concord such as these plains never saw nor heard.

I also heard the whooping of the ice in the pond,
my great bed-fellow in that part of Concord, as if it
were restless in its bed and would fain turn over, were
troubled with flatulency and bad dreams; or I was
waked by the cracking of the ground by the frost, as if
some one had driven a team against my door, and in
the morning would find a crack in the earth a quarter
of a mile long and a third of an inch wide.

Sometimes I heard the foxes as they ranged over the
snow-crust, in moonlight nights, in search of a partridge
or other game, barking raggedly and demoniacally like
forest dogs, as if laboring with some anxiety, or seeking
expression, struggling for light and to be dogs outright
and run freely in the streets; for if we take the ages
into our account, may there not be a civilization going
on among brutes as well as men? They seemed to me
to be rudimental, burrowing men, still standing on their
defence, awaiting their transformation. Sometimes one
came near to my window, attracted by my light, barked
a vulpine curse at me, and then retreated.

Usually the red squirrel (*Sciurus Hudsonius*) waked
me in the dawn, coursing over the roof and up and
down the sides of the house, as if sent out of the woods
for this purpose. In the course of the winter I threw
out half a bushel of ears of sweet corn, which had not

got ripe, on to the snow-crust by my door, and was amused by watching the motions of the various animals which were baited by it. In the twilight and the night the rabbits came regularly and made a hearty meal. All day long the red squirrels came and went, and afforded me much entertainment by their manœuvres. One would approach at first warily through the shrub oaks, running over the snow-crust by fits and starts like a leaf blown by the wind, now a few paces this way, with wonderful speed and waste of energy, making inconceivable haste with his "trotters," as if it were for a wager, and now as many paces that way, but never getting on more than half a rod at a time; and then suddenly pausing with a ludicrous expression and a gratuitous somerset, as if all the eyes in the universe were fixed on him, — for all the motions of a squirrel, even in the most solitary recesses of the forest, imply spectators as much as those of a dancing girl, — wasting more time in delay and circumspection than would have sufficed to walk the whole distance, — I never saw one walk, — and then suddenly, before you could say Jack Robinson, he would be in the top of a young pitch pine, winding up his clock and chiding all imaginary spectators, soliloquizing and talking to all the universe at the same time, — for no reason that I could ever detect, or he himself was aware of, I suspect. At length he would reach the corn, and selecting a suitable ear, frisk about in the same uncertain trigonometrical way to the topmost stick of my wood-pile, before my window, where he looked me in the face, and there sit for hours, supplying himself with a new ear from time to time, nibbling at first voraciously and throwing the half-naked cobs about; till at length he grew more dainty still and played with his food, tasting only the inside of the kernel, and the ear, which was held balanced over the stick by one paw, slipped from his careless grasp and fell to the ground, when he would look over at it with a ludicrous expression of uncertainty, as if suspecting that it had life, with a mind not made up whether to get it again, or a new one, or be off; now thinking of corn, then listening to hear what was in the wind. So the little impudent fellow would waste many an ear in a forenoon; till at last, seizing some longer and plumper one, considerably bigger than himself, and skilfully balancing it, he would set out with it to the woods, like a tiger with a buffalo, by the same zigzag course and frequent pauses, scratching along with it as if it were too heavy for him and falling all the while, making its fall a diagonal between a perpendicular and horizontal, being determined to put it through at any rate; — a singularly frivolous and whimsical fellow; — and so he would get off with it to where he lived, perhaps carry it to the top of a pine tree forty or fifty rods distant, and I would afterwards find the cobs strewn about the woods in various directions.

At length the jays arrive, whose discordant screams were heard long before, as they were warily making their approach an eighth of a mile off, and in a stealthy and sneaking manner they flit from tree to tree, nearer and nearer, and pick up the kernels which the squirrels have dropped. Then, sitting on a pitch pine bough, they attempt to swallow in their haste a kernel which is too

big for their throats and chokes them; and after great
labor they disgorge it, and spend an hour in the endeavor to crack it by repeated blows with their bills.
They were manifestly thieves, and I had not much respect for them; but the squirrels, though at first shy,
went to work as if they were taking what was their
own.

Meanwhile also came the chickadees in flocks, which,
picking up the crumbs the squirrels had dropped, flew
to the nearest twig, and, placing them under their claws,
hammered away at them with their little bills, as if it
were an insect in the bark, till they were sufficiently reduced for their slender throats. A little flock of these tit-
mice came daily to pick a dinner out of my wood-pile, or
the crumbs at my door, with faint flitting lisping notes,
like the tinkling of icicles in the grass, or else with
sprightly *day day day*, or more rarely, in springlike days,
a wiry summery *phe-be* from the woodside. They were
so familiar that at length one alighted on an armful of
wood which I was carrying in, and pecked at the sticks
without fear. I once had a sparrow alight upon my
shoulder for a moment while I was hoeing in a village
garden, and I felt that I was more distinguished by that
circumstance than I should have been by any epaulet I
could have worn. The squirrels also grew at last to be
quite familiar, and occasionally stepped upon my shoe,
when that was the nearest way.

When the ground was not yet quite covered, and again
near the end of winter, when the snow was melted on my
south hillside and about my wood-pile, the partridges
came out of the woods morning and evening to feed

there. Whichever side you walk in the woods the partridge bursts away on whirring wings, jarring the snow from the dry leaves and twigs on high, which comes sifting down in the sunbeams like golden dust, for this brave bird is not to be scared by winter. It is frequently covered up by drifts, and, it is said, "sometimes plunges from on wing into the soft snow, where it remains concealed for a day or two." I used to start them in the open land also, where they had come out of the woods at sunset to "bud" the wild apple trees. They will come regularly every evening to particular trees, where the cunning sportsman lies in wait for them, and the distant orchards next the woods suffer thus not a little. I am glad that the partridge gets fed, at any rate. It is Nature's own bird which lives on buds and diet-drink.

In dark winter mornings, or in short winter afternoons, I sometimes heard a pack of hounds threading all the woods with hounding cry and yelp, unable to resist the instinct of the chase, and the note of the hunting-horn at intervals, proving that man was in the rear. The woods ring again, and yet no fox bursts forth on to the open level of the pond, nor following pack pursuing their Actæon. And perhaps at evening I see the hunters returning with a single brush trailing from their sleigh for a trophy, seeking their inn. They tell me that if the fox would remain in the bosom of the frozen earth he would be safe, or if he would run in a straight line away no foxhound could overtake him; but, having left his pursuers far behind, he stops to rest and listen till they come up, and when he runs he circles round to his old haunts, where the hunters await him. Sometimes, however, he will run upon a wall many rods, and then leap off far to one side, and he appears to know that water will not retain his scent. A hunter told me that he once saw a fox pursued by hounds burst out on to Walden when the ice was covered with shallow puddles, run part way across, and then return to the same shore. Ere long the hounds arrived, but here they lost the scent. Sometimes a pack hunting by themselves would pass my door, and circle round my house, and yelp and hound without regarding me, as if afflicted by a species of madness, so that nothing could divert them from the pursuit. Thus they circle until they fall upon the recent trail of a fox, for a wise hound will forsake everything else for this. One day a man came to my hut from Lexington to inquire after his hound that made a large track, and had been hunting for a week by himself. But I fear that he was not the wiser for all I told him, for every time I attempted to answer his questions he interrupted me by asking, "What do you do here?" He had lost a dog, but found a man.

One old hunter who has a dry tongue, who used to come to bathe in Walden once every year when the water was warmest, and at such times looked in upon me, told me that many years ago he took his gun one afternoon and went out for a cruise in Walden Wood; and as he walked the Wayland road he heard the cry of hounds approaching, and ere long a fox leaped the wall into the road, and as quick as thought leaped the other wall out of the road, and his swift bullet had not touched him. Some way behind came an old hound and her

three pups in full pursuit, hunting on their own account,
and disappeared again in the woods. Late in the afternoon, as he was resting in the thick woods south of Walden, he heard the voice of the hounds far over toward
Fair Haven still pursuing the fox; and on they came,
their hounding cry which made all the woods ring sounding nearer and nearer, now from Well Meadow, now
from the Baker Farm. For a long time he stood still and
listened to their music, so sweet to a hunter's ear, when
suddenly the fox appeared, threading the solemn aisles
with an easy coursing pace, whose sound was concealed
by a sympathetic rustle of the leaves, swift and still,
keeping the ground, leaving his pursuers far behind;
and, leaping upon a rock amid the woods, he sat erect
and listening, with his back to the hunter. For a moment compassion restrained the latter's arm; but that
was a short-lived mood, and as quick as thought can
follow thought his piece was levelled, and *whang!* — the
fox rolling over the rock lay dead on the ground. The
hunter still kept his place and listened to the hounds.
Still on they came, and now the near woods resounded
through all their aisles with their demoniac cry. At
length the old hound burst into view with muzzle to the
ground, and snapping the air as if possessed, and ran
directly to the rock; but spying the dead fox she suddenly
ceased her hounding, as if struck dumb with amazement,
and walked round and round him in silence ; and one
by one her pups arrived, and, like their mother, were
sobered into silence by the mystery. Then the hunter
came forward and stood in their midst, and the mystery was solved. They waited in silence while he skinned

the fox, then followed the brush a while, and at length turned off into the woods again. That evening a Weston squire came to the Concord hunter's cottage to inquire for his hounds, and told how for a week they had been hunting on their own account from Weston woods. The Concord hunter told him what he knew and offered him the skin; but the other declined it and departed. He did not find his hounds that night, but the next day learned that they had crossed the river and put up at a farm-house for the night, whence, having been well fed, they took their departure early in the morning.

The hunter who told me this could remember one Sam Nutting, who used to hunt bears on Fair Haven Ledges, and exchange their skins for rum in Concord village; who told him, even, that he had seen a moose there. Nutting had a famous foxhound named Bur-goyne, — he pronounced it Bugine, — which my inform-ant used to borrow. In the "Wast Book" of an old trader of this town, who was also a captain, town-clerk, and representative, I find the following entry. Jan. 18th, 1742-3, "John Melven Cr. by 1 Grey Fox 0 — 2 — 3;" they are not now found here; and in his ledger, Feb. 7th, 1743, Hezekiah Stratton has credit "by $\frac{1}{2}$ a Catt skin 0 — 1 — 4$\frac{1}{2}$;" of course, a wild-cat, for Stratton was a sergeant in the old French war, and would not have got credit for hunting less noble game. Credit is given for deerskins also, and they were daily sold. One man still preserves the horns of the last deer that was killed in this vicinity, and another has told me the particulars of the hunt in which his uncle was engaged. The hunters were formerly a numerous and merry crew here. I remember

well one gaunt Nimrod who would catch up a leaf by
the roadside and play a strain on it wilder and more
melodious, if my memory serves me, than any hunting-
horn.

At midnight, when there was a moon, I sometimes
met with hounds in my path prowling about the woods,
which would skulk out of my way, as if afraid, and stand
silent amid the bushes till I had passed.

Squirrels and wild mice disputed for my store of nuts.
There were scores of pitch pines around my house, from
one to four inches in diameter, which had been gnawed
by mice the previous winter, — a Norwegian winter for
them, for the snow lay long and deep, and they were
obliged to mix a large proportion of pine bark with their
other diet. These trees were alive and apparently flourishing at midsummer, and many of them had grown a
foot, though completely girdled; but after another winter such were without exception dead. It is remarkable
that a single mouse should thus be allowed a whole pine
tree for its dinner, gnawing round instead of up and
down it; but perhaps it is necessary in order to thin these
trees, which are wont to grow up densely.

The hares (*Lepus Americanus*) were very familiar.
One had her form under my house all winter, separated
from me only by the flooring, and she startled me each
morning by her hasty departure when I began to stir, —
thump, thump, thump, striking her head against the
floor timbers in her hurry. They used to come round my
door at dusk to nibble the potato parings which I had
thrown out, and were so nearly the color of the ground
that they could hardly be distinguished when still. Some-

times in the twilight I alternately lost and recovered
sight of one sitting motionless under my window. When
I opened my door in the evening, off they would go with
a squeak and a bounce. Near at hand they only excited
my pity. One evening one sat by my door two paces
from me, at first trembling with fear, yet unwilling to
move; a poor wee thing, lean and bony, with ragged
ears and sharp nose, scant tail and slender paws. It
looked as if Nature no longer contained the breed of
nobler bloods, but stood on her last toes. Its large eyes
appeared young and unhealthy, almost dropsical. I took
a step, and lo, away it scud with an elastic spring over
the snow-crust, straightening its body and its limbs into
graceful length, and soon put the forest between me and
itself, — the wild free venison, asserting its vigor and
the dignity of Nature. Not without reason was its slenderness. Such then was its nature. (*Lepus*, *levipes*, light-
foot, some think.)

What is a country without rabbits and partridges?
They are among the most simple and indigenous animal
products; ancient and venerable families known to antiquity as to modern times; of the very hue and substance
of Nature, nearest allied to leaves and to the ground, —
and to one another; it is either winged or it is legged.
It is hardly as if you had seen a wild creature when a
rabbit or a partridge bursts away, only a natural one, as
much to be expected as rustling leaves. The partridge
and the rabbit are still sure to thrive, like true natives
of the soil, whatever revolutions occur. If the forest is
cut off, the sprouts and bushes which spring up afford
them concealment, and they become more numerous

than ever. That must be a poor country indeed that does not support a hare. Our woods teem with them both, and around every swamp may be seen the partridge or rabbit walk, beset with twiggy fences and horse-hair snares, which some cow-boy tends.

XVI

THE POND IN WINTER

Aᴅᴛᴇʀ a still winter night I awoke with the impression that some question had been put to me, which I had been endeavoring in vain to answer in my sleep, as what — how — when — where? But there was dawning Nature, in whom all creatures live, looking in at my broad windows with serene and satisfied face, and no question on *her* lips. I awoke to an answered question, to Nature and daylight. The snow lying deep on the earth dotted with young pines, and the very slope of the hill on which my house is placed, seemed to say, Forward! Nature puts no question and answers none which we mortals ask. She has long ago taken her resolution. "O Prince, our eyes contemplate with admiration and transmit to the soul the wonderful and varied spectacle of this universe. The night veils without doubt a part of this glorious creation; but day comes to reveal to us this great work, which extends from earth even into the plains of the ether."

Then to my morning work. First I take an axe and pail and go in search of water, if that be not a dream. After a cold and snowy night it needed a divining-rod to find it. Every winter the liquid and trembling surface of the pond, which was so sensitive to every breath, and reflected every light and shadow, becomes solid to the depth of a foot or a foot and a half, so that it will support the heaviest teams, and perchance the snow covers it to an equal depth, and it is not to be distinguished from any level field. Like the marmots in the surrounding hills, it closes its eyelids and becomes dormant for three months or more. Standing on the snow-covered plain, as if in a pasture amid the hills, I cut my way first through a foot of snow, and then a foot of ice, and open a window under my feet, where, kneeling to drink, I look down into the quiet parlor of the fishes, pervaded by a softened light as through a window of ground glass, with its bright sanded floor the same as in summer; there a perennial waveless serenity reigns as in the amber twilight sky, corresponding to the cool and even temperament of the inhabitants. Heaven is under our feet as well as over our heads.

Early in the morning, while all things are crisp with frost, men come with fishing-reels and slender lunch, and let down their fine lines through the snowy field to take pickerel and perch; wild men, who instinctively follow other fashions and trust other authorities than their townsmen, and by their goings and comings stitch towns together in parts where else they would be ripped. They sit and eat their luncheon in stout fear-naughts on the dry oak leaves on the shore, as wise in natural lore as the citizen is in artificial. They never consulted with books, and know and can tell much less than they have done. The things which they practice are said not yet to be known. Here is one fishing for pickerel with grown perch for bait. You look into his pail with wonder as into a summer pond, as if he kept summer locked up at home, or knew where she had retreated. How, pray, did he get these in midwinter? Oh, he got worms out of rotten logs since the ground froze, and so he caught them. His life itself passes deeper in nature than the studies of the naturalist penetrate; himself a subject for the naturalist. The latter raises the moss and bark gently with his knife in search of insects; the former lays open logs to their core with his axe, and moss and bark fly far and wide. He gets his living by barking trees. Such a man has some right to fish, and I love to see nature carried out in him. The perch swallows the grub-worm, the pickerel swallows the perch, and the fisherman swallows the pickerel; and so all the chinks in the scale of being are filled.

When I strolled around the pond in misty weather I was sometimes amused by the primitive mode which some ruder fisherman had adopted. He would perhaps have placed alder branches over the narrow holes in the ice, which were four or five rods apart and an equal distance from the shore, and having fastened the end of the line to a stick to prevent its being pulled through, have passed the slack line over a twig of the alder, a foot or more above the ice, and tied a dry oak leaf to it, which, being pulled down, would show when he had a bite. These alders loomed through the mist at regular intervals as you walked half way round the pond.

Ah, the pickerel of Walden! when I see them lying on the ice, or in the well which the fisherman cuts in the ice, making a little hole to admit the water, I am always surprised by their rare beauty, as if they were fabulous fishes, they are so foreign to the streets, even to the

woods, foreign as Arabia to our Concord life. They
possess a quite dazzling and transcendent beauty which
separates them by a wide interval from the cadaverous
cod and haddock whose fame is trumpeted in our streets.
They are not green like the pines, nor gray like the
stones, nor blue like the sky; but they have, to my eyes,
if possible, yet rarer colors, like flowers and precious
stones, as if they were the pearls, the animalized *nuclei*
or crystals of the Walden water. They, of course, are
Walden all over and all through; are themselves small
Waldens in the animal kingdom, Waldenses. It is surprising that they are caught here, — that in this deep
and capacious spring, far beneath the rattling teams and
chaises and tinkling sleighs that travel the Walden road,
this great gold and emerald fish swims. I never chanced
to see its kind in any market; it would be the cynosure
of all eyes there. Easily, with a few convulsive quirks,
they give up their watery ghosts, like a mortal translated before his time to the thin air of heaven.

As I was desirous to recover the long lost bottom of
Walden Pond, I surveyed it carefully, before the ice
broke up, early in '46, with compass and chain and
sounding line. There have been many stories told about
the bottom, or rather no bottom, of this pond, which
certainly had no foundation for themselves. It is remarkable how long men will believe in the bottomless-
ness of a pond without taking the trouble to sound it. I
have visited two such Bottomless Ponds in one walk in
this neighborhood. Many have believed that Walden
reached quite through to the other side of the globe.

Some who have lain flat on the ice for a long time, looking down through the illusive medium, perchance with watery eyes into the bargain, and driven to hasty conclusions by the fear of catching cold in their breasts, have seen vast holes "into which a load of hay might be driven," if there were anybody to drive it, the undoubted source of the Styx and entrance to the Infernal Regions from these parts. Others have gone down from the village with a "fifty-six" and a wagon load of inch rope, but yet have failed to find any bottom; for while the "fifty-six" was resting by the way, they were paying out the rope in the vain attempt to fathom their truly immeasurable capacity for marvellousness. But I can assure my readers that Walden has a reasonably tight bottom at a not unreasonable, though at an unusual, depth. I fathomed it easily with a cod-line and a stone weighing about a pound and a half, and could tell accurately when the stone left the bottom, by having to pull so much harder before the water got underneath to help me. The greatest depth was exactly one hundred and two feet; to which may be added the five feet which it has risen since, making one hundred and seven. This is a remarkable depth for so small an area; yet not an inch of it can be spared by the imagination. What if all ponds were shallow? Would it not react on the minds of men? I am thankful that this pond was made deep and pure for a symbol. While men believe in the infinite some ponds will be thought to be bottomless.

A factory-owner, hearing what depth I had found, thought that it could not be true, for, judging from his acquaintance with dams, sand would not lie at so steep an

angle. But the deepest ponds are not so deep in proportion to their area as most suppose, and, if drained, would
not leave very remarkable valleys. They are not like
cups between the hills; for this one, which is so unusually
deep for its area, appears in a vertical section through its
centre not deeper than a shallow plate. Most ponds,
emptied, would leave a meadow no more hollow than
we frequently see. William Gilpin, who is so admirable
in all that relates to landscapes, and usually so correct,
standing at the head of Loch Fyne, in Scotland, which
he describes as "a bay of salt water, sixty or seventy
fathoms deep, four miles in breadth," and about fifty
miles long, surrounded by mountains, observes, "If we
could have seen it immediately after the diluvian crash,
or whatever convulsion of nature occasioned it, before
the waters gushed in, what a horrid chasm must it have
appeared!

> "So high as heaved the tumid hills, so low
> Down sunk a hollow bottom, broad, and deep,
> Capacious bed of waters ——."

But if, using the shortest diameter of Loch Fyne, we
apply these proportions to Walden, which, as we have
seen, appears already in a vertical section only like a
shallow plate, it will appear four times as shallow. So
much for the *increased* horrors of the chasm of Loch
Fyne when emptied. No doubt many a smiling valley
with its stretching cornfields occupies exactly such a
"horrid chasm," from which the waters have receded,
though it requires the insight and the far sight of the
geologist to convince the unsuspecting inhabitants of
this fact. Often an inquisitive eye may detect the shores

of a primitive lake in the low horizon hills, and no subsequent elevation of the plain have been necessary to conceal their history. But it is easiest, as they who work on the highways know, to find the hollows by the puddles after a shower. The amount of it is, the imagination, give it the least license, dives deeper and soars higher than Nature goes. So, probably, the depth of the ocean will be found to be very inconsiderable compared with its breadth.

As I sounded through the ice I could determine the shape of the bottom with greater accuracy than is possible in surveying harbors which do not freeze over, and I was surprised at its general regularity. In the deepest part there are several acres more level than almost any field which is exposed to the sun, wind, and plow. In one instance, on a line arbitrarily chosen, the depth did not vary more than one foot in thirty rods; and generally, near the middle, I could calculate the variation for each one hundred feet in any direction beforehand within three or four inches. Some are accustomed to speak of deep and dangerous holes even in quiet sandy ponds like this, but the effect of water under these circumstances is to level all inequalities. The regularity of the bottom and its conformity to the shores and the range of the neighboring hills were so perfect that a distant promontory betrayed itself in the soundings quite across the pond, and its direction could be determined by observing the opposite shore. Cape becomes bar, and plain shoal, and valley and gorge deep water and channel.

When I had mapped the pond by the scale of ten

Walden in early winter

Walden Pond in winter

rods to an inch, and put down the soundings, more than
a hundred in all, I observed this remarkable coincidence. Having noticed that the number indicating the
greatest depth was apparently in the centre of the map,
I laid a rule on the map lengthwise, and then breadth-
wise, and found, to my surprise, that the line of greatest
length intersected the line of greatest breadth *exactly*
at the point of greatest depth, notwithstanding that the
middle is so nearly level, the outline of the pond far
from regular, and the extreme length and breadth were
got by measuring into the coves; and I said to myself,
Who knows but this hint would conduct to the deepest
part of the ocean as well as of a pond or puddle? Is not
this the rule also for the height of mountains, regarded
as the opposite of valleys? We know that a hill is not
highest at its narrowest part.

Of five coves, three, or all which had been sounded,
were observed to have a bar quite across their mouths
and deeper water within, so that the bay tended to be
an expansion of water within the land not only hori-
zontally but vertically, and to form a basin or independent pond, the direction of the two capes showing the
course of the bar. Every harbor on the sea-coast, also,
has its bar at its entrance. In proportion as the mouth
of the cove was wider compared with its length, the water
over the bar was deeper compared with that in the
basin. Given, then, the length and breadth of the cove,
and the character of the surrounding shore, and you
have almost elements enough to make out a formula
for all cases.

In order to see how nearly I could guess, with this

experience, at the deepest point in a pond, by observing the outlines of its surface and the character of its shores alone, I made a plan of White Pond, which contains about forty-one acres, and, like this, has no island in it, nor any visible inlet or outlet; and as the line of greatest breadth fell very near the line of least breadth, where two opposite capes approached each other and two opposite bays receded, I ventured to mark a point a short distance from the latter line, but still on the line of greatest length, as the deepest. The deepest part was found to be within one hundred feet of this, still farther in the direction to which I had inclined, and was only one foot deeper, namely, sixty feet. Of course, a stream running through, or an island in the pond, would make the problem much more complicated.

If we knew all the laws of Nature, we should need only one fact, or the description of one actual phenomenon, to infer all the particular results at that point. Now we know only a few laws, and our result is vitiated, not, of course, by any confusion or irregularity in Nature, but by our ignorance of essential elements in the calculation. Our notions of law and harmony are commonly confined to those instances which we detect; but the harmony which results from a far greater number of seemingly conflicting, but really concurring, laws, which we have not detected, is still more wonderful. The particular laws are as our points of view, as, to the traveller, a mountain outline varies with every step, and it has an infinite number of profiles, though absolutely but one form. Even when cleft or bored through it is not comprehended in its entirety.

What I have observed of the pond is no less true in ethics. It is the law of average. Such a rule of the two diameters not only guides us toward the sun in the system and the heart in man, but draw lines through the length and breadth of the aggregate of a man's particular daily behaviors and waves of life into his coves and inlets, and where they intersect will be the height or depth of his character. Perhaps we need only to know how his shores trend and his adjacent country or circumstances, to infer his depth and concealed bottom. If he is surrounded by mountainous circumstances, an Achillean shore, whose peaks overshadow and are reflected in his bosom, they suggest a corresponding depth in him. But a low and smooth shore proves him shallow on that side. In our bodies, a bold projecting brow falls off to and indicates a corresponding depth of thought. Also there is a bar across the entrance of our every cove, or particular inclination ; each is our harbor for a season, in which we are detained and partially land-locked. These inclinations are not whimsical usually, but their form, size, and direction are determined by the promontories of the shore, the ancient axes of elevation. When this bar is gradually increased by storms, tides, or currents, or there is a subsidence of the waters, so that it reaches to the surface, that which was at first but an inclination in the shore in which a thought was harbored becomes an individual lake, cut off from the ocean, wherein the thought secures its own conditions, — changes, perhaps, from salt to fresh, becomes a sweet sea, dead sea, or a marsh. At the advent of each individual into this life, may we not suppose that such a bar has risen to the surface somewhere? It is true, we are such poor navigators that our thoughts, for the most part, stand off and on upon a harborless coast, are conversant only with the bights of the bays of poesy, or steer for the public ports of entry, and go into the dry docks of science, where they merely refit for this world, and no natural currents concur to individualize them.

As for the inlet or outlet of Walden, I have not discovered any but rain and snow and evaporation, though perhaps, with a thermometer and a line, such places may be found, for where the water flows into the pond it will probably be coldest in summer and warmest in winter. When the ice-men were at work here in '46–7, the cakes sent to the shore were one day rejected by those who were stacking them up there, not being thick enough to lie side by side with the rest; and the cutters thus discovered that the ice over a small space was two or three inches thinner than elsewhere, which made them think that there was an inlet there. They also showed me in another place what they thought was a "leach-hole," through which the pond leaked out under a hill into a neighboring meadow, pushing me out on a cake of ice to see it. It was a small cavity under ten feet of water; but I think that I can warrant the pond not to need soldering till they find a worse leak than that. One has suggested, that if such a "leach-hole" should be found, its connection with the meadow, if any existed, might be proved by conveying some colored powder or sawdust to the mouth of the hole, and then putting a strainer over the spring in the meadow, which would catch some of the particles carried through by the current.

While I was surveying, the ice, which was sixteen inches thick, undulated under a slight wind like water. It is well known that a level cannot be used on ice. At one rod from the shore its greatest fluctuation, when observed by means of a level on land directed toward a graduated staff on the ice, was three quarters of an inch, though the ice appeared firmly attached to the shore. It was probably greater in the middle. Who knows but if our instruments were delicate enough we might detect an undulation in the crust of the earth? When two legs of my level were on the shore and the third on the ice, and the sights were directed over the latter, a rise or fall of the ice of an almost infinitesimal amount made a difference of several feet on a tree across the pond. When I began to cut holes for sounding there were three or four inches of water on the ice under a deep snow which had sunk it thus far; but the water began immediately to run into these holes, and continued to run for two days in deep streams, which wore away the ice on every side, and contributed essentially, if not mainly, to dry the surface of the pond; for, as the water ran in, it raised and floated the ice. This was somewhat like cutting a hole in the bottom of a ship to let the water out. When such holes freeze, and a rain succeeds, and finally a new freezing forms a fresh smooth ice over all, it is beautifully mottled internally by dark figures, shaped somewhat like a spider's web, what you may call ice rosettes, produced by the channels worn by the water flowing from all sides to a centre. Sometimes, also, when the ice was covered with shallow puddles, I saw a double shadow of myself, one standing on the head of the other, one on the ice, the other on the trees or hillside.

While yet it is cold January, and snow and ice are thick and solid, the prudent landlord comes from the village to get ice to cool his summer drink; impressively, even pathetically, wise, to foresee the heat and thirst of July now in January, — wearing a thick coat and mittens ! when so many things are not provided for. It may be that he lays up no treasures in this world which will cool his summer drink in the next. He cuts and saws the solid pond, unroofs the house of fishes, and carts off their very element and air, held fast by chains and stakes like corded wood, through the favoring winter air, to wintry cellars, to underlie the summer there. It looks like solidified azure, as, far off, it is drawn through the streets. These ice-cutters are a merry race, full of jest and sport, and when I went among them they were wont to invite me to saw pit-fashion with them, I standing underneath.

In the winter of '46-7 there came a hundred men of Hyperborean extraction swoop down on to our pond one morning, with many carloads of ungainly-looking farming tools, — sleds, plows, drill-barrows, turf-knives, spades, saws, rakes, and each man was armed with a double-pointed pike-staff, such as is not described in the New-England Farmer or the Cultivator. I did not know whether they had come to sow a crop of winter rye, or some other kind of grain recently intro-

duced from Iceland. As I saw no manure, I judged that
they meant to skim the land, as I had done, thinking
the soil was deep and had lain fallow long enough.
They said that a gentleman farmer, who was behind
the scenes, wanted to double his money, which, as I
understood, amounted to half a million already; but in
order to cover each one of his dollars with another, he
took off the only coat, ay, the skin itself, of Walden
Pond in the midst of a hard winter. They went to work
at once, plowing, harrowing, rolling, furrowing, in admirable order, as if they were bent on making this a
model farm; but when I was looking sharp to see what
kind of seed they dropped into the furrow, a gang of
fellows by my side suddenly began to hook up the
virgin mould itself, with a peculiar jerk, clean down
to the sand, or rather the water, — for it was a very
springy soil, — indeed all the *terra firma* there was, —
and haul it away on sleds, and then I guessed that they
must be cutting peat in a bog. So they came and went
every day, with a peculiar shriek from the locomotive,
from and to some point of the polar regions, as it seemed
to me, like a flock of arctic snowbirds. But sometimes
Squaw Walden had her revenge, and a hired man, walking behind his team, slipped through a crack in the
ground down toward Tartarus, and he who was so
brave before suddenly became but the ninth part of a
man, almost gave up his animal heat, and was glad to
take refuge in my house, and acknowledged that there
was some virtue in a stove; or sometimes the frozen
soil took a piece of steel out of a plowshare, or a plow got
set in the furrow and had to be cut out.

To speak literally, a hundred Irishmen, with Yankee overseers, came from Cambridge every day to get out the ice. They divided it into cakes by methods too well known to require description, and these, being sledded to the shore, were rapidly hauled off on to an ice plat-form, and raised by grappling irons and block and tackle, worked by horses, on to a stack, as surely as so many barrels of flour, and there placed evenly side by side, and row upon row, as if they formed the solid base of an obelisk designed to pierce the clouds. They told me that in a good day they could get out a thousand tons, which was the yield of about one acre. Deep ruts and "cradle-holes" were worn in the ice, as on *terra firma*, by the passage of the sleds over the same track, and the horses invariably ate their oats out of cakes of ice hollowed out like buckets. They stacked up the cakes thus in the open air in a pile thirty-five feet high on one side and six or seven rods square, putting hay between the outside layers to exclude the air; for when the wind, though never so cold, finds a passage through, it will wear large cavities, leaving slight supports or studs only here and there, and finally topple it down. At first it looked like a vast blue fort or Valhalla; but when they began to tuck the coarse meadow hay into the crevices, and this became covered with rime and icicles, it looked like a venerable moss-grown and hoary ruin, built of azure-tinted marble, the abode of Winter, that old man we see in the almanac, — his shanty, as if he had a design to estivate with us. They calculated that not twenty-five per cent. of this would reach its destination, and that two or three per cent. would be wasted in the cars. However, a still greater part of this heap had a different destiny from what was intended; for, either because the ice was found not to keep so well as was expected, containing more air than usual, or for some other reason, it never got to market. This heap, made in the winter of '46–7 and estimated to contain ten thousand tons, was finally covered with hay and boards; and though it was unroofed the following July, and a part of it carried off, the rest remaining exposed to the sun, it stood over that summer and the next winter, and was not quite melted till September, 1848. Thus the pond recovered the greater part.

Like the water, the Walden ice, seen near at hand, has a green tint, but at a distance is beautifully blue, and you can easily tell it from the white ice of the river, or the merely greenish ice of some ponds, a quarter of a mile off. Sometimes one of those great cakes slips from the ice-man's sled into the village street, and lies there for a week like a great emerald, an object of interest to all passers. I have noticed that a portion of Walden which in the state of water was green will often, when frozen, appear from the same point of view blue. So the hollows about this pond will, sometimes, in the winter, be filled with a greenish water somewhat like its own, but the next day will have frozen blue. Perhaps the blue color of water and ice is due to the light and air they contain, and the most transparent is the bluest. Ice is an interesting subject for contemplation. They told me that they had some in the ice-houses at Fresh Pond five years old which was as good as ever. Why is it that a bucket of water soon becomes putrid, but frozen remains sweet forever? It is commonly said that this is the difference between the affections and the intellect.

Thus for sixteen days I saw from my window a hundred men at work like busy husbandmen, with teams and horses and apparently all the implements of farming, such a picture as we see on the first page of the almanac; and as often as I looked out I was reminded of the fable of the lark and the reapers, or the parable of the sower, and the like; and now they are all gone, and in thirty days more, probably, I shall look from the same window on the pure sea-green Walden water there, reflecting the clouds and the trees, and sending up its evaporations in solitude, and no traces will appear that a man has ever stood there. Perhaps I shall hear a solitary loon laugh as hc dives and plumes himself, or shall see a lonely fisher in his boat, like a floating leaf, beholding his form reflected in the waves, where lately a hundred men securely labored.

Thus it appears that the sweltering inhabitants of Charleston and New Orleans, of Madras and Bombay and Calcutta, drink at my well. In the morning I bathe my intellect in the stupendous and cosmogonal philosophy of the Bhagvat-Geeta, since whose composition years of the gods have elapsed, and in comparison with which our modern world and its literature seem puny and trivial; and I doubt if that philosophy is not to be referred to a previous state of existence, so remote is its sublimity from our conceptions. I lay down the book and go to my well for water, and lo! there I meet the servant of the Bramin, priest of Brahma and Vishnu and

Indra, who still sits in his temple on the Ganges reading the Vedas, or dwells at the root of a tree with his crust and water jug. I meet his servant come to draw water for his master, and our buckets as it were grate together in the same well. The pure Walden water is mingled with the sacred water of the Ganges. With favoring winds it is wafted past the site of the fabulous islands of Atlantis and the Hesperides, makes the periplus of Hanno, and, floating by Ternate and Tidore and the mouth of the Persian Gulf, melts in the tropic gales of the Indian seas, and is landed in ports of which Alexander only heard the names.

XVII

SPRING

THE opening of large tracts by the ice-cutters commonly causes a pond to break up earlier; for the water, agitated by the wind, even in cold weather, wears away the surrounding ice. But such was not the effect on Walden that year, for she had soon got a thick new garment to take the place of the old. This pond never breaks up so soon as the others in this neighborhood, on account both of its greater depth and its having no stream passing through it to melt or wear away the ice. I never knew it to open in the course of a winter, not excepting that of '52–3, which gave the ponds so severe a trial. It commonly opens about the first of April, a week or ten days later than Flint's Pond and Fair Haven, beginning to melt on the north side and in the shallower parts where it began to freeze. It indicates better than any water hereabouts the absolute progress of the season, being least affected by transient changes of temperature. A severe cold of a few days' duration in March may very much retard the opening of the former ponds, while the temperature of Walden increases almost uninterruptedly. A thermometer thrust into the middle of Walden on the 6th of March, 1847, stood at 32°, or freezing point; near the shore at 33°; in the middle of Flint's Pond, the same day, at 32½°;

at a dozen rods from the shore, in shallow water, under
ice a foot thick, at 36°. This difference of three and a
half degrees between the temperature of the deep water
and the shallow in the latter pond, and the fact that a
great proportion of it is comparatively shallow, show
why it should break up so much sooner than Walden.
The ice in the shallowest part was at this time several
inches thinner than in the middle. In midwinter the
middle had been the warmest and the ice thinnest there.
So, also, every one who has waded about the shores
of a pond in summer must have perceived how much
warmer the water is close to the shore, where only three
or four inches deep, than a little distance out, and on
the surface where it is deep, than near the bottom. In
spring the sun not only exerts an influence through
the increased temperature of the air and earth, but its
heat passes through ice a foot or more thick, and is reflected from the bottom in shallow water, and so also
warms the water and melts the under side of the ice, at
the same time that it is melting it more directly above,
making it uneven, and causing the air bubbles which
it contains to extend themselves upward and downward until it is completely honeycombed, and at last
disappears suddenly in a single spring rain. Ice has its
grain as well as wood, and when a cake begins to rot or
"comb," that is, assume the appearance of honeycomb,
whatever may be its position, the air cells are at right
angles with what was the water surface. Where there
is a rock or a log rising near to the surface the ice over
it is much thinner, and is frequently quite dissolved by
this reflected heat; and I have been told that in the

experiment at Cambridge to freeze water in a shallow wooden pond, though the cold air circulated underneath, and so had access to both sides, the reflection of the sun from the bottom more than counterbalanced this advantage. When a warm rain in the middle of the winter melts off the snow ice from Walden, and leaves a hard dark or transparent ice on the middle, there will be a strip of rotten though thicker white ice, a rod or more wide, about the shores, created by this reflected heat. Also, as I have said, the bubbles themselves within the ice operate as burning-glasses to melt the ice beneath.

The phenomena of the year take place every day in a pond on a small scale. Every morning, generally speaking, the shallow water is being warmed more rapidly than the deep, though it may not be made so warm after all, and every evening it is being cooled more rapidly until the morning. The day is an epitome of the year. The night is the winter, the morning and evening are the spring and fall, and the noon is the summer. The cracking and booming of the ice indicate a change of temperature. One pleasant morning after a cold night, February 24th, 1850, having gone to Flint's Pond to spend the day, I noticed with surprise, that when I struck the ice with the head of my axe, it resounded like a gong for many rods around, or as if I had struck on a tight drum-head. The pond began to boom about an hour after sunrise, when it felt the influence of the sun's rays slanted upon it from over the hills; it stretched itself and yawned like a waking man with a gradually increasing tumult, which was kept up three or four hours. It took a short siesta at noon, and boomed once more toward night, as the sun was withdrawing his influence. In the right stage of the weather a pond fires its evening gun with great regularity. But in the middle of the day, being full of cracks, and the air also being less elastic, it had completely lost its resonance, and probably fishes and muskrats could not then have been stunned by a blow on it. The fishermen say that the "thundering of the pond" scares the fishes and prevents their biting. The pond does not thunder every evening, and I cannot tell surely when to expect its thundering; but though I may perceive no difference in the weather, it does. Who would have suspected so large and cold and thick-skinned a thing to be so sensitive? Yet it has its law to which it thunders obedience when it should as surely as the buds expand in the spring. The earth is all alive and covered with papillæ. The largest pond is as sensitive to atmospheric changes as the globule of mercury in its tube.

One attraction in coming to the woods to live was that I should have leisure and opportunity to see the Spring come in. The ice in the pond at length begins to be honeycombed, and I can set my heel in it as I walk. Fogs and rains and warmer suns are gradually melting the snow; the days have grown sensibly longer; and I see how I shall get through the winter without adding to my wood-pile, for large fires are no longer necessary. I am on the alert for the first signs of spring, to hear the chance note of some arriving bird, or the striped squirrel's chirp, for his stores must be now nearly exhausted, or see the woodchuck venture out of his winter quarters. On the 13th of March, after I had

heard the bluebird, song sparrow, and red-wing, the
ice was still nearly a foot thick. As the weather grew
warmer it was not sensibly worn away by the water,
nor broken up and floated off as in rivers, but, though
it was completely melted for half a rod in width about
the shore, the middle was merely honeycombed and
saturated with water, so that you could put your foot
through it when six inches thick; but by the next day
evening, perhaps, after a warm rain followed by fog,
it would have wholly disappeared, all gone off with the
fog, spirited away. One year I went across the middle
only five days before it disappeared entirely. In 1845
Walden was first completely open on the 1st of April;
in '46, the 25th of March; in '47, the 8th of April; in
'51, the 28th of March; in '52, the 18th of April; in '53,
the 23d of March; in '54, about the 7th of April.

Every incident connected with the breaking up of the
rivers and ponds and the settling of the weather is
particularly interesting to us who live in a climate of
so great extremes. When the warmer days come, they
who dwell near the river hear the ice crack at night
with a startling whoop as loud as artillery, as if its icy
fetters were rent from end to end, and within a few days
see it rapidly going out. So the alligator comes out of
the mud with quakings of the earth. One old man, who
has been a close observer of Nature, and seems as
thoroughly wise in regard to all her operations as if she
had been put upon the stocks when he was a boy, and
he had helped to lay her keel, — who has come to his
growth, and can hardly acquire more of natural lore
if he should live to the age of Methuselah, — told me —

and I was surprised to hear him express wonder at any
of Nature's operations, for I thought that there were
no secrets between them — that one spring day he took
his gun and boat, and thought that he would have a
little sport with the ducks. There was ice still on the
meadows, but it was all gone out of the river, and he
dropped down without obstruction from Sudbury,
where he lived, to Fair Haven Pond, which he found,
unexpectedly, covered for the most part with a firm
field of ice. It was a warm day, and he was surprised to
see so great a body of ice remaining. Not seeing any
ducks, he hid his boat on the north or back side of an
island in the pond, and then concealed himself in the
bushes on the south side, to await them. The ice was
melted for three or four rods from the shore, and there
was a smooth and warm sheet of water, with a muddy
bottom, such as the ducks love, within, and he thought
it likely that some would be along pretty soon. After
he had lain still there about an hour he heard a low
and seemingly very distant sound, but singularly grand
and impressive, unlike anything he had ever heard,
gradually swelling and increasing as if it would have a
universal and memorable ending, a sullen rush and
roar, which seemed to him all at once like the sound of
a vast body of fowl coming in to settle there, and, seizing his gun, he started up in haste and excited; but he
found, to his surprise, that the whole body of the ice
had started while he lay there, and drifted in to the
shore, and the sound he had heard was made by its
edge grating on the shore, — at first gently nibbled and
crumbled off, but at length heaving up and scattering

its wrecks along the island to a considerable height before it came to a stand still.

At length the sun's rays have attained the right angle, and warm winds blow up mist and rain and melt the snowbanks, and the sun dispersing the mist smiles on a checkered landscape of russet and white smoking with incense, through which the traveller picks his way from islet to islet, cheered by the music of a thousand tinkling rills and rivulets whose veins are filled with the blood of winter which they are bearing off.

Few phenomena gave me more delight than to observe the forms which thawing sand and clay assume in flowing down the sides of a deep cut on the railroad through which I passed on my way to the village, a phenomenon not very common on so large a scale, though the number of freshly exposed banks of the right material must have been greatly multiplied since railroads were invented. The material was sand of every degree of fineness and of various rich colors, commonly mixed with a little clay. When the frost comes out in the spring, and even in a thawing day in the winter, the sand begins to flow down the slopes like lava, sometimes bursting out through the snow and overflowing it where no sand was to be seen before. Innumerable little streams overlap and interlace one with another, exhibiting a sort of hybrid product, which obeys half way the law of currents, and half way that of vegetation. As it flows it takes the forms of sappy leaves or vines, making heaps of pulpy sprays a foot or more in depth, and resembling, as you look down on them, the laciniated, lobed, and imbricated thalluses of some lichens; or you are re-

minded of coral, of leopards' paws or birds' feet, of
brains or lungs or bowels, and excrements of all kinds.
It is a truly *grotesque* vegetation, whose forms and color
we see imitated in bronze, a sort of architectural foliage
more ancient and typical than acanthus, chiccory, ivy,
vine, or any vegetable leaves; destined perhaps, under
some circumstances, to become a puzzle to future
geologists. The whole cut impressed me as if it were a
cave with its stalactites laid open to the light. The various shades of the sand are singularly rich and agreeable, embracing the different iron colors, brown, gray,
yellowish, and reddish. When the flowing mass reaches
the drain at the foot of the bank it spreads out flatter
into *strands*, the separate streams losing their semi-
cylindrical form and gradually becoming more flat and
broad, running together as they are more moist, till they
form an almost flat *sand*, still variously and beautifully
shaded, but in which you can trace the original forms
of vegetation; till at length, in the water itself, they are
converted into *banks*, like those formed off the mouths
of rivers, and the forms of vegetation are lost in the
ripple-marks on the bottom.

The whole bank, which is from twenty to forty feet
high, is sometimes overlaid with a mass of this kind of
foliage, or sandy rupture, for a quarter of a mile on one
or both sides, the produce of one spring day. What
makes this sand foliage remarkable is its springing into
existence thus suddenly. When I see on the one side
the inert bank, — for the sun acts on one side first, —
and on the other this luxuriant foliage, the creation of
an hour, I am affected as if in a peculiar sense I stood

in the laboratory of the Artist who made the world and me, — had come to where he was still at work, sporting on this bank, and with excess of energy strewing his fresh designs about. I feel as if I were nearer to the vitals of the globe, for this sandy overflow is something such a foliaceous mass as the vitals of the animal body. You find thus in the very sands an anticipation of the vegetable leaf. No wonder that the earth expresses itself outwardly in leaves, it so labors with the idea inwardly. The atoms have already learned this law, and are pregnant by it. The overhanging leaf sees here its prototype. *Internally*, whether in the globe or animal body, it is a moist thick *lobe*, a word especially applicable to the liver and lungs and the *leaves* of fat (λείβω, *labor*, *lapsus*, to flow or slip downward, a lapsing; λοβός, *globus*, lobe, globe; also lap, flap, and many other words); *externally*, a dry thin *leaf*, even as the *f* and *v* are a pressed and dried *b*. The radicals of *lobe* are *lb*, the soft mass of the *b* (single-lobed, or B, double-lobed), with the liquid *l* behind it pressing it forward. In globe, *glb*, the guttural *g* adds to the meaning the capacity of the throat. The feathers and wings of birds are still drier and thinner leaves. Thus, also, you pass from the lumpish grub in the earth to the airy and fluttering butterfly. The very globe continually transcends and translates itself, and becomes winged in its orbit. Even ice begins with delicate crystal leaves, as if it had flowed into moulds which the fronds of water-plants have impressed on the watery mirror. The whole tree itself is but one leaf, and rivers are still vaster leaves whose pulp is intervening earth, and towns and cities are the ova of insects in their axils.

When the sun withdraws the sand ceases to flow,
but in the morning the streams will start once more and
branch and branch again into a myriad of others. You
here see perchance how blood-vessels are formed. If you
look closely you observe that first there pushes forward
from the thawing mass a stream of softened sand with
a drop-like point, like the ball of the finger, feeling its
way slowly and blindly downward, until at last with
more heat and moisture, as the sun gets higher, the
most fluid portion, in its effort to obey the law to which
the most inert also yields, separates from the latter
and forms for itself a meandering channel or artery
within that, in which is seen a little silvery stream glancing like lightning from one stage of pulpy leaves or
branches to another, and ever and anon swallowed up
in the sand. It is wonderful how rapidly yet perfectly
the sand organizes itself as it flows, using the best
material its mass affords to form the sharp edges of its
channel. Such are the sources of rivers. In the silicious
matter which the water deposits is perhaps the bony
system, and in the still finer soil and organic matter the
fleshy fibre or cellular tissue. What is man but a mass
of thawing clay? The ball of the human finger is but a
drop congealed. The fingers and toes flow to their extent from the thawing mass of the body. Who knows
what the human body would expand and flow out to
under a more genial heaven? Is not the hand a spreading *palm* leaf with its lobes and veins? The ear may be
regarded, fancifully, as a lichen, *umbilicaria*, on the
side of the head, with its lobe or drop. The lip —
labium, from *labor* (?) — laps or lapses from the sides

of the cavernous mouth. The nose is a manifest congealed drop or stalactite. The chin is a still larger drop,
the confluent dripping of the face. The cheeks are a
slide from the brows into the valley of the face, opposed
and diffused by the cheek bones. Each rounded lobe
of the vegetable leaf, too, is a thick and now loitering
drop, larger or smaller; the lobes are the fingers of the
leaf; and as many lobes as it has, in so many directions
it tends to flow, and more heat or other genial influences
would have caused it to flow yet farther.

Thus it seemed that this one hillside illustrated the
principle of all the operations of Nature. The Maker
of this earth but patented a leaf. What Champollion
will decipher this hieroglyphic for us, that we may turn
over a new leaf at last? This phenomenon is more
exhilarating to me than the luxuriance and fertility of
vineyards. True, it is somewhat excrementitious in its
character, and there is no end to the heaps of liver,
lights, and bowels, as if the globe were turned wrong
side outward; but this suggests at least that Nature has
some bowels, and there again is mother of humanity.
This is the frost coming out of the ground; this is
Spring. It precedes the green and flowery spring, as
mythology precedes regular poetry. I know of nothing
more purgative of winter fumes and indigestions. It
convinces me that Earth is still in her swaddling-
clothes, and stretches forth baby fingers on every side.
Fresh curls spring from the baldest brow. There is nothing inorganic. These foliaceous heaps lie along the
bank like the slag of a furnace, showing that Nature
is "in full blast" within. The earth is not a mere frag-

ment of dead history, stratum upon stratum like the
leaves of a book, to be studied by geologists and anti-
quaries chiefly, but living poetry like the leaves of a
tree, which precede flowers and fruit, — not a fossil
earth, but a living earth; compared with whose great
central life all animal and vegetable life is merely parasitic. Its throes will heave our exuviæ from their graves.
You may melt your metals and cast them into the most
beautiful moulds you can; they will never excite me
like the forms which this molten earth flows out into.
And not only it, but the institutions upon it are plastic
like clay in the hands of the potter.

Ere long, not only on these banks, but on every hill
and plain and in every hollow, the frost comes out of the
ground like a dormant quadruped from its burrow,
and seeks the sea with music, or migrates to other
climes in clouds. Thaw with his gentle persuasion is
more powerful than Thor with his hammer. The one
melts, the other but breaks in pieces.

When the ground was partially bare of snow, and a
few warm days had dried its surface somewhat, it was
pleasant to compare the first tender signs of the infant
year just peeping forth with the stately beauty of the
withered vegetation which had withstood the winter, —
life-everlasting, goldenrods, pinweeds, and graceful wild
grasses, more obvious and interesting frequently than
in summer even, as if their beauty was not ripe till
then ; even cotton-grass, cat-tails, mulleins, johnswort,
hardhack, meadow-sweet, and other strong-stemmed
plants, those unexhausted granaries which entertain
the earliest birds, — decent weeds, at least, which

widowed Nature wears. I am particularly attracted
by the arching and sheaf-like top of the wool-grass;
it brings back the summer to our winter memories,
and is among the forms which art loves to copy, and
which, in the vegetable kingdom, have the same relation
to types already in the mind of man that astronomy
has. It is an antique style, older than Greek or Egyptian. Many of the phenomena of Winter are suggestive
of an inexpressible tenderness and fragile delicacy.
We are accustomed to hear this king described as a rude
and boisterous tyrant; but with the gentleness of a
lover he adorns the tresses of Summer.

At the approach of spring the red squirrels got under
my house, two at a time, directly under my feet as I sat
reading or writing, and kept up the queerest chuckling
and chirruping and vocal pirouetting and gurgling
sounds that ever were heard; and when I stamped
they only chirruped the louder, as if past all fear and
respect in their mad pranks, defying humanity to stop
them. No, you don't — chickaree — chickaree. They
were wholly deaf to my arguments, or failed to perceive
their force, and fell into a strain of invective that was
irresistible.

The first sparrow of spring! The year beginning with
younger hope than ever! The faint silvery warblings
heard over the partially bare and moist fields from the
bluebird, the song sparrow, and the red-wing, as if the
last flakes of winter tinkled as they fell! What at such
a time are histories, chronologies, traditions, and all
written revelations? The brooks sing carols and glees
to the spring. The marsh hawk, sailing low over the

meadow, is already seeking the first slimy life that
awakes. The sinking sound of melting snow is heard in
all dells, and the ice dissolves apace in the ponds. The
grass flames up on the hillsides like a spring fire, — " et
primitus oritur herba imbribus primoribus evocata,"
— as if the earth sent forth an inward heat to greet the
returning sun; not yellow but green is the color of its
flame; — the symbol of perpetual youth, the grass-blade,
like a long green ribbon, streams from the sod into the
summer, checked indeed by the frost, but anon pushing
on again, lifting its spear of last year's hay with the
fresh life below. It grows as steadily as the rill oozes
out of the ground. It is almost identical with that, for
in the growing days of June, when the rills are dry, the
grass-blades are their channels, and from year to year
the herds drink at this perennial green stream, and the
mower draws from it betimes their winter supply. So
our human life but dies down to its root, and still puts
forth its green blade to eternity.

Walden is melting apace. There is a canal two rods
wide along the northerly and westerly sides, and wider
still at the east end. A great field of ice has cracked off
from the main body. I hear a song sparrow singing
from the bushes on the shore, — *olit, olit, olit,* — *chip,
chip, chip, che char,* — *che wiss, wiss, wiss.* He too is
helping to crack it. How handsome the great sweeping
curves in the edge of the ice, answering somewhat to
those of the shore, but more regular ! It is unusually
hard, owing to the recent severe but transient cold, and
all watered or waved like a palace floor. But the wind
slides eastward over its opaque surface in vain, till it

reaches the living surface beyond. It is glorious to behold this ribbon of water sparkling in the sun, the bare face of the pond full of glee and youth, as if it spoke the joy of the fishes within it, and of the sands on its shore, — a silvery sheen as from the scales of a leuciscus, as it were all one active fish. Such is the contrast between winter and spring. Walden was dead and is alive again. But this spring it broke up more steadily, as I have said.

The change from storm and winter to serene and mild weather, from dark and sluggish hours to bright and elastic ones, is a memorable crisis which all things proclaim. It is seemingly instantaneous at last. Suddenly an influx of light filled my house, though the evening was at hand, and the clouds of winter still overhung it, and the eaves were dripping with sleety rain. I looked out the window, and lo! where yesterday was cold gray ice there lay the transparent pond already calm and full of hope as in a summer evening, reflecting a summer evening sky in its bosom, though none was visible overhead, as if it had intelligence with some remote horizon. I heard a robin in the distance, the first I had heard for many a thousand years, methought, whose note I shall not forget for many a thousand more, — the same sweet and powerful song as of yore. O the evening robin, at the end of a New England summer day! If I could ever find the twig he sits upon! I mean *he;* I mean *the twig*. This at least is not the *Turdus migratorius*. The pitch pines and shrub oaks about my house, which had so long drooped, suddenly resumed their several characters, looked brighter, greener, and more erect and alive, as if effectually cleansed and restored by the rain. I knew

that it would not rain any more. You may tell by looking at any twig of the forest, ay, at your very wood-pile,
whether its winter is past or not. As it grew darker, I was
startled by the honking of geese flying low over the woods,
like weary travellers getting in late from Southern lakes,
and indulging at last in unrestrained complaint and
mutual consolation. Standing at my door, I could hear
the rush of their wings; when, driving toward my house,
they suddenly spied my light, and with hushed clamor
wheeled and settled in the pond. So I came in, and shut
the door, and passed my first spring night in the woods.

In the morning I watched the geese from the door
through the mist, sailing in the middle of the pond, fifty
rods off, so large and tumultuous that Walden appeared
like an artificial pond for their amusement. But when
I stood on the shore they at once rose up with a great
flapping of wings at the signal of their commander, and
when they had got into rank circled about over my
head, twenty-nine of them, and then steered straight
to Canada, with a regular *honk* from the leader at intervals, trusting to break their fast in muddier pools. A
"plump" of ducks rose at the same time and took the
route to the north in the wake of their noisier cousins.

For a week I heard the circling, groping clangor of
some solitary goose in the foggy mornings, seeking its
companion, and still peopling the woods with the sound
of a larger life than they could sustain. In April the
pigeons were seen again flying express in small flocks,
and in due time I heard the martins twittering over my
clearing, though it had not seemed that the township
contained so many that it could afford me any, and I

fancied that they were peculiarly of the ancient race that dwelt in hollow trees ere white men came. In almost all climes the tortoise and the frog are among the precursors and heralds of this season, and birds fly with song and glancing plumage, and plants spring and bloom, and winds blow, to correct this slight oscillation of the poles and preserve the equilibrium of nature.

As every season seems best to us in its turn, so the coming in of spring is like the creation of Cosmos out of Chaos and the realization of the Golden Age. —

"Eurus ad Auroram, Nabathacaque regna recessit,
Persidaque, et radiis juga subdita matutinis."

"The East-Wind withdrew to Aurora and the Nabathæan kingdom,
And the Persian, and the ridges placed under the morning rays.
. . . .
Man was born. Whether that Artificer of things,
The origin of a better world, made him from the divine seed;
Or the earth, being recent and lately sundered from the high
Ether, retained some seeds of cognate heaven."

A single gentle rain makes the grass many shades greener. So our prospects brighten on the influx of better thoughts. We should be blessed if we lived in the present always, and took advantage of every accident that befell us, like the grass which confesses the influence of the slightest dew that falls on it; and did not spend our time in atoning for the neglect of past opportunities, which we call doing our duty. We loiter in winter while it is already spring. In a pleasant spring morning all men's sins are forgiven. Such a day is a truce to vice. While such a sun holds out to burn, the vilest sinner may return. Through our own recovered innocence

we discern the innocence of our neighbors. You may
have known your neighbor yesterday for a thief, a drunk-
ard, or a sensualist, and merely pitied or despised him,
and despaired of the world; but the sun shines bright and
warm this first spring morning, recreating the world, and
you meet him at some serene work, and see how his
exhausted and debauched veins expand with still joy
and bless the new day, feel the spring influence with the
innocence of infancy, and all his faults are forgotten.
There is not only an atmosphere of good will about him,
but even a savor of holiness groping for expression,
blindly and ineffectually perhaps, like a new-born instinct, and for a short hour the south hillside echoes to
no vulgar jest. You see some innocent fair shoots preparing to burst from his gnarled rind and try another
year's life, tender and fresh as the youngest plant.
Even he has entered into the joy of his Lord. Why the
jailer does not leave open his prison doors, — why the
judge does not dismiss his case, — why the preacher
does not dismiss his congregation! It is because they do
not obey the hint which God gives them, nor accept the
pardon which he freely offers to all.

"A return to goodness produced each day in the tran-
quil and beneficent breath of the morning, causes that in
respect to the love of virtue and the hatred of vice, one
approaches a little the primitive nature of man, as the
sprouts of the forest which has been felled. In like manner the evil which one does in the interval of a day prevents the germs of virtues which began to spring up again
from developing themselves and destroys them.

"After the germs of virtue have thus been prevented

many times from developing themselves, then the beneficent breath of evening does not suffice to preserve them. As soon as the breath of evening does not suffice longer to preserve them, then the nature of man does not differ much from that of the brute. Men seeing the nature of this man like that of the brute, think that he has never possessed the innate faculty of reason. Are those the true and natural sentiments of man?"

"The Golden Age was first created, which without any avenger
Spontaneously without law cherished fidelity and rectitude.
Punishment and fear were not; nor were threatening words read
On suspended brass; nor did the suppliant crowd fear
The words of their judge; but were safe without an avenger.
Not yet the pine felled on its mountains had descended
To the liquid waves that it might see a foreign world,
And mortals knew no shores but their own.
.   .   .   .
There was eternal spring, and placid zephyrs with warm
Blasts soothed the flowers born without seed."

On the 29th of April, as I was fishing from the bank of the river near the Nine-Acre-Corner bridge, standing on the quaking grass and willow roots, where the muskrats lurk, I heard a singular rattling sound, somewhat like that of the sticks which boys play with their fingers, when, looking up, I observed a very slight and graceful hawk, like a nighthawk, alternately soaring like a ripple and tumbling a rod or two over and over, showing the under side of its wings, which gleamed like a satin ribbon in the sun, or like the pearly inside of a shell. This sight reminded me of falconry and what nobleness and poetry are associated with that sport. The merlin it seemed to me it might be called: but I care not for its name. It was the most ethereal flight I had ever witnessed. It did not simply flutter like a butterfly, nor soar like the larger hawks, but it sported with proud reliance in the fields of air; mounting again and again with its strange chuckle, it repeated its free and beautiful fall, turning over and over like a kite, and then recovering from its lofty tumbling, as if it had never set its foot on *terra firma*. It appeared to have no companion in the universe, — sporting there alone, — and to need none but the morning and the ether with which it played. It was not lonely, but made all the earth lonely beneath it. Where was the parent which hatched it, its kindred, and its father in the heavens? The tenant of the air, it seemed related to the earth but by an egg hatched some time in the crevice of a crag; — or was its native nest made in the angle of a cloud, woven of the rainbow's trimmings and the sunset sky, and lined with some soft midsummer haze caught up from earth? Its eyry now some cliffy cloud.

Beside this I got a rare mess of golden and silver and bright cupreous fishes, which looked like a string of jewels. Ah! I have penetrated to those meadows on the morning of many a first spring day, jumping from hummock to hummock, from willow root to willow root, when the wild river valley and the woods were bathed in so pure and bright a light as would have waked the dead, if they had been slumbering in their graves, as some suppose. There needs no stronger proof of immortality. All things must live in such a light. O Death, where was thy sting? O Grave, where was thy victory, then?

Our village life would stagnate if it were not for the un-

explored forests and meadows which surround it. We
need the tonic of wildness, — to wade sometimes in
marshes where the bittern and the meadow-hen lurk,
and hear the booming of the snipe; to smell the whisper-
ing sedge where only some wilder and more solitary fowl
builds her nest, and the mink crawls with its belly close
to the ground. At the same time that we are earnest to
explore and learn all things, we require that all things be
mysterious and unexplorable, that land and sea be infinitely wild, unsurveyed and unfathomed by us because
unfathomable. We can never have enough of nature.
We must be refreshed by the sight of inexhaustible vigor,
vast and titanic features, the sea-coast with its wrecks,
the wilderness with its living and its decaying trees, the
thunder-cloud, and the rain which lasts three weeks and
produces freshets. We need to witness our own limits
transgressed, and some life pasturing freely where we
never wander. We are cheered when we observe the vul-
ture feeding on the carrion which disgusts and disheart-
ens us, and deriving health and strength from the repast.
There was a dead horse in the hollow by the path to my
house, which compelled me sometimes to go out of my
way, especially in the night when the air was heavy, but
the assurance it gave me of the strong appetite and in-
violable health of Nature was my compensation for this.
I love to see that Nature is so rife with life that myriads
can be afforded to be sacrificed and suffered to prey on
one another; that tender organizations can be so serenely
squashed out of existence like pulp, — tadpoles which
herons gobble up, and tortoises and toads run over in the
road; and that sometimes it has rained flesh and blood!

With the liability to accident, we must see how little account is to be made of it. The impression made on a wise man is that of universal innocence. Poison is not poisonous after all, nor are any wounds fatal. Compassion is a very untenable ground. It must be expeditious. Its pleadings will not bear to be stereotyped.

Early in May, the oaks, hickories, maples, and other trees, just putting out amidst the pine woods around the pond, imparted a brightness like sunshine to the landscape, especially in cloudy days, as if the sun were breaking through mists and shining faintly on the hillsides here and there. On the third or fourth of May I saw a loon in the pond, and during the first week of the month I heard the whip-poor-will, the brown thrasher, the veery, the wood pewee, the chewink, and other birds. I had heard the wood thrush long before. The phœbe had already come once more and looked in at my door and window, to see if my house was cavern-like enough for her, sustaining herself on humming wings with clinched talons, as if she held by the air, while she surveyed the premises. The sulphur-like pollen of the pitch pine soon covered the pond and the stones and rotten wood along the shore, so that you could have collected a barrelful. This is the "sulphur showers" we hear of. Even in Calidas' drama of Sacontala, we read of "rills dyed yellow with the golden dust of the lotus." And so the seasons went rolling on into summer, as one rambles into higher and higher grass.

Thus was my first year's life in the woods completed; and the second year was similar to it. I finally left Walden September 6th, 1847.

XVIII

CONCLUSION

To the sick the doctors wisely recommend a change of air and scenery. Thank Heaven, here is not all the world. The buckeye does not grow in New England, and the mockingbird is rarely heard here. The wild goose is more of a cosmopolite than we; he breaks his fast in Canada, takes a luncheon in the Ohio, and plumes himself for the night in a southern bayou. Even the bison, to some extent, keeps pace with the seasons, cropping the pastures of the Colorado only till a greener and sweeter grass awaits him by the Yellowstone. Yet we think that if rail fences are pulled down, and stone walls piled up on our farms, bounds are henceforth set to our lives and our fates decided. If you are chosen town clerk, forsooth, you cannot go to Tierra del Fuego this summer: but you may go to the land of infernal fire nevertheless. The universe is wider than our views of it.

Yet we should oftener look over the tafferel of our craft, like curious passengers, and not make the voyage like stupid sailors picking oakum. The other side of the globe is but the home of our correspondent. Our voyaging is only great-circle sailing, and the doctors prescribe for diseases of the skin merely. One hastens to southern Africa to chase the giraffe; but surely that is

not the game he would be after. How long, pray, would
a man hunt giraffes if he could? Snipes and woodcocks
also may afford rare sport; but I trust it would be nobler
game to shoot one's self. —

> "Direct your eye right inward, and you'll find
> A thousand regions in your mind
> Yet undiscovered. Travel them, and be
> Expert in home-cosmography."

What does Africa, — what does the West stand for? Is
not our own interior white on the chart? black though
it may prove, like the coast, when discovered. Is it the
source of the Nile, or the Niger, or the Mississippi, or
a Northwest Passage around this continent, that we
would find? Are these the problems which most concern
mankind? Is Franklin the only man who is lost, that his
wife should be so earnest to find him? Does Mr. Grin-
nell know where he himself is? Be rather the Mungo
Park, the Lewis and Clark and Frobisher, of your own
streams and oceans; explore your own higher latitudes,
— with shiploads of preserved meats to support you, if
they be necessary; and pile the empty cans sky-high for
a sign. Were preserved meats invented to preserve meat
merely? Nay, be a Columbus to whole new continents
and worlds within you, opening new channels, not of
trade, but of thought. Every man is the lord of a realm
beside which the earthly empire of the Czar is but a petty
state, a hummock left by the ice. Yet some can be pa-
triotic who have no *self*-respect, and sacrifice the greater
to the less. They love the soil which makes their graves,
but have no sympathy with the spirit which may still
animate their clay. Patriotism is a maggot in their heads.

What was the meaning of that South-Sea Exploring Expedition, with all its parade and expense, but an indirect recognition of the fact that there are continents and seas in the moral world to which every man is an isthmus or an inlet, yet unexplored by him, but that it is easier to sail many thousand miles through cold and storm and cannibals, in a government ship, with five hundred men and boys to assist one, than it is to explore the private sea, the Atlantic and Pacific Ocean of one's being alone. —

> "Erret, et extremos alter scrutetur Iberos.
> Plus habet hic vitae, plus habet ille viae."

Let them wander and scrutinize the outlandish Australians.
I have more of God, they more of the road.

It is not worth the while to go round the world to count the cats in Zanzibar. Yet do this even till you can do better, and you may perhaps find some "Symmes' Hole" by which to get at the inside at last. England and France, Spain and Portugal, Gold Coast and Slave Coast, all front on this private sea; but no bark from them has ventured out of sight of land, though it is without doubt the direct way to India. If you would learn to speak all tongues and conform to the customs of all nations, if you would travel farther than all travellers, be naturalized in all climes, and cause the Sphinx to dash her head against a stone, even obey the precept of the old philosopher, and Explore thyself. Herein are demanded the eye and the nerve. Only the defeated and deserters go to the wars, cowards that run away and enlist. Start now on that farthest western way, which does not pause at the

Mississippi or the Pacific, nor conduct toward a worn-out China or Japan, but leads on direct, a tangent to this sphere, summer and winter, day and night, sun down, moon down, and at last earth down too.

It is said that Mirabeau took to highway robbery "to ascertain what degree of resolution was necessary in order to place one's self in formal opposition to the most sacred laws of society." He declared that "a soldier who fights in the ranks does not require half so much courage as a foot-pad," — "that honor and religion have never stood in the way of a well-considered and a firm resolve." This was manly, as the world goes; and yet it was idle, if not desperate. A saner man would have found himself often enough "in formal opposition" to what are deemed "the most sacred laws of society," through obedience to yet more sacred laws, and so have tested his resolution without going out of his way. It is not for a man to put himself in such an attitude to society, but to maintain himself in whatever attitude he find himself through obedience to the laws of his being, which will never be one of opposition to a just government, if he should chance to meet with such.

I left the woods for as good a reason as I went there. Perhaps it seemed to me that I had several more lives to live, and could not spare any more time for that one. It is remarkable how easily and insensibly we fall into a particular route, and make a beaten track for ourselves. I had not lived there a week before my feet wore a path from my door to the pond-side; and though it is five or six years since I trod it, it is still quite distinct. It is true, I fear that others may have fallen into it, and so helped to keep it open. The surface of the earth is soft and impressible by the feet of men; and so with the paths which the mind travels. How worn and dusty, then, must be the highways of the world, how deep the ruts of tradition and conformity! I did not wish to take a cabin passage, but rather to go before the mast and on the deck of the world, for there I could best see the moonlight amid the mountains. I do not wish to go below now.

I learned this, at least, by my experiment; that if one advances confidently in the direction of his dreams, and endeavors to live the life which he has imagined, he will meet with a success unexpected in common hours. He will put some things behind, will pass an invisible boundary; new, universal, and more liberal laws will begin to establish themselves around and within him; or the old laws be expanded, and interpreted in his favor in a more liberal sense, and he will live with the license of a higher order of beings. In proportion as he simplifies his life, the laws of the universe will appear less complex, and solitude will not be solitude, nor poverty poverty, nor weakness weakness. If you have built castles in the air, your work need not be lost; that is where they should be. Now put the foundations under them.

It is a ridiculous demand which England and America make, that you shall speak so that they can understand you. Neither men nor toadstools grow so. As if that were important, and there were not enough to understand you without them. As if Nature could support but one order of understandings, could not sustain birds as well as quadrupeds, flying as well as creeping things, and *hīsh* and *whoa*, which Bright can understand, were the best English. As if there were safety in stupidity alone. I fear chiefly lest my expression may not be *extra-vagant* enough, may not wander far enough beyond the narrow limits of my daily experience, so as to be adequate to the truth of which I have been convinced. *Extra vagance!* it depends on how you are yarded. The migrating buffalo, which seeks new pastures in another latitude, is not extravagant like the cow which kicks over the pail, leaps the cowyard fence, and runs after her calf, in milking time. I desire to speak somewhere *without* bounds; like a man in a waking moment, to men in their waking moments; for I am convinced that I cannot exaggerate enough even to lay the foundation of a true expression. Who that has heard a strain of music feared then lest he should speak extravagantly any more forever? In view of the future or possible, we should live quite laxly and undefined in front, our outlines dim and misty on that side; as our shadows reveal an insensible perspiration toward the sun. The volatile truth of our words should continually betray the inadequacy of the residual statement. Their truth is instantly *translated;* its literal monument alone remains. The words which express our faith and piety are not definite; yet they are significant and fragrant like frankincense to superior natures.

Why level downward to our dullest perception always, and praise that as common sense? The commonest sense is the sense of men asleep, which they express by snoring. Sometimes we are inclined to class those who are once-and-a-half-witted with the half-witted, because we appreciate only a third part of their wit. Some would find fault with the morning red, if they ever got up early enough. "They pretend," as I hear, "that the verses of Kabir have four different senses; illusion, spirit, intellect, and the exoteric doctrine of the Vedas;" but in this part of the world it is considered a ground for complaint if a man's writings admit of more than one interpretation. While England endeavors to cure the potato-rot, will not any endeavor to cure the brain-rot, which prevails so much more widely and fatally?

I do not suppose that I have attained to obscurity, but I should be proud if no more fatal fault were found with my pages on this score than was found with the Walden ice. Southern customers objected to its blue color, which is the evidence of its purity, as if it were muddy, and preferred the Cambridge ice, which is white, but tastes of weeds. The purity men love is like the mists which envelop the earth, and not like the azure ether beyond.

Some are dinning in our ears that we Americans, and moderns generally, are intellectual dwarfs compared with the ancients, or even the Elizabethan men. But what is that to the purpose? A living dog is better than a dead lion. Shall a man go and hang himself because he belongs to the race of pygmies, and not be the biggest pygmy that he can? Let every one mind his own business, and endeavor to be what he was made.

Why should we be in such desperate haste to succeed and in such desperate enterprises? If a man does not keep pace with his companions, perhaps it is because he hears a different drummer. Let him step to the music which he hears, however measured or far away. It is not important that he should mature as soon as an apple tree or an oak. Shall he turn his spring into summer? If the condition of things which we were made for is not yet, what were any reality which we can substitute? We will not be shipwrecked on a vain‘reality. Shall we with pains erect a heaven of blue glass over ourselves, though when it is done we shall be sure to gaze still at the true ethereal heaven far above, as if the former were not?

There was an artist in the city of Kouroo who was disposed to strive after perfection. One day it came into his mind to make a staff. Having considered that in an imperfect work time is an ingredient, but into a perfect work time does not enter, he said to himself, It shall be perfect in all respects, though I should do nothing else in my life. He proceeded instantly to the forest for wood, being resolved that it should not be made of unsuitable material; and as he searched for and rejected stick after stick, his friends gradually deserted him, for they grew old in their works and died, but he grew not older by a moment. His singleness of purpose and resolution, and his elevated piety, endowed him, without his knowledge, with perennial youth. As he made no compromise with Time, Time kept out of his way, and only sighed at a distance because he could not overcome him. Before he had found a stock in all respects suitable the city of Kouroo was a hoary ruin, and he sat on one of its mounds to peel the stick. Before he had given it the proper shape the dynasty of the Candahars was at an end, and with the

point of the stick he wrote the name of the last of that
race in the sand, and then resumed his work. By the
time he had smoothed and polished the staff Kalpa
was no longer the pole-star; and ere he had put on the
ferule and the head adorned with precious stones,
Brahma had awoke and slumbered many times. But
why do I stay to mention these things? When the
finishing stroke was put to his work, it suddenly expanded before the eyes of the astonished artist into the
fairest of all the creations of Brahma. He had made a
new system in making a staff, a world with full and fair
proportions; in which, though the old cities and dynas-
ties had passed away, fairer and more glorious ones had
taken their places. And now he saw by the heap of
shavings still fresh at his feet, that, for him and his
work, the former lapse of time had been an illusion,
and that no more time had elapsed than is required for
a single scintillation from the brain of Brahma to fall on
and inflame the tinder of a mortal brain. The material
was pure, and his art was pure; how could the result
be other than wonderful?

No face which we can give to a matter will stead us
so well at last as the truth. This alone wears well. For
the most part, we are not where we are, but in a false
position. Through an infirmity of our natures, we suppose a case, and put ourselves into it, and hence are in
two cases at the same time, and it is doubly difficult
to get out. In sane moments we regard only the facts,
the case that is. Say what you have to say, not what
you ought. Any truth is better than make-believe. Tom
Hyde, the tinker, standing on the gallows, was asked if

he had anything to say. "Tell the tailors," said he, "to remember to make a knot in their thread before they take the first stitch." His companion's prayer is forgotten.

However mean your life is, meet it and live it; do not shun it and call it hard names. It is not so bad as you are. It looks poorest when you are richest. The faultfinder will find faults even in paradise. Love your life, poor as it is. You may perhaps have some pleasant, thrilling, glorious hours, even in a poor-house. The setting sun is reflected from the windows of the almshouse as brightly as from the rich man's abode; the snow melts before its door as early in the spring. I do not see but a quiet mind may live as contentedly there, and have as cheering thoughts, as in a palace. The town's poor seem to me often to live the most independent lives of any. Maybe they are simply great enough to receive without misgiving. Most think that they are above being supported by the town; but it oftener happens that they are not above supporting themselves by dishonest means, which should be more disreputable. Cultivate poverty like a garden herb, like sage. Do not trouble yourself much to get new things, whether clothes or friends. Turn the old; return to them. Things do not change; we change. Sell your clothes and keep your thoughts. God will see that you do not want society. If I were confined to a corner of a garret all my days, like a spider, the world would be just as large to me while I had my thoughts about me. The philosopher said: "From an army of three divisions one can take away its general, and put it in disorder;

from the man the most abject and vulgar one cannot take away his thought." Do not seek so anxiously to be developed, to subject yourself to many influences to be played on; it is all dissipation. Humility like darkness reveals the heavenly lights. The shadows of poverty and meanness gather around us, "and lo! creation widens to our view." We are often reminded that if there were bestowed on us the wealth of Crœsus, our aims must still be the same, and our means essentially the same. Moreover, if you are restricted in your range by poverty, if you cannot buy books and newspapers, for instance, you are but confined to the most significant and vital experiences; you are compelled to deal with the material which yields the most sugar and the most starch. It is life near the bone where it is sweetest. You are defended from being a trifler. No man loses ever on a lower level by magnanimity on a higher. Superfluous wealth can buy superfluities only. Money is not required to buy one necessary of the soul.

I live in the angle of a leaden wall, into whose composition was poured a little alloy of bell-metal. Often, in the repose of my mid-day, there reaches my ears a confused *tintinnabulum* from without. It is the noise of my contemporaries. My neighbors tell me of their adventures with famous gentlemen and ladies, what notabilities they met at the dinner-table; but I am no more interested in such things than in the contents of the Daily Times. The interest and the conversation are about costume and manners chiefly; but a goose is a goose still, dress it as you will. They tell me of California and Texas, of England and the Indies, of the

Hon. Mr. —— of Georgia or of Massachusetts, all
transient and fleeting phenomena, till I am ready to
leap from their court-yard like the Mameluke bey. I
delight to come to my bearings, — not walk in procession with pomp and parade, in a conspicuous place, but
to walk even with the Builder of the universe, if I may,
— not to live in this restless, nervous, bustling, trivial
Nineteenth Century, but stand or sit thoughtfully while
it goes by. What are men celebrating? They are all
on a committee of arrangements, and hourly expect a
speech from somebody. God is only the president of
the day, and Webster is his orator. I love to weigh, to
settle, to gravitate toward that which most strongly
and rightfully attracts me; — not hang by the beam of
the scale and try to weigh less, — not suppose a case,
but take the case that is; to travel the only path I can,
and that on which no power can resist me. It affords
me no satisfaction to commence to spring an arch before
I have got a solid foundation. Let us not play at kittly-
benders. There is a solid bottom everywhere. We read
that the traveller asked the boy if the swamp before him
had a hard bottom. The boy replied that it had. But
presently the traveller's horse sank in up to the girths,
and he observed to the boy, "I thought you said that
this bog had a hard bottom." "So it has," answered
the latter, "but you have not got half way to it yet."
So it is with the bogs and quicksands of society; but
he is an old boy that knows it. Only what is thought,
said, or done at a certain rare coincidence is good.
I would not be one of those who will foolishly drive a
nail into mere lath and plastering; such a deed would

keep me awake nights. Give me a hammer, and let me feel for the furrowing. Do not depend on the putty. Drive a nail home and clinch it so faithfully that you can wake up in the night and think of your work with satisfaction, — a work at which you would not be ashamed to invoke the Muse. So will help you God, and so only. Every nail driven should be as another rivet in the machine of the universe, you carrying on the work.

Rather than love, than money, than fame, give me truth. I sat at a table where were rich food and wine in abundance, and obsequious attendance, but sincerity and truth were not; and I went away hungry from the inhospitable board. The hospitality was as cold as the ices. I thought that there was no need of ice to freeze them. They talked to me of the age of the wine and the fame of the vintage; but I thought of an older, a newer, and purer wine, of a more glorious vintage, which they had not got, and could not buy. The style, the house and grounds and "entertainment" pass for nothing with me. I called on the king, but he made me wait in his hall, and conducted like a man incapacitated for hospitality. There was a man in my neighborhood who lived in a hollow tree. His manners were truly regal. I should have done better had I called on him.

How long shall we sit in our porticoes practising idle and musty virtues, which any work would make impertinent? As if one were to begin the day with long-suffering, and hire a man to hoe his potatoes; and in the afternoon go forth to practise Christian meekness and charity with goodness aforethought! Consider the

China pride and stagnant self-complacency of mankind. This generation inclines a little to congratulate itself on being the last of an illustrious line; and in Boston and London and Paris and Rome, thinking of its long descent, it speaks of its progress in art and science and literature with satisfaction. There are the Records of the Philosophical Societies, and the public Eulogies of *Great Men!* It is the good Adam contemplating his own virtue. "Yes, we have done great deeds, and sung divine songs, which shall never die," — that is, as long as *we* can remember them. The learned societies and great men of Assyria, — where are they? What youthful philosophers and experimentalists we are! There is not one of my readers who has yet lived a whole human life. These may be but the spring months in the life of the race. If we have had the seven-years' itch, we have not seen the seventeen-year locust yet in Concord. We are acquainted with a mere pellicle of the globe on which we live. Most have not delved six feet beneath the surface, nor leaped as many above it. We know not where we are. Beside, we are sound asleep nearly half our time. Yet we esteem ourselves wise, and have an established order on the surface. Truly, we are deep thinkers, we are ambitious spirits! As I stand over the insect crawling amid the pine needles on the forest floor, and endeavoring to conceal itself from my sight, and ask myself why it will cherish those humble thoughts, and hide its head from me who might, perhaps, be its benefactor, and impart to its race some cheering information, I am reminded of the greater Benefactor and Intelligence that stands over me the human insect.

There is an incessant influx of novelty into the world, and yet we tolerate incredible dulness. I need only suggest what kind of sermons are still listened to in the most enlightened countries. There are such words as joy and sorrow, but they are only the burden of a psalm, sung with a nasal twang, while we believe in the ordinary and mean. We think that we can change our clothes only. It is said that the British Empire is very large and respectable, and that the United States are a first-rate power. We do not believe that a tide rises and falls behind every man which can float the British Empire like a chip, if he should ever harbor it in his mind. Who knows what sort of seventeen-year locust will next come out of the ground? The government of the world I live in was not framed, like that of Britain, in after-dinner conversations over the wine.

The life in us is like the water in the river. It may rise this year higher than man has ever known it, and flood the parched uplands; even this may be the eventful year, which will drown out all our muskrats. It was not always dry land where we dwell. I see far inland the banks which the stream anciently washed, before science began to record its freshets. Every one has heard the story which has gone the rounds of New England, of a strong and beautiful bug which came out of the dry leaf of an old table of apple-tree wood, which had stood in a farmer's kitchen for sixty years, first in Connecticut, and afterward in Massachusetts, — from an egg deposited in the living tree many years earlier still, as appeared by counting the annual layers beyond it; which was heard gnawing out for several weeks, hatched perchance by the heat of an urn. Who does not feel his faith in a resurrection and immortality strengthened by hearing of this? Who knows what beautiful and winged life, whose egg has been buried for ages under many concentric layers of woodenness in the dead dry life of society, deposited at first in the alburnum of the green and living tree, which has been gradually converted into the semblance of its well-seasoned tomb, — heard perchance gnawing out now for years by the astonished family of man, as they sat round the festive board, — may unexpectedly come forth from amidst society's most trivial and handselled furniture, to enjoy its perfect summer life at last!

I do not say that John or Jonathan will realize all this; but such is the character of that morrow which mere lapse of time can never make to dawn. The light which puts out our eyes is darkness to us. Only that day dawns to which we are awake. There is more day to dawn. The sun is but a morning star.

Walden woods

WALKING

Ferns

WALKING

I wish to speak a word for Nature, for absolute freedom and wildness, as contrasted with a freedom and
culture merely civil, — to regard man as an inhabitant,
or a part and parcel of Nature, rather than a member
of society. I wish to make an extreme statement, if so
I may make an emphatic one, for there are enough
champions of civilization: the minister and the school
committee and every one of you will take care of that.

I have met with but one or two persons in the course
of my life who understood the art of Walking, that is,
of taking walks, — who had a genius, so to speak, for
sauntering, which word is beautifully derived "from
idle people who roved about the country, in the Middle
Ages, and asked charity, under pretense of going *à la
Sainte Terre*," to the Holy Land, till the children
exclaimed, "There goes a *Sainte-Terrer*," a Saunterer,
a Holy-Lander. They who never go to the Holy Land in
their walks, as they pretend, are indeed mere idlers and
vagabonds; but they who do go there are saunterers in
the good sense, such as I mean. Some, however, would
derive the word from *sans terre*, without land or a home,
which, therefore, in the good sense, will mean, having no
particular home, but equally at home everywhere. For
this is the secret of successful sauntering. He who sits
still in a house all the time may be the greatest vagrant
of all; but the saunterer, in the good sense, is no more

vagrant than the meandering river, which is all the while
sedulously seeking the shortest course to the sea. But I
prefer the first, which, indeed, is the most probable
derivation. For every walk is a sort of crusade, preached
by some Peter the Hermit in us, to go forth and recon-
quer this Holy Land from the hands of the Infidels.

It is true, we are but faint-hearted crusaders, even
the walkers, nowadays, who undertake no persevering,
never-ending enterprises. Our expeditions are but tours,
and come round again at evening to the old hearth-side
from which we set out. Half the walk is but retracing
our steps. We should go forth on the shortest walk,
perchance, in the spirit of undying adventure, never to
return, — prepared to send back our embalmed hearts
only as relics to our desolate kingdoms. If you are ready
to leave father and mother, and brother and sister, and
wife and child and friends, and never see them again, —
if you have paid your debts, and made your will, and
settled all your affairs, and are a free man, then you are
ready for a walk.

To come down to my own experience, my companion
and I, for I sometimes have a companion, take pleasure
in fancying ourselves knights of a new, or rather an old,
order, — not Equestrians or Chevaliers, not Ritters or
Riders, but Walkers, a still more ancient and honorable
class, I trust. The chivalric and heroic spirit which
once belonged to the Rider seems now to reside in, or
perchance to have subsided into, the Walker, — not the
Knight, but Walker, Errant. He is a sort of fourth
estate, outside of Church and State and People.

We have felt that we almost alone hereabouts prac-

ticed this noble art; though, to tell the truth, at least
if their own assertions are to be received, most of my
townsmen would fain walk sometimes, as I do, but
they cannot. No wealth can buy the requisite leisure,
freedom, and independence which are the capital in
this profession. It comes only by the grace of God.
It requires a direct dispensation from Heaven to become a walker. You must be born into the family of
the Walkers. *Ambulator nascitur, non fit.* Some of my
townsmen, it is true, can remember and have described
to me some walks which they took ten years ago, in
which they were so blessed as to lose themselves for
half an hour in the woods; but I know very well that
they have confined themselves to the highway ever
since, whatever pretensions they may make to belong
to this select class. No doubt they were elevated for a
moment as by the reminiscence of a previous state of
existence, when even they were foresters and outlaws.

> "When he came to grene wode,
> In a mery mornynge,
> There he herde the notes small
> Of byrdes mery syngynge.

> "It is ferre gone, sayd Robyn,
> That I was last here;
> Me lyste a lytell for to shote
> At the donne dere."

I think that I cannot preserve my health and spirits,
unless I spend four hours a day at least — and it is
commonly more than that — sauntering through the
woods and over the hills and fields, absolutely free from
all worldly engagements. You may safely say, A penny

for your thoughts, or a thousand pounds. When sometimes I am reminded that the mechanics and shopkeepers stay in their shops not only all the forenoon, but all the afternoon too, sitting with crossed legs, so many of them, — as if the legs were made to sit upon, and not to stand or walk upon, — I think that they deserve some credit for not having all committed suicide long ago.

I, who cannot stay in my chamber for a single day without acquiring some rust, and when sometimes I have stolen forth for a walk at the eleventh hour, or four o'clock in the afternoon, too late to redeem the day, when the shades of night were already beginning to be mingled with the daylight, have felt as if I had committed some sin to be atoned for, — I confess that I am astonished at the power of endurance, to say nothing of the moral insensibility, of my neighbors who confine themselves to shops and offices the whole day for weeks and months, aye, and years almost together. I know not what manner of stuff they are of, — sitting there now at three o'clock in the afternoon, as if it were three o'clock in the morning. Bonaparte may talk of the three-o'clock-in-the-morning courage, but it is nothing to the courage which can sit down cheerfully at this hour in the afternoon over against one's self whom you have known all the morning, to starve out a garrison to whom you are bound by such strong ties of sympathy. I wonder that about this time, or say between four and five o'clock in the afternoon, too late for the morning papers and too early for the evening ones, there is not a general explosion heard up and down the street, scattering a legion of antiquated and house-bred notions and whims to the four winds for an airing, — and so the evil cure itself.

How womankind, who are confined to the house still more than men, stand it I do not know; but I have ground to suspect that most of them do not *stand* it at all. When, early in a summer afternoon, we have been shaking the dust of the village from the skirts of our garments, making haste past those houses with purely Doric or Gothic fronts, which have such an air of repose about them, my companion whispers that probably about these times their occupants are all gone to bed. Then it is that I appreciate the beauty and the glory of architecture, which itself never turns in, but forever stands out and erect, keeping watch over the slumberers.

No doubt temperament, and, above all, age, have a good deal to do with it. As a man grows older, his ability to sit still and follow indoor occupations increases. He grows vespertinal in his habits as the evening of life approaches, till at last he comes forth only just before sundown, and gets all the walk that he requires in half an hour.

But the walking of which I speak has nothing in it akin to taking exercise, as it is called, as the sick take medicine at stated hours, — as the swinging of dumb-bells or chairs; but is itself the enterprise and adventure of the day. If you would get exercise, go in search of the springs of life. Think of a man's swinging dumb-bells for his health, when those springs are bubbling up in far-off pastures unsought by him!

Moreover, you must walk like a camel, which is said to be the only beast which ruminates when walking. When a traveler asked Wordsworth's servant to show him her master's study, she answered, "Here is his library, but his study is out of doors."

Living much out of doors, in the sun and wind, will no doubt produce a certain roughness of character, — will cause a thicker cuticle to grow over some of the finer qualities of our nature, as on the face and hands, or as severe manual labor robs the hands of some of their delicacy of touch. So staying in the house, on the other hand, may produce a softness and smoothness, not to say thinness of skin, accompanied by an increased sensibility to certain impressions. Perhaps we should be more susceptible to some influences important to our intellectual and moral growth, if the sun had shone and the wind blown on us a little less; and no doubt it is a nice matter to proportion rightly the thick and thin skin. But methinks that is a scurf that will fall off fast enough, — that the natural remedy is to be found in the proportion which the night bears to the day, the winter to the summer, thought to experience. There will be so much the more air and sunshine in our thoughts. The callous palms of the laborer are conversant with finer tissues of self-respect and heroism, whose touch thrills the heart, than the languid fingers of idleness. That is mere sentimentality that lies abed by day and thinks itself white, far from the tan and callus of experience.

When we walk, we naturally go to the fields and woods: what would become of us, if we walked only in a garden or a mall? Even some sects of philosophers have felt the necessity of importing the woods to themselves, since they did not go to the woods. "They planted groves and walks of Platanes," where they took *subdiales ambulationes* in porticos open to the air. Of course it is of no use to direct our steps to the woods, if they do not carry us thither. I am alarmed when it happens that I have walked a mile into the woods bodily, without getting there in spirit. In my afternoon walk I would fain forget all my morning occupations and my obligations to society. But it sometimes happens that I cannot easily shake off the village. The thought of some work will run in my head and I am not where my body is, — I am out of my senses. In my walks I would fain return to my senses. What business have I in the woods, if I am thinking of something out of the woods? I suspect myself, and cannot help a shudder, when I find myself so implicated even in what are called good works, — for this may sometimes happen.

My vicinity affords many good walks; and though for so many years I have walked almost every day, and sometimes for several days together, I have not yet exhausted them. An absolutely new prospect is a great happiness, and I can still get this any afternoon. Two or three hours' walking will carry me to as strange a country as I expect ever to see. A single farmhouse which I had not seen before is sometimes as good as the dominions of the King of Dahomey. There is in fact a sort of harmony discoverable between the capabilities of the landscape within a circle of ten miles' radius, or the limits of an afternoon walk, and the threescore years and ten of human life. It will never become quite familiar to you.

Nowadays almost all man's improvements, so called, as the building of houses and the cutting down of the forest and of all large trees, simply deform the landscape, and make it more and more tame and cheap. A people who would begin by burning the fences and let the forest stand! I saw the fences half consumed, their ends lost in the middle of the prairie, and some worldly miser with a surveyor looking after his bounds, while heaven had taken place around him, and he did not see the angels going to and fro, but was looking for an old post-hole in the midst of paradise. I looked again, and saw him standing in the middle of a boggy Stygian fen, surrounded by devils, and he had found his bounds without a doubt, three little stones, where a stake had been driven, and looking nearer, I saw that the Prince of Darkness was his surveyor.

I can easily walk ten, fifteen, twenty, any number of miles, commencing at my own door, without going by any house, without crossing a road except where the fox and the mink do: first along by the river, and then the brook, and then the meadow and the woodside. There are square miles in my vicinity which have no inhabitant. From many a hill I can see civilization and the abodes of man afar. The farmers and their works are scarcely more obvious than woodchucks and their burrows. Man and his affairs, church and state and school, trade and commerce, and manufactures and agriculture, even politics, the most alarming of them all, — I am pleased to see how little space they occupy

in the landscape. Politics is but a narrow field, and
that still narrower highway yonder leads to it. I sometimes direct the traveler thither. If you would go to the
political world, follow the great road, — follow that
market-man, keep his dust in your eyes, and it will
lead you straight to it; for it, too, has its place merely,
and does not occupy all space. I pass from it as from
a bean-field into the forest, and it is forgotten. In one
half-hour I can walk off to some portion of the earth's
surface where a man does not stand from one year's
end to another, and there, consequently, politics are
not, for they are but as the cigar-smoke of a man.

The village is the place to which the roads tend, a
sort of expansion of the highway, as a lake of a river.
It is the body of which roads are the arms and legs, —
a trivial or quadrivial place, the thoroughfare and ordinary of travelers. The word is from the Latin *villa*,
which together with *via*, a way, or more anciently *ved*
and *vella*, Varro derives from *veho*, to carry, because
the villa is the place to and from which things are carried. They who got their living by teaming were said
vellaturam facere. Hence, too, the Latin word *vilis*
and our vile, also *villain*. This suggests what kind of
degeneracy villagers are liable to. They are wayworn by
the travel that goes by and over them, without traveling
themselves.

Some do not walk at all; others walk in the highways;
a few walk across lots. Roads are made for horses and
men of business. I do not travel in them much, comparatively, because I am not in a hurry to get to any
tavern or grocery or livery-stable or depot to which

they lead. I am a good horse to travel, but not from choice a roadster. The landscape-painter uses the figures of men to mark a road. He would not make that use of my figure. I walk out into a nature such as the old prophets and poets, Menu, Moses, Homer, Chaucer, walked in. You may name it America, but it is not America; neither Americus Vespucius, nor Columbus, nor the rest were the discoverers of it. There is a truer account of it in mythology than in any history of America, so called, that I have seen.

However, there are a few old roads that may be trodden with profit, as if they led somewhere now that they are nearly discontinued. There is the Old Marlborough Road, which does not go to Marlborough now, methinks, unless that is Marlborough where it carries me. I am the bolder to speak of it here, because I presume that there are one or two such roads in every town.

THE OLD MARLBOROUGH ROAD

Where they once dug for money,
But never found any;
Where sometimes Martial Miles
Singly files,
And Elijah Wood,
I fear for no good:
No other man,
Save Elisha Dugan, —
O man of wild habits,
Partridges and rabbits,
Who hast no cares
Only to set snares,
Who liv'st all alone,
Close to the bone,

And where life is sweetest
Constantly eatest.
When the spring stirs my blood
With the instinct to travel,
I can get enough gravel
On the Old Marlborough Road.
Nobody repairs it,
For nobody wears it;
It is a living way,
As the Christians say.
Not many there be
Who enter therein,
Only the guests of the
Irishman Quin.
What is it, what is it,
But a direction out there,
And the bare possibility
Of going somewhere?
Great guide-boards of stone,
But travelers none;
Cenotaphs of the towns
Named on their crowns.
It is worth going to see
Where you *might* be.
What king
Did the thing,
I am still wondering;
Set up how or when,
By what selectmen,
Gourgas or Lee,
Clark or Darby?
They 're a great endeavor
To be something forever;
Blank tablets of stone,
Where a traveler might groan,
And in one sentence
Grave all that is known;
Which another might read,
In his extreme need.

> I know one or two
> Lines that would do,
> Literature that might stand
> All over the land,
> Which a man could remember
> Till next December,
> And read again in the spring,
> After the thawing.
> If with fancy unfurled
> You leave your abode,
> You may go round the world
> By the Old Marlborough Road.

At present, in this vicinity, the best part of the land is not private property; the landscape is not owned, and the walker enjoys comparative freedom. But possibly the day will come when it will be partitioned off into so-called pleasure-grounds, in which a few will take a narrow and exclusive pleasure only, — when fences shall be multiplied, and man-traps and other engines invented to confine men to the *public* road, and walking over the surface of God's earth shall be construed to mean trespassing on some gentleman's grounds. To enjoy a thing exclusively is commonly to exclude yourself from the true enjoyment of it. Let us improve our opportunities, then, before the evil days come.

What is it that makes it so hard sometimes to determine whither we will walk? I believe that there is a subtle magnetism in Nature, which, if we unconsciously yield to it, will direct us aright. It is not indifferent to us which way we walk. There is a right way; but we are very liable from heedlessness and stupidity to take the wrong one. We would fain take that walk, never yet

The Old Marlborough Road

Midwinter

taken by us through this actual world, which is perfectly symbolical of the path which we love to travel in
the interior and ideal world; and sometimes, no doubt,
we find it difficult to choose our direction, because it
does not yet exist distinctly in our idea.

When I go out of the house for a walk, uncertain as
yet whither I will bend my steps, and submit myself to
my instinct to decide for me, I find, strange and whimsical as it may seem, that I finally and inevitably settle
southwest, toward some particular wood or meadow or
deserted pasture or hill in that direction. My needle
is slow to settle, — varies a few degrees, and does not
always point due southwest, it is true, and it has good
authority for this variation, but it always settles between
west and south-southwest. The future lies that way to
me, and the earth seems more unexhausted and richer on
that side. The outline which would bound my walks
would be, not a circle, but a parabola, or rather like one
of those cometary orbits which have been thought to be
non-returning curves, in this case opening westward,
in which my house occupies the place of the sun. I turn
round and round irresolute sometimes for a quarter of
an hour, until I decide, for a thousandth time, that I will
walk into the southwest or west. Eastward I go only by
force; but westward I go free. Thither no business leads
me. It is hard for me to believe that I shall find fair
landscapes or sufficient wildness and freedom behind the
eastern horizon. I am not excited by the prospect of a
walk thither; but I believe that the forest which I see in
the western horizon stretches uninterruptedly toward
the setting sun, and there are no towns nor cities in it of

enough consequence to disturb me. Let me live where I will, on this side is the city, on that the wilderness, and ever I am leaving the city more and more, and withdrawing into the wilderness. I should not lay so much stress on this fact, if I did not believe that something like this is the prevailing tendency of my countrymen. I must walk toward Oregon, and not toward Europe. And that way the nation is moving, and I may say that mankind progress from east to west. Within a few years we have witnessed the phenomenon of a southeastward migration, in the settlement of Australia; but this affects us as a retrograde movement, and, judging from the moral and physical character of the first generation of Australians, has not yet proved a successful experiment. The eastern Tartars think that there is nothing west beyond Thibet. "The world ends there," say they; "beyond there is nothing but a shoreless sea." It is unmitigated East where they live.

We go eastward to realize history and study the works of art and literature, retracing the steps of the race; we go westward as into the future, with a spirit of enterprise and adventure. The Atlantic is a Lethean stream, in our passage over which we have had an opportunity to forget the Old World and its institutions. If we do not succeed this time, there is perhaps one more chance for the race left before it arrives on the banks of the Styx; and that is in the Lethe of the Pacific, which is three times as wide.

I know not how significant it is, or how far it is an evidence of singularity, that an individual should thus consent in his pettiest walk with the general movement

of the race; but I know that something akin to the
migratory instinct in birds and quadrupeds, — which,
in some instances, is known to have affected the squirrel
tribe, impelling them to a general and mysterious movement, in which they were seen, say some, crossing the
broadest rivers, each on its particular chip, with its
tail raised for a sail, and bridging narrower streams
with their dead, — that something like the *furor* which
affects the domestic cattle in the spring, and which is
referred to a worm in their tails, affects both nations
and individuals, either perennially or from time to time.
Not a flock of wild geese cackles over our town, but it to
some extent unsettles the value of real estate here, and,
if I were a broker, I should probably take that disturbance into account.

> " Than longen folk to gon on pilgrimages,
> And palmeres for to seken strange strondes."

Every sunset which I witness inspires me with the
desire to go to a West as distant and as fair as that into
which the sun goes down. He appears to migrate westward daily, and tempt us to follow him. He is the Great
Western Pioneer whom the nations follow. We dream
all night of those mountain-ridges in the horizon, though
they may be of vapor only, which were last gilded by his
rays. The island of Atlantis, and the islands and gardens
of the Hesperides, a sort of terrestrial paradise, appear
to have been the Great West of the ancients, enveloped
in mystery and poetry. Who has not seen in imagination,
when looking into the sunset sky, the gardens of the
Hesperides, and the foundation of all those fables?

Columbus felt the westward tendency more strongly

than any before. He obeyed it, and found a New World
for Castile and Leon. The herd of men in those days
scented fresh pastures from afar.

> "And now the sun had stretched out all the hills,
> And now was dropped into the western bay;
> At last *he* rose, and twitched his mantle blue;
> To-morrow to fresh woods and pastures new."

Where on the globe can there be found an area of
equal extent with that occupied by the bulk of our
States, so fertile and so rich and varied in its productions, and at the same time so habitable by the European, as this is? Michaux, who knew but part of them,
says that "the species of large trees are much more
numerous in North America than in Europe; in the
United States there are more than one hundred and
forty species that exceed thirty feet in height; in France
there are but thirty that attain this size." Later botanists more than confirm his observations. Humboldt
came to America to realize his youthful dreams of a
tropical vegetation, and he beheld it in its greatest perfection in the primitive forests of the Amazon, the most
gigantic wilderness on the earth, which he has so eloquently described. The geographer Guyot, himself a
European, goes farther, — farther than I am ready to
follow him; yet not when he says: "As the plant is made
for the animal, as the vegetable world is made for the
animal world, America is made for the man of the Old
World. . . . The man of the Old World sets out upon
his way. Leaving the highlands of Asia, he descends
from station to station towards Europe. Each of his
steps is marked by a new civilization superior to the

preceding, by a greater power of development. Arrived at the Atlantic, he pauses on the shore of this unknown ocean, the bounds of which he knows not, and turns upon his footprints for an instant." When he has exhausted the rich soil of Europe, and reinvigorated himself, "then recommences his adventurous career westward as in the earliest ages." So far Guyot.

From this western impulse coming in contact with the barrier of the Atlantic sprang the commerce and enterprise of modern times. The younger Michaux, in his "Travels West of the Alleghanies in 1802," says that the common inquiry in the newly settled West was, "'From what part of the world have you come?' As if these vast and fertile regions would naturally be the place of meeting and common country of all the inhabitants of the globe."

To use an obsolete Latin word, I might say, *Ex Oriente lux; ex Occidente* FRUX. From the East light; from the West fruit.

Sir Francis Head, an English traveler and a Governor-General of Canada, tells us that "in both the northern and southern hemispheres of the New World, Nature has not only outlined her works on a larger scale, but has painted the whole picture with brighter and more costly colors than she used in delineating and in beautifying the Old World. . . . The heavens of America appear infinitely higher, the sky is bluer, the air is fresher, the cold is intenser, the moon looks larger, the stars are brighter, the thunder is louder, the lightning is vivider, the wind is stronger, the rain is heavier, the mountains are higher, the rivers longer, the forests bigger, the plains broader." This statement will do at least to set against Buffon's account of this part of the world and its productions.

Linnæus said long ago, "Nescio quae facies *laeta, glabra* plantis Americanis" (I know not what there is of joyous and smooth in the aspect of American plants); and I think that in this country there are no, or at most very few, *Africanae bestiae*, African beasts, as the Romans called them, and that in this respect also it is peculiarly fitted for the habitation of man. We are told that within three miles of the centre of the East-Indian city of Singapore, some of the inhabitants are annually carried off by tigers; but the traveler can lie down in the woods at night almost anywhere in North America without fear of wild beasts.

These are encouraging testimonies. If the moon looks larger here than in Europe, probably the sun looks larger also. If the heavens of America appear infinitely higher, and the stars brighter, I trust that these facts are symbolical of the height to which the philosophy and poetry and religion of her inhabitants may one day soar. At length, perchance, the immaterial heaven will appear as much higher to the American mind, and the intimations that star it as much brighter. For I believe that climate does thus react on man, — as there is something in the mountain air that feeds the spirit and inspires. Will not man grow to greater perfection intellectually as well as physically under these influences? Or is it unimportant how many foggy days there are in his life? I trust that we shall be more imaginative, that our thoughts will be clearer, fresher, and more ethereal, as our sky, — our understanding more comprehensive and broader, like our plains, — our intellect generally on a grander scale, like our thunder and lightning, our rivers and mountains and forests, — and our hearts shall even correspond in breadth and depth and grandeur to our inland seas. Perchance there will appear to the traveler something, he knows not what, of *laeta* and *glabra*, of joyous and serene, in our very faces. Else to what end does the world go on, and why was America discovered?

To Americans I hardly need to say, —

> "Westward the star of empire takes its way."

As a true patriot, I should be ashamed to think that Adam in paradise was more favorably situated on the whole than the backwoodsman in this country.

Our sympathies in Massachusetts are not confined to New England; though we may be estranged from the South, we sympathize with the West. There is the home of the younger sons, as among the Scandinavians they took to the sea for their inheritance. It is too late to be studying Hebrew; it is more important to understand even the slang of to-day.

Some months ago I went to see a panorama of the Rhine. It was like a dream of the Middle Ages. I floated down its historic stream in something more than imagination, under bridges built by the Romans, and repaired by later heroes, past cities and castles whose very names were music to my ears, and each of which was the subject of a legend. There were Ehrenbreitstein and Rolandseck and Coblentz, which I knew only in

history.   They were ruins that interested me chiefly.
There seemed to come up from its waters and its vine-
clad hills and valleys a hushed music as of Crusaders
departing for the Holy Land. I floated along under the
spell of enchantment, as if I had been transported to an
heroic age, and breathed an atmosphere of chivalry.

Soon after, I went to see a panorama of the Mississippi, and as I worked my way up the river in the light
of to-day, and saw the steamboats wooding up, counted
the rising cities, gazed on the fresh ruins of Nauvoo,
beheld the Indians moving west across the stream, and,
as before I had looked up the Moselle, now looked up the
Ohio and the Missouri and heard the legends of Dubuque
and of Wenona's Cliff, — still thinking more of the
future than of the past or present, — I saw that this was
a Rhine stream of a different kind; that the foundations
of castles were yet to be laid, and the famous bridges
were yet to be thrown over the river; and I felt that
this was the heroic age itself, though we know it not, for
the hero is commonly the simplest and obscurest of men.

The West of which I speak is but another name for
the Wild; and what I have been preparing to say is,
that in Wildness is the preservation of the World. Every
tree sends its fibres forth in search of the Wild. The
cities import it at any price. Men plow and sail for it.
From the forest and wilderness come the tonics and
barks which brace mankind. Our ancestors were savages. The story of Romulus and Remus being suckled
by a wolf is not a meaningless fable. The founders
of every state which has risen to eminence have drawn

their nourishment and vigor from a similar wild source. It was because the children of the Empire were not suckled by the wolf that they were conquered and displaced by the children of the northern forests who were.

I believe in the forest, and in the meadow, and in the night in which the corn grows. We require an infusion of hemlock spruce or arbor-vitæ in our tea. There is a difference between eating and drinking for strength and from mere gluttony. The Hottentots eagerly devour the marrow of the koodoo and other antelopes raw, as a matter of course. Some of our northern Indians eat raw the marrow of the Arctic reindeer, as well as various other parts, including the summits of the antlers, as long as they are soft. And herein, perchance, they have stolen a march on the cooks of Paris. They get what usually goes to feed the fire: This is probably better than stall-fed beef and slaughter-house pork to make a man of. Give me a wildness whose glance no civilization can endure, — as if we lived on the marrow of koodoos devoured raw.

There are some intervals which border the strain of the wood thrush, to which I would migrate, — wild lands where no settler has squatted; to which, methinks, I am already acclimated.

The African hunter Cumming tells us that the skin of the eland, as well as that of most other antelopes just killed, emits the most delicious perfume of trees and grass. I would have every man so much like a wild antelope, so much a part and parcel of nature, that his very person should thus sweetly advertise our senses of his presence, and remind us of those parts of nature which he most haunts. I feel no disposition to be satirical, when the trapper's coat emits the odor of musquash even; it is a sweeter scent to me than that which commonly exhales from the merchant's or the scholar's garments. When I go into their wardrobes and handle their vestments, I am reminded of no grassy plains and flowery meads which they have frequented, but of dusty merchants' exchanges and libraries rather.

A tanned skin is something more than respectable, and perhaps olive is a fitter color than white for a man, — a denizen of the woods. "The pale white man!" I do not wonder that the African pitied him. Darwin the naturalist says, "A white man bathing by the side of a Tahitian was like a plant bleached by the gardener's art, compared with a fine, dark green one, growing vigorously in the open fields."

Ben Jonson exclaims, —

"How near to good is what is fair!"

So I would say, —

How near to good is what is *wild!*

Life consists with wildness. The most alive is the wildest. Not yet subdued to man, its presence refreshes him. One who pressed forward incessantly and never rested from his labors, who grew fast and made infinite demands on life, would always find himself in a new country or wilderness, and surrounded by the raw material of life. He would be climbing over the prostrate stems of primitive forest-trees.

Hope and the future for me are not in lawns and cultivated fields, not in towns and cities, but in the impervious and quaking swamps. When, formerly, I have analyzed my partiality for some farm which I had contemplated purchasing, I have frequently found that I was attracted solely by a few square rods of impermeable and unfathomable bog, — a natural sink in one corner of it. That was the jewel which dazzled me. I derive more of my subsistence from the swamps which surround my native town than from the cultivated gardens in the village. There are no richer parterres to my eyes than the dense beds of dwarf andromeda (*Cassandra calyculata*) which cover these tender places on the earth's surface. Botany cannot go farther than tell me the names of the shrubs which grow there, — the high blueberry, panicled andromeda, lambkill, azalea, and rhodora, — all standing in the quaking sphagnum. I often think that I should like to have my house front on this mass of dull red bushes, omitting other flower plots and borders, transplanted spruce and trim box, even graveled walks, — to have this fertile spot under my windows, not a few imported barrowfuls of soil only to cover the sand which was thrown out in digging the cellar. Why not put my house, my parlor, behind this plot, instead of behind that meagre assemblage of curiosities, that poor apology for a Nature and Art, which I call my front yard? It is an effort to clear up and make a decent appearance when the carpenter and mason have departed, though done as much for the passer-by as the dweller within. The most tasteful front-yard fence was never an agreeable object of study to me; the most elaborate ornaments, acorn tops, or what not, soon wearied and disgusted me. Bring your sills up to the very edge of the swamp, then (though it may not be the best place for a dry cellar), so that there be no access on that side to citizens. Front yards are not made to walk in, but, at most, through, and you could go in the back way.

Yes, though you may think me perverse, if it were proposed to me to dwell in the neighborhood of the most beautiful garden that ever human art contrived, or else of a Dismal Swamp, I should certainly decide for the swamp. How vain, then, have been all your labors, citizens, for me!

My spirits infallibly rise in proportion to the outward dreariness. Give me the ocean, the desert, or the wilderness! In the desert, pure air and solitude compensate for want of moisture and fertility. The traveler Burton says of it: "Your *morale* improves; you become frank and cordial, hospitable and single-minded. . . . In the desert, spirituous liquors excite only disgust. There is a keen enjoyment in a mere animal existence." They who have been traveling long on the steppes of Tartary say, "On reëntering cultivated lands, the agitation, perplexity, and turmoil of civilization oppressed and suffocated us; the air seemed to fail us, and we felt every moment as if about to die of asphyxia." When I would recreate myself, I seek the darkest wood, the thickest and most interminable and, to the citizen, most dismal, swamp. I enter a swamp as a sacred place, a *sanctum sanctorum*. There is the strength, the marrow, of Nature. The wildwood covers the virgin mould, and the same soil is good for men and for trees. A man's health requires as many acres of meadow to his prospect as his farm does loads of muck. There are the strong meats on which he feeds. A town is saved, not more by the righteous men in it than by the woods and swamps that surround it. A township where one primitive forest waves above while another primitive forest rots below, — such a town is fitted to raise not only corn and potatoes, but poets and philosophers for the coming ages. In such a soil grew Homer and Confucius and the rest, and out of such a wilderness comes the Reformer eating locusts and wild honey.

To preserve wild animals implies generally the creation of a forest for them to dwell in or resort to. So it is with man. A hundred years ago they sold bark in our streets peeled from our own woods. In the very aspect of those primitive and rugged trees there was, methinks, a tanning principle which hardened and consolidated the fibres of men's thoughts. Ah! already I shudder for these comparatively degenerate days of my native village, when you cannot collect a load of bark of good thickness, and we no longer produce tar and turpentine.

The civilized nations — Greece, Rome, England — have been sustained by the primitive forests which anciently rotted where they stand. They survive as long as the soil is not exhausted. Alas for human culture! little is to be expected of a nation, when the vegetable mould is exhausted, and it is compelled to make manure of the bones of its fathers. There the poet sustains himself merely by his own superfluous fat, and the philosopher comes down on his marrow-bones.

It is said to be the task of the American "to work

the virgin soil," and that "agriculture here already
assumes proportions unknown everywhere else." I
think that the farmer displaces the Indian even because he redeems the meadow, and so makes himself
stronger and in some respects more natural. I was
surveying for a man the other day a single straight
line one hundred and thirty-two rods long, through a
swamp at whose entrance might have been written the
words which Dante read over the entrance to the infernal regions, "Leave all hope, ye that enter," — that
is, of ever getting out again; where at one time I saw
my employer actually up to his neck and swimming
for his life in his property, though it was still winter.
He had another similar swamp which I could not survey at all, because it was completely under water, and
nevertheless, with regard to a third swamp, which I
did *survey* from a distance, he remarked to me, true
to his instincts, that he would not part with it for any
consideration, on account of the mud which it contained. And that man intends to put a girdling ditch
round the whole in the course of forty months, and so
redeem it by the magic of his spade. I refer to him
only as the type of a class.

The weapons with which we have gained our most
important victories, which should be handed down as
heirlooms from father to son, are not the sword and the
lance, but the bushwhack, the turf-cutter, the spade,
and the bog hoe, rusted with the blood of many a
meadow, and begrimed with the dust of many a hard-
fought field. The very winds blew the Indian's cornfield into the meadow, and pointed out the way which

he had not the skill to follow. He had no better implement with which to intrench himself in the land than a clamshell. But the farmer is armed with plow and spade.

In literature it is only the wild that attracts us. Dullness is but another name for tameness. It is the uncivilized free and wild thinking in Hamlet and the Iliad, in all the scriptures and mythologies, not learned in the schools, that delights us. As the wild duck is more swift and beautiful than the tame, so is the wild — the mallard — thought, which 'mid falling dews wings its way above the fens. A truly good book is something as natural, and as unexpectedly and unaccountably fair and perfect, as a wild-flower discovered on the prairies of the West or in the jungles of the East. Genius is a light which makes the darkness visible, like the lightning's flash, which perchance shatters the temple of knowledge itself, — and not a taper lighted at the hearth-stone of the race, which pales before the light of common day.

English literature, from the days of the minstrels to the Lake Poets, — Chaucer and Spenser and Milton, and even Shakespeare, included, — breathes no quite fresh and, in this sense, wild strain. It is an essentially tame and civilized literature, reflecting Greece and Rome. Her wilderness is a greenwood, her wild man a Robin Hood. There is plenty of genial love of Nature, but not so much of Nature herself. Her chronicles inform us when her wild animals, but not when the wild man in her, became extinct.

The science of Humboldt is one thing, poetry is another thing. The poet to-day, notwithstanding all the discoveries of science, and the accumulated learning of mankind, enjoys no advantage over Homer.

Where is the literature which gives expression ‘to Nature? He would be a poet who could impress the winds and streams into his service, to speak for him; who nailed words to their primitive senses, as farmers drive down stakes in the spring, which the frost has heaved; who derived his words as often as he used them, — transplanted them to his page with earth adhering to their roots; whose words were so true and fresh and natural that they would appear to expand like the buds at the approach of spring, though they lay half smothered between two musty leaves in a library, — aye, to bloom and bear fruit there, after their kind, annually, for the faithful reader, in sympathy with surrounding Nature.

I do not know of any poetry to quote which adequately expresses this yearning for the Wild. Approached from this side, the best poetry is tame. I do not know where to find in any literature, ancient or modern, any account which contents me of that Nature with which even I am acquainted. You will perceive that I demand something which no Augustan nor Elizabethan age, which no *culture*, in short, can give. Mythology comes nearer to it than anything. How much more fertile a Nature, at least, has Grecian mythology its root in than English literature! Mythology is the crop which the Old World bore before its soil was exhausted, before the fancy and imagination were affected with blight; and which it still bears,

wherever its pristine vigor is unabated. All other literatures endure only as the elms which overshadow
our houses; but this is like the great dragon-tree of
the Western Isles, as old as mankind, and, whether
that does or not, will endure as long; for the decay of
other literatures makes the soil in which it thrives.

The West is preparing to add its fables to those of
the East. The valleys of the Ganges, the Nile, and
the Rhine having yielded their crop, it remains to be
seen what the valleys of the Amazon, the Plate, the
Orinoco, the St. Lawrence, and the Mississippi will
produce. Perchance, when, in the course of ages,
American liberty has become a fiction of the past, — as
it is to some extent a fiction of the present, — the poets
of the world will be inspired by American mythology.

The wildest dreams of wild men, even, are not the
less true, though they may not recommend themselves
to the sense which is most common among Englishmen
and Americans to-day. It is not every truth that recommends itself to the common sense. Nature has a place
for the wild clematis as well as for the cabbage. Some
expressions of truth are reminiscent, — others merely
sensible, as the phrase is, — others prophetic. Some
forms of disease, even, may prophesy forms of health.
The geologist has discovered that the figures of serpents,
griffins, flying dragons, and other fanciful embellish-
ments of heraldry, have their prototypes in the forms
of fossil species which were extinct before man was
created, and hence "indicate a faint and shadowy
knowledge of a previous state of organic existence."
The Hindoos dreamed that the earth rested on an ele-

phant, and the elephant on a tortoise, and the tortoise on a serpent; and though it may be an unimportant coincidence, it will not be out of place here to state, that a fossil tortoise has lately been discovered in Asia large enough to support an elephant. I confess that I am partial to these wild fancies, which transcend the order of time and development. They are the sublimest recreation of the intellect. The partridge loves peas, but not those that go with her into the pot.

In short, all good things are wild and free. There is something in a strain of music, whether produced by an instrument or by the human voice, — take the sound of a bugle in a summer night, for instance, — which by its wildness, to speak without satire, reminds me of the cries emitted by wild beasts in their native forests. It is so much of their wildness as I can understand. Give me for my friends and neighbors wild men, not tame ones. The wildness of the savage is but a faint symbol of the awful ferity with which good men and lovers meet.

I love even to see the domestic animals reassert their native rights, — any evidence that they have not wholly lost their original wild habits and vigor; as when my neighbor's cow breaks out of her pasture early in the spring and boldly swims the river, a cold, gray tide, twenty-five or thirty rods wide, swollen by the melted snow. It is the buffalo crossing the Mississippi. This exploit confers some dignity on the herd in my eyes, — already dignified. The seeds of instinct are preserved under the thick hides of cattle and horses, like seeds in the bowels of the earth, an indefinite period.

Any sportiveness in cattle is unexpected. I saw one day a herd of a dozen bullocks and cows running about and frisking in unwieldy sport, like huge rats, even like kittens. They shook their heads, raised their tails, and rushed up and down a hill, and I perceived by their horns, as well as by their activity, their relation to the deer tribe. But, alas! a sudden loud *Whoa!* would have damped their ardor at once, reduced them from venison to beef, and stiffened their sides and sinews like the locomotive. Who but the Evil One has cried "Whoa!" to mankind? Indeed, the life of cattle, like that of many men, is but a sort of locomotiveness; they move a side at a time, and man, by his machinery, is meeting the horse and the ox half-way. Whatever part the whip has touched is thenceforth palsied. Who would ever think of a *side* of any of the supple cat tribe, as we speak of a *side* of beef?

I rejoice that horses and steers have to be broken before they can be made the slaves of men, and that men themselves have some wild oats still left to sow before they become submissive members of society. Undoubtedly, all men are not equally fit subjects for civilization; and because the majority, like dogs and sheep, are tame by inherited disposition, this is no reason why the others should have their natures broken that they may be reduced to the same level. Men are in the main alike, but they were made several in order that they might be various. If a low use is to be served, one man will do nearly or quite as well as another; if a high one, individual excellence is to be regarded. Any man can stop a hole to keep the wind away, but no other man could serve so rare a use as the author of this illustration did. Confucius says, "The skins of the tiger and the leopard, when they are tanned, are as the skins of the dog and the sheep tanned." But it is not the part of a true culture to tame tigers, any more than it is to make sheep ferocious; and tanning their skins for shoes is not the best use to which they can be put.

When looking over a list of men's names in a foreign language, as of military officers, or of authors who have written on a particular subject, I am reminded once more that there is nothing in a name. The name Menschikoff, for instance, has nothing in it to my ears more human than a whisker, and it may belong to a rat. As the names of the Poles and Russians are to us, so are ours to them. It is as if they had been named by the child's rigmarole, *Iery wiery ichery van, tittle-tol-tan.* I see in my mind a herd of wild creatures swarming over the earth, and to each the herdsman has affixed some barbarous sound in his own dialect. The names of men are, of course, as cheap and meaningless as *Bose* and *Tray,* the names of dogs.

Methinks it would be some advantage to philosophy if men were named merely in the gross, as they are known. It would be necessary only to know the genus and perhaps the race or variety, to know the individual. We are not prepared to believe that every private soldier in a Roman army had a name of his own, — because we have not supposed that he had a character of his own.

At present our only true names are nicknames. I knew a boy who, from his peculiar energy, was called

"Buster" by his playmates, and this rightly supplanted his Christian name. Some travelers tell us that an Indian had no name given him at first, but earned it, and his name was his fame; and among some tribes he acquired a new name with every new exploit. It is pitiful when a man bears a name for convenience merely, who has earned neither name nor fame.

I will not allow mere names to make distinctions for me, but still see men in herds for all them. A familiar name cannot make a man less strange to me. It may be given to a savage who retains in secret his own wild title earned in the woods. We have a wild savage in us, and a savage name is perchance somewhere recorded as ours. I see that my neighbor, who bears the familiar epithet William or Edwin, takes it off with his jacket. It does not adhere to him when asleep or in anger, or aroused by any passion or inspiration. I seem to hear pronounced by some of his kin at such a time his original wild name in some jaw-breaking or else melodious tongue.

Here is this vast, savage, howling mother of ours, Nature, lying all around, with such beauty, and such affection for her children, as the leopard; and yet we are so early weaned from her breast to society, to that culture which is exclusively an interaction of man on man, — a sort of breeding in and in, which produces at most a merely English nobility, a civilization destined to have a speedy limit.

In society, in the best institutions of men, it is easy to detect a certain precocity. When we should still be growing children, we are already little men. Give me a culture which imports much muck from the meadows, and deepens the soil, — not that which trusts to heating manures, and improved implements and modes of culture only!

Many a poor sore-eyed student that I have heard of would grow faster, both intellectually and physically, if, instead of sitting up so very late, he honestly slumbered a fool's allowance.

There may be an excess even of informing light. Niepce, a Frenchman, discovered "actinism," that power in the sun's rays which produces a chemical effect; that granite rocks, and stone structures, and statues of metal "are all alike destructively acted upon during the hours of sunshine, and, but for provisions of Nature no less wonderful, would soon perish under the delicate touch of the most subtile of the agencies of the universe." But he observed that "those bodies which underwent this change during the daylight possessed the power of restoring themselves to their original conditions during the hours of night, when this excitement was no longer influencing them." Hence it has been inferred that "the hours of darkness are as necessary to the inorganic creation as we know night and sleep are to the organic kingdom." Not even does the moon shine every night, but gives place to darkness.

I would not have every man nor every part of a man cultivated, any more than I would have every acre of earth cultivated: part will be tillage, but the greater part will be meadow and forest, not only serving an immediate use, but preparing a mould against a distant future, by the annual decay of the vegetation which it supports.

There are other letters for the child to learn than those which Cadmus invented. The Spaniards have a good term to express this wild and dusky knowledge, *Gramática parda*, tawny grammar, a kind of mother-wit derived from that same leopard to which I have referred.

We have heard of a Society for the Diffusion of Useful Knowledge. It is said that knowledge is power, and the like. Methinks there is equal need of a Society for the Diffusion of Useful Ignorance, what we will call Beautiful Knowledge, a knowledge useful in a higher sense: for what is most of our boasted so-called knowledge but a conceit that we know something, which robs us of the advantage of our actual ignorance? What we call knowledge is often our positive ignorance; ignorance our negative knowledge. By long years of patient industry and reading of the newspapers, — for what are the libraries of science but files of newspapers? — a man accumulates a myriad facts, lays them up in his memory, and then when in some spring of his life he saunters abroad into the Great Fields of thought, he, as it were, goes to grass like a horse and leaves all his harness behind in the stable. I would say to the Society for the Diffusion of Useful Knowledge, sometimes, — Go to grass. You have eaten hay long enough. The spring has come with its green crop. The very cows are driven to their country pastures before the end of May; though I have heard of one unnatural farmer who kept his cow in the barn and fed her on hay all the year round. So, frequently, the Society for the Diffusion of Useful Knowledge treats its cattle.

A man's ignorance sometimes is not only useful, but beautiful, — while his knowledge, so called, is oftentimes worse than useless, besides being ugly. Which is the best man to deal with, — he who knows nothing about a subject, and, what is extremely rare, knows that he knows nothing, or he who really knows something about it, but thinks that he knows all?

My desire for knowledge is intermittent, but my desire to bathe my head in atmospheres unknown to my feet is perennial and constant. The highest that we can attain to is not Knowledge, but Sympathy with Intelligence. I do not know that this higher knowledge amounts to anything more definite than a novel and grand surprise on a sudden revelation of the insufficiency of all that we called Knowledge before, — a discovery that there are more things in heaven and earth than are dreamed of in our philosophy. It is the lighting up of the mist by the sun. Man cannot *know* in any higher sense than this, any more than he can look serenely and with impunity in the face of the sun: Ὡς τὶ νοῶν, οὐ κεῖνον νοήσεις, "You will not perceive that, as perceiving a particular thing," say the Chaldean Oracles.

There is something servile in the habit of seeking after a law which we may obey. We may study the laws of matter at and for our convenience, but a successful life knows no law. It is an unfortunate discovery certainly, that of a law which binds us where we did not know before that we were bound. Live free, child of the mist, — and with respect to knowledge we are all children of the mist. The man who takes the liberty to live is superior to all the laws, by virtue of his relation to the lawmaker. "That is active duty," says the Vishnu Purana, "which is not for our bondage; that is knowledge which is for our liberation: all other duty is good only unto weariness; all other knowledge is only the cleverness of an artist."

It is remarkable how few events or crises there are in our histories, how little exercised we have been in our minds, how few experiences we have had. I would fain be assured that I am growing apace and rankly, though my very growth disturb this dull equanimity, — though it be with struggle through long, dark, muggy nights or seasons of gloom. It would be well if all our lives were a divine tragedy even, instead of this trivial comedy or farce. Dante, Bunyan, and others appear to have been exercised in their minds more than we: they were subjected to a kind of culture such as our district schools and colleges do not contemplate. Even Mahomet, though many may scream at his name, had a good deal more to live for, aye, and to die for, than they have commonly.

When, at rare intervals, some thought visits one, as perchance he is walking on a railroad, then, indeed, the cars go by without his hearing them. But soon, by some inexorable law, our life goes by and the cars return.

> "Gentle breeze, that wanderest unseen,
> And bendest the thistles round Loira of storms,
> Traveler of the windy glens,
> Why hast thou left my ear so soon?"

While almost all men feel an attraction drawing them to society, few are attracted strongly to Nature. In their reaction to Nature men appear to me for the most part, notwithstanding their arts, lower than the animals. It is not often a beautiful relation, as in the case of the animals. How little appreciation of the beauty of the landscape there is among us! We have to be told that the Greeks called the world Κόσμος, Beauty, or Order, but we do not see clearly why they did so, and we esteem it at best only a curious philological fact.

For my part, I feel that with regard to Nature I live a sort of border life, on the confines of a world into which I make occasional and transient forays only, and my patriotism and allegiance to the state into whose territories I seem to retreat are those of a moss-trooper. Unto a life which I call natural I would gladly follow even a will-o'-the-wisp through bogs and sloughs unimaginable, but no moon nor firefly has shown me the causeway to it. Nature is a personality so vast and universal that we have never seen one of her features. The walker in the familiar fields which stretch around my native town sometimes finds himself in another land than is described in their owners' deeds, as it were in some faraway field on the confines of the actual Concord, where her jurisdiction ceases, and the idea which the word Concord suggests ceases to be suggested. These farms which I have myself surveyed, these bounds which I have set up, appear dimly still as through a mist; but they have no chemistry to fix them; they fade from the surface of the glass, and the picture which the painter painted stands out dimly from beneath. The world with which we are commonly acquainted leaves no trace, and it will have no anniversary.

I took a walk on Spaulding's Farm the other afternoon. I saw the setting sun lighting up the opposite
side of a stately pine wood. Its golden rays straggled into
the aisles of the wood as into some noble hall. I was
impressed as if some ancient and altogether admirable
and shining family had settled there in that part of the
land called Concord, unknown to me, — to whom the
sun was servant, — who had not gone into society in
the village, — who had not been called on. I saw their
park, their pleasure-ground, beyond through the wood,
in Spaulding's cranberry-meadow. The pines furnished
them with gables as they grew. Their house was not
obvious to vision; the trees grew through it. I do not
know whether I heard the sounds of a suppressed
hilarity or not. They seemed to recline on the sunbeams.
They have sons and daughters. They are quite well.
The farmer's cart-path, which leads directly through
their hall, does not in the least put them out, as the
muddy bottom of a pool is sometimes seen through the
reflected skies. They never heard of Spaulding, and do
not know that he is their neighbor, — notwithstanding
I heard him whistle as he drove his team through the
house. Nothing can equal the serenity of their lives.
Their coat-of-arms is simply a lichen. I saw it painted
on the pines and oaks. Their attics were in the tops of
the trees. They are of no politics. There was no noise
of labor. I did not perceive that they were weaving or
spinning. Yet I did detect, when the wind lulled and
hearing was done away, the finest imaginable sweet
musical hum, — as of a distant hive in May, — which
perchance was the sound of their thinking. They had no

idle thoughts, and no one without could see their work, for their industry was not as in knots and excrescences embayed.

But I find it difficult to remember them. They fade irrevocably out of my mind even now while I speak, and endeavor to recall them and recollect myself. It is only after a long and serious effort to recollect my best thoughts that I become again aware of their cohabitancy. If it were not for such families as this, I think I should move out of Concord.

We are accustomed to say in New England that few and fewer pigeons visit us every year. Our forests furnish no mast for them. So, it would seem, few and fewer thoughts visit each growing man from year to year, for the grove in our minds is laid waste, — sold to feed unnecessary fires of ambition, or sent to mill, — and there is scarcely a twig left for them to perch on. They no longer build nor breed with us. In some more genial season, perchance, a faint shadow flits across the landscape of the mind, cast by the *wings* of some thought in its vernal or autumnal migration, but, looking up, we are unable to detect the substance of the thought itself. Our winged thoughts are turned to poultry. They no longer soar, and they attain only to a Shanghai and Cochin-China grandeur. Those *gra-a-ate thoughts*, those *gra-a-ate men* you hear of!

We hug the earth, — how rarely we mount! Methinks we might elevate ourselves a little more. We might climb a tree, at least. I found my account in climbing a tree once. It was a tall white pine, on the top of a hill; and though I got well pitched, I was well paid for it, for I discovered new mountains in the horizon which I had never seen before, — so much more of the earth and the heavens. I might have walked about the foot of the tree for threescore years and ten, and yet I certainly should never have seen them. But, above all, I discovered around me, — it was near the end of June, — on the ends of the topmost branches only, a few minute and delicate red cone-like blossoms, the fertile flower of the white pine looking heavenward. I carried straightway to the village the topmost spire, and showed it to stranger jurymen who walked the streets, — for it was court week, — and to farmers and lumber-dealers and woodchoppers and hunters, and not one had ever seen the like before, but they wondered as at a star dropped down. Tell of ancient architects finishing their works on the tops of columns as perfectly as on the lower and more visible parts! Nature has from the first expanded the minute blossoms of the forest only toward the heavens, above men's heads and unobserved by them. We see only the flowers that are under our feet in the meadows. The pines have developed their delicate blossoms on the highest twigs of the wood every summer for ages, as well over the heads of Nature's red children as of her white ones; yet scarcely a farmer or hunter in the land has ever seen them.

Above all, we cannot afford not to live in the present. He is blessed over all mortals who loses no moment of the passing life in remembering the past. Unless our philosophy hears the cock crow in every barn-yard within our horizon, it is belated. That sound commonly reminds us that we are growing rusty and antique in our employments and habits of thought. His philosophy comes down to a more recent time than ours. There is something suggested by it that is a newer testament, — the gospel according to this moment. He has not fallen astern; he has got up early and kept up early, and to be where he is is to be in season, in the foremost rank of time. It is an expression of the health and soundness of Nature, a brag for all the world, — healthiness as of a spring burst forth, a new fountain of the Muses, to celebrate this last instant of time. Where he lives no fugitive slave laws are passed. Who has not betrayed his master many times since last he heard that note?

The merit of this bird's strain is in its freedom from all plaintiveness. The singer can easily move us to tears or to laughter, but where is he who can excite in us a pure morning joy? When, in doleful dumps, breaking the awful stillness of our wooden sidewalk on a Sunday, or, perchance, a watcher in the house of mourning, I hear a cockerel crow far or near, I think to myself, "There is one of us well, at any rate," — and with a sudden gush return to my senses.

We had a remarkable sunset one day last November. I was walking in a meadow, the source of a small brook, when the sun at last, just before setting, after a cold, gray day, reached a clear stratum in the horizon, and

the softest, brightest morning sunlight fell on the dry
grass and on the stems of the trees in the opposite horizon and on the leaves of the shrub oaks on the hillside,
while our shadows stretched long over the meadow
eastward, as if we were the only motes in its beams.
It was such a light as we could not have imagined a
moment before, and the air also was so warm and serene
that nothing was wanting to make a paradise of that
meadow. When we reflected that this was not a solitary
phenomenon, never to happen again, but that it would
happen forever and ever, an infinite number of evenings,
and cheer and reassure the latest child that walked
there, it was more glorious still.

The sun sets on some retired meadow, where no
house is visible, with all the glory and splendor that it
lavishes on cities, and perchance as it has never set
before, — where there is but a solitary marsh hawk
to have his wings gilded by it, or only a musquash
looks out from his cabin, and there is some little black-
veined brook in the midst of the marsh, just beginning to meander, winding slowly round a decaying
stump. We walked in so pure and bright a light,
gilding the withered grass and leaves, so softly and
serenely bright, I thought I had never bathed in such
a golden flood, without a ripple or a murmur to it.
The west side of every wood and rising ground gleamed
like the boundary of Elysium, and the sun on our
backs seemed like a gentle herdsman driving us home
at evening.

So we saunter toward the Holy Land, till one day
the sun shall shine more brightly than ever he has done,

shall perchance shine into our minds and hearts, and
light up our whole lives with a great awakening light,
as warm and serene and golden as on a bankside in
autumn.

CIVIL DISOBEDIENCE

CIVIL DISOBEDIENCE

I HEARTILY accept the motto, "That government is best which governs least;" and I should like to see it acted up to more rapidly and systematically. Carried out, it finally amounts to this, which also I believe, — "That government is best which governs not at all;" and when men are prepared for it, that will be the kind of government which they will have. Government is at best but an expedient; but most governments are usually, and all governments are sometimes, inexpedient. The objections which have been brought against a standing army, and they are many and weighty, and deserve to prevail, may also at last be brought against a standing government. The standing army is only an arm of the standing government. The government itself, which is only the mode which the people have chosen to execute their will, is equally liable to be abused and perverted before the people can act through it. Witness the present Mexican war, the work of comparatively a few individuals using the standing government as their tool; for, in the outset, the people would not have consented to this measure.

This American government, — what is it but a tradition, though a recent one, endeavoring to transmit itself unimpaired to posterity, but each instant losing some of its integrity? It has not the vitality and force of a single living man; for a single man can bend it to his will. It is a sort of wooden gun to the people themselves. But it is not the less necessary for this; for the people must have some complicated machinery or other, and hear its din, to satisfy that idea of government which they have. Governments show thus how successfully men can be imposed on, even impose on themselves, for their own advantage. It is excellent, we must all allow. Yet this government never of itself furthered any enterprise, but by the alacrity with which it got out of its way. *It* does not keep the country free. *It* does not settle the West. *It* does not educate. The character inherent in the American people has done all that has been accomplished; and it would have done somewhat more, if the government had not sometimes got in its way. For government is an expedient by which men would fain succeed in letting one another alone; and, as has been said, when it is most expedient, the governed are most let alone by it. Trade and commerce, if they were not made of india-rubber, would never manage to bounce over the obstacles which legislators are continually putting in their way; and, if one were to judge these men wholly by the effects of their actions and not partly by their intentions, they would deserve to be classed and punished with those mischievous persons who put obstructions on the railroads.

But, to speak practically and as a citizen, unlike those who call themselves no-government men, I ask for, not at once no government, but *at once* a better government. Let every man make known what kind of government would command his respect, and that will be one step toward obtaining it.

After all, the practical reason why, when the power is once in the hands of the people, a majority are permitted, and for a long period continue, to rule is not because they are most likely to be in the right, nor because this seems fairest to the minority, but because they are physically the strongest. But a government in which the majority rule in all cases cannot be based on justice, even as far as men understand it. Can there not be a government in which majorities do not virtually decide right and wrong, but conscience? — in which majorities decide only those questions to which the rule of expediency is applicable? Must the citizen ever for a moment, or in the least degree, resign his conscience to the legislator? Why has every man a conscience, then? I think that we should be men first, and subjects afterward. It is not desirable to cultivate a respect for the law, so much as for the right. The only obligation which I have a right to assume is to do at any time what I think right. It is truly enough said that a corporation has no conscience; but a corporation of conscientious men is a corporation *with* a conscience. Law never made men a whit more just; and, by means of their respect for it, even the well-disposed are daily made the agents of injustice. A common and natural result of an undue respect for law is, that you may see a file of soldiers, colonel, captain, corporal, privates, powder-monkeys, and all, marching in admirable order over hill and dale to the wars, against their wills, ay, against their common sense and consciences, which makes it very steep marching indeed, and produces a palpitation of the heart. They have no doubt that it is a damnable business in which they are concerned; they are all peaceably inclined. Now, what are they? Men at all? or small movable forts and magazines, at the service of some unscrupulous man in power? Visit the Navy-Yard, and behold a marine, such a man as an American government can make, or such as it can make a man with its black arts, — a mere shadow and reminiscence of humanity, a man laid out alive and standing, and already, as one may say, buried under arms with funeral accompaniments, though it may be, —

> " Not a drum was heard, not a funeral note,
>   As his corse to the rampart we hurried;
>   Not a soldier discharged his farewell shot
>   O'er the grave where our hero we buried."

The mass of men serve the state thus, not as men mainly, but as machines, with their bodies. They are the standing army, and the militia, jailers, constables, *posse comitatus*, etc. In most cases there is no free exercise whatever of the judgment or of the moral sense; but they put themselves on a level with wood and earth and stones; and wooden men can perhaps be manufactured that will serve the purpose as well. Such command no more respect than men of straw or a lump of dirt. They have the same sort of worth only as horses and dogs. Yet such as these even are commonly esteemed good citizens. Others — as most legislators, politicians, lawyers, ministers, and office-holders — serve the state chiefly with their heads; and, as they rarely make any moral distinctions, they are as likely to serve the devil, without *intending* it, as God. A very few — as heroes, patriots, martyrs, reformers in the great sense, and *men* — serve the state with their consciences also, and so necessarily resist it for the most part; and they are commonly treated as enemies by it. A wise man will only be useful as a man, and will not submit to be "clay," and "stop a hole to keep the wind away," but leave that office to his dust at least:—

> "I am too high-born to be propertied,
> To be a secondary at control,
> Or useful serving-man and instrument
> To any sovereign state throughout the world."

He who gives himself entirely to his fellow-men appears to them useless and selfish; but he who gives himself partially to them is pronounced a benefactor and philanthropist.

How does it become a man to behave toward this American government to-day? I answer, that he cannot without disgrace be associated with it. I cannot for an instant recognize that political organization as *my* government which is the *slave's* government also.

All men recognize the right of revolution; that is, the right to refuse allegiance to, and to resist, the government, when its tyranny or its inefficiency are great and unendurable. But almost all say that such is not the case now. But such was the case, they think, in the Revolution of '75. If one were to tell me that this was a bad government because it taxed certain foreign commodities brought to its ports, it is most probable that I should not make an ado about it, for I can do without them. All machines have their friction; and possibly this does enough good to counterbalance the evil. At any rate, it is a great evil to make a stir about it. But when the friction comes to have its machine, and oppression and robbery are organized, I say, let us not have such a machine any longer. In other words, when a sixth of the population of a nation which has undertaken to be the refuge of liberty are slaves, and a whole country is unjustly overrun and conquered by a foreign army, and subjected to military law, I think that it is not too soon for honest men to rebel and revolutionize. What makes this duty the more urgent is the fact that the country so overrun is not our own, but ours is the invading army.

Paley, a common authority with many on moral questions, in his chapter on the " Duty of Submission to Civil Government," resolves all civil obligation into expediency; and he proceeds to say that " so long as the interest of the whole society requires it, that is, so long as the established government cannot be resisted or changed without public inconveniency, it is the will of God . . . that the established government be obeyed, — and no longer. This principle being admitted, the justice of every particular case of resistance is reduced to a computation of the quantity of the danger and grievance on the one side, and of the probability and expense of redressing it on the other." Of this, he says, every man shall judge for himself. But Paley appears never to have contemplated those cases to which the rule of expediency does not apply, in which a people, as well as an individual, must do justice, cost what it may. If I have unjustly wrested a plank from a drowning man, I must restore it to him though I drown myself.

This, according to Paley, would be inconvenient. But he that would save his life, in such a case, shall lose it. This people must cease to hold slaves, and to make war on Mexico, though it cost them their existence as a people.

In their practice, nations agree with Paley; but does any one think that Massachusetts does exactly what is right at the present crisis?

> "A drab of state, a cloth-o'-silver slut,
>   To have her train borne up, and her soul trail in the dirt."

Practically speaking, the opponents to a reform in Massachusetts are not a hundred thousand politicians at the South, but a hundred thousand merchants and farmers here, who are more interested in commerce and agriculture than they are in humanity, and are not prepared to do justice to the slave and to Mexico, *cost what it may*. I quarrel not with far-off foes, but with those who, near at home, coöperate with, and do the bidding of, those far away, and without whom the latter would be harmless. We are accustomed to say, that the mass of men are unprepared; but improvement is slow, because the few are not materially wiser or better than the many. It is not so important that many should be as good as you, as that there be some absolute goodness somewhere; for that will leaven the whole lump. There are thousands who are *in opinion* opposed to slavery and to the war, who yet in effect do nothing to put an end to them; who, esteeming themselves children of Washington and Franklin, sit down with their hands in their pockets, and say that they know not what to do, and do nothing; who even postpone the question of freedom to the question of free trade, and quietly read the prices-current along with the latest advices from Mexico, after dinner, and, it may be, fall asleep over them both. What is the price-current of an honest man and patriot to-day? They hesitate, and they regret, and sometimes they petition; but they do nothing in earnest and with effect. They will wait, well disposed, for others to remedy the evil, that they may no longer have it to regret. At most, they give only a cheap vote, and a feeble countenance and God-speed, to the right, as it goes by them. There are nine hundred and ninety-nine patrons of virtue to one virtuous man. But it is easier to deal with the real possessor of a thing than with the temporary guardian of it.

All voting is a sort of gaming, like checkers or backgammon, with a slight moral tinge to it, a playing with right and wrong, with moral questions; and betting naturally accompanies it. The character of the voters is not staked. I cast my vote, perchance, as I think right; but I am not vitally concerned that that right should prevail. I am willing to leave it to the majority. Its obligation, therefore, never exceeds that of expediency. Even voting *for the right* is *doing* nothing for it. It is only expressing to men feebly your desire that it should prevail. A wise man will not leave the right to the mercy of chance, nor wish it to prevail through the power of the majority. There is but little virtue in the action of masses of men. When the majority shall at length vote for the abolition of slavery, it will be because they are indifferent to slavery, or because there is but little slavery left to be abolished by their vote. *They* will then be the only slaves. Only *his* vote can hasten the abolition of slavery who asserts his own freedom by his vote.

I hear of a convention to be held at Baltimore, or elsewhere, for the selection of a candidate for the Presidency, made up chiefly of editors, and men who are politicians by profession; but I think, what is it to any independent, intelligent, and respectable man what decision they may come to? Shall we not have the advantage of his wisdom and honesty, nevertheless? Can we not count upon some independent votes? Are there not many individuals in the country who do not attend conventions? But no: I find that the respectable man, so called, has immediately drifted from his position, and despairs of his country, when his country has more reason to despair of him. He forthwith adopts one of the candidates thus selected as the only *available* one, thus proving that he is himself *available* for any purposes of the demagogue. His vote is of no more worth than that of any unprincipled foreigner or hireling native, who may have been bought. O for a man who is a *man*, and, as my neighbor says, has a bone in his back which you cannot pass your hand through! Our statistics are at fault: the population has been returned too large. How many *men* are there to a square thousand miles in this country? Hardly one. Does not America offer any inducement for men to settle here? The American has dwindled into an Odd Fellow, — one who may be known by the development of his organ of gregariousness, and a manifest lack of intellect and cheerful self-reliance; whose first and chief concern, on coming into the world, is to see that the almshouses are in good repair; and, before yet he has lawfully donned the virile garb, to collect a fund for the support of the widows and orphans that may be; who, in short, ventures to live only by the aid of the Mutual Insurance company, which has promised to bury him decently.

It is not a man's duty, as a matter of course, to devote himself to the eradication of any, even the most enormous, wrong; he may still properly have other concerns to engage him; but it is his duty, at least, to wash his hands of it, and, if he gives it no thought longer, not to give it practically his support. If I devote myself to other pursuits and contemplations, I must first see, at least, that I do not pursue them sitting upon another man's shoulders. I must get off him first, that he may pursue his contemplations too. See what gross inconsistency is tolerated. I have heard some of my townsmen say, " I should like to have them order me out to help put down an insurrection of the slaves, or to march to Mexico; — see if I would go;" and yet these very men have each, directly by their allegiance, and so indirectly, at least, by their money, furnished a substitute. The soldier is applauded who refuses to serve in an unjust war by those who do not refuse to sustain the unjust government which makes the war; is applauded by those whose own act and authority he disregards and sets at naught; as if the state were penitent to that degree that it hired one to scourge it while it sinned, but not to that degree that it left off sinning for a moment. Thus, under the name of Order and Civil Government, we are all made at last to pay homage to and support our own meanness. After the first blush of sin comes its indifference; and from immoral it becomes, as it were, *un*moral, and not quite unnecessary to that life which we have made.

The broadest and most prevalent error requires the most disinterested virtue to sustain it. The slight reproach to which the virtue of patriotism is commonly liable, the noble are most likely to incur. Those who, while they disapprove of the character and measures of a government, yield to it their allegiance and support are undoubtedly its most conscientious supporters, and so frequently the most serious obstacles to reform. Some are petitioning the State to dissolve the Union, to disregard the requisitions of the President. Why do they not dissolve it themselves, — the union between themselves and the State, — and refuse to pay their quota into its treasury ? Do not they stand in the same relation to the State that the State does to the Union ? And have not the same reasons prevented the State from resisting the Union which have prevented them from resisting the State ?

How can a man be satisfied to entertain an opinion merely, and enjoy *it* ? Is there any enjoyment in it, if his opinion is that he is aggrieved ? If you are cheated out of a single dollar by your neighbor, you do not rest satisfied with knowing that you are cheated, or with saying that you are cheated, or even with petitioning him to pay you your due; but you take effectual steps at once to obtain the full amount, and see that you are never cheated again. Action from principle, the perception and the performance of right, changes things and relations; it is essentially revolutionary, and does not consist wholly with anything which was. It not only divides States and churches, it divides families; ay, it divides the *individual*, separating the diabolical in him from the divine.

Unjust laws exist: shall we be content to obey them, or shall we endeavor to amend them, and obey them until we have succeeded, or shall we transgress them at once? Men generally, under such a government as this, think that they ought to wait until they have persuaded the majority to alter them. They think that, if they should resist, the remedy would be worse than the evil. But it is the fault of the government itself that the remedy *is* worse than the evil. *It* makes it worse. Why is it not more apt to anticipate and provide for reform? Why does it not cherish its wise minority? Why does it cry and resist before it is hurt? Why does it not encourage its citizens to be on the alert to point out its faults, and *do* better than it would have them? Why does it always crucify Christ, and excommunicate Copernicus and Luther, and pronounce Washington and Franklin rebels?

One would think, that a deliberate and practical denial of its authority was the only offence never contemplated by government; else, why has it not assigned its definite, its suitable and proportionate, penalty? If a man who has no property refuses but once to earn nine shillings for the State, he is put in prison for a period unlimited by any law that I know, and determined only by the discretion of those who placed him there; but if he should steal ninety times nine shillings from the State, he is soon permitted to go at large again.

If the injustice is part of the necessary friction of the machine of government, let it go, let it go: perchance it will wear smooth, — certainly the machine will wear out. If the injustice has a spring, or a pulley, or a rope, or a crank, exclusively for itself, then perhaps you may consider whether the remedy will not be worse than the evil; but if it is of such a nature that it requires you to be the agent of injustice to another, then, I say, break the law. Let your life be a counter-friction to stop the machine. What I have to do is to see, at any rate, that I do not lend myself to the wrong which I condemn.

As for adopting the ways which the State has provided for remedying the evil, I know not of such ways. They take too much time, and a man's life will be gone. I have other affairs to attend to. I came into this world, not chiefly to make this a good place to live in, but to live in it, be it good or bad. A man has not everything to do, but something; and because he cannot do *everything*, it is not necessary that he should do *something* wrong. It is not my business to be petitioning the Governor or the Legislature any more than it is theirs to petition me; and if they should not hear my petition, what should I do then? But in this case the State has provided no way: its very Constitution is the evil. This may seem to be harsh and stubborn and unconciliatory; but it is to treat with the utmost kindness and consideration the only spirit that can appreciate or deserves it. So is all change for the better, like birth and death, which convulse the body.

I do not hesitate to say, that those who call themselves Abolitionists should at once effectually withdraw their support, both in person and property, from the government of Massachusetts, and not wait till they constitute a majority of one, before they suffer the right to prevail through them. I think that it is enough if they have God on their side, without waiting for that other one. Moreover, any man more right than his neighbors constitutes a majority of one already.

I meet this American government, or its representative, the State government, directly, and face to face, once a year — no more — in the person of its tax-gatherer; this is the only mode in which a man situated as I am necessarily meets it; and it then says distinctly, Recognize me; and the simplest, the most effectual, and, in the present posture of affairs, the indispensablest mode of treating with it on this head, of expressing your little satisfaction with and love for it, is to deny it then. My civil neighbor, the tax-gatherer, is the very man I have to deal with, — for it is, after all, with men and not with parchment that I quarrel, — and he has voluntarily chosen to be an agent of the government. How shall he ever know well what he is and does as an officer of the government, or as a man, until he is obliged to consider whether he shall treat me, his neighbor, for whom he has respect, as a neighbor and well-disposed man, or as a maniac and disturber of the peace, and see if he can get over this obstruction

to his neighborliness without a ruder and more impetuous thought or speech corresponding with his action.
I know this well, that if one thousand, if one hundred,
if ten men whom I could name, — if ten *honest* men
only, — ay, if *one* HONEST man, in this State of Massachusetts, *ceasing to hold slaves*, were actually to withdraw from this copartnership, and be locked up in the
county jail therefor, it would be the abolition of slavery
in America. For it matters not how small the beginning may seem to be: what is once well done is done
forever. But we love better to talk about it: that
we say is our mission. Reform keeps many scores of
newspapers in its service, but not one man. If my
esteemed neighbor, the State's ambassador, who will
devote his days to the settlement of the question of
human rights in the Council Chamber, instead of being
threatened with the prisons of Carolina, were to sit
down the prisoner of Massachusetts, that State which
is so anxious to foist the sin of slavery upon her sister,
— though at present she can discover only an act of
inhospitality to be the ground of a quarrel with her, —
the Legislature would not wholly waive the subject the
following winter.

Under a government which imprisons any unjustly,
the true place for a just man is also a prison. The
proper place to-day, the only place which Massachusetts has provided for her freer and less desponding
spirits, is in her prisons, to be put out and locked out
of the State by her own act, as they have already put
themselves out by their principles. It is there that the
fugitive slave, and the Mexican prisoner on parole,

and the Indian come to plead the wrongs of his race should find them; on that separate, but more free and honorable, ground, where the State places those who are not *with* her, but *against* her, — the only house in a slave State in which a free man can abide with honor. If any think that their influence would be lost there, and their voices no longer afflict the ear of the State, that they would not be as an enemy within its walls, they do not know by how much truth is stronger than error, nor how much more eloquently and effectively he can combat injustice who has experienced a little in his own person. Cast your whole vote, not a strip of paper merely, but your whole influence. A minority is powerless while it conforms to the majority; it is not even a minority then; but it is irresistible when it clogs by its whole weight. If the alternative is to keep all just men in prison, or give up war and slavery, the State will not hesitate which to choose. If a thousand men were not to pay their tax-bills this year, that would not be a violent and bloody measure, as it would be to pay them, and enable the State to commit violence and shed innocent blood. This is, in fact, the definition of a peaceable revolution, if any such is possible. If the tax-gatherer, or any other public officer, asks me, as one has done, " But what shall I do?" my answer is, " If you really wish to do anything, resign your office." When the subject has refused allegiance, and the officer has resigned his office, then the revolution is accomplished. But even suppose blood should flow. Is there not a sort of blood shed when the conscience is wounded? Through this wound a man's real manhood and immortality flow out, and he bleeds to an everlasting death. I see this blood flowing now.

I have contemplated the imprisonment of the offender, rather than the seizure of his goods, — though both will serve the same purpose, — because they who assert the purest right, and consequently are most dangerous to a corrupt State, commonly have not spent much time in accumulating property. To such the State renders comparatively small service, and a slight tax is wont to appear exorbitant, particularly if they are obliged to earn it by special labor with their hands. If there were one who lived wholly without the use of money, the State itself would hesitate to demand it of him. But the rich man — not to make any invidious comparison — is always sold to the institution which makes him rich. Absolutely speaking, the more money, the less virtue; for money comes between a man and his objects, and obtains them for him; and it was certainly no great virtue to obtain it. It puts to rest many questions which he would otherwise be taxed to answer; while the only new question which it puts is the hard but superfluous one, how to spend it. Thus his moral ground is taken from under his feet. The opportunities of living are diminished in proportion as what are called the "means" are increased. The best thing a man can do for his culture when he is rich is to endeavor to carry out those schemes which he entertained when he was poor. Christ answered the Herodians according to their condition. "Show me the tribute-money," said he; — and one took a penny out of his pocket; — if you use money which has the image of Cæsar on it, and which he has made current and valuable, that is, *if you are men of the State*, and gladly enjoy the advantages of Cæsar's government, then pay him back some of his own when he demands it. " Render therefore to Cæsar that which is Cæsar's, and to God those things which are God's," — leaving them no wiser than before as to which was which; for they did not wish to know.

When I converse with the freest of my neighbors, I perceive that, whatever they may say about the magnitude and seriousness of the question, and their regard for the public tranquillity, the long and the short of the matter is, that they cannot spare the protection of the existing government, and they dread the consequences to their property and families of disobedience to it. For my own part, I should not like to think that I ever rely on the protection of the State. But, if I deny the authority of the State when it presents its tax-bill, it will soon take and waste all my property, and so harass me and my children without end. This is hard. This makes it impossible for a man to live honestly, and at the same time comfortably, in outward respects. It will not be worth the while to accumulate property; that would be sure to go again. You must hire or squat somewhere, and raise but a small crop, and eat that soon. You must live within yourself, and depend upon yourself always tucked up and ready for a start, and not have many affairs. A man may grow rich in Turkey even, if he will be in all respects a good subject of the Turkish government. Confucius said: " If a state is governed by the principles of reason, poverty and misery are subjects of shame; if a state is not governed by the principles of reason, riches and honors are the subjects of shame." No: until I want the protection of Massachusetts to be extended to me in some distant Southern port, where my liberty is endangered, or until I am bent solely on building up an estate at home by peaceful enterprise, I can afford to refuse allegiance to Massachusetts, and her right to my property and life. It costs me less in every sense to incur the penalty of disobedience to the State than it would to obey. I should feel as if I were worth less in that case.

Some years ago, the State met me in behalf of the Church, and commanded me to pay a certain sum toward the support of a clergyman whose preaching my father attended, but never I myself. "Pay," it said, " or be locked up in the jail." I declined to pay. But, unfortunately, another man saw fit to pay it. I did not see why the schoolmaster should be taxed to support the priest, and not the priest the schoolmaster; for I was not the State's schoolmaster, but I supported myself by voluntary subscription. I did not see why the lyceum should not present its tax-bill, and have the State to back its demand, as well as the Church. However, at the request of the selectmen, I condescended to make some such statement as this in writing: — " Know all men by these presents, that I, Henry Thoreau, do not wish to be regarded as a member of any incorporated society which I have not joined." This I gave to the town clerk; and he has it. The State, having thus learned that I did not wish to be regarded as a member of that church, has never made a like demand on me since; though it said that it must adhere to its original presumption that time. If I had known how to name them, I should then have signed off in detail from all the societies which I never signed on to; but I did not know where to find a complete list.

I have paid no poll-tax for six years. I was put into a jail once on this account, for one night; and, as I stood considering the walls of solid stone, two or three feet thick, the door of wood and iron, a foot thick, and the iron grating which strained the light, I could not help being struck with the foolishness of that institution which treated me as if I were mere flesh and blood and bones, to be locked up. I wondered that it should have concluded at length that this was the best use it could put me to, and had never thought to avail itself of my services in some way. I saw that, if there was a wall of stone between me and my townsmen, there was a still more difficult one to climb or break through before they could get to be as free as I was. I did not for a moment feel confined, and the walls seemed a great waste of stone and mortar. I felt as if I alone of all my townsmen had paid my tax. They plainly did not know how to treat me, but behaved like persons who are underbred. In every threat and in every compliment there was a blunder; for they thought that my chief desire was to stand the other side of that stone wall. I could not but smile to see how industriously they locked the door on my meditations, which followed them out again without let or hindrance, and *they* were really all that was dangerous. As they could not reach me, they had resolved to punish my body; just as boys, if they cannot come at some person against whom they have a spite, will abuse his dog. I saw that the State was half-witted, that it was timid as a lone woman with her silver spoons, and that it did not know its friends from its foes, and I lost all my remaining respect for it, and pitied it.

Thus the State never intentionally confronts a man's sense, intellectual or moral, but only his body, his senses. It is not armed with superior wit or honesty, but with superior physical strength. I was not born to be forced. I will breathe after my own fashion. Let us see who is the strongest. What force has a multitude? They only can force me who obey a higher law than I. They force me to become like themselves. I do not hear of *men* being *forced* to live this way or that by masses of men. What sort of life were that to live? When I meet a government which says to me, " Your money or your life," why should I be in haste to give it my money? It may be in a great strait, and not know what to do: I cannot help that. It must help itself; do as I do. It is not worth the while to snivel about it. I am not responsible for the successful working of the machinery of society. I am not the son of the engineer. I perceive that, when an acorn and a chestnut fall side by side, the one does not remain inert to make way for the other, but both obey their own laws, and spring and grow and flourish as best they can, till one, perchance, overshadows and destroys the other. If a plant cannot live according to its nature, it dies; and so a man.

Old chestnut trees on a hilltop

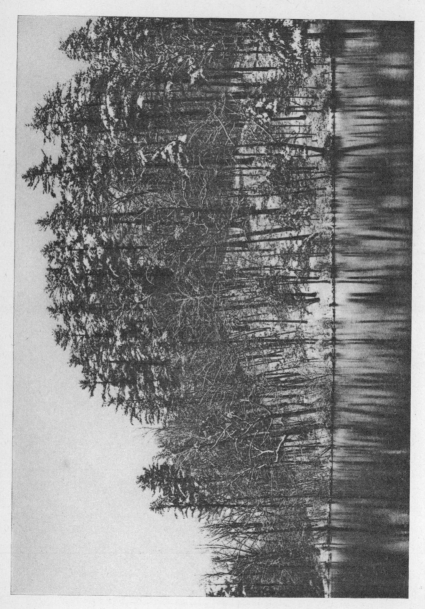

First snow

The night in prison was novel and interesting enough. The prisoners in their shirt-sleeves were enjoying a chat and the evening air in the doorway, when I entered. But the jailer said, " Come, boys, it is time to lock up;" and so they dispersed, and I heard the sound of their steps returning into the hollow apartments. My room-mate was introduced to me by the jailer as " a first-rate fellow and a clever man." When the door was locked, he showed me where to hang my hat, and how he managed matters there. The rooms were whitewashed once a month; and this one, at least, was the whitest, most simply furnished, and probably the neatest apartment in the town. He naturally wanted to know where I came from, and what brought me there; and, when I had told him, I asked him in my turn how he came there, presuming him to be an honest man, of course; and, as the world goes, I believe he was. " Why," said he, " they accuse me of burning a barn; but I never did it." As near as I could discover, he had probably gone to bed in a barn when drunk, and smoked his pipe there; and so a barn was burnt. He had the reputation of being a clever man, had been there some three months waiting for his trial to come on, and would have to wait as much longer; but he was quite domesticated and contented, since he got his board for nothing, and thought that he was well treated.

He occupied one window, and I the other; and I saw that if one stayed there long, his principal business would be to look out the window. I had soon read all the tracts that were left there, and examined where former prisoners had broken out, and where a grate had been sawed off, and heard the history of the various occupants of that room; for I found that even here there was a history and a gossip which never circulated beyond the walls of the jail. Probably this is the only house in the town where verses are composed, which are afterward printed in a circular form, but not published. I was shown quite a long list of verses which were composed by some young men who had been detected in an attempt to escape, who avenged themselves by singing them.

I pumped my fellow-prisoner as dry as I could, for fear I should never see him again; but at length he showed me which was my bed, and left me to blow out the lamp.

It was like traveling into a far country, such as I had never expected to behold, to lie there for one night. It seemed to me that I never had heard the town clock strike before, nor the evening sounds of the village; for we slept with the windows open, which were inside the grating. It was to see my native village in the light of the Middle Ages, and our Concord was turned into a Rhine stream, and visions of knights and castles passed before me. They were the voices of old burghers that I heard in the streets. I was an involuntary spectator and auditor of whatever was done and said in the kitchen of the adjacent village inn, — a wholly new and rare experience to me. It was a closer view of my native town. I was fairly inside of it. I never had seen its institutions before. This is one of its peculiar institutions; for it is a shire town. I began to comprehend what its inhabitants were about.

In the morning, our breakfasts were put through the hole in the door, in small oblong-square tin pans, made to fit, and holding a pint of chocolate, with brown bread, and an iron spoon. When they called for the vessels again, I was green enough to return what bread I had left; but my comrade seized it, and said that I should lay that up for lunch or dinner. Soon after he was let out to work at haying in a neighboring field, whither he went every day, and would not be back till noon; so he bade me good-day, saying that he doubted if he should see me again.

When I came out of prison, — for some one interfered, and paid that tax, — I did not perceive that great changes had taken place on the common, such as he observed who went in a youth and emerged a tottering and gray-headed man; and yet a change had to my eyes come over the scene, — the town, and State, and country, — greater than any that mere time could effect. I saw yet more distinctly the State in which I lived. I saw to what extent the people among whom I lived could be trusted as good neighbors and friends; that their friendship was for summer weather only; that they did not greatly propose to do right; that they were a distinct race from me by their prejudices and superstitions, as the Chinamen and Malays are; that in their sacrifices to humanity they ran no risks, not even to their property; that after all they were not so noble but they treated the thief as he had treated them, and hoped, by a certain outward observance and a few prayers, and by walking in a particular straight though useless path from time to time, to save their souls.

This may be to judge my neighbors harshly; for I believe that many of them are not aware that they have such an institution as the jail in their village.

It was formerly the custom in our village, when a poor debtor came out of jail, for his acquaintances to salute him, looking through their fingers, which were crossed to represent the grating of a jail window, "How do ye do?" My neighbors did not thus salute me, but first looked at me, and then at one another, as if I had returned from a long journey. I was put into jail as I was going to the shoemaker's to get a shoe which was mended. When I was· let out the next morning, I proceeded to finish my errand, and, having put on my mended shoe, joined a huckleberry party, who were impatient to put themselves under my conduct; and in half an hour, — for the horse was soon tackled, — was in the midst of a huckleberry field, on one of our highest hills, two miles off, and then the State was nowhere to be seen.

This is the whole history of "My Prisons."

I have never declined paying the highway tax, because I am as desirous of being a good neighbor as I am of being a bad subject; and as for supporting schools, I am doing my part to educate my fellow-countrymen now. It is for no particular item in the tax-bill that I refuse to pay it. I simply wish to refuse allegiance to the State, to withdraw and stand aloof from it effectually. I do not care to trace the course of my dollar, if I could, till it buys a man or a musket to shoot one with, — the dollar is innocent, — but I am concerned to trace the effects of my allegiance. In fact, I quietly declare war with the State, after my fashion, though I will still make what use and get what advantage of her I can, as is usual in such cases.

If others pay the tax which is demanded of me, from a sympathy with the State, they do but what they have already done in their own case, or rather they abet injustice to a greater extent than the State requires. If they pay the tax from a mistaken interest in the individual taxed, to save his property, or prevent his going to jail, it is because they have not considered wisely how far they let their private feelings interfere with the public good.

This, then, is my position at present. But one cannot be too much on his guard in such a case, lest his action be biased by obstinacy or an undue regard for the opinions of men. Let him see that he does only what belongs to himself and to the hour.

I think sometimes, Why, this people mean well, they are only ignorant; they would do better if they knew how: why give your neighbors this pain to treat you as they are not inclined to? But I think again, This is no reason why I should do as they do, or permit others to suffer much greater pain of a different kind. Again, I sometimes say to myself, When many millions of men, without heat, without ill will, without personal feeling of any kind, demand of you a few shillings only, without the possibility, such is their constitution, of retracting or altering their present demand, and without the possibility, on your side, of appeal to any other millions, why expose yourself to this overwhelming brute force? You do not resist cold and hunger, the winds and the waves, thus obstinately; you quietly submit to a thousand similar necessities. You do not put your head into the fire. But just in proportion as I regard this as not wholly a brute force, but partly a human force, and consider that I have relations to those millions as to so many millions of men, and not of mere brute or inanimate things, I see that appeal is possible, first and instantaneously, from them to the Maker of them, and, secondly, from them to themselves. But if I put my head deliberately into the fire, there is no appeal to fire or to the Maker of fire, and I have only myself to blame. If I could convince myself that I have any right to be satisfied with men as they are, and to treat them accordingly, and not according, in some respects, to my requisitions and expectations of what they and I ought to be, then, like a good Mussulman and fatalist, I should endeavor to be satisfied with things as they are, and say it is the will of God. And, above all, there is this difference between resisting this and a purely brute or natural force, that I can resist this with some effect; but I cannot expect, like Orpheus, to change the nature of the rocks and trees and beasts.

I do not wish to quarrel with any man or nation. I do not wish to split hairs, to make fine distinctions, or set myself up as better than my neighbors. I seek rather, I may say, even an excuse for conforming to the laws of the land. I am but too ready to conform to them. Indeed, I have reason to suspect myself on this head; and each year, as the tax-gatherer comes round, I find myself disposed to review the acts and position of the general and State governments, and the spirit of the people, to discover a pretext for conformity.

"We must affect our country as our parents,
And if at any time we alienate
Our love or industry from doing it honor,
We must respect effects and teach the soul
Matter of conscience and religion,
And not desire of rule or benefit."

I believe that the State will soon be able to take all my work of this sort out of my hands, and then I shall be no better a patriot than my fellow-countrymen. Seen from a lower point of view, the Constitution, with all its faults, is very good; the law and the courts are very respectable; even this State and this American government are, in many respects, very admirable, and rare things, to be thankful for, such as a great many have described them; but seen from a point of view a little higher, they are what I have described them; seen from a higher still, and the highest, who shall say what they are, or that they are worth looking at or thinking of at all?

However, the government does not concern me much, and I shall bestow the fewest possible thoughts on it. It is not many moments that I live under a government, even in this world. If a man is thought-free, fancy-free, imagination-free, that which *is not* never for a long time appearing *to be* to him, unwise rulers or reformers cannot fatally interrupt him.

I know that most men think differently from myself; but those whose lives are by profession devoted to the study of these or kindred subjects content me as little as any. Statesmen and legislators, standing so completely within the institution, never distinctly and nakedly behold it. They speak of moving society, but have no resting-place without it. They may be men of a certain experience and discrimination, and have no doubt invented ingenious and even useful systems, for which we sincerely thank them; but all their wit and usefulness lie within certain not very wide limits. They are wont to forget that the world is not governed by policy and expediency. Webster never goes behind government, and so cannot speak with authority about it. His words are wisdom to those legislators who contemplate no essential reform in the existing government; but for thinkers, and those who legislate for all time, he never once glances at the subject. I know of those whose serene and wise speculations on this theme would soon reveal the limits of his mind's range and hospitality. Yet, compared with the cheap professions of most reformers, and the still cheaper wisdom and eloquence of politicians in general, his are almost the only sensible and valuable words, and we thank Heaven for him. Comparatively, he is always strong, original, and, above all, practical. Still, his quality is not wisdom, but prudence. The lawyer's truth is not Truth, but consistency or a consistent expediency. Truth is always in harmony with herself, and is not concerned chiefly to reveal the justice that may consist with wrong-doing. He well deserves to be called, as he has been called, the Defender of the Constitution. There are really no blows to be given by him but defensive ones. He is not a leader, but a follower. His leaders are the men of '87. " I have never made an effort," he says, " and never propose to make an effort; I have never countenanced an effort, and never mean to countenance an effort, to disturb the arrangement as originally made, by which the various States came into the Union." Still thinking of the sanction which the Constitution gives to slavery, he says, " Because it was a part of the original compact, — let it stand." Notwithstanding his special acuteness and ability, he is unable to take a fact out of its merely political relations, and behold it as it lies absolutely to be disposed of by the intellect, — what, for instance, it behooves a man to do here in America to-day with regard to slavery, — but ventures, or is driven, to make some such desperate answer as the following, while professing to speak absolutely, and as a private man, — from which what new and singular code of social duties might be inferred ? " The manner," says he, " in which the governments of those States where slavery exists are to regulate it is for their own consideration, under their responsibility to their constituents, to the general laws of propriety, humanity, and justice, and to God. Associations formed elsewhere, springing from a feeling of humanity, or any other cause, have nothing whatever to do with it. They have never received any encouragement from me, and they never will." [1]

They who know of no purer sources of truth, who have traced up its stream no higher, stand, and wisely stand, by the Bible and the Constitution, and drink at

[1] These extracts have been inserted since the lecture was read.

it there with reverence and humility; but they who behold where it comes trickling into this lake or that pool, gird up their loins once more, and continue their pilgrimage toward its fountain-head.

No man with a genius for legislation has appeared in America. They are rare in the history of the world. There are orators, politicians, and eloquent men, by the thousand; but the speaker has not yet opened his mouth to speak who is capable of settling the much-vexed questions of the day. We love eloquence for its own sake, and not for any truth which it may utter, or any heroism it may inspire. Our legislators have not yet learned the comparative value of free trade and of freedom, of union, and of rectitude, to a nation. They have no genius or talent for comparatively humble questions of taxation and finance, commerce and manufactures and agriculture. If we were left solely to the wordy wit of legislators in Congress for our guidance, uncorrected by the seasonable experience and the effectual complaints of the people, America would not long retain her rank among the nations. For eighteen hundred years, though perchance I have no right to say it, the New Testament has been written; yet where is the legislator who has wisdom and practical talent enough to avail himself of the light which it sheds on the science of legislation?

The authority of government, even such as I am willing to submit to, — for I will cheerfully obey those who know and can do better than I, and in many things even those who neither know nor can do so well, — is still an impure one: to be strictly just, it must have the sanction and consent of the governed. It can have no pure right over my person and property but what I concede to it. The progress from an absolute to a limited monarchy, from a limited monarchy to a democracy, is a progress toward a true respect for the individual. Even the Chinese philosopher was wise enough to regard the individual as the basis of the empire. Is a democracy, such as we know it, the last improvement possible in government? Is it not possible to take a step further towards recognizing and organizing the rights of man? There will never be a really free and enlightened State until the State comes to recognize the individual as a higher and independent power, from which all its own power and authority are derived, and treats him accordingly. I please myself with imagining a State at last which can afford to be just to all men, and to treat the individual with respect as a neighbor; which even would not think it inconsistent with its own repose if a few were to live aloof from it, not meddling with it, nor embraced by it, who fulfilled all the duties of neighbors and fellow-men. A State which bore this kind of fruit, and suffered it to drop off as fast as it ripened, would prepare the way for a still more perfect and glorious State, which also I have imagined, but not yet anywhere seen.

Snow statuary

CAPE COD

Shells on the beach

THE SHIPWRECK

Wishing to get a better view than I had yet had of the ocean, which, we are told, covers more than two thirds of the globe, but of which a man who lives a few miles inland may never see any trace, more than of another world, I made a visit to Cape Cod in October, 1849, another the succeeding June, and another to Truro in July, 1855; the first and last time with a single companion, the second time alone. I have spent, in all, about three weeks on the Cape; walked from Eastham to Provincetown twice on the Atlantic side, and once on the Bay side also, excepting four or five miles, and crossed the Cape half a dozen times on my way; but having come so fresh to the sea, I have got but little salted. My readers must expect only so much saltness as the land breeze acquires from blowing over an arm of the sea, or is tasted on the windows and the bark of trees twenty miles inland, after September gales. I have been accustomed to make excursions to the ponds within ten miles of Concord, but latterly I have extended my excursions to the seashore.

I did not see why I might not make a book on Cape Cod, as well as my neighbor on "Human Culture." It is but another name for the same thing, and hardly a sandier phase of it. As for my title, I suppose that the word Cape is from the French *cap*; which is from the Latın *caput*, a head ; which is, perhaps, from the verb *capere*, to take, — that being the part by which we take hold of a thing : — Take Time by the forelock. It is also the safest part to take a serpent by. And as for Cod, that was derived directly from that " great store of cod-fish " which Captain Bartholomew Gosnold caught there in 1602 ; which fish appears to have been so called from the Saxon word *codde*, " a case in which seeds are lodged," either from the form of the fish, or the quantity of spawn it contains ; whence also, perhaps, codling (" *pomum coctile* " ?) and coddle, — to cook green like peas. (V. Dic.)

Cape Cod is the bared and bended arm of Massachusetts: the shoulder is at Buzzard's Bay; the elbow, or crazy-bone, at Cape Mallebarre; the wrist at Truro; and the sandy fist at Provincetown, — behind which the State stands on her guard, with her back to the Green Mountains, and her feet planted on the floor of the ocean, like an athlete protecting her Bay, — boxing with northeast storms, and, ever and anon, heaving up her Atlantic adversary from the lap of earth, — ready to thrust forward her other fist, which keeps guard the while upon her breast at Cape Ann.

On studying the map, I saw that there must be an uninterrupted beach on the east or outside of the forearm of the Cape, more than thirty miles from the general line of the coast, which would afford a good sea view, but that, on account of an opening in the beach, forming the entrance to Nauset Harbor, in Orleans, I must strike it in Eastham, if I approached it by land, and probably I could walk thence straight to Race

Point, about twenty-eight miles, and not meet with any obstruction.

We left Concord, Massachusetts, on Tuesday, October 9, 1849. On reaching Boston, we found that the Provincetown steamer, which should have got in the day before, had not yet arrived, on account of a violent storm ; and, as we noticed in the streets a handbill headed, " Death ! one hundred and forty-five lives lost at Cohasset," we decided to go by way of Cohasset. We found many Irish in the cars, going to identify bodies and to sympathize with the survivors, and also to attend the funeral which was to take place in the afternoon; and when we arrived at Cohasset, it appeared that nearly all the passengers were bound for the beach, which was about a mile distant, and many other persons were flocking in from the neighboring country. There were several hundreds of them streaming off over Cohasset Common in that direction, some on foot and some in wagons; and among them were some sportsmen in their hunting-jackets, with their guns, and game-bags, and dogs. As we passed the graveyard we saw a large hole, like a cellar, freshly dug there, and, just before reaching the shore, by a pleasantly winding and rocky road, we met several hay-riggings and farm-wagons coming away toward the meeting-house, each loaded with three large, rough deal boxes. We did not need to ask what was in them. The owners of the wagons were made the undertakers. Many horses in carriages were fastened to the fences near the shore, and, for a mile or more, up and down, the beach was covered with people looking out for bodies, and examining the fragments of the wreck. There was a small island called Brook Island, with a hut on it, lying just off the shore. This is said to be the rockiest shore in Massachusetts, — from Nantasket to Scituate, — hard sienitic rocks, which the waves have laid bare, but have not been able to crumble. It has been the scene of many a shipwreck.

The brig St. John, from Galway, Ireland, laden with emigrants, was wrecked on Sunday morning ; it was now Tuesday morning, and the sea was still breaking violently on the rocks. There were eighteen or twenty of the same large boxes that I have mentioned, lying on a green hillside, a few rods from the water, and surrounded by a crowd. The bodies which had been recovered, twenty-seven or eight in all, had been collected there. Some were rapidly nailing down the lids, others were carting the boxes away, and others were lifting the lids, which were yet loose, and peeping under the cloths, — for each body, with such rags as still adhered to it, was covered loosely with a white sheet. I witnessed no signs of grief, but there was a sober dispatch of business which was affecting. One man was seeking to identify a particular body, and one undertaker or carpenter was calling to another to know in what box a certain child was put. I saw many marble feet and matted heads as the cloths were raised, and one livid, swollen, and mangled body of a drowned girl, — who probably had intended to go out to service in some American family, — to which some rags still adhered, with a string, half concealed by the flesh, about its swollen neck; the coiled-up wreck of a human hulk, gashed by the rocks or fishes, so that the bone and muscle were exposed, but quite bloodless, — merely red and white, — with wide-open and staring eyes, yet lustreless, deadlights; or like the cabin windows of a stranded vessel, filled with sand. Sometimes there were two or more children, or a parent and child, in the same box, and on the lid would, perhaps, be written with red chalk, " Bridget such-a-one, and sister's child." The surrounding sward was covered with bits of sails and clothing. I have since heard, from one who lives by this beach, that a woman who had come over before, but had left her infant behind for her sister to bring, came and looked into these boxes, and saw in one — probably the same whose superscription I have quoted — her child in her sister's arms, as if the sister had meant to be found thus; and within three days after, the mother died from the effect of that sight.

We turned from this and walked along the rocky shore. In the first cove were strewn what seemed the fragments of a vessel, in small pieces mixed with sand and seaweed, and great quantities of feathers; but it looked so old and rusty, that I at first took it to be some old wreck which had lain there many years. I even thought of Captain Kidd, and that the feathers were those which sea-fowl had cast there; and perhaps there might be some tradition about it in the neighborhood. I asked a sailor if that was the St. John. He said it was. I asked him where she struck. He pointed to a rock in front of us, a mile from the shore, called the Grampus Rock, and added, —

" You can see a part of her now sticking up; it looks like a small boat."

I saw it. It was thought to be held by the chain-cables and the anchors. I asked if the bodies which I saw were all that were drowned.

" Not a quarter of them," said he.

" Where are the rest ? "

" Most of them right underneath that piece you see."

It appeared to us that there was enough rubbish to make the wreck of a large vessel in this cove alone, and that it would take many days to cart it off. It was several feet deep, and here and there was a bonnet or a jacket on it. In the very midst of the crowd about this wreck, there were men with carts busily collecting the seaweed which the storm had cast up, and conveying it beyond the reach of the tide, though they were often obliged to separate fragments of clothing from it, and they might at any moment have found a human body under it. Drown who might, they did not forget that this weed was a valuable manure. This shipwreck had not produced a visible vibration in the fabric of society.

About a mile south we could see, rising above the rocks, the masts of the British brig which the St. John had endeavored to follow, which had slipped her cables, and, by good luck, run into the mouth of Cohasset Harbor. A little further along the shore we saw a man's clothes on a rock; further, a woman's scarf, a gown, a straw bonnet, the brig's caboose, and one of her masts high and dry, broken into several pieces. In another

rocky cove, several rods from the water, and behind
rocks twenty feet high, lay a part of one side of the
vessel, still hanging together. It was, perhaps, forty
feet long, by fourteen wide. I was even more surprised
at the power of the waves, exhibited on this shattered
fragment, than I had been at the sight of the smaller
fragments before. The largest timbers and iron braces
were broken superfluously, and I saw that no material
could withstand the power of the waves; that iron must
go to pieces in such a case, and an iron vessel would
be cracked up like an egg-shell on the rocks. Some
of these timbers, however, were so rotten that I could
almost thrust my umbrella through them. They told
us that some were saved on this piece, and also showed
where the sea had heaved it into this cove which was
now dry. When I saw where it had come in, and in
what condition, I wondered that any had been saved
on it. A little further on, a crowd of men was collected
around the mate of the St. John, who was telling his
story. He was a slim-looking youth, who spoke of the
captain as the master, and seemed a little excited. He
was saying that when they jumped into the boat, she
filled, and, the vessel lurching, the weight of the water in
the boat caused the painter to break, and so they were
separated. Whereat one man came away, saying, —

"Well, I don't see but he tells a straight story enough.
You see, the weight of the water in the boat broke the
painter. A boat full of water is very heavy," — and so
on, in a loud and impertinently earnest tone, as if he
had a bet depending on it, but had no humane interest in the matter.

Another, a large man, stood near by upon a rock, gazing into the sea, and chewing large quids of tobacco, as if that habit were forever confirmed with him.

" Come," says another to his companion, " let's be off. We've seen the whole of it. It's no use to stay to the funeral."

Further, we saw one standing upon a rock, who, we were told, was one that was saved. He was a sober-looking man, dressed in a jacket and gray pantaloons, with his hands in the pockets. I asked him a few questions, which he answered; but he seemed unwilling to talk about it, and soon walked away. By his side stood one of the life-boat men, in an oilcloth jacket, who told us how they went to the relief of the British brig, thinking that the boat of the St. John, which they passed on the way, held all her crew, — for the waves prevented their seeing those who were on the vessel, though they might have saved some had they known there were any there. A little further was the flag of the St. John, spread on a rock to dry, and held down by stones at the corners. This frail, but essential and significant portion of the vessel, which had so long been the sport of the winds, was sure to reach the shore. There were one or two houses visible from these rocks, in which were some of the survivors recovering from the shock which their bodies and minds had sustained. One was not expected to live.

We kept on down the shore as far as a promontory called Whitehead, that we might see more of the Cohasset Rocks. In a little cove, within half a mile, there were an old man and his son collecting, with their team, the seaweed which that fatal storm had cast up, as serenely employed as if there had never been a wreck in the world, though they were within sight of the Grampus Rock, on which the St. John had struck. The old man had heard that there was a wreck and knew most of the particulars, but he said that he had not been up there since it happened. It was the wrecked weed that concerned him most, rockweed, kelp, and seaweed, as he named them, which he carted to his barnyard; and those bodies were to him but other weeds which the tide cast up, but which were of no use to him. We afterwards came to the life-boat in its harbor, waiting for another emergency; and in the afternoon we saw the funeral procession at a distance, at the head of which walked the captain with the other survivors.

On the whole, it was not so impressive a scene as I might have expected. If I had found one body cast upon the beach in some lonely place, it would have affected me more. I sympathized rather with the winds and waves, as if to toss and mangle these poor human bodies was the order of the day. If this was the law of Nature, why waste any time in awe or pity? If the last day were come, we should not think so much about the separation of friends or the blighted prospects of individuals. I saw that corpses might be multiplied, as on the field of battle, till they no longer affected us in any degree as exceptions to the common lot of humanity. Take all the graveyards together, they are always the majority. It is the individual and private that demands our sympathy. A man can attend but one funeral in the course of his life, can behold but

one corpse. Yet I saw that the inhabitants of the
shore would be not a little affected by this event. They
would watch there many days and nights for the sea to
give up its dead, and their imaginations and sympathies would supply the place of mourners far away,
who as yet knew not of the wreck. Many days after
this, something white was seen floating on the water
by one who was sauntering on the beach. It was approached in a boat, and found to be the body of
a woman, which had risen in an upright position,
whose white cap was blown back with the wind. I
saw that the beauty of the shore itself was wrecked
for many a lonely walker there, until he could perceive,
at last, how its beauty was enhanced by wrecks like
this, and it acquired thus a rarer and sublimer beauty
still.

Why care for these dead bodies? They really have
no friends but the worms or fishes. Their owners were
coming to the New World, as Columbus and the Pilgrims did; they were within a mile of its shores ; but,
before they could reach it, they emigrated to a newer
world than ever Columbus dreamed of, yet one of
whose existence we believe that there is far more universal and convincing evidence — though it has not yet
been discovered by science — than Columbus had of
this: not merely mariners' tales and some paltry driftwood and seaweed, but a continual drift and instinct
to all our shores. I saw their empty hulks that came
to land; but they themselves, meanwhile, were cast
upon some shore yet further west, toward which we
are all tending, and which we shall reach at last, it

may be through storm and darkness, as they did. No doubt, we have reason to thank God that they have not been "shipwrecked into life again." The mariner who makes the safest port in heaven, perchance, seems to his friends on earth to be shipwrecked, for they deem Boston Harbor the better place; though perhaps, invisible to them, a skillful pilot comes to meet him, and the fairest and balmiest gales blow off that coast, his good ship makes the land in halcyon days, and he kisses the shore in rapture there, while his old hulk tosses in the surf here. It is hard to part with one's body, but, no doubt, it is easy enough to do without it when once it is gone. All their plans and hopes burst like a bubble! Infants by the score dashed on the rocks by the enraged Atlantic Ocean! No, no! If the St. John did not make her port here, she has been telegraphed there. The strongest wind cannot stagger a Spirit; it is a Spirit's breath. A just man's purpose cannot be split on any Grampus or material rock, but itself will split rocks till it succeeds.

The verses addressed to Columbus dying may, with slight alterations, be applied to the passengers of the St. John, —

> "Soon with them will all be over,
> Soon the voyage will be begun
> That shall bear them to discover,
> Far away, a land unknown.

> "Land that each, alone, must visit,
> But no tidings bring to men;
> For no sailor, once departed,
> Ever hath returned again.

"No carved wood, no broken branches
  Ever drift from that far wild;
He who on that ocean launches
  Meets no corse of angel child.

"Undismayed, my noble sailors,
  Spread, then spread your canvas out;
Spirits! on a sea of ether
  Soon shall ye serenely float!

"Where the deep no plummet soundeth,
  Fear no hidden breakers there,
And the fanning wing of angels
  Shall your bark right onward bear.

"Quit, now, full of heart and comfort,
  These rude shores, they are of earth;
Where the rosy clouds are parting,
  There the blessed isles loom forth."

One summer day, since this, I came this way, on foot, along the shore from Boston. It was so warm that some horses had climbed to the very top of the ramparts of the old fort at Hull, where there was hardly room to turn round, for the sake of the breeze. The *Datura Stramonium*, or thorn-apple, was in full bloom along the beach; and, at sight of this cosmopolite, this Captain Cook among plants, carried in ballast all over the world, I felt as if I were on the highway of nations. Say, rather, this Viking, king of the Bays, for it is not an innocent plant; it suggests not merely commerce, but its attendant vices, as if its fibres were the stuff of which pirates spin their yarns. I heard the voices of men shouting aboard a vessel, half a mile from the shore, which sounded as if they were in a barn in the country, they being between the sails. It was a purely rural sound. As I looked over the water, I saw the isles rapidly wasting away, the sea nibbling voraciously at the continent, the springing arch of a hill suddenly interrupted, as at Point Allerton, — what botanists might call premorse, — showing, by its curve against the sky, how much space it must have occupied, where now was water only. On the other hand, these wrecks of isles were being fancifully arranged into new shores, as at Hog Island, inside of Hull, where everything seemed to be gently lapsing into futurity. This isle had got the very form of a ripple, and I thought that the inhabitants should bear a ripple for device on their shields, a wave passing over them, with the datura, which is said to produce mental alienation of long duration without affecting the bodily health,[1] springing from its edge. The most interesting thing which I heard of, in

[1] The Jamestown-weed, or thorn-apple. "This, being an early plant, was gathered very young for a boiled salad, by some of the soldiers sent thither [*i. e.*, to Virginia] to quell the rebellion of Bacon; and some of them ate plentifully of it, the effect of which was a very pleasant comedy, for they turned natural fools upon it for several days: one would blow up a feather in the air; another would dart straws at it with much fury; and another, stark naked, was sitting up in a corner like a monkey, grinning and making mows at them; a fourth would fondly kiss and paw his companions, and sneer in their faces, with a countenance more antic than any in a Dutch droll. In this frantic condition they were confined, lest they should, in their folly, destroy themselves, — though it was observed that all their actions were full of innocence and good nature. Indeed, they were not very cleanly. A thousand such simple tricks they played, and after eleven days returned to themselves again, not remembering anything that had passed." — Beverley's *History of Virginia*, p. 120.

this township of Hull, was an unfailing spring, whose locality was pointed out to me on the side of a distant hill, as I was panting along the shore, though I did not visit it. Perhaps, if I should go through Rome, it would be some spring on the Capitoline Hill I should remember the longest. It is true, I was somewhat interested in the well at the old French fort, which was said to be ninety feet deep, with a cannon at the bottom of it. On Nantasket Beach I counted a dozen chaises from the public house. From time to time the riders turned their horses toward the sea, standing in the water for the coolness; and I saw the value of beaches to cities for the sea-breeze and the bath.

At Jerusalem Village, the inhabitants were collecting in haste, before a thunder-shower now approaching, the Irish moss which they had spread to dry. The shower passed on one side, and gave me a few drops only, which did not cool the air. I merely felt a puff upon my cheek, though, within sight, a vessel was capsized in the bay, and several others dragged their anchors, and were near going ashore. The sea bathing at Cohasset Rocks was perfect. The water was purer and more transparent than any I had ever seen. There was not a particle of mud or slime about it. The bottom being sandy, I could see the sea perch swimming about. The smooth and fantastically worn rocks, and the perfectly clean and tress-like rockweeds falling over you, and attached so firmly to the rocks that you could pull yourself up by them, greatly enhanced the luxury of the bath. The stripe of barnacles just above the weeds reminded me of some vegetable growth,— the buds, and

petals, and seed-vessels of flowers. They lay along the
seams of the rock like buttons on a waistcoat. It was
one of the hottest days in the year, yet I found the
water so icy cold that I could swim but a stroke or two,
and thought that, in case of shipwreck, there would
be more danger of being chilled to death than simply
drowned. One immersion was enough to make you forget the dog-days utterly. Though you were sweltering
before, it will take you half an hour now to remember
that it was ever warm. There were the tawny rocks,
like lions couchant, defying the ocean, whose waves
incessantly dashed against and scoured them with vast
quantities of gravel. The water held in their little hollows on the receding of the tide was so crystalline that
I could not believe it salt, but wished to drink it; and
higher up were basins of fresh water left by the rain,
— all which, being also of different depths and temperature, were convenient for different kinds of baths.
Also, the larger hollows in the smoothed rocks formed
the most convenient of seats and dressing-rooms. In
these respects it was the most perfect seashore that I
had seen.

I saw in Cohasset, separated from the sea only by a
narrow beach, a handsome but shallow lake of some
four hundred acres, which, I was told, the sea had
tossed over the beach in a great storm in the spring,
and, after the alewives had passed into it, it had stopped
up its outlet, and now the alewives were dying by
thousands, and the inhabitants were apprehending a
pestilence as the water evaporated. It had five rocky
islets in it.

This rocky shore is called Pleasant Cove on some maps; on the map of Cohasset, that name appears to be confined to the particular cove where I saw the wreck of the St. John. The ocean did not look, now, as if any were ever shipwrecked in it; it was not grand and sublime, but beautiful as a lake. Not a vestige of a wreck was visible, nor could I believe that the bones of many a shipwrecked man were buried in that pure sand. But to go on with our first excursion.

Highland Light, Cape Cod

Beach Bluffs, Wellfleet Shore

THE WELLFLEET OYSTERMAN

Having walked about eight miles since we struck the beach, and passed the boundary between Wellfleet and Truro, a stone post in the sand, — for even this sand comes under the jurisdiction of one town or another, — we turned inland over barren hills and valleys, whither the sea, for some reason, did not follow us, and, tracing up a Hollow, discovered two or three sober-looking houses within half a mile, uncommonly near the eastern coast. Their garrets were apparently so full of chambers, that their roofs could hardly lie down straight, and we did not doubt that there was room for us there. Houses near the sea are generally low and broad. These were a story and a half high; but if you merely counted the windows in their gable ends, you would think that there were many stories more, or, at any rate, that the half-story was the only one thought worthy of being illustrated. The great number of windows in the ends of the houses, and their irregularity in size and position, here and elsewhere on the Cape, struck us agreeably, — as if each of the various occupants who had their *cunabula* behind had punched a hole where his necessities required it, and according to his size and stature, without regard to outside effect. There were windows for the grown folks, and windows for the children, — three or four apiece; as a certain man had a large hole cut in his barn-door for the cat, and another smaller one for the kitten. Sometimes they were so low under the eaves that I thought they must have perforated the plate beam for another apartment, and I noticed some which were triangular, to fit that part more exactly. The ends of the houses had thus as many muzzles as a revolver, and, if the inhabitants have the same habit of staring out the windows that some of our neighbors have, a traveler must stand a small chance with them.

Generally, the old-fashioned and unpainted houses on the Cape looked more comfortable, as well as picturesque, than the modern and more pretending ones, which were less in harmony with the scenery, and less firmly planted.

These houses were on the shores of a chain of ponds, seven in number, the source of a small stream called Herring River, which empties into the Bay. There are many Herring Rivers on the Cape; they will, perhaps, be more numerous than herrings soon. We knocked at the door of the first house, but its inhabitants were all gone away. In the meanwhile, we saw the occupants of the next one looking out the window at us, and before we reached it an old woman came out and fastened the door of her bulkhead, and went in again. Nevertheless, we did not hesitate to knock at her door, when a grizzly-looking man appeared, whom we took to be sixty or seventy years old. He asked us, at first, suspiciously, where we were from, and what our business was; to which we returned plain answers.

" How far is Concord from Boston?" he inquired.

" Twenty miles by railroad."

" Twenty miles by railroad," he repeated.

" Did n't you ever hear of Concord of Revolutionary fame ? "

" Did n't I ever hear of Concord? Why, I heard guns fire at the battle of Bunker Hill. [They hear the sound of heavy cannon across the Bay.] I am almost ninety; I am eighty-eight year old. I was fourteen year old at the time of Concord Fight, — and where were you then ? "

We were obliged to confess that we were not in the fight.

" Well, walk in, we 'll leave it to the women," said he.

So we walked in, surprised, and sat down, an old woman taking our hats and bundles, and the old man continued, drawing up to the large, old-fashioned fireplace, —

" I am a poor, good-for-nothing crittur, as Isaiah says; I am all broken down this year. I am under petticoat government here."

The family consisted of the old man, his wife, and his daughter, who appeared nearly as old as her mother, a fool, her son (a brutish-looking, middle-aged man, with a prominent lower face, who was standing by the hearth when we entered, but immediately went out), and a little boy of ten.

While my companion talked with the women, I talked with the old man. They said that he was old and foolish, but he was evidently too knowing for them.

" These women," said he to me, " are both of them poor good-for-nothing critturs. This one is my wife.

I married her sixty-four years ago. She is eighty-four years old, and as deaf as an adder, and the other is not much better."

He thought well of the Bible, or at least he *spoke* well, and did not *think* ill, of it, for that would not have been prudent for a man of his age. He said that he had read it attentively for many years, and he had much of it at his tongue's end. He seemed deeply impressed with a sense of his own nothingness, and would repeatedly exclaim, —

" I am a nothing. What I gather from my Bible is just this; that man is a poor good-for-nothing crittur, and everything is just as God sees fit and disposes."

" May I ask your name? " I said.

" Yes," he answered, " I am not ashamed to tell my name. My name is ——. My great-grandfather came over from England and settled here."

He was an old Wellfleet oysterman, who had acquired a competency in that business, and had sons still engaged in it.

Nearly all the oyster shops and stands in Massachusetts, I am told, are supplied and kept by natives of Wellfleet, and a part of this town is still called Billingsgate from the oysters having been formerly planted there; but the native oysters are said to have died in 1770. Various causes are assigned for this, such as a ground frost, the carcasses of blackfish, kept to rot in the harbor, and the like, but the most common account of the matter is, — and I find that a similar superstition with regard to the disappearance of fishes exists almost everywhere, — that when Wellfleet began to quarrel with the neighboring towns about the right to gather them, yellow specks appeared in them, and Providence caused them to disappear. A few years ago sixty thousand bushels were annually brought from the South and planted in the harbor of Wellfleet till they attained "the proper relish of Billingsgate;" but now they are imported commonly full-grown, and laid down near their markets, at Boston and elsewhere, where the water, being a mixture of salt and fresh, suits them better. The business was said to be still good and improving.

The old man said that the oysters were liable to freeze in the winter, if planted too high; but if it were not "so cold as to strain their eyes" they were not injured. The inhabitants of New Brunswick have noticed that "ice will not form over an oyster-bed, unless the cold is very intense indeed, and when the bays are frozen over the oyster-beds are easily discovered by the water above them remaining unfrozen, or as the French residents say, dégelée." Our host said that they kept them in cellars all winter.

"Without anything to eat or drink?" I asked.

"Without anything to eat or drink," he answered.

"Can the oysters move?"

"Just as much as my shoe."

But when I caught him saying that they "bedded themselves down in the sand, flat side up, round side down," I told him that my shoe could not do that, without the aid of my foot in it; at which he said that they merely settled down as they grew; if put down in a square they would be found so; but the clam could move quite fast. I have since been told by oystermen of Long Island, where the oyster is still indigenous and abundant, that they are found in large masses attached to the parent in their midst, and are so taken up with their tongs; in which case, they say, the age of the young proves that there could have been no motion for five or six years at least. And Buckland in his "Curiosities of Natural History" (page 50) says: "An oyster, who has once taken up his position and fixed himself when quite young, can never make a change. Oysters, nevertheless, that have not fixed themselves, but remain loose at the bottom of the sea, have the power of locomotion; they open their shells to their fullest extent, and then suddenly contracting them, the expulsion of the water forwards gives a motion backwards. A fisherman at Guernsey told me that he had frequently seen oysters moving in this way."

Some still entertain the question "whether the oyster was indigenous in Massachusetts Bay," and whether Wellfleet Harbor was a "natural habitat" of this fish; but, to say nothing of the testimony of old oystermen, which, I think, is quite conclusive, though the native oyster may now be extinct there, I saw that their shells, opened by the Indians, were strewn all over the Cape. Indeed, the Cape was at first thickly settled by Indians on account of the abundance of these and other fish. We saw many traces of their occupancy after this, in Truro, near Great Hollow, and at High Head, near East Harbor River, — oysters, clams, cockles, and other shells, mingled with ashes and the bones of deer and other quadrupeds. I picked up half a dozen arrowheads, and in an hour or two could have filled my pockets with them. The Indians lived about the edges of the swamps, then probably in some instances ponds, for shelter and water. Moreover, Champlain, in the edition of his " Voyages " printed in 1613, says that in the year 1606 he and Poitrincourt explored a harbor (Barnstable Harbor?) in the southerly part of what is now called Massachusetts Bay, in latitude 42°, about five leagues south, one point west of *Cap Blanc* (Cape Cod), and there they found many good oysters, and they named it " *le Port aux Huistres* " [sic] (Oyster Harbor). In one edition of his map (1632), the " *R. aux Escailles* " is drawn emptying into the same part of the bay, and on the map " *Novi Belgii*," in Ogilby's America (1670), the words " *Port aux Huistres* " are placed against the same place. Also William Wood, who left New England in 1633, speaks, in his " New England's Prospect," published in 1634, of " a great oyster-bank " in Charles River, and of another in the Mistick, each of which obstructed the navigation of its river. " The oysters," says he, " be great ones in form of a shoe-horn; some be a foot long; these breed on certain banks that are bare every spring tide. This fish without the shell is so big, that it must admit of a division before you can well get it into your mouth." Oysters are still found there.[1]

Our host told us that the sea-clam, or hen, was not easily obtained; it was raked up, but never on the Atlantic side, only cast ashore there in small quantities in storms. The fisherman sometimes wades in

[1] Also, see Thomas Morton's *New English Canaan*, p. 90.

water several feet deep, and thrusts a pointed stick into the sand before him. When this enters between the valves of a clam, he closes them on it, and is drawn out. It has been known to catch and hold coot and teal which were preying on it. I chanced to be on the bank of the Acushnet at New Bedford one day since this, watching some ducks, when a man informed me that, having let out his young ducks to seek their food amid the samphire (*Salicornia*) and other weeds along the riverside at low tide that morning, at length he noticed that one remained stationary, amid the weeds, something preventing it from following the others, and going to it he found its foot tightly shut in a quahog's shell. He took up both together, carried them to his home, and his wife opening the shell with a knife released the duck and cooked the quahog. The old man said that the great clams were good to eat, but that they always took out a certain part which was poisonous, before they cooked them. " People said it would kill a cat." I did not tell him that I had eaten a large one entire that afternoon, but began to think that I was tougher than a cat. He stated that pedlers came round there, and sometimes tried to sell the women folks a skimmer, but he told them that their women had got a better skimmer than *they* could make, in the shell of their clams; it was shaped just right for this purpose. — They call them " skim-alls " in some places. He also said that the sun-squall was poisonous to handle, and when the sailors came across it, they did not meddle with it, but heaved it out of their way. I told him that I had handled it that afternoon, and had felt no ill effects as yet. But he said it made the hands itch, especially if they had previously been scratched, or if I put it into my bosom, I should find out what it was.

He informed us that no ice ever formed on the back side of the Cape, or not more than once in a century, and but little snow lay there, it being either absorbed or blown or washed away. Sometimes in winter, when the tide was down, the beach was frozen, and afforded a hard road up the back side for some thirty miles, as smooth as a floor. One winter when he was a boy, he and his father "took right out into the Back Side before daylight, and walked to Provincetown and back to dinner."

When I asked what they did with all that barren-looking land, where I saw so few cultivated fields, — "Nothing," he said.

" Then why fence your fields ? "

" To keep the sand from blowing and covering up the whole."

" The yellow sand," said he, " has some life in it, but the white little or none."

When, in answer to his questions, I told him that I was a surveyor, he said that they who surveyed his farm were accustomed, where the ground was uneven, to loop up each chain as high as their elbows; that was the allowance they made, and he wished to know if I could tell him why they did not come out according to his deed, or twice alike. He seemed to have more respect for surveyors of the old school, which I did not wonder at. " King George the Third," said he, " laid out a road four rods wide and straight, the whole length of the Cape," but where it was now he could not tell.

This story of the surveyors reminded me of a Long-Islander, who once, when I had made ready to jump from the bow of his boat to the shore, and he thought that I underrated the distance and would fall short, — though I found afterward that he judged of the elasticity of my joints by his own, — told me that when he came to a brook which he wanted to get over, he held up one leg, and then, if his foot appeared to cover any part of the opposite bank, he knew that he could jump it. "Why," I told him, " to say nothing of the Mississippi, and other small watery streams, I could blot out a star with my foot, but I would not engage to jump that distance," and asked how he knew when he had got his leg at the right elevation. But he regarded his legs as no less accurate than a pair of screw dividers or an ordinary quadrant, and appeared to have a painful recollection of every degree and minute in the arc which they described; and he would have had me believe that there was a kind of hitch in his hip-joint which answered the purpose. I suggested that he should connect his two ankles by a string of the proper length, which should be the chord of an arc, measuring his jumping ability on horizontal surfaces, — assuming one leg to be a perpendicular to the plane of the horizon, which, however, may have been too bold an assumption in this case. Nevertheless, this was a kind of geometry in the legs which it interested me to hear of.

Our host took pleasure in telling us the names of the ponds, most of which we could see from his windows, and making us repeat them after him, to see if we had got them right. They were Gull Pond, the largest and a very handsome one, clear and deep, and more than a mile in circumference, Newcomb's, Swett's, Slough, Horse-Leech, Round, and Herring Ponds, all connected at high water, if I do not mistake. The coast-surveyors had come to him for their names, and he told them of one which they had not detected. He said that they were not so high as formerly. There was an earthquake about four years before he was born, which cracked the pans of the ponds, which were of iron, and caused them to settle. I did not remember to have read of this. Innumerable gulls used to resort to them; but the large gulls were now very scarce, for, as he said, the English robbed their nests far in the north, where they breed. He remembered well when gulls were taken in the gull-house, and when small birds were killed by means of a frying-pan and fire at night. His father once lost a valuable horse from this cause. A party from Wellfleet having lighted their fire for this purpose, one dark night, on Billingsgate Island, twenty horses which were pastured there, and this colt among them, being frightened by it, and endeavoring in the dark to cross the passage which separated them from the neighboring beach, and which was then fordable at low tide, were all swept out to sea and drowned. I observed that many horses were still turned out to pasture all summer on the islands and beaches in Wellfleet, Eastham, and Orleans, as a kind of common. He also described the killing of what he called " wild hens," here, after they had gone to roost in the woods, when he was a boy. Perhaps they were " prairie hens " (pinnated grouse).

He liked the beach pea (*Lathyrus maritimus*), cooked green, as well as the cultivated. He had seen it growing very abundantly in Newfoundland, where also the inhabitants ate them, but he had never been able to obtain any ripe for seed. We read, under the head of Chatham, that " in 1555, during a time of great scarcity, the people about Orford, in Sussex [England] were preserved from perishing by eating the seeds of this plant, which grew there in great abundance upon the sea coast. Cows, horses, sheep, and goats eat it." But the writer who quoted this could not learn that they had ever been used in Barnstable County.

He had been a voyager, then? Oh, he had been about the world in his day. He once considered himself a pilot for all our coast; but now they had changed the names so he might be bothered.

He gave us to taste what he called the Summer Sweeting, a pleasant apple which he raised, and frequently grafted from, but had never seen growing elsewhere, except once, — three trees on Newfoundland, or at the Bay of Chaleur, I forget which, as he was sailing by. He was sure that he could tell the tree at a distance.

At length the fool, whom my companion called the wizard, came in, muttering between his teeth, " Damn book-pedlers, — all the time talking about books. Better do something. Damn 'em. I 'll shoot 'em. Got a doctor down here. Damn him, I 'll get a gun and shoot him; " never once holding up his head. Whereat the old man stood up and said in a loud voice, as if he was accustomed to command, and this was not the first time he had been obliged to exert his authority there: "John, go sit down, mind your business, — we've heard you talk before, — precious little you'll do, — your bark is worse than your bite." But, without minding, John muttered the same gibberish over again, and then sat down at the table which the old folks had left. He ate all there was on it, and then turned to the apples, which his aged mother was paring, that she might give her guests some apple-sauce for breakfast, but she drew them away and sent him off.

When I approached this house the next summer, over the desolate hills between it and the shore, which are worthy to have been the birthplace of Ossian, I saw the wizard in the midst of a corn-field on the hillside, but, as usual, he loomed so strangely, that I mistook him for a scarecrow.

This was the merriest old man that we had ever seen, and one of the best preserved. His style of conversation was coarse and plain enough to have suited Rabelais. He would have made a good Panurge. Or rather he was a sober Silenus, and we were the boys Chromis and Mnasilus, who listened to his story.

> "Not by Hæmonian hills the Thracian bard,
> Nor awful Phœbus was on Pindus heard
> With deeper silence or with more regard."

There was a strange mingling of past and present in his conversation, for he had lived under King George, and might have remembered when Napoleon and the moderns generally were born. He said that one day, when the troubles between the Colonies and the mother country first broke out, as he, a boy of fifteen, was pitching hay out of a cart, one Donne, an old Tory, who was talking with his father, a good Whig, said to him, " Why, Uncle Bill, you might as well undertake to pitch that pond into the ocean with a pitchfork, as for the Colonies to undertake to gain their independence." He remembered well General Washington, and how he rode his horse along the streets of Boston, and he stood up to show us how he looked.

" He was a r—a—ther large and portly-looking man, a manly and resolute-looking officer, with a pretty good leg as he sat on his horse." — " There, I 'll tell you, this was the way with Washington." Then he jumped up again, and bowed gracefully to right and left, making show as if he were waving his hat. Said he, " *That* was Washington."

He told us many anecdotes of the Revolution, and was much pleased when we told him that we had read the same in history, and that his account agreed with the written.

" Oh," he said, " I know, I know! I was a young fellow of sixteen, with my ears wide open; and a fellow of that age, you know, is pretty wide awake, and likes to know everything that 's going on. Oh, I know!"

He told us the story of the wreck of the Franklin, which took place there the previous spring; how a boy came to his house early in the morning to know whose boat that was by the shore, for there was a vessel in distress, and he, being an old man, first ate his breakfast, and then walked over to the top of the hill by the shore, and sat down there, having found a comfortable seat, to see the ship wrecked. She was on the bar, only a quarter of a mile from him, and still nearer to the men on the beach, who had got a boat ready, but could render no assistance on account of the breakers, for there was a pretty high sea running. There were the passengers all crowded together in the forward part of the ship, and some were getting out of the cabin windows and were drawn on deck by the others.

" I saw the captain get out his boat," said he; " he had one little one; and then they jumped into it one after another, down as straight as an arrow. I counted them. There were nine. One was a woman, and she jumped as straight as any of them. Then they shoved off. The sea took them back, one wave went over them, and when they came up there were six still clinging to the boat; I counted them. The next wave turned the boat bottom upward, and emptied them all out. None of them ever came ashore alive. There were the rest of them all crowded together on the forecastle, the other parts of the ship being under water. They had seen all that happened to the boat. At length a heavy sea separated the forecastle from the rest of the wreck, and set it inside of the worst breaker, and the boat was able to reach them, and it saved all that were left, but one woman."

He also told us of the steamer Cambria's getting aground on this shore a few months before we were there, and of her English passengers who roamed over his grounds, and who, he said, thought the prospect from the high hill by the shore, " the most delightsome they had ever seen," and also of the pranks which the ladies played with his scoop-net in the ponds. He spoke of these travelers with their purses full of guineas, just as our provincial fathers used to speak of British bloods in the time of King George the Third.

Quid loquar? Why repeat what he told us?

> " Aut Scyllam Nisi, quam fama secuta est,
> Candida succinctam latrantibus inguina monstris,
> Dulichias vexâsse rates, et gurgite in alto
> Ah! timidos nautas canibus lacerâsse marinis?"

In the course of the evening I began to feel the potency of the clam which I had eaten, and I was obliged to confess to our host that I was no tougher than the cat he told of; but he answered, that he was a plain-spoken man, and he could tell me that it was all imagination. At any rate, it proved an emetic in my case, and I was made quite sick by it for a short time, while he laughed at my expense. I was pleased to read afterward, in Mourt's Relation of the landing of the Pilgrims in Provincetown Harbor, these words: " We found great muscles [the old editor says that they were undoubtedly sea-clams] and very fat and full of sea-pearl; but we could not eat them, for they made us all sick that did eat, as well sailors as passengers, . . . but they were soon well again." It brought me nearer to the Pilgrims to be thus reminded by a similar experience that I was so like them. Moreover, it was a valuable confirmation of their story, and I am prepared now to believe every word of Mourt's Relation. I was also pleased to find that man and the clam lay still at the same angle to one another. But I did not notice sea-pearl. Like Cleopatra, I must have swallowed it. I have since dug these clams on a flat in the Bay and observed them. They could squirt full ten feet before the wind, as appeared by the marks of the drops on the sand.

" Now I am going to ask you a question," said the old man, " and I don't know as you can tell me; but you are a learned man, and I never had any learning, only what I got by natur." — It was in vain that we reminded him that he could quote Josephus to our confusion. — " I 've thought, if I ever met a learned man I should like to ask him this question. Can you tell me how *Axy* is spelt, and what it means ? *Axy,*" says he; " there 's a girl over here is named *Axy*. Now what is it ? What does it mean ? Is it Scripture ? I 've read my Bible twenty-five years over and over, and I never came across it."

" Did you read it twenty-five years for this object ? " I asked.

" Well, *how* is it spelt ? Wife, how is it spelt ? " She said, " It is in the Bible; I 've seen it."

" Well, how do you spell it ? "

" I don't know. A c h, ach, s e h, sch, — Achsch."

" Does that spell Axy ? Well, do *you* know what it means ? " asked he, turning to me.

" No," I replied, " I never heard the sound before."

" There was a schoolmaster down here once, and they asked him what it meant, and he said it had no more meaning than a bean-pole."

I told him that I held the same opinion with the schoolmaster. I had been a schoolmaster myself, and had had strange names to deal with. I also heard of such names as Zoheth, Beriah, Amaziah, Bethuel, and Shearjashub, hereabouts.

At length the little boy, who had a seat quite in the chimney-corner, took off his stockings and shoes, warmed his feet, and having had his sore leg freshly salved, went off to bed; then the fool made bare his knotty-looking feet and legs, and followed him; and finally the old man exposed his calves also to our gaze. We had never had the good fortune to see an old man's legs before, and were surprised to find them fair and plump as an infant's, and we thought that he took a pride in exhibiting them. He then proceeded to make preparations for retiring, discoursing meanwhile with Panurgic plainness of speech on the ills to which old humanity is subject. We were a rare haul for him. He could commonly get none but ministers to talk to, though sometimes ten of them at once, and he was glad to meet some of the laity at leisure. The evening was not long enough for him. As I had been sick, the old lady asked if I would not go to bed, — it was getting late for old people; but the old man, who had not yet done his stories, said, "You ain't particular, are you?"

"Oh, no," said I, "I am in no hurry. I believe I have weathered the Clam cape."

"They are good," said he; "I wish I had some of them now."

"They never hurt me," said the old lady.

"But then you took out the part that killed a cat," said I.

At last we cut him short in the midst of his stories, which he promised to resume in the morning. Yet, after all, one of the old ladies who came into our room in the night to fasten the fire-board, which rattled, as she went out took the precaution to fasten us in. Old women are by nature more suspicious than old men. However, the winds howled around the house, and made the fire-boards as well as the casements rattle well that night. It was probably a windy night for any locality, but we could not distinguish the roar which was proper to the ocean from that which was due to the wind alone.

The sounds which the ocean makes must be very significant and interesting to those who live near it. When I was leaving the shore at this place the next summer, and had got a quarter of a mile distant, ascending a hill, I was startled by a sudden, loud sound from the sea, as if a large steamer were letting off steam by the shore, so that I caught my breath and felt my blood run cold for an instant, and I turned about, expecting to see one of the Atlantic steamers thus far out of her course, but there was nothing unusual to be seen. There was a low bank at the entrance of the Hollow, between me and the ocean, and suspecting that I might have risen into another stratum of air in ascending the hill, — which had wafted to me only the ordinary roar of the sea, — I immediately descended again, to see if I lost hearing of it; but, without regard to my ascending or descending, it died away in a minute or two, and yet there was scarcely any wind all the while. The old man said that this was what they called the "rut," a peculiar roar of the sea before the wind changes, which, however, he could not account for. He thought that he could tell all about the weather from the sounds which the sea made.

Old Josselyn, who came to New England in 1638, has it among his weather-signs, that "the resounding of the sea from the shore, and murmuring of the winds in the woods, without apparent wind, sheweth wind to follow."

Being on another part of the coast one night since this, I heard the roar of the surf a mile distant, and the inhabitants said it was a sign that the wind would work round east, and we should have rainy weather. The ocean was heaped up somewhere at the eastward, and this roar was occasioned by its effort to preserve its equilibrium, the wave reaching the shore before the wind. Also the captain of a packet between this country and England told me that he sometimes met with a wave on the Atlantic coming against the wind, perhaps in a calm sea, which indicated that at a distance the wind was blowing from an opposite quarter, but the undulation had traveled faster than it. Sailors tell of "tide-rips" and "ground-swells," which they suppose to have been occasioned by hurricanes and earthquakes, and to have traveled many hundred, and sometimes even two or three thousand miles.

Before sunrise the next morning they let us out again, and I ran over to the beach to see the sun come out of the ocean. The old woman of eighty-four winters was already out in the cold morning wind, bareheaded, tripping about like a young girl, and driving up the cow to milk. She got the breakfast with dispatch, and without noise or bustle; and meanwhile the old man resumed his stories, standing before us, who were sitting, with his back to the chimney, and ejecting his tobacco-juice right and left into the fire behind him, without regard to the various dishes which were there preparing. At breakfast we had eels, buttermilk cake, cold bread, green beans, doughnuts, and tea. The old man talked a steady stream; and when his wife told him he had better eat his breakfast, he said, "Don't hurry me; I have lived too long to be hurried." I ate of the apple-sauce and the doughnuts, which I thought had sustained the least detriment from the old man's shots, but my companion refused the apple-sauce, and ate of the hot cake and green beans, which had appeared to him to occupy the safest part of the hearth. But on comparing notes afterward, I told him that the buttermilk cake was particularly exposed, and I saw how it suffered repeatedly, and therefore I avoided it; but he declared that, however that might be, he witnessed that the apple-sauce was seriously injured, and had therefore declined that. After breakfast we looked at his clock, which was out of order, and oiled it with some "hen's grease," for want of sweet oil, for he scarcely could believe that we were not tinkers or pedlers; meanwhile, he told a story about visions, which had reference to a crack in the clock-case made by frost one night. He was curious to know to what religious sect we belonged. He said that he had been to hear thirteen

kinds of preaching in one month, when he was young,
but he did not join any of them, — he stuck to his
Bible. There was nothing like any of them in his
Bible. While I was shaving in the next room, I heard
him ask my companion to what sect he belonged, to
which he answered, —

"Oh, I belong to the Universal Brotherhood."

"What's that?" he asked, "Sons o' Temperance?"

Finally, filling our pockets with doughnuts, which he
was pleased to find that we called by the same name
that he did, and paying for our entertainment, we took
our departure; but he followed us out of doors, and
made us tell him the names of the vegetables which he
had raised from seeds that came out of the Franklin.
They were cabbage, broccoli, and parsley. As I had
asked him the names of so many things, he tried me
in turn with all the plants which grew in his garden,
both wild and cultivated. It was about half an acre,
which he cultivated wholly himself. Besides the common garden vegetables, there were yellow dock, lemon
balm, hyssop, gill-go-over-the-ground, mouse-ear, chick-
weed, Roman wormwood, elecampane, and other plants.
As we stood there, I saw a fish hawk stoop to pick a
fish out of his pond.

"There," said I, "he has got a fish."

"Well," said the old man, who was looking all the
while, but could see nothing, "he did n't dive, he just
wet his claws."

And, sure enough, he did not this time, though it is
said that they often do, but he merely stooped low
enough to pick him out with his talons; but as he bore

his shining prey over the bushes, it fell to the ground, and we did not see that he recovered it. That is not their practice.

Thus, having had another crack with the old man, he standing bareheaded under the eaves, he directed us " athwart the fields," and we took to the beach again for another day, it being now late in the morning.

It was but a day or two after this that the safe of the Provincetown Bank was broken open and robbed by two men from the interior, and we learned that our hospitable entertainers did at least transiently harbor the suspicion that we were the men.

Provincetown

THE MAINE WOODS

Maine wilderness

KTAADN

On the 31st of August, 1846, I left Concord in Massachusetts for Bangor and the backwoods of Maine, by way of the railroad and steamboat, intending to accompany a relative of mine, engaged in the lumber trade in Bangor, as far as a dam on the West Branch of the Penobscot, in which property he was interested. From this place, which is about one hundred miles by the river above Bangor, thirty miles from the Houlton military road, and five miles beyond the last log hut, I proposed to make excursions to Mount Ktaadn, the second highest mountain in New England, about thirty miles distant, and to some of the lakes of the Penobscot, either alone or with such company as I might pick up there. It is unusual to find a camp so far in the woods at that season, when lumbering operations have ceased, and I was glad to avail myself of the circumstance of a gang of men being employed there at that time in repairing the injuries caused by the great freshet in the spring. The mountain may be approached more easily and directly on horseback and on foot from the northeast side, by the Aroostook road, and the Wassataquoik River; but in that case you see much less of the wilderness, none of the glorious river and lake scenery, and have no experience of the batteau and the boatman's life. I was fortunate also in the season of the year, for in the summer myriads of black flies, mosquitoes, and midges, or, as the Indians call them, "no-see-ems," make traveling in the woods almost impossible; but now their reign was nearly over.

Ktaadn, whose name is an Indian word signifying highest land, was first ascended by white men in 1804. It was visited by Professor J. W. Bailey of West Point in 1836; by Dr. Charles T. Jackson, the State Geologist, in 1837; and by two young men from Boston in 1845. All these have given accounts of their expeditions. Since I was there, two or three other parties have made the excursion, and told their stories. Besides these, very few, even among backwoodsmen and hunters, have ever climbed it, and it will be a long time before the tide of fashionable travel sets that way. The mountainous region of the State of Maine stretches from near the White Mountains, northeasterly one hundred and sixty miles, to the head of the Aroostook River, and is about sixty miles wide. The wild or unsettled portion is far more extensive. So that some hours only of travel in this direction will carry the curious to the verge of a primitive forest, more interesting, perhaps, on all accounts, than they would reach by going a thousand miles westward.

The next forenoon, Tuesday, September 1, I started with my companion in a buggy from Bangor for "up river," expecting to be overtaken the next day night at Mattawamkeag Point, some sixty miles off, by two more Bangoreans, who had decided to join us in a trip to the mountain. We had each a knapsack or bag filled with such clothing and articles as were indispensable, and my companion carried his gun.

Within a dozen miles of Bangor we passed through the villages of Stillwater and Oldtown, built at the falls of the Penobscot, which furnish the principal power by which the Maine woods are converted into lumber. The mills are built directly over and across the river. Here is a close jam, a hard rub, at all seasons; and then the once green tree, long since white, I need not say as the driven snow, but as a driven log, becomes lumber merely. Here your inch, your two and your three inch stuff begin to be, and Mr. Sawyer marks off those spaces which decide the destiny of so many prostrate forests. Through this steel riddle, more or less coarse, is the arrowy Maine forest, from Ktaadn and Chesuncook, and the head-waters of the St. John, relentlessly sifted, till it comes out boards, clapboards, laths, and shingles such as the wind can take, still, perchance, to be slit and slit again, till men get a size that will suit. Think how stood the white pine tree on the shore of Chesuncook, its branches soughing with the four winds, and every individual needle trembling in the sunlight, — think how it stands with it now, — sold, perchance, to the New England Friction-Match Company! There were in 1837, as I read, two hundred and fifty sawmills on the Penobscot and its tributaries above Bangor, the greater part of them in this immediate neighborhood, and they sawed two hundred millions of feet of boards annually. To this is to be added the lumber of the Kennebec, Androscoggin, Saco, Passamaquoddy, and other streams. No wonder that we hear so often of vessels which are becalmed off our coast being surrounded a week at a time by floating lumber from the Maine woods. The mission of men there seems to be, like so many busy demons, to drive the forest all out of the country, from every solitary beaver swamp and mountain-side, as soon as possible.

At Oldtown, we walked into a batteau-manufactory. The making of batteaux is quite a business here for the supply of the Penobscot River. We examined some on the stocks. They are light and shapely vessels, calculated for rapid and rocky streams, and to be carried over long portages on men's shoulders, from twenty to thirty feet long, and only four or four and a half wide, sharp at both ends like a canoe, though broadest forward on the bottom, and reaching seven or eight feet over the water, in order that they may slip over rocks as gently as possible. They are made very slight, only two boards to a side, commonly secured to a few light maple or other hard-wood knees, but inward are of the clearest and widest white pine stuff, of which there is a great waste on account of their form, for the bottom is left perfectly flat, not only from side to side, but from end to end. Sometimes they become "hogging" even, after long use, and the boatmen then turn them over and straighten them by a weight at each end. They told us that one wore out in two years, or often in a single trip, on the rocks, and sold for from fourteen to sixteen dollars. There was something refreshing and wildly musical to my ears in the very name of the white man's canoe, reminding me of Charlevoix and Canadian Voyageurs. The batteau is a sort of mongrel between the canoe and the boat, a fur-trader's boat.

The ferry here took us past the Indian island. As we left the shore, I observed a short, shabby, washerwoman-looking Indian, — they commonly have the woebegone

look of the girl that cried for spilt milk, — just from
"up river," land on the Oldtown side near a grocery,
and, drawing up his canoe, take out a bundle of skins
in one hand, and an empty keg or half-barrel in the other,
and scramble up the bank with them. This picture will
do to put before the Indian's history, that is, the history
of his extinction. In 1837 there were three hundred and
sixty-two souls left of this tribe. The island seemed deserted to-day, yet I observed some new houses among
the weather-stained ones, as if the tribe had still a design
upon life; but generally they have a very shabby, forlorn, and cheerless look, being all back side and woodshed, not homesteads, even Indian homesteads, but instead of home or abroad-steads, for their life is *domi aut
militiæ*, at home or at war, or now rather *venatus*, that
is, a hunting, and most of the latter. The church is the
only trim-looking building, but that is not Abenaki,
that was Rome's doings. Good Canadian it may be,
but it is poor Indian. These were once a powerful tribe.
Politics are all the rage with them now. I even thought
that a row of wigwams, with a dance of powwows, and
a prisoner tortured at the stake, would be more respectable than this.

We landed in Milford, and rode along on the east side
of the Penobscot, having a more or less constant view of
the river, and the Indian islands in it, for they retain all
the islands as far up as Nicketow, at the mouth of the
East Branch. They are generally well-timbered, and
are said to be better soil than the neighboring shores.
The river seemed shallow and rocky, and interrupted by
rapids, rippling and gleaming in the sun. We paused a

moment to see a fish hawk dive for a fish down straight as an arrow, from a great height, but he missed his prey this time. It was the Houlton road on which we were now traveling, over which some troops were marched once towards Mars' Hill, though not to Mars' *field*, as it proved. It is the main, almost the only, road in these parts, as straight and well made, and kept in as good repair as almost any you will find anywhere. Everywhere we saw signs of the great freshet, — this house standing awry, and that where it was not founded, but where it was found, at any rate, the next day; and that other with a waterlogged look, as if it were still airing and drying its basement, and logs with everybody's marks upon them, and sometimes the marks of their having served as bridges, strewn along the road. We crossed the Sunkhaze, a summery Indian name, the Olemmon, Passadumkeag, and other streams, which make a greater show on the map than they now did on the road. At Passadumkeag we found anything but what the name implies, — earnest politicians, to wit, — white ones, I mean, — on the alert to know how the election was likely to go; men who talked rapidly, with subdued voice, and a sort of factitious earnestness you could not help believing, hardly waiting for an introduction, one on each side of your buggy, endeavoring to say much in little, for they see you hold the whip impatiently, but always saying little in much. Caucuses they have had, it seems, and caucuses they are to have again, — victory and defeat. Somebody may be elected, somebody may not. One man, a total stranger, who stood by our carriage in the dusk, actually frightened the horse with

his asseverations, growing more solemnly positive as
there was less in him to be positive about. So Passadumkeag did not look on the map. At sundown, leaving
the river road awhile for shortness, we went by way of
Enfield, where we stopped for the night. This, like most
of the localities bearing names on this road, was a place
to name which, in the midst of the unnamed and unin-
corporated wilderness, was to make a distinction without a difference, it seemed to me. Here, however, I noticed quite an orchard of healthy and well-grown apple
trees, in a bearing state, it being the oldest settler's house
in this region, but all natural fruit and comparatively
worthless for want of a grafter. And so it is generally,
lower down the river. It would be a good speculation,
as well as a favor conferred on the settlers, for a Massachusetts boy to go down there with a trunk full of choice
scions, and his grafting apparatus, in the spring.

The next morning we drove along through a high and
hilly country, in view of Cold-Stream Pond, a beautiful
lake four or five miles long, and came into the Houlton
road again, here called the military road, at Lincoln,
forty-five miles from Bangor, where there is quite a village for this country, — the principal one above Oldtown. Learning that there were several wigwams here,
on one of the Indian islands, we left our horse and wagon
and walked through the forest half a mile to the river,
to procure a guide to the mountain. It was not till after
considerable search that we discovered their habitations, — small huts, in a retired place, where the scenery
was unusually soft and beautiful, and the shore skirted
with pleasant meadows and graceful elms. We paddled

ourselves across to the island side in a canoe, which we found on the shore. Near where we landed sat an Indian girl, ten or twelve years old, on a rock in the water, in the sun, washing, and humming or moaning a song meanwhile. It was an aboriginal strain. A salmon-spear, made wholly of wood, lay on the shore, such as they might have used before white men came. It had an elastic piece of wood fastened to one side of its point, which slipped over and closed upon the fish, somewhat like the contrivance for holding a bucket at the end of a well-pole. As we walked up to the nearest house, we were met by a sally of a dozen wolfish-looking dogs, which may have been lineal descendants from the ancient Indian dogs, which the first voyageurs describe as "their wolves." I suppose they were. The occupant soon appeared, with a long pole in his hand, with which he beat off the dogs, while he parleyed with us, — a stalwart, but dull and greasy-looking fellow, who told us, in his sluggish way, in answer to our questions, as if it were the first serious business he had to do that day, that there *were* Indians going "up river" — he and one other — to-day, before noon. And who was the other? Louis Neptune, who lives in the next house. Well, let us go over and see Louis together. The same doggish reception, and Louis Neptune makes his appearance, — a small, wiry man, with puckered and wrinkled face, yet he seemed the chief man of the two; the same, as I remembered, who had accompanied Jackson to the mountain in '37. The same questions were put to Louis, and the same information obtained, while the other Indian stood by. It appeared that they were going to start by noon,

with two canoes, to go up to Chesuncook to hunt moose,
— to be gone a month. "Well, Louis, suppose you get
to the Point (to the Five Islands, just below Mattawamkeag) to camp, we walk on up the West Branch to-
morrow, — four of us, — and wait for you at the dam,
or this side. You overtake us to-morrow or next day,
and take us into your canoes. We stop for you, you stop
for us. We pay you for your trouble." "Ye'," replied
Louis, "may be you carry some provision for all, —
some pork, — some bread, — and so pay." He said,
"Me sure get some moose;" and when I asked if he
thought Pomola would let us go up, he answered that
we must plant one bottle of rum on the top; he had
planted good many; and when he looked again, the
rum was all gone. He had been up two or three times;
he had planted letter, — English, German, French,
etc. These men were slightly clad in shirt and pantaloons, like laborers with us in warm weather. They did
not invite us into their houses, but met us outside. So
we left the Indians, thinking ourselves lucky to have
secured such guides and companions.

There were very few houses along the road, yet they
did not altogether fail, as if the law by which men are
dispersed over the globe were a very stringent one, and
not to be resisted with impunity or for slight reasons.
There were even the germs of one or two villages just
beginning to expand. The beauty of the road itself was
remarkable. The various evergreens, many of which are
rare with us, — delicate and beautiful specimens of the
larch, arbor-vitæ, ball-spruce, and fir-balsam, from a
few inches to many feet in height, — lined its sides, in

some places like a long front yard, springing up from
the smooth grass-plots which uninterruptedly border it,
and are made fertile by its wash; while it was but a step
on either hand to the grim, untrodden wilderness, whose
tangled labyrinth of living, fallen, and decaying trees
only the deer and moose, the bear and wolf can easily
penetrate. More perfect specimens than any front-yard
plot can show grew there to grace the passage of the
Houlton teams.

About noon we reached the Mattawamkeag, fifty-six
miles from Bangor by the way we had come, and put up
at a frequented house still on the Houlton road, where
the Houlton stage stops. Here was a substantial covered bridge over the Mattawamkeag, built, I think they
said, some seventeen years before. We had dinner, —
where, by the way, and even at breakfast, as well as
supper, at the public-houses on this road, the front rank
is composed of various kinds of "sweet cakes," in a continuous line from one end of the table to the other. I
think I may safely say that there was a row of ten or a
dozen plates of this kind set before us two here. To
account for which, they say that, when the lumberers
come out of the woods, they have a craving for cakes
and pies, and such sweet things, which there are almost
unknown, and this is the *supply* to satisfy that *demand*.
The supply is always equal to the demand, and these
hungry men think a good deal of getting their money's
worth. No doubt the balance of victuals is restored by
the time they reach Bangor, — Mattawamkeag takes
off the raw edge. Well, over this front rank, I say you,
coming from the "sweet cake" side, with a cheap phi-

losophic indifference though it may be, have to assault
what there is behind, which I do not by any means
mean to insinuate is insufficient in quantity or quality
to supply that other demand, of men, not from the woods
but from the towns, for venison and strong country fare.
After dinner we strolled down to the "Point," formed by
the junction of the two rivers, which is said to be the
scene of an ancient battle between the Eastern Indians
and the Mohawks, and searched there carefully for
relics, though the men at the bar-room had never heard
of such things; but we found only some flakes of arrow-
head stone, some points of arrowheads, one small leaden
bullet, and some colored beads, the last to be referred,
perhaps, to early fur-trader days. The Mattawamkeag,
though wide, was a mere river's bed, full of rocks and
shallows at this time, so that you could cross it almost
dry-shod in boots; and I could hardly believe my companion, when he told me that he had been fifty or sixty
miles up it in a batteau, through distant and still uncut
forests. A batteau could hardly find a harbor now at its
mouth. Deer and caribou, or reindeer, are taken here
in the winter, in sight of the house.

Before our companions arrived, we rode on up the
Houlton road seven miles to Molunkus, where the Aroostook road comes into it, and where there is a spacious
public house in the woods, called the "Molunkus
House," kept by one Libbey, which looked as if it had
its hall for dancing and for military drills. There was
no other evidence of man but this huge shingle palace
in this part of the world; but sometimes even this is
filled with travelers. I looked off the piazza round the

corner of the house up the Aroostook road, on which
there was no clearing in sight. There was a man just
adventuring upon it this evening in a rude, original,
what you may call Aroostook wagon, — a mere seat,
with a wagon swung under it, a few bags on it, and a
dog asleep to watch them. He offered to carry a message for us to anybody in that country, cheerfully. I
suspect that, if you should go to the end of the world,
you would find somebody there going farther, as if just
starting for home at sundown, and having a last word
before he drove off. Here, too, *was* a small trader,
whom I did not see at first, who kept a store, — but no
great store, certainly, — in a small box over the way,
behind the Molunkus sign-post. It looked like the bal-
ance-box of a patent hay-scales. As for his house, we
could only conjecture where that was; he may have
been a boarder in the Molunkus House. I saw him
standing in his shop door, — his shop was so small, that,
if a traveler should make demonstrations of entering in,
he would have to go out by the back way, and confer
with his customer through a window, about his goods
in the cellar, or, more probably, bespoken, and yet on
the way. I should have gone in, for I felt a real impulse
to trade, if I had not stopped to consider what would
become of him. The day before, we had walked into
a shop, over against an inn where we stopped, the puny
beginning of trade, which would grow at last into a firm
copartnership in the future town or city, — indeed, it
was already "Somebody & Co.," I forget who. The
woman came forward from the penetralia of the attached house, for "Somebody & Co." was in the burn-

ing, and she sold us percussion-caps, canalés and smooth, and knew their prices and qualities, and which the hunters preferred. Here was a little of everything in a small compass to satisfy the wants and the ambition of the woods, — a stock selected with what pains and care, and brought home in the wagon-box, or a corner of the Houlton team; but there seemed to me, as usual, a preponderance of children's toys, — dogs to bark, and cats to mew, and trumpets to blow, where natives there hardly are yet. As if a child born into the Maine woods, among the pine cones and cedar berries, could not do without such a sugar-man or skipping-jack as the young Rothschild has.

I think that there was not more than one house on the road to Molunkus, or for seven miles. At that place we got over the fence into a new field, planted with potatoes, where the logs were still burning between the hills; and, pulling up the vines, found good-sized potatoes, nearly ripe, growing like weeds, and turnips mixed with them. The mode of clearing and planting is to fell the trees, and burn once what will burn, then cut them up into suitable lengths, roll into heaps, and burn again; then, with a hoe, plant potatoes where you can come at the ground between the stumps and charred logs; for a first crop the ashes sufficing for manure, and no hoeing being necessary the first year. In the fall, cut, roll, and burn again, and so on, till the land is cleared; and soon it is ready for grain, and to be laid down. Let those talk of poverty and hard times who will in the towns and cities; cannot the emigrant who can pay his fare to New York or Boston pay five dollars more to get here, —

I paid three, all told, for my passage from Boston to
Bangor, two hundred and fifty miles, — and be as rich
as he pleases, where land virtually costs nothing, and
houses only the labor of building, and he may begin life
as Adam did? If he will still remember the distinction
of poor and rich, let him bespeak him a narrower house
forthwith.

When we returned to the Mattawamkeag, the Houlton stage had already put up there; and a Province
man was betraying his greenness to the Yankees by his
questions. Why Province money won't pass here at par,
when States' money is good at Fredericton, — though
this, perhaps, was sensible enough. From what I saw
then, it appears that the Province man was now the only
real Jonathan, or raw country bumpkin, left so far behind by his enterprising neighbors that he did n't know
enough to put a question to them. No people can long
continue provincial in character who have the propen-
sity for politics and whittling, and rapid traveling, which
the Yankees have, and who are leaving the mother country behind in the variety of their notions and inventions.
The possession and exercise of practical talent merely
are a sure and rapid means of intellectual culture and
independence.

The last edition of Greenleaf's Map of Maine hung
on the wall here, and, as we had no pocket-map, we resolved to trace a map of the lake country. So, dipping
a wad of tow into the lamp, we oiled a sheet of paper on
the oiled table-cloth, and, in good faith, traced what we
afterwards ascertained to be a labyrinth of errors, carefully following the outlines of the imaginary lakes which

the map contains. The Map of the Public Lands of
Maine and Massachusetts is the only one I have seen
that at all deserves the name. It was while we were
engaged in this operation that our companions arrived.
They had seen the Indians' fire on the Five Islands,
and so we concluded that all was right.

Early the next morning we had mounted our packs,
and prepared for a tramp up the West Branch, my companion having turned his horse out to pasture for a week
or ten days, thinking that a bite of fresh grass and a
taste of running water would do him as much good as
backwoods fare and new country influences his master.
Leaping over a fence, we began to follow an obscure
trail up the northern bank of the Penobscot. There was
now no road further, the river being the only highway,
and but half a dozen log huts, confined to its banks, to
be met with for thirty miles. On either hand, and beyond, was a wholly uninhabited wilderness, stretching
to Canada. Neither horse nor cow, nor vehicle of any
kind, had ever passed over this ground; the cattle, and
the few bulky articles which the loggers use, being got
up in the winter on the ice, and down again before it
breaks up. The evergreen woods had a decidedly sweet
and bracing fragrance; the air was a sort of diet-drink,
and we walked on buoyantly in Indian file, stretching
our legs. Occasionally there was a small opening on the
bank, made for the purpose of log-rolling, where we got
a sight of the river, — always a rocky and rippling
stream. The roar of the rapids, the note of a whistler
duck on the river, of the jay and chickadee around us,
and of the pigeon woodpecker in the openings, were the

sounds that we heard. This was what you might call a bran-new country; the only roads were of Nature's making, and the few houses were camps. Here, then, one could no longer accuse institutions and society, but must front the true source of evil.

There are three classes of inhabitants who either frequent or inhabit the country which we had now entered: first, the loggers, who, for a part of the year, the winter and spring, are far the most numerous, but in the summer, except a few explorers for timber, completely desert it; second, the few settlers I have named, the only permanent inhabitants, who live on the verge of it, and help raise supplies for the former; third, the hunters, mostly Indians, who range over it in their season.

At the end of three miles we came to the Mattaseunk stream and mill, where there was even a rude wooden railroad running down to the Penobscot, the last railroad we were to see. We crossed one tract, on the bank of the river, of more than a hundred acres of heavy timber, which had just been felled and burnt over, and was still smoking. Our trail lay through the midst of it, and was well-nigh blotted out. The trees lay at full length, four or five feet deep, and crossing each other in all directions, all black as charcoal, but perfectly sound within, still good for fuel or for timber; soon they would be cut into lengths and burnt again. Here were thousands of cords, enough to keep the poor of Boston and New York amply warm for a winter, which only cumbered the ground and were in the settler's way. And the whole of that solid and interminable forest is doomed to be gradually devoured thus by fire, like shavings, and

no man be warmed by it. At Crocker's log-hut, at the
mouth of Salmon River, seven miles from the Point,
one of the party commenced distributing a store of
small, cent picture-books among the children, to teach
them to read, and also newspapers, more or less recent,
among the parents, than which nothing can be more
acceptable to a backwoods people. It was really an important item in our outfit, and, at times, the only cur-
rency that would circulate. I walked through Salmon
River with my shoes on, it being low water, but not
without wetting my feet. A few miles farther we came
to "Marm Howard's," at the end of an extensive clearing, where there were two or three log huts in sight at
once, one on the opposite side of the river, and a few
graves even, surrounded by a wooden paling, where
already the rude forefathers of *a* hamlet lie, and a
thousand years hence, perchance, some poet will write
his "Elergy in a Country Churchyard." The "Village
Hampdens," the "mute, inglorious Miltons," and
Cromwells, "guiltless of" their "country's blood,"
were yet unborn.

> "Perchance in this *wild* spot *there will be* laid
> Some heart once pregnant with celestial fire;
> Hands that the rod of empire might have swayed,
> Or waked to ecstasy the living lyre."

The next house was Fisk's, ten miles from the Point
at the mouth of the East Branch, opposite to the island
Nicketow, or the Forks, the last of the Indian islands.
I am particular to give the names of the settlers and the
distances, since every log hut in these woods is a public
house, and such information is of no little consequence

to those who may have occasion to travel this way. Our course here crossed the Penobscot, and followed the southern bank. One of the party, who entered the house in search of some one to set us over, reported a very neat dwelling, with plenty of books, and a new wife, just imported from Boston, wholly new to the woods. We found the East Branch a large and rapid stream at its mouth and much deeper than it appeared. Having with some difficulty discovered the trail again, we kept up the south side of the West Branch, or main river, passing by some rapids called Rock-Ebeeme, the roar of which we heard through the woods, and, shortly after, in the thickest of the wood, some empty loggers' camps, still new, which were occupied the previous winter. Though we saw a few more afterwards, I will make one account serve for all. These were such houses as the lumberers of Maine spend the winter in, in the wilderness. There were the camps and the hovels for the cattle, hardly distinguishable, except that the latter had no chimney. These camps were about twenty feet long by fifteen wide, built of logs, — hemlock, cedar, spruce or yellow birch, — one kind alone, or all together, with the bark on; two or three large ones first, one directly above another, and notched together at the ends, to the height of three or four feet, then of smaller logs resting upon transverse ones at the ends, each of the last successively shorter than the other, to form the roof. The chimney was an oblong square hole in the middle, three or four feet in diameter, with a fence of logs as high as the ridge. The interstices were filled with moss, and the roof was shingled with long and handsome splints of cedar, or spruce, or pine, rifted with a sledge and cleaver. The fireplace, the most important place of all, was in shape and size like the chimney, and directly under it, defined by a log fence or fender on the ground, and a heap of ashes, a foot or two deep within, with solid benches of split logs running round it. Here the fire usually melts the snow, and dries the rain before it can descend to quench it. The faded beds of arbor-vitæ leaves extended under the eaves on either hand. There was the place for the water-pail, pork-barrel, and wash-basin, and generally a dingy pack of cards left on a log. Usually a good deal of whittling was expended on the latch, which was made of wood, in the form of an iron one. These houses are made comfortable by the huge fires, which can be afforded night and day. Usually the scenery about them is drear and savage enough; and the loggers' camp is as completely in the woods as a fungus at the foot of a pine in a swamp; no outlook but to the sky overhead; no more clearing than is made by cutting down the trees of which it is built, and those which are necessary for fuel. If only it be well sheltered and convenient to his work, and near a spring, he wastes no thought on the prospect. They are very proper forest houses, the stems of the trees collected together and piled up around a man to keep out wind and rain, — made of living green logs, hanging with moss and lichen, and with the curls and fringes of the yellow birch bark, and dripping with resin, fresh and moist, and redolent of swampy odors, with that sort of vigor and perennialness even about them that toadstools suggest.[1] The

[1] Springer, in his *Forest Life* (1851), says that they first remove the

logger's fare consists of tea, molasses, flour, pork (sometimes beef), and beans. A great proportion of the beans
raised in Massachusetts find their market here. On
expeditions it is only hard bread and pork, often raw,
slice upon slice, with tea or water, as the case may be.

The primitive wood is always and everywhere damp
and mossy, so that I traveled constantly with the impression that I was in a swamp; and only when it was
remarked that this or that tract, judging from the quality of the timber on it, would make a profitable clearing,
was I reminded, that if the sun were let in it would make
a dry field, like the few I had seen, at once. The best
shod for the most part travel with wet feet. If the ground
was so wet and spongy at this, the dryest part of a dry
season, what must it be in the spring? The woods hereabouts abounded in beech and yellow birch, of which
last there were some very large specimens; also spruce,
cedar, fir, and hemlock; but we saw only the stumps
of the white pine here, some of them of great size, these
having been already culled out, being the only tree
much sought after, even as low down as this. Only a
little spruce and hemlock beside had been logged here.
The Eastern wood which is sold for fuel in Massachu-

leaves and turf from the spot where they intend to build a camp, for
fear of fire; also, that "the spruce-tree is generally selected for camp-
building, it being light, straight, and quite free from sap;" that "the
roof is finally covered with the boughs of the fir, spruce, and hemlock,
so that when the snow falls upon the whole, the warmth of the camp
is preserved in the coldest weather;" and that they make the log seat
before the fire, called the "Deacon's Seat," of a spruce or fir split in
halves, with three or four stout limbs left on one side for legs, which are
not likely to get loose.

setts all comes from below Bangor. It was the pine
alone, chiefly the white pine, that had tempted any but
the hunter to precede us on this route.

Waite's farm, thirteen miles from the Point, is an
extensive and elevated clearing, from which we got a
fine view of the river, rippling and gleaming far beneath us. My companions had formerly had a good
view of Ktaadn and the other mountains here, but
to-day it was so smoky that we could see nothing of
them. We could overlook an immense country of uninterrupted forest, stretching away up the East Branch
toward Canada on the north and northwest, and toward the Aroostook valley on the northeast; and imagine what wild life was stirring in its midst. Here was
quite a field of corn for this region, whose peculiar dry
scent we perceived a third of a mile off, before we saw it.

Eighteen miles from the Point brought us in sight of
McCauslin's, or "Uncle George's," as he was familiarly
called by my companions, to whom he was well known,
where we intended to break our long fast. His house
was in the midst of an extensive clearing or intervale,
at the mouth of the Little Schoodic River, on the opposite or north bank of the Penobscot. So we collected
on a point of the shore, that we might be seen, and fired
our gun as a signal, which brought out his dogs forthwith, and thereafter their master, who in due time took
us across in his batteau. This clearing was bounded
abruptly, on all sides but the river, by the naked stems
of the forest, as if you were to cut only a few feet square
in the midst of a thousand acres of mowing, and set
down a thimble therein. He had a whole heaven and

horizon to himself, and the sun seemed to be journey-
ing over his clearing only the livelong day. Here we
concluded to spend the night, and wait for the Indians,
as there was no stopping-place so convenient above.
He had seen no Indians pass, and this did not often
happen without his knowledge. He thought that his
dogs sometimes gave notice of the approach of Indians
half an hour before they arrived.

McCauslin was a Kennebec man, of Scotch descent,
who had been a waterman twenty-two years, and had
driven on the lakes and headwaters of the Penobscot
five or six springs in succession, but was now settled
here to raise supplies for the lumberers and for himself.
He entertained us a day or two with true Scotch hospitality, and would accept no recompense for it. A man
of a dry wit and shrewdness, and a general intelligence
which I had not looked for in the back woods. In fact,
the deeper you penetrate into the woods, the more intelligent, and, in one sense, less countrified do you find
the inhabitants; for always the pioneer has been a
traveler, and, to some extent, a man of the world; and,
as the distances with which he is familiar are greater,
so is his information more general and far reaching
than the villager's. If I were to look for a narrow, un-
informed, and countrified mind, as opposed to the intelligence and refinement which are thought to emanate
from cities, it would be among the rusty inhabitants
of an old-settled country, on farms all run out and
gone to seed with life-everlasting, in the towns about
Boston, even on the high-road in Concord, and not in
the back woods of Maine.

Supper was got before our eyes in the ample kitchen, by a fire which would have roasted an ox; many whole logs, four feet long, were consumed to boil our tea-kettle, — birch, or beech, or maple, the same summer and winter; and the dishes were soon smoking on the table, late the arm-chair, against the wall, from which one of the party was expelled. The arms of the chair formed the frame on which the table rested; and, when the round top was turned up against the wall, it formed the back of the chair, and was no more in the way than the wall itself. This, we noticed, was the prevailing fashion in these log houses, in order to economize in room. There were piping-hot wheaten cakes, the flour having been brought up the river in batteaux, — no Indian bread, for the upper part of Maine, it will be remembered, is a wheat country, — and ham, eggs, and potatoes, and milk and cheese, the produce of the farm; and also shad and salmon, tea sweetened with molasses, and sweet cakes, in contradistinction to the hot cakes not sweetened, the one white, the other yellow, to wind up with. Such we found was the prevailing fare, ordinary and extraordinary, along this river. Mountain cranberries (*Vaccinium Vitis-Idæa*), stewed and sweetened, were the common dessert. Everything here was in profusion, and the best of its kind. Butter was in such plenty that it was commonly used, before it was salted, to grease boots with.

In the night we were entertained by the sound of rain-drops on the cedar splints which covered the roof, and awaked the next morning with a drop or two in our eyes. It had set in for a storm, and we made up our minds not to forsake such comfortable quarters with this prospect, but wait for Indians and fair weather. It rained and drizzled and gleamed by turns, the livelong day. What we did there, how we killed the time would perhaps be idle to tell; how many times we buttered our boots, and how often a drowsy one was seen to sidle off to the bedroom. When it held up, I strolled up and down the bank, and gathered the harebell and cedar berries, which grew there; or else we tried by turns the long-handled axe on the logs before the door. The axe-helves here were made to chop standing on the log, — a primitive log of course, — and were, therefore, nearly a foot longer than with us. One while we walked over the farm and visited his well-filled barns with McCaus-lin. There were one other man and two women only here. He kept horses, cows, oxen, and sheep. I think he said that he was the first to bring a plow and a cow so far; and he might have added the last, with only two exceptions. The potato-rot had found him out here, too, the previous year, and got half or two thirds of his crop, though the seed was of his own raising. Oats, grass, and potatoes were his staples; but he raised, also, a few carrots and turnips, and "a little corn for the hens," for this was all that he dared risk, for fear that it would not ripen. Melons, squashes, sweet corn, beans, tomatoes, and many other vegetables, could not be ripened there.

The very few settlers along this stream were obviously tempted by the cheapness of the land mainly. When I asked McCauslin why more settlers did not come in, he answered, that one reason was, they could

not buy the land, it belonged to individuals or companies who were afraid that their wild lands would be settled, and so incorporated into towns, and they be taxed
for them; but to settling on the State's land there was
no such hindrance. For his own part, he wanted no
neighbors, — he did n't wish to see any road by his
house. Neighbors, even the best, were a trouble and
expense, especially on the score of cattle and fences.
They might live across the river, perhaps, but not on
the same side.

The chickens here were protected by the dogs. As
McCauslin said, " The old one took it up first, and she
taught the pup, and now they had got it into their heads
that it would n't do to have anything of the bird kind
on the premises." A hawk hovering over was not
allowed to alight, but barked off by the dogs circling
underneath; and a pigeon, or a " yellow-hammer," as
they called the pigeon woodpecker, on a dead limb or
stump, was instantly expelled. It was the main business
of their day, and kept them constantly coming and
going. One would rush out of the house on the least
alarm given by the other.

When it rained hardest, we returned to the house,
and took down a tract from the shelf. There was the
" Wandering Jew," cheap edition, and fine print, the
" Criminal Calendar," and " Parish's Geography,"
and flash novels two or three. Under the pressure of
circumstances, we read a little in these. With such aid,
the press is not so feeble an engine, after all. This house,
which was a fair specimen of those on this river, was
built of huge logs, which peeped out everywhere, and

were chinked with clay and moss. It contained four or
five rooms. There were no sawed boards, or shingles,
or clapboards, about it; and scarcely any tool but the
axe had been used in its construction. The partitions
were made of long clapboard-like splints, of spruce or
cedar, turned to a delicate salmon-color by the smoke.
The roof and sides were covered with the same, instead
of shingles and clapboards, and some of a much thicker
and larger size were used for the floor. These were all
so straight and smooth, that they answered the purpose
admirably, and a careless observer would not have suspected that they were not sawed and planed. The chimney and hearth were of vast size, and made of stone.
The broom was a few twigs of arbor-vitæ tied to a stick;
and a pole was suspended over the hearth, close to the
ceiling, to dry stockings and clothes on. I noticed that
the floor was full of small, dingy holes, as if made with
a gimlet, but which were, in fact, made by the spikes,
nearly an inch long, which the lumberers wear in their
boots to prevent their slipping on wet logs. Just above
McCauslin's, there is a rocky rapid, where logs jam in
the spring; and many "drivers" are there collected,
who frequent his house for supplies; these were their
tracks which I saw.

At sundown McCauslin pointed away over the forest,
across the river, to signs of fair weather amid the clouds,
— some evening redness there. For even there the
points of compass held; and there was a quarter of the
heavens appropriated to sunrise and another to sunset.

The next morning, the weather proving fair enough
for our purpose, we prepared to start, and, the Indians

having failed us, persuaded McCauslin, who was not
unwilling to revisit the scenes of his driving, to accompany us in their stead, intending to engage one other
boatman on the way. A strip of cotton cloth for a tent,
a couple of blankets, which would suffice for the whole
party, fifteen pounds of hard bread, ten pounds of
"clear" pork, and a little tea, made up "Uncle George's"
pack. The last three articles were calculated to be provision enough for six men for a week, with what we
might pick up. A tea-kettle, a frying-pan, and an axe,
to be obtained at the last house, would complete our
outfit.

We were soon out of McCauslin's clearing, and in
the evergreen woods again. The obscure trail made
by the two settlers above, which even the woodman is
sometimes puzzled to discern, ere long crossed a narrow,
open strip in the woods overrun with weeds, called
the Burnt Land, where a fire had raged formerly,
stretching northward nine or ten miles, to Millinocket
Lake. At the end of three miles, we reached Shad Pond,
or Noliseemack, an expansion of the river. Hodge, the
Assistant State Geologist, who passed through this on
the 25th of June, 1837, says, "We pushed our boat
through an acre or more of buck-beans, which had taken
root at the bottom, and bloomed above the surface in
the greatest profusion and beauty." Thomas Fowler's
house is four miles from McCauslin's, on the shore of
the pond, at the mouth of the Millinocket River, and
eight miles from the lake of the same name, on the latter
stream. This lake affords a more direct course to
Ktaadn, but we preferred to follow the Penobscot and

the Pamadumcook lakes. Fowler was just completing a new log hut, and was sawing out a window through the logs, nearly two feet thick, when we arrived. He had begun to paper his house with spruce bark, turned inside out, which had a good effect, and was in keeping with the circumstances. Instead of water we got here a draught of beer, which, it was allowed, would be better; clear and thin, but strong and stringent as the cedar sap. It was as if we sucked at the very teats of Nature's pine-clad bosom in these parts, — the sap of all Millinocket botany commingled, — the topmost, most fantastic, and spiciest sprays of the primitive wood, and whatever invigorating and stringent gum or essence it afforded steeped and dissolved in it, — a lumberer's drink, which would acclimate and naturalize a man at once, — which would make him see green, and, if he slept, dream that he heard the wind sough among the pines. Here was a fife, praying to be played on, through which we breathed a few tuneful strains, — brought hither to tame wild beasts. As we stood upon the pile of chips by the door, fish hawks were sailing overhead; and here, over Shad Pond, might daily be witnessed the tyranny of the bald eagle over that bird. Tom pointed away over the lake to a bald eagle's nest, which was plainly visible more than a mile off, on a pine, high above the surrounding forest, and was frequented from year to year by the same pair, and held sacred by him. There were these two houses only there, his low hut and the eagles' airy cart-load of fagots. Thomas Fowler, too, was persuaded to join us, for two men were necessary to manage the bat-teau, which was soon to be our carriage, and these men needed to be cool and skillful for the navigation of the Penobscot. Tom's pack was soon made, for he had not far to look for his waterman's boots, and a red flannel shirt. This is the favorite color with lumbermen; and red flannel is reputed to possess some mysterious virtues, to be most healthful and convenient in respect to perspiration. In every gang there will be a large proportion of red birds. We took here a poor and leaky batteau, and began to pole up the Millinocket two miles, to the elder Fowler's, in order to avoid the Grand Falls of the Penobscot, intending to exchange our batteau there for a better. The Millinocket is a small, shallow, and sandy stream, full of what I took to be lamprey-eels' or suckers' nests, and lined with musquash-cabins, but free from rapids, according to Fowler, excepting at its outlet from the lake. He was at this time engaged in cutting the native grass — rush-grass and meadow-clover, as he called it — on the meadows and small, low islands of this stream. We noticed flattened places in the grass on either side, where, he said, a moose had laid down the night before, adding, that there were thousands in these meadows.

Old Fowler's, on the Millinocket, six miles from McCauslin's, and twenty-four from the Point, is the last house. Gibson's, on the Sowadnehunk, is the only clearing above, but that had proved a failure, and was long since deserted. Fowler is the oldest inhabitant of these woods. He formerly lived a few miles from here, on the south side of the West Branch, where he built his house sixteen years ago, the first house built above the Five Islands. Here our new batteau was to be carried

over the first portage of two miles, round the Grand
Falls of the Penobscot, on a horse-sled made of saplings,
to jump the numerous rocks in the way; but we had to
wait a couple of hours for them to catch the horses,
which were pastured at a distance, amid the stumps, and
had wandered still farther off. The last of the salmon
for this season had just been caught, and were still fresh
in pickle, from which enough was extracted to fill our
empty kettle, and so graduate our introduction to simpler forest fare. The week before they had lost nine
sheep here out of their first flock, by the wolves. The
surviving sheep came round the house, and seemed
frightened, which induced them to go and look for the
rest, when they found seven dead and lacerated, and
two still alive. These last they carried to the house, and,
as Mrs. Fowler said, they were merely scratched in the
throat, and had no more visible wound than would be
produced by the prick of a pin. She sheared off the wool
from their throats, and washed them, and put on some
salve, and turned them out, but in a few moments they
were missing, and had not been found since. In fact,
they were all poisoned, and those that were found swelled
up at once, so that they saved neither skin nor wool.
This realized the old fables of the wolves and the sheep,
and convinced me that that ancient hostility still existed. Verily, the shepherd-boy did not need to sound
a false alarm this time. There were steel traps by the
door, of various sizes, for wolves, otter, and bears, with
large claws instead of teeth, to catch in their sinews.
Wolves are frequently killed with poisoned bait.

At length, after we had dined here on the usual back-

woods fare, the horses arrived, and we hauled our batteau out of the water, and lashed it to its wicker carriage,
and, throwing in our packs, walked on before, leaving
the boatmen and driver, who was Tom's brother, to
manage the concern. The route, which led through the
wild pasture where the sheep were killed, was in some
places the roughest ever traveled by horses, over rocky
hills, where the sled bounced and slid along, like a vessel pitching in a storm; and one man was as necessary
to stand at the stern, to prevent the boat from being
wrecked, as a helmsman in the roughest sea. The philosophy of our progress was something like this: when
the runners struck a rock three or four feet high, the
sled bounced back and upwards at the same time; but,
as the horses never ceased pulling, it came down on
the top of the rock, and so we got over. This portage
probably followed the trail of an ancient Indian carry
round these falls. By two o'clock we, who had walked
on before, reached the river above the falls, not far from
the outlet of Quakish Lake, and waited for the batteau
to come up. We had been here but a short time, when
a thunder-shower was seen coming up from the west,
over the still invisible lakes, and that pleasant wilderness which we were so eager to become acquainted with;
and soon the heavy drops began to patter on the leaves
around us. I had just selected the prostrate trunk of a
huge pine, five or six feet in diameter, and was crawling
under it, when, luckily, the boat arrived. It would have
amused a sheltered man to witness the manner in which
it was unlashed, and whirled over, while the first waterspout burst upon us. It was no sooner in the hands of

the eager company than it was abandoned to the first revolutionary impulse, and to gravity, to adjust it; and they might have been seen all stooping to its shelter, and wriggling under like so many eels, before it was fairly deposited on the ground. When all were under, we propped up the lee side, and busied ourselves there whittling thole-pins for rowing, when we should reach the lakes; and made the woods ring, between the claps of thunder, with such boat-songs as we could remember. The horses stood sleek and shining with the rain, all drooping and crestfallen, while deluge after deluge washed over us; but the bottom of a boat may be relied on for a tight roof. At length, after two hours' delay at this place, a streak of fair weather appeared in the northwest, whither our course now lay, promising a serene evening for our voyage; and the driver returned with his horses, while we made haste to launch our boat, and commence our voyage in good earnest.

There were six of us, including the two boatmen. With our packs heaped up near the bows, and ourselves disposed as baggage to trim the boat, with instructions not to move in case we should strike a rock, more than so many barrels of pork, we pushed out into the first rapid, a slight specimen of the stream we had to navigate. With Uncle George in the stern, and Tom in the bows, each using a spruce pole about twelve feet long, pointed with iron,[1] and poling on the same side, we shot up the rapids like a salmon, the water rushing and roaring around, so that only a practiced eye could distinguish a safe course, or tell what was deep water and

---

[1] The Canadians call it *picquer de fond.*

what rocks, frequently grazing the latter on one or both sides, with a hundred as narrow escapes as ever the Argo had in passing through the Symplegades. I, who had had some experience in boating, had never experienced any half so exhilarating before. We were lucky to have exchanged our Indians, whom we did not know, for these men, who, together with Tom's brother, were reputed the best boatmen on the river, and were at once indispensable pilots and pleasant companions. The canoe is smaller, more easily upset, and sooner worn out; and the Indian is said not to be so skillful in the management of the batteau. He is, for the most part, less to be relied on, and more disposed to sulks and whims. The utmost familiarity with dead streams, or with the ocean, would not prepare a man for this peculiar navigation ; and the most skillful boatman anywhere else would here be obliged to take out his boat and carry round a hundred times, still with great risk, as well as delay, where the practiced batteau-man poles up with comparative ease and safety. The hardy "voyageur" pushes with incredible perseverance and success quite up to the foot of the falls, and then only carries round some perpendicular ledge, and launches again in

"The torrent's smoothness, ere it dash below,"

to struggle with the boiling rapids above. The Indians say that the river once ran both ways, one half up and the other down, but that, since the white man came, it all runs down, and now they must laboriously pole their canoes against the stream, and carry them

over numerous portages. In the summer, all stores —
the grindstone and the plow of the pioneer, flour, pork,
and utensils for the explorer — must be conveyed up
the river in batteaux; and many a cargo and many a
boatman is lost in these waters. In the winter, however,
which is very equable and long, the ice is the great
highway, and the loggers' team penetrates to Chesuncook Lake, and still higher up, even two hundred miles
above Bangor. Imagine the solitary sled-track running far up into the snowy and evergreen wilderness,
hemmed in closely for a hundred miles by the forest,
and again stretching straight across the broad surfaces
of concealed lakes!

We were soon in the smooth water of the Quakish
Lake, and took our turns at rowing and paddling across
it. It is a small, irregular, but handsome lake, shut in
on all sides by the forest, and showing no traces of man
but some low boom in a distant cove, reserved for
spring use. The spruce and cedar on its shores, hung
with gray lichens, looked at a distance like the ghosts
of trees. Ducks were sailing here and there on its
surface, and a solitary loon, like a more living wave,
— a vital spot on the lake's surface, — laughed and
frolicked, and showed its straight leg, for our amusement. Joe Merry Mountain appeared in the northwest,
as if it were looking down on this lake especially; and
we had our first, but a partial view of Ktaadn, its summit veiled in clouds, like a dark isthmus in that quarter,
connecting the heavens with the earth. After two miles
of smooth rowing across this lake, we found ourselves
in the river again, which was a continuous rapid for one

mile, to the dam, requiring all the strength and skill of our boatmen to pole up it.

This dam is a quite important and expensive work for this country, whither cattle and horses cannot penetrate in the summer, raising the whole river ten feet, and flooding, as they said, some sixty square miles by means of the innumerable lakes with which the river connects. It is a lofty and solid structure, with sloping piers, some distance above, made of frames of logs filled with stones, to break the ice.[1] Here every log pays toll as it passes through the sluices.

We filed into the rude loggers' camp at this place, such as I have described, without ceremony, and the cook, at that moment the sole occupant, at once set about preparing tea for his visitors. His fireplace, which the rain had converted into a mud-puddle, was soon blazing again, and we sat down on the log benches around it to dry us. On the well-flattened and somewhat faded beds of arbor-vitæ leaves, which stretched on either hand under the eaves behind us, lay an odd leaf of the Bible, some genealogical chapter out of the Old Testament; and, half buried by the leaves, we found Emerson's Address on West India Emancipation, which had been left here formerly by one of our company, and *had made two converts to the Liberty party here*, as I was told; also, an odd number of the *Westminster Review*, for 1834, and a pamphlet entitled

---

[1] Even the Jesuit missionaries, accustomed to the St. Lawrence and other rivers of Canada, in their first expeditions to the Abenaquinois, speak of rivers *ferrées de rochers*, shod with rocks. See also No. 10 *Relations*, for 1647, p. 185.

" History of the Erection of the Monument on the Grave of Myron Holly." This was the readable or reading matter in a lumberer's camp in the Maine woods, thirty miles from a road, which would be given up to the bears in a fortnight. These things were well thumbed and soiled. This gang was headed by one John Morrison, a good specimen of a Yankee; and was necessarily composed of men not bred to the business of dam-building, but who were jacks-at-all-trades, handy with the axe, and other simple implements, and well skilled in wood and water craft. We had hot cakes for our supper even here, white as snowballs, but without butter, and the never-failing sweet cakes, with which we filled our pockets, foreseeing that we should not soon meet with the like again. Such delicate puffballs seemed a singular diet for backwoodsmen. There was also tea without milk, sweetened with molasses. And so, exchanging a word with John Morrison and his gang when we had returned to the shore, and also exchanging our batteau for a better still, we made haste to improve the little daylight that remained. This camp, exactly twenty-nine miles from Mattawamkeag Point by the way we had come, and about one hundred from Bangor by the river, was the last human habitation of any kind in this direction. Beyond, there was no trail, and the river and lakes, by batteaux and canoes, was considered the only practicable route. We were about thirty miles by the river from the summit of Ktaadn, which was in sight, though not more than twenty, perhaps, in a straight line.

It being about the full of the moon, and a warm and

pleasant evening, we decided to row five miles by moonlight to the head of the North Twin Lake, lest the wind should rise on the morrow. After one mile of river, or what the boatmen call " thoroughfare," — for the river becomes at length only the connecting link between the lakes, — and some slight rapid which had been mostly made smooth water by the dam, we entered the North Twin Lake just after sundown, and steered across for the river " thoroughfare," four miles distant. This is a noble sheet of water, where one may get the impression which a new country and a " lake of the woods " are fitted to create. There was the smoke of no log hut nor camp of any kind to greet us, still less was any lover of nature or musing traveler watching our batteau from the distant hills; not even the Indian hunter was there, for he rarely climbs them, but hugs the river like ourselves. No face welcomed us but the fine fantastic sprays of free and happy evergreen trees, waving one above another in their ancient home. At first the red clouds hung over the western shore as gorgeously as if over a city, and the lake lay open to the light with even a civilized aspect, as if expecting trade and commerce, and towns and villas. We could distinguish the inlet to the South Twin, which is said to be the larger, where the shore was misty and blue, and it was worth the while to look thus through a narrow opening across the entire expanse of a concealed lake to its own yet more dim and distant shore. The shores rose gently to ranges of low hills covered with forests; and though, in fact, the most valuable white-pine timber, even about this lake, had been culled out, this would never have been suspected by the voyager. The impression, which indeed corresponded with the fact, was, as if we were upon a high table-land between the States and Canada, the northern side of which is drained by the St. John and Chaudière, the southern by the Penobscot and Kennebec. There was no bold, mountainous shore, as we might have expected, but only isolated hills and mountains rising here and there from the plateau. The country is an archipelago of lakes, — the lake-country of New England. Their levels vary but a few feet, and the boatmen, by short portages, or by none at all, pass easily from one to another. They say that at very high water the Penobscot and the Kennebec flow into each other, or at any rate, that you may lie with your face in the one and your toes in the other. Even the Penobscot and St. John have been connected by a canal, so that the lumber of the Allegash, instead of going down the St. John, comes down the Penobscot; and the Indian's tradition, that the Penobscot once ran both ways for his convenience, is, in one sense, partially realized to-day.

None of our party but McCauslin had been above this lake, so we trusted to him to pilot us, and we could not but confess the importance of a pilot on these waters. While it is river, you will not easily forget which way is up-stream; but when you enter a lake, the river is completely lost, and you scan the distant shores in vain to find where it comes in. A stranger is, for the time at least, lost, and must set about a voyage of discovery first of all to find the river. To follow the windings of the shore when the lake is ten miles, or even more, in length, and of an irregularity which will not soon be mapped, is a wearisome voyage, and will spend his time and his provisions. They tell a story of a gang of experienced woodmen sent to a location on this stream, who were thus lost in the wilderness of lakes. They cut their way through thickets, and carried their baggage and their boats over from lake to lake, sometimes several miles. They carried into Millinocket Lake, which is on another stream, and is ten miles square, and contains a hundred islands. They explored its shores thoroughly, and then carried into another, and another, and it was a week of toil and anxiety before they found the Penobscot River again, and then their provisions were exhausted, and they were obliged to return.

While Uncle George steered for a small island near the head of the lake, now just visible, like a speck on the water, we rowed by turns swiftly over its surface, singing such boat songs as we could remember. The shores seemed at an indefinite distance in the moonlight. Occasionally we paused in our singing and rested on our oars, while we listened to hear if the wolves howled, for this is a common serenade, and my companions affirmed that it was the most dismal and unearthly of sounds; but we heard none this time. If we did not *hear*, however, we did *listen*, not without a reasonable expectation; that at least I have to tell, — only some utterly uncivilized, big-throated owl hooted loud and dismally in the drear and boughy wilderness, plainly not nervous about his solitary life, nor afraid to hear the echoes of his voice there. We remembered also that possibly moose were silently watching us from the distant coves, or some surly bear or timid caribou had been startled by our singing. It was with new emphasis that we sang there the Canadian boat song, —

> " Row, brothers, row, the stream runs fast,
>   The rapids are near and the daylight 's past ! "

which describes precisely our own adventure, and was inspired by the experience of a similar kind of life, — for the rapids were ever near, and the daylight long past; the woods on shore looked dim, and many an Utawas' tide here emptied into the lake.

> " Why should we yet our sail unfurl ?
>   There is not a breath the blue wave to curl !
>   But, when the wind blows off the shore,
>   Oh, sweetly we 'll rest our weary oar."

> " Utawas' tide ! this trembling moon
>   Shall see us float o'er thy surges soon."

At last we glided past the " green isle," which had been our landmark, all joining in the chorus; as if by the watery links of rivers and of lakes we were about to float over unmeasured zones of earth, bound on un-imaginable adventures, —

> " Saint of this green isle ! hear our prayers,
>   Oh, grant us cool heavens and favoring airs ! "

About nine o'clock we reached the river, and ran our boat into a natural haven between some rocks, and drew her out on the sand. This camping-ground McCauslin had been familiar with in his lumbering days, and he now struck it unerringly in the moonlight, and we heard the sound of the rill which would supply

us with cool water emptying into the lake. The first
business was to make a fire, an operation which was a
little delayed by the wetness of the fuel and the ground,
owing to the heavy showers of the afternoon. The fire
is the main comfort of the camp, whether in summer
or winter, and is about as ample at one season as at
another. It is as well for cheerfulness as for warmth
and dryness. It forms one side of the camp; one bright
side at any rate. Some were dispersed to fetch in dead
trees and boughs, while Uncle George felled the birches
and beeches which stood convenient, and soon we had
a fire some ten feet long by three or four high, which
rapidly dried the sand before it. This was calculated
to burn all night. We next proceeded to pitch our tent;
which operation was performed by sticking our two
spike-poles into the ground in a slanting direction,
about ten feet apart, for rafters, and then drawing our
cotton cloth over them, and tying it down at the ends,
leaving it open in front, shed-fashion. But this evening
the wind carried the sparks on to the tent and burned
it. So we hastily drew up the batteau just within the
edge of the woods before the fire, and propping up
one side three or four feet high, spread the tent on the
ground to lie on; and with the corner of a blanket, or
what more or less we could get to put over us, lay down
with our heads and bodies under the boat, and our
feet and legs on the sand toward the fire. At first we
lay awake, talking of our course, and finding ourselves
in so convenient a posture for studying the heavens,
with the moon and stars shining in our faces, our conversation naturally turned upon astronomy, and we

recounted by turns the most interesting discoveries in that science. But at length we composed ourselves seriously to sleep. It was interesting, when awakened at midnight, to watch the grotesque and fiend-like forms and motions of some one of the party, who, not being able to sleep, had got up silently to arouse the fire, and add fresh fuel, for a change; now stealthily lugging a dead tree from out the dark, and heaving it on, now stirring up the embers with his fork, or tiptoeing about to observe the stars, watched, perchance, by half the prostrate party in breathless silence; so much the more intense because they were awake, while each supposed his neighbor sound asleep. Thus aroused, I, too, brought fresh fuel to the fire, and then rambled along the sandy shore in the moonlight, hoping to meet a moose come down to drink, or else a wolf. The little rill tinkled the louder, and peopled all the wilderness for me· and the glassy smoothness of the sleeping lake, laving the shores of a new world, with the dark, fantastic rocks rising here and there from its surface, made a scene not easily described. It has left such an impression of stern, yet gentle, wildness on my memory as will not soon be effaced. Not far from midnight we were one after another awakened by rain falling on our extremities; and as each was made aware of the fact by cold or wet, he drew a long sigh and then drew up his legs, until gradually we had all sidled round from lying at right angles with the boat, till our bodies formed an acute angle with it, and were wholly protected. When next we awoke, the moon and stars were shining again, and there were signs of dawn in the

east. I have been thus particular in order to convey
some idea of a night in the woods.

We had soon launched and loaded our boat, and,
leaving our fire blazing, were off again before breakfast. The lumberers rarely trouble themselves to put
out their fires, such is the dampness of the primitive
forest; and this is one cause, no doubt, of the frequent
fires in Maine, of which we hear so much on smoky
days in Massachusetts. The forests are held cheap
after the white pine has been culled out; and the explorers and hunters pray for rain only to clear the
atmosphere of smoke. The woods were so wet to-day,
however, that there was no danger of our fire spreading.
After poling up half a mile of river, or thoroughfare,
we rowed a mile across the foot of Pamadumcook
Lake, which is the name given on the map to this
whole chain of lakes, as if there was but one, though
they are, in each instance, distinctly separated by a
reach of the river, with its narrow and rocky channel
and its rapids. This lake, which is one of the largest,
stretched northwest ten miles, to hills and mountains
in the distance. McCauslin pointed to some distant,
and as yet inaccessible, forests of white pine, on the
sides of a mountain in that direction. The Joe Merry
Lakes, which lay between us and Moosehead, on the
west, were recently, if they are not still, "surrounded
by some of the best timbered land in the State." By
another thoroughfare we passed into Deep Cove, a part
of the same lake, which makes up two miles, toward
the northeast, and rowing two miles across this, by
another short thoroughfare, entered Ambejijis Lake.

At the entrance to a lake we sometimes observed what is technically called "fencing-stuff," or the unhewn timbers of which booms are formed, either secured together in the water, or laid up on the rocks and lashed to trees, for spring use. But it was always startling to discover so plain a trail of civilized man there. I remember that I was strangely affected, when we were returning, by the sight of a ring-bolt well drilled into a rock, and fastened with lead, at the head of this solitary Ambejijis Lake.

It was easy to see that driving logs must be an exciting as well as arduous and dangerous business. All winter long the logger goes on piling up the trees which he has trimmed and hauled in some dry ravine at the head of a stream, and then in the spring he stands on the bank and whistles for Rain and Thaw, ready to wring the perspiration out of his shirt to swell the tide, till suddenly, with a whoop and halloo from him, shutting his eyes, as if to bid farewell to the existing state of things, a fair proportion of his winter's work goes scrambling down the country, followed by his faithful dogs, Thaw and Rain and Freshet and Wind, the whole pack in full cry, toward the Orono Mills. Every log is marked with the owner's name, cut in the sapwood with an axe or bored with an auger, so deep as not to be worn off in the driving, and yet not so as to injure the timber; and it requires considerable ingenuity to invent new and simple marks where there are so many owners. They have quite an alphabet of their own, which only the practiced can read. One of my companions read off from his memorandum book some

marks of his own logs, among which there were crosses,
belts, crow's feet, girdles, etc., as, " Y — girdle—crow-
foot," and various other devices. When the logs have
run the gauntlet of innumerable rapids and falls, each
on its own account, with more or less jamming and
bruising, those bearing various owners' marks being
mixed up together, — since all must take advantage of
the same freshet, —they are collected together at the
heads of the lakes, and surrounded by a boom fence of
floating logs, to prevent their being dispersed by the
wind, and are thus towed all together, like a flock of
sheep, across the lake, where there is no current, by
a windlass, or boom-head, such as we sometimes saw
standing on an island or headland, and, if circumstances permit, with the aid of sails and oars. Sometimes, notwithstanding, the logs are dispersed over many
miles of lake surface in a few hours by winds and freshets, and thrown up on distant shores, where the driver
can pick up only one or two at a time, and return with
them to the thoroughfare; and before he gets his flock
well through Ambejijis or Pamadumcook, he makes
many a wet and uncomfortable camp on the shore. He
must be able to navigate a log as if it were a canoe,
and be as indifferent to cold and wet as a muskrat.
He uses a few efficient tools, — a lever commonly of
rock maple, six or seven feet long, with a stout spike
in it, strongly ferruled on, and a long spike-pole, with
a screw at the end of the spike to make it hold. The
boys along shore learn to walk on floating logs as city
boys on sidewalks. Sometimes the logs are thrown up
on rocks in such positions as to be irrecoverable but by

another freshet as high, or they jam together at rapids
and falls, and accumulate in vast piles, which the driver
must start at the risk of his life. Such is the lumber
business, which depends on many accidents, as the
early freezing of the rivers, that the teams may get up
in season, a sufficient freshet in the spring, to fetch the
logs down, and many others.[1] I quote Michaux on
Lumbering on the Kennebec, then the source of the
best white pine lumber carried to England. "The persons engaged in this branch of industry are generally
emigrants from New Hampshire. . . . In the summer
they unite in small companies, and traverse these vast
solitudes in every direction, to ascertain the places in
which the pines abound. After cutting the grass and
converting it into hay for the nourishment of the cattle
to be employed in their labor, they return home. In
the beginning of the winter they enter the forests again,
establish themselves in huts covered with the bark of
the canoe-birch, or the arbor-vitæ; and, though the cold
is so intense that the mercury sometimes remains for
several weeks from 40° to 50° [Fahr.] below the point
of congelation, they persevere, with unabated courage,
in their work." According to Springer, the company
consists of choppers, swampers, — who make roads, —
barker and loader, teamster, and cook. "When the

[1] "A steady current or pitch of water is preferable to one either
rising or diminishing; as, when rising rapidly, the water at the middle
of the river is considerably higher than at the shores, — so much so
as to be distinctly perceived by the eye of a spectator on the banks,
presenting an appearance like a turnpike road. The lumber, therefore, is always sure to incline from the centre of the channel toward
either shore." — Springer.

trees are felled, they cut them into logs from fourteen to eighteen feet long, and, by means of their cattle, which they employ with great dexterity, drag them to the river, and, after stamping on them a mark of property, roll them on its frozen bosom. At the breaking of the ice, in the spring, they float down with the current. . . . The logs that are not drawn the first year," adds Michaux, "are attacked by large worms, which form holes about two lines in diameter, in every direction; but, if stripped of their bark, they will remain uninjured for thirty years."

Ambejijis, this quiet Sunday morning, struck me as the most beautiful lake we had seen. It is said to be one of the deepest. We had the fairest view of Joe Merry, Double Top, and Ktaadn, from its surface. The summit of the latter had a singularly flat, table-land appearance, like a short highway, where a demigod might be let down to take a turn or two in an afternoon, to settle his dinner. We rowed a mile and a half to near the head of the lake, and, pushing through a field of lily-pads, landed, to cook our breakfast, by the side of a large rock, known to McCauslin. Our breakfast consisted of tea, with hard-bread and pork, and fried salmon, which we ate with forks neatly whittled from alder twigs, which grew there, off strips of birch-bark for plates. The tea was black tea, without milk to color or sugar to sweeten it, and two tin dippers were our tea cups. This beverage is as indispensable to the loggers as to any gossiping old women in the land, and they, no doubt, derive great comfort from it. Here was the site of an old logger's camp, remembered by McCauslin, now overgrown with weeds and bushes. In the midst of a dense underwood we noticed a whole brick, on a rock, in a small run, clean and red and square as in a brick-yard, which had been brought thus far formerly for tamping. Some of us afterward regretted that we had not carried this on with us to the top of the mountain, to be left there for our mark. It would certainly have been a simple evidence of civilized man. McCauslin said that large wooden crosses, made of oak, still sound, were sometimes found standing in this wilderness, which were set up by the first Catholic missionaries who came through to the Kennebec.

In the next nine miles, which were the extent of our voyage, and which it took us the rest of the day to get over, we rowed across several small lakes, poled up numerous rapids and thoroughfares, and carried over four portages. I will give the names and distances, for the benefit of future tourists. First, after leaving Ambejijis Lake, we had a quarter of a mile of rapids to the portage, or carry of ninety rods around Ambejijis Falls; then a mile and a half through Passamagamet Lake, which is narrow and river-like, to the falls of the same name, — Ambejijis stream coming in on the right; then two miles through Katepskonegan Lake to the portage of ninety rods around Katepskonegan Falls, which name signifies "carrying-place," — Passamagamet stream coming in on the left; then three miles through Pockwockomus Lake, a slight expansion of the river, to the portage of forty rods around the falls of the same name, — Katepskonegan stream coming in on the left; then three quarters of a mile through

Aboljacarmegus Lake, similar to the last, to the portage of forty rods around the falls of the same name; then half a mile of rapid water to the Sowadnehunk deadwater, and the Aboljacknagesic stream.

This is generally the order of names as you ascend the river: First, the lake, or, if there is no expansion, the deadwater; then the falls; then the stream emptying into the lake, or river above, all of the same name. First we came to Passamagamet Lake, then to Passamagamet Falls, then to Passamagamet Stream, emptying in. This order and identity of names, it will be perceived, is quite philosophical, since the deadwater or lake is always at least partially produced by the stream emptying in above; and the first fall below, which is the outlet of that lake, and where that tributary water makes its first plunge, also naturally bears the same name.

At the portage around Ambejijis Falls I observed a pork-barrel on the shore, with a hole eight or nine inches square cut in one side, which was set against an upright rock; but the bears, without turning or upsetting the barrel, had gnawed a hole in the opposite side, which looked exactly like an enormous rat-hole, big enough to put their heads in; and at the bottom of the barrel were still left a few mangled and slabbered slices of pork. It is usual for the lumberers to leave such supplies as they cannot conveniently carry along with them at carries or camps, to which the next comers do not scruple to help themselves, they being the property, commonly, not of an individual, but a company, who can afford to deal liberally.

I will describe particularly how we got over some of these portages and rapids, in order that the reader may get an idea of the boatman's life. At Ambejijis Falls, for instance, there was the roughest path imaginable cut through the woods; at first up hill, at an angle of nearly forty-five degrees, over rocks and logs without end. This was the manner of the portage. We first carried over our baggage, and deposited it on the shore at the other end; then, returning to the batteau, we dragged it up the hill by the painter, and onward, with frequent pauses, over half the portage. But this was a bungling way, and would soon have worn out the boat. Commonly, three men walk over with a batteau weighing from three to five or six hundred pounds on their heads and shoulders, the tallest standing under the middle of the boat, which is turned over, and one at each end, or else there are two at the bows. More cannot well take hold at once. But this requires some practice, as well as strength, and is in any case extremely laborious, and wearing to the constitution, to follow. We were, on the whole, rather an invalid party, and could render our boatmen but little assistance. Our two men at length took the batteau upon their shoulders, and, while two of us steadied it, to prevent it from rocking and wearing into their shoulders, on which they placed their hats folded, walked bravely over the remaining distance, with two or three pauses. In the same manner they accomplished the other portages. With this crushing weight they must climb and stumble along over fallen trees and slippery rocks of all sizes, where those who walked by the sides were continually brushed off, such was the narrowness of the path. But we were fortunate not to have to cut our path in the first place. Before we launched our boat, we scraped the bottom smooth again, with our knives, where it had rubbed on the rocks, to save friction.

To avoid the difficulties of the portage, our men determined to "warp up" the Passamagamet Falls; so while the rest walked over the portage with the baggage, I remained in the batteau, to assist in warping up. We were soon in the midst of the rapids, which were more swift and tumultuous than any we had poled up, and had turned to the side of the stream for the purpose of warping, when the boatmen, who felt some pride in their skill, and were ambitious to do something more than usual, for my benefit, as I surmised, took one more view of the rapids, or rather the falls; and, in answer to our question, whether we couldn't get up there, the other answered that he guessed he'd try it. So we pushed again into the midst of the stream, and began to struggle with the current. I sat in the middle of the boat to trim it, moving slightly to the right or left as it grazed a rock. With an uncertain and wavering motion we wound and bolted our way up, until the bow was actually raised two feet above the stern at the steepest pitch; and then, when everything depended upon his exertions, the bowman's pole snapped in two; but before he had time to take the spare one, which I reached him, he had saved himself with the fragment upon a rock; and so we got up by a hair's breadth; and Uncle George exclaimed that that was never done before, and he had not tried it if he had not known whom he had got in the bow, nor he in the bow, if he had not known him in the stern. At this place there was a regular portage cut through the woods, and our boatmen had never known a batteau to ascend the falls. As near as I can remember, there was a perpendicular fall here, at the worst place of the whole Penobscot River, two or three feet at least. I could not sufficiently admire the skill and coolness with which they performed this feat, never speaking to each other. The bowman, not looking behind, but knowing exactly what the other is about, works as if he worked alone. Now sounding in vain for a bottom in fifteen feet of water, while the boat falls back several rods, held straight only with the greatest skill and exertion; or, while the sternman obstinately holds his ground, like a turtle, the bowman springs from side to side with wonderful suppleness and dexterity, scanning the rapids and the rocks with a thousand eyes; and now, having got a bite at last, with a lusty shove, which makes his pole bend and quiver, and the whole boat tremble, he gains a few feet upon the river. To add to the danger, the poles are liable at any time to be caught between the rocks, and wrenched out of their hands, leaving them at the mercy of the rapids, — the rocks, as it were, lying in wait, like so many alligators, to catch them in their teeth, and jerk them from your hands, before you have stolen an effectual shove against their palates. The pole is set close to the boat, and the prow is made to overshoot, and just turn the corners of the rocks, in the very teeth of the rapids. Nothing but the length and lightness, and the slight draught of the batteau, enables them to make any headway. The bowman must quickly choose his course; there is no time to deliberate. Frequently the boat is shoved between rocks where both sides touch, and the waters on either hand are a perfect maelstrom.

Half a mile above this two of us tried our hands at poling up a slight rapid; and we were just surmounting the last difficulty, when an unlucky rock confounded our calculations; and while the batteau was sweeping round irrecoverably amid the whirlpool, we were obliged to resign the poles to more skillful hands.

Katepskonegan is one of the shallowest and weediest of the lakes, and looked as if it might abound in pickerel. The falls of the same name, where we stopped to dine, are considerable and quite picturesque. Here Uncle George had seen trout caught by the barrelful; but they would not rise to our bait at this hour. Halfway over this carry, thus far in the Maine wilderness on its way to the Provinces, we noticed a large, flaming, Oak Hall handbill, about two feet long, wrapped round the trunk of a pine, from which the bark had been stripped, and to which it was fast glued by the pitch. This should be recorded among the advantages of this mode of advertising, that so, possibly, even the bears and wolves, moose, deer, otter, and beaver, not to mention the Indian, may learn where they can fit themselves according to the latest fashion, or, at least, recover some of their own lost garments. We christened this the Oak Hall carry.

The forenoon was as serene and placid on this wild stream in the woods, as we are apt to imagine that Sunday in summer usually is in Massachusetts. We were occasionally startled by the scream of a bald eagle, sailing over the stream in front of our batteau; or of the fish hawks on whom he levies his contributions. There were, at intervals, small meadows of a few acres on the sides of the stream, waving with uncut grass, which attracted the attention of our boatmen, who regretted that they were not nearer to their clearings, and calculated how many stacks they might cut. Two or three men sometimes spend the summer by themselves, cutting the grass in these meadows, to sell to the loggers in the winter, since it will fetch a higher price on the spot than in any market in the State. On a small isle, covered with this kind of rush, or cut-grass, on which we landed to consult about our further course, we noticed the recent track of a moose, a large, roundish hole in the soft, wet ground, evincing the great size and weight of the animal that made it. They are fond of the water, and visit all these island meadows, swimming as easily from island to island as they make their way through the thickets on land. Now and then we passed what McCauslin called a pokelogan, an Indian term for what the drivers might have reason to call a poke-logs-in, an inlet that leads nowhere. If you get in, you have got to get out again the same way. These, and the frequent " runrounds " which come into the river again, would embarrass an inexperienced voyager not a little.

The carry around Pockwockomus Falls was exceed-

ingly rough and rocky, the batteau having to be lifted
directly from the water up four or five feet on to a rock,
and launched again down a similar bank. The rocks
on this portage were covered with the *dents* made by
the spikes in the lumberers' boots while staggering
over under the weight of their batteaux; and you could
see where the surface of some large rocks on which
they had rested their batteaux was worn quite smooth
with use. As it was, we had carried over but half the
usual portage at this place for this stage of the water,
and launched our boat in the smooth wave just curving
to the fall, prepared to struggle with the most violent
rapid we had to encounter. The rest of the party
walked over the remainder of the portage, while I remained with the boatmen to assist in warping up. One
had to hold the boat while the others got in to prevent
it from going over the falls. When we had pushed up
the rapids as far as possible, keeping close to the shore,
Tom seized the painter and leaped out upon a rock
just visible in the water, but he lost his footing, notwithstanding his spiked boots, and was instantly amid
the rapids; but recovering himself by good luck, and
reaching another rock, he passed the painter to me,
who had followed him, and took his place again in the
bows. Leaping from rock to rock in the shoal water,
close to the shore, and now and then getting a bite
with the rope round an upright one, I held the boat
while one reset his pole, and then all three forced it
upward against any rapid. This was " warping up."
When a part of us walked round at such a place, we
generally took the precaution to take out the most

valuable part of the baggage for fear of being swamped.

As we poled up a swift rapid for half a mile above Aboljacarmegus Falls, some of the party read their own marks on the huge logs which lay piled up high and dry on the rocks on either hand, the relics prob- ably of a jam which had taken place here in the Great Freshet in the spring. Many of these would have to wait for another great freshet, perchance, if they lasted so long, before they could be got off. It was singular enough to meet with property of theirs which they had never seen, and where they had never been before, thus detained by freshets and rocks when on its way to them. Methinks that must be where all my property lies, cast up on the rocks on some distant and unex- plored stream, and waiting for an unheard-of freshet to fetch it down. O make haste, ye gods, with your winds and rains, and start the jam before it rots!

The last half mile carried us to the Sowadnehunk Deadwater, so called from the stream of the same name, signifying " running between mountains," an important tributary which comes in a mile above. Here we decided to camp, about twenty miles from the Dam, at the mouth of Murch Brook and the Aboljacknagesic, mountain streams, broad off from Ktaadn, and about a dozen miles from its summit, having made fifteen miles this day.

We had been told by McCauslin that we should here find trout enough; so, while some prepared the camp, the rest fell to fishing. Seizing the birch poles which some party of Indians, or white hunters, had left on the shore, and baiting our hooks with pork, and with trout, as soon as they were caught, we cast our lines into the mouth of the Aboljacknagesic, a clear, swift, shallow stream, which came in from Ktaadn. Instantly a shoal of white chivin (*Leuciscus pulchellus*), silvery roaches, cousin-trout, or what not, large and small, prowling thereabouts, fell upon our bait, and one after another were landed amidst the bushes. Anon their cousins, the true trout, took their turn, and alternately the speckled trout, and the silvery roaches, swallowed the bait as fast as we could throw in; and the finest specimens of both that I have ever seen, the largest one weighing three pounds, were heaved upon the shore, though at first in vain, to wriggle down into the water again, for we stood in the boat; but soon we learned to remedy this evil; for one, who had lost his hook, stood on shore to catch them as they fell in a perfect shower around him, — sometimes, wet and slippery, full in his face and bosom, as his arms were outstretched to receive them. While yet alive, before their tints had faded, they glistened like the fairest flowers, the product of primitive rivers; and he could hardly trust his senses, as he stood over them, that these jewels should have swam away in that Aboljacknagesic water for so long, so many dark ages; — these bright fluviatile flowers, seen of Indians only, made beautiful, the Lord only knows why, to swim there! I could understand better for this, the truth of mythology, the fables of Proteus, and all those beautiful sea-monsters, — how all history, indeed, put to a terrestrial use, is mere history; but put to a celestial, is mythology always.

But there is the rough voice of Uncle George, who

commands at the frying-pan, to send over what you 've got, and then you may stay till morning. The pork sizzles and cries for fish. Luckily for the foolish race, and this particularly foolish generation of trout, the night shut down at last, not a little deepened by the dark side of Ktaadn, which, like a permanent shadow, reared itself from the eastern bank. Lescarbot, writing in 1609, tells us that the Sieur Champdoré, who, with one of the people of the Sieur de Monts, ascended some fifty leagues up the St. John in 1608, found the fish so plenty, " qu'en mettant la chaudière sur le feu ils en avoient pris suffisamment pour eux disner avant que l'eau fust chaude." Their descendants here are no less numerous. So we accompanied Tom into the woods to cut cedar twigs for our bed. While he went ahead with the axe and lopped off the smallest twigs of the flat-leaved cedar, the arbor-vitæ of the gardens, we gathered them up, and returned with them to the boat, until it was loaded. Our bed was made with as much care and skill as a roof is shingled; beginning at the foot, and laying the twig end of the cedar upward, we advanced to the head, a course at a time, thus successively covering the stub-ends, and producing a soft and level bed. For us six it was about ten feet long by six in breadth. This time we lay under our tent, having pitched it more prudently with reference to the wind and the flame, and the usual huge fire blazed in front. Supper was eaten off a large log, which some freshet had thrown up. This night we had a dish of arbor-vitæ or cedar tea, which the lumberer sometimes uses when other herbs fail, —

"A quart of arbor-vitæ,
To make him strong and mighty," —

but I had no wish to repeat the experiment. It had
too medicinal a taste for my palate. There was the
skeleton of a moose here, whose bones some Indian
hunters had picked on this very spot.

In the night I dreamed of trout-fishing; and, when
at length I awoke, it seemed a fable that this painted
fish swam there so near my couch, and rose to our
hooks the last evening, and I doubted if I had not
dreamed it all. So I arose before dawn to test its truth,
while my companions were still sleeping. There stood
Ktaadn with distinct and cloudless outline in the
moonlight; and the rippling of the rapids was the only
sound to break the stillness. Standing on the shore, I
once more cast my line into the stream, and found the
dream to be real and the fable true. The speckled trout
and silvery roach, like flying-fish, sped swiftly through
the moonlight air, describing bright arcs on the dark
side of Ktaadn, until moonlight, now fading into daylight, brought satiety to my mind, and the minds of my
companions, who had joined me.

By six o'clock, having mounted our packs and a good
blanketful of trout, ready dressed, and swung up such
baggage and provision as we wished to leave behind
upon the tops of saplings, to be out of the reach of
bears, we started for the summit of the mountain, distant, as Uncle George said the boatmen called it, about
four miles, but as I judged, and as it proved, nearer
fourteen. He had never been any nearer the mountain
than this, and there was not the slightest trace of man

to guide us farther in this direction. At first, pushing a few rods up the Aboljacknagesic, or " open-land
stream," we fastened our batteau to a tree, and traveled
up the north side, through burnt lands, now partially
overgrown with young aspens and other shrubbery;
but soon, recrossing this stream, where it was about
fifty or sixty feet wide, upon a jam of logs and rocks,
— and you could cross it by this means almost anywhere, — we struck at once for the highest peak, over
a mile or more of comparatively open land, still very
gradually ascending the while. Here it fell to my lot,
as the oldest mountain-climber, to take the lead. So,
scanning the woody side of the mountain, which lay
still at an indefinite distance, stretched out some seven
or eight miles in length before us, we determined to
steer directly for the base of the highest peak, leaving a
large slide, by which, as I have since learned, some of our
predecessors ascended, on our left. This course would
lead us parallel to a dark seam in the forest, which
marked the bed of a torrent, and over a slight spur,
which extended southward from the main mountain,
from whose bare summit we could get an outlook over
the country, and climb directly up the peak, which
would then be close at hand. Seen from this point, a
bare ridge at the extremity of the open land, Ktaadn
presented a different aspect from any mountain I have
seen, there being a greater proportion of naked rock
rising abruptly from the forest; and we looked up at
this blue barrier as if it were some fragment of a wall
which anciently bounded the earth in that direction.
Setting the compass for a northeast course, which was

Mount Kineo Cliff, Maine

Squaw Mountain, Moosehead Lake

the bearing of the southern base of the highest peak,
we were soon buried in the woods.

We soon began to meet with traces of bears and
moose, and those of rabbits were everywhere visible.
The tracks of moose, more or less recent, to speak literally, covered every square rod on the sides of the
mountain; and these animals are probably more numerous there now than ever before, being driven into this
wilderness, from all sides, by the settlements. The track
of a full-grown moose is like that of a cow, or larger,
and of the young, like that of a calf. Sometimes we
found ourselves traveling in faint paths, which they had
made, like cow-paths in the woods, only far more indistinct, being rather openings, affording imperfect vistas through the dense underwood, than trodden paths;
and everywhere the twigs had been browsed by them,
clipped as smoothly as if by a knife. The bark of trees
was stripped up by them to the height of eight or nine
feet, in long, narrow strips, an inch wide, still showing
the distinct marks of their teeth. We expected nothing
less than to meet a herd of them every moment, and
our Nimrod held his shooting-iron in readiness; but
we did not go out of our way to look for them, and,
though numerous, they are so wary that the unskillful
hunter might range the forest a long time before he
could get sight of one. They are sometimes dangerous
to encounter, and will not turn out for the hunter, but
furiously rush upon him and trample him to death, unless he is lucky enough to avoid them by dodging round
a tree. The largest are nearly as large as a horse, and
weigh sometimes one thousand pounds; and it is said

that they can step over a five-foot gate in their ordinary
walk. They are described as exceedingly awkward-look-
ing animals, with their long legs and short bodies,
making a ludicrous figure when in full run, but making
great headway, nevertheless. It seemed a mystery to us
how they could thread these woods, which it required
all our suppleness to accomplish, — climbing, stooping,
and winding, alternately. They are said to drop their
long and branching horns, which usually spread five
or six feet, on their backs, and make their way easily
by the weight of their bodies. Our boatmen said, but
I know not with how much truth, that their horns are
apt to be gnawed away by vermin while they sleep.
Their flesh, which is more like beef than venison, is
common in Bangor market.

We had proceeded on thus seven or eight miles, till
about noon, with frequent pauses to refresh the weary
ones, crossing a considerable mountain stream, which
we conjectured to be Murch Brook, at whose mouth we
had camped, all the time in woods, without having once
seen the summit, and rising very gradually, when the
boatmen beginning to despair a little, and fearing that
we were leaving the mountain on one side of us, for
they had not entire faith in the compass, McCauslin
climbed a tree, from the top of which he could see the
peak, when it appeared that we had not swerved from
a right line, the compass down below still ranging with
his arm, which pointed to the summit. By the side of
a cool mountain rill, amid the woods, where the water
began to partake of the purity and transparency of the
air, we stopped to cook some of our fishes, which we had

brought thus far in order to save our hard-bread and pork, in the use of which we had put ourselves on short allowance. We soon had a fire blazing, and stood around it, under the damp and sombre forest of firs and birches, each with a sharpened stick, three or four feet in length, upon which he had spitted his trout, or roach, previously well gashed and salted, our sticks radiating like the spokes of a wheel from one centre, and each crowding his particular fish into the most desirable exposure, not with the truest regard always to his neighbor's rights. Thus we regaled ourselves, drinking meanwhile at the spring, till one man's pack, at least, was considerably lightened, when we again took up our line of march.

At length we reached an elevation sufficiently bare to afford a view of the summit, still distant and blue, almost as if retreating from us. A torrent, which proved to be the same we had crossed, was seen tumbling down in front, literally from out of the clouds. But this glimpse at our whereabouts was soon lost, and we were buried in the woods again. The wood was chiefly yellow birch, spruce, fir, mountain-ash, or round-wood, as the Maine people call it, and moose-wood. It was the worst kind of traveling; sometimes like the densest scrub oak patches with us. The cornel, or bunch-berries, were very abundant, as well as Solomon's-seal and moose-berries. Blueberries were distributed along our whole route: and in one place the bushes were drooping with the weight of the fruit, still as fresh as ever. It was the 7th of September. Such patches afforded a grateful repast, and served to bait the tired party forward. When any lagged behind, the cry of "blueber-ries" was most effectual to bring them up. Even at this elevation we passed through a moose-yard, formed by a large flat rock, four or five rods square, where they tread down the snow in winter. At length, fearing that if we held the direct course to the summit, we should not find any water near our camping-ground, we gradually swerved to the west, till, at four o'clock, we struck again the torrent which I have mentioned, and here, in view of the summit, the weary party de-cided to camp that night.

While my companions were seeking a suitable spot for this purpose, I improved the little daylight that was left in climbing the mountain alone. We were in a deep and narrow ravine, sloping up to the clouds, at an angle of nearly forty-five degrees, and hemmed in by walls of rock, which were at first covered with low trees, then with impenetrable thickets of scraggy birches and spruce trees, and with moss, but at last bare of all vegetation but lichens, and almost continually draped in clouds. Following up the course of the torrent which occupied this, — and I mean to lay some emphasis on this word *up*, — pulling myself up by the side of per-pendicular falls of twenty or thirty feet, by the roots of firs and birches, and then, perhaps, walking a level rod or two in the thin stream, for it took up the whole road, ascending by huge steps, as it were, a giant's stairway, down which a river flowed, I had soon cleared the trees, and paused on the successive shelves, to look back over the country. The torrent was from fifteen to thirty feet wide, without a tributary, and seemingly not diminishing in breadth as I advanced; but still it came rushing and roaring down, with a copious tide, over and amidst masses of bare rock, from the very clouds, as though a waterspout had just burst over the mountain. Leaving this at last, I began to work my way, scarcely less arduous than Satan's anciently through Chaos, up the nearest though not the highest peak. At first scrambling on all fours over the tops of ancient black spruce trees (*Abies nigra*), old as the flood, from two to ten or twelve feet in height, their tops flat and spreading, and their foliage blue, and nipped with cold, as if for centuries they had ceased growing upward against the bleak sky, the solid cold. I walked some good rods erect upon the tops of these trees, which were overgrown with moss and mountain cranberries. It seemed that in the course of time they had filled up the intervals between the huge rocks, and the cold wind had uniformly leveled all over. Here the principle of vegetation was hard put to it. There was apparently a belt of this kind running quite round the mountain, though, perhaps, nowhere so remarkable as here. Once, slumping through, I looked down ten feet, into a dark and cavernous region, and saw the stem of a spruce, on whose top I stood, as on a mass of coarse basket-work, fully nine inches in diameter at the ground. These holes were bears' dens, and the bears were even then at home. This was the sort of garden I made my way *over*, for an eighth of a mile, at the risk, it is true, of treading on some of the plants, not seeing any path *through* it, — certainly the most treacherous and porous country I ever traveled.

> " Nigh foundered on he fares,
> Treading the crude consistence, half on foot,
> Half flying,"

But nothing could exceed the toughness of the twigs,
— not one snapped under my weight, for they had
slowly grown. Having slumped, scrambled, rolled,
bounced, and walked, by turns, over this scraggy coun
try, I arrived upon a side-hill, or rather side-mountain,
where rocks, gray, silent rocks, were the flocks and
herds that pastured, chewing a rocky cud at sunset.
They looked at me with hard gray eyes, without a bleat
or a low. This brought me to the skirt of a cloud, and
bounded my walk that night. But I had already seen
that Maine country when I turned about, waving, flowing, rippling, down below.

When I returned to my companions, they had selected a camping-ground on the torrent's edge, and
were resting on the ground; one was on the sick list,
rolled in a blanket, on a damp shelf of rock. It was
a savage and dreary scenery enough, so wildly rough,
that they looked long to find a level and open space
for the tent. We could not well camp higher, for want
of fuel; and the trees here seemed so evergreen and
sappy, that we almost doubted if they would acknow-
ledge the influence of fire; but fire prevailed at last, and
blazed here, too, like a good citizen of the world. Even
at this height we met with frequent traces of moose,
as well as of bears. As here was no cedar, we made
our bed of coarser feathered spruce; but at any rate
the feathers were plucked from the live tree. It was,
perhaps, even a more grand and desolate place for a

night's lodging than the summit would have been, being
in the neighborhood of those wild trees, and of the
torrent. Some more aërial and finer-spirited winds
rushed and roared through the ravine all night, from
time to time arousing our fire, and dispersing the embers about. It was as if we lay in the very nest of a
young whirlwind. At midnight, one of my bed-fellows,
being startled in his dreams by the sudden blazing
up to its top of a fir tree, whose green boughs were
dried by the heat, sprang up, with a cry, from his bed,
thinking the world on fire, and drew the whole camp
after him.

In the morning, after whetting our appetite on some
raw pork, a wafer of hard-bread, and a dipper of condensed cloud or waterspout, we all together began to
make our way up the falls, which I have described;
this time choosing the right hand, or highest peak,
which was not the one I had approached before. But
soon my companions were lost to my sight behind the
mountain ridge in my rear, which still seemed ever retreating before me, and I climbed alone over huge rocks,
loosely poised, a mile or more, still edging toward the
clouds; for though the day was clear elsewhere, the
summit was concealed by mist. The mountain seemed
a vast aggregation of loose rocks, as if some time it had
rained rocks, and they lay as they fell on the mountain sides, nowhere fairly at rest, but leaning on each
other, all rocking stones, with cavities between, but
scarcely any soil or smoother shelf. They were the raw
materials of a planet dropped from an unseen quarry,
which the vast chemistry of nature would anon work

up, or work down, into the smiling and verdant plains
and valleys of earth. This was an undone extremity
of the globe; as in lignite we see coal in the process of
formation.

At length I entered within the skirts of the cloud
which seemed forever drifting over the summit, and yet
would never be gone, but was generated out of that
pure air as fast as it flowed away; and when, a quarter
of a mile farther, I reached the summit of the ridge,
which those who have seen in clearer weather say is
about five miles long, and contains a thousand acres of
table-land, I was deep within the hostile ranks of clouds,
and all objects were obscured by them. Now the wind
would blow me out a yard of clear sunlight, wherein I
stood; then a gray, dawning light was all it could accomplish, the cloud-line ever rising and falling with the
wind's intensity. Sometimes it seemed as if the summit would be cleared in a few moments, and smile in
sunshine; but what was gained on one side was lost on
another. It was like sitting in a chimney and waiting
for the smoke to blow away. It was, in fact, a cloud-
factory, — these were the cloud-works, and the wind
turned them off done from the cool, bare rocks. Occasionally, when the windy columns broke in to me, I
caught sight of a dark, damp crag to the right or left;
the mist driving ceaselessly between it and me. It
reminded me of the creations of the old epic and dra-
matic poets, of Atlas, Vulcan, the Cyclops, and Prome-
theus. Such was Caucasus and the rock where Prome-
theus was bound. Æschylus had no doubt visited such
scenery as this. It was vast, Titanic, and such as man

never inhabits. Some part of the beholder, even some vital part, seems to escape through the loose grating of his ribs as he ascends. He is more lone than you can imagine. There is less of substantial thought and fair understanding in him than in the plains where men inhabit. His reason is dispersed and shadowy, more thin and subtile, like the air. Vast, Titanic, inhuman Nature has got him at disadvantage, caught him alone, and pilfers him of some of his divine faculty. She does not smile on him as in the plains. She seems to say sternly, Why came ye here before your time. This ground is not prepared for you. Is it not enough that I smile in the valleys? I have never made this soil for thy feet, this air for thy breathing, these rocks for thy neighbors. I cannot pity nor fondle thee here, but forever relentlessly drive thee hence to where I *am* kind. Why seek me where I have not called thee, and then complain because you find me but a stepmother? Shouldst thou freeze or starve, or shudder thy life away, here is no shrine, nor altar, nor any access to my ear.

> "Chaos and ancient Night, I come no spy
> With purpose to explore or to disturb
> The secrets of your realm, but . . .
> .   .   .   .   .   .   as my way
> Lies through your spacious empire up to light."

The tops of mountains are among the unfinished parts of the globe, whither it is a slight insult to the gods to climb and pry into their secrets, and try their effect on our humanity. Only daring and insolent men, perchance, go there. Simple races, as savages, do not climb mountains, — their tops are sacred and mysteri-

ous tracts never visited by them. Pomola is always
angry with those who climb to the summit of Ktaadn.

According to Jackson, who, in his capacity of geological surveyor of the State, has accurately measured
it, the altitude of Ktaadn is 5300 feet, or a little more
than one mile above the level of the sea, and he adds,
" It is then evidently the highest point in the State of
Maine, and is the most abrupt granite mountain in New
England." The peculiarities of that spacious table-land
on which I was standing, as well as the remarkable
semicircular precipice or basin on the eastern side, were
all concealed by the mist. I had brought my whole
pack to the top, not knowing but I should have to
make my descent to the river, and possibly to the settled
portion of the State alone, and by some other route, and
wishing to have a complete outfit with me. But at length
fearing that my companions would be anxious to reach
the river before night, and knowing that the clouds
might rest on the mountain for days, I was compelled
to descend. Occasionally, as I came down, the wind
would blow me a vista open, through which I could see
the country eastward, boundless forests, and lakes, and
streams, gleaming in the sun, some of them emptying
into the East Branch. There were also new mountains
in sight in that direction. Now and then some small
bird of the sparrow family would flit away before me,
unable to command its course, like a fragment of the
gray rock blown off by the wind.

I found my companions where I had left them, on
the side of the peak, gathering the mountain cranberries,
which filled every crevice between the rocks, together

with blueberries, which had a spicier flavor the higher
up they grew, but were not the less agreeable to our
palates. When the country is settled, and roads are
made, these cranberries will perhaps become an article of
commerce. From this elevation, just on the skirts of the
clouds, we could overlook the country, west and south,
for a hundred miles. There it was, the State of Maine,
which we had seen on the map, but not much like that, —
immeasurable forest for the sun to shine on, that eastern *stuff* we hear of in Massachusetts. No clearing, no
house. It did not look as if a solitary traveler had cut
so much as a walking-stick there. Countless lakes, —
Moosehead in the southwest, forty miles long by ten
wide, like a gleaming silver platter at the end of the
table; Chesuncook, eighteen long by three wide, without
an island; Millinocket, on the south, with its hundred
islands; and a hundred others without a name; and
mountains, also, whose names, for the most part, are
known only to the Indians. The forest looked like a
firm grass sward, and the effect of these lakes in its
midst has been well compared, by one who has since
visited this same spot, to that of a " mirror broken into
a thousand fragments, and wildly scattered over the
grass, reflecting the full blaze of the sun." It was a
large farm for somebody, when cleared. According to
the Gazetteer, which was printed before the boundary
question was settled, this single Penobscot County, in
which we were, was larger than the whole State of
Vermont, with its fourteen counties; and this was only
a part of the wild lands of Maine. We are concerned
now, however, about natural, not political limits. We

were about eighty miles, as the bird flies, from Bangor, or one hundred and fifteen, as we had ridden, and walked, and paddled. We had to console ourselves with the reflection that this view was probably as good as that from the peak, as far as it went; and what were a mountain without its attendant clouds and mists? Like ourselves, neither Bailey nor Jackson had obtained a clear view from the summit.

Setting out on our return to the river, still at an early hour in the day, we decided to follow the course of the torrent, which we supposed to be Murch Brook, as long as it would not lead us too far out of our way. We thus traveled about four miles in the very torrent itself, continually crossing and recrossing it, leaping from rock to rock, and jumping with the stream down falls of seven or eight feet, or sometimes sliding down on our backs in a thin sheet of water. This ravine had been the scene of an extraordinary freshet in the spring, apparently accompanied by a slide from the mountain. It must have been filled with a stream of stones and water, at least twenty feet above the present level of the torrent. For a rod or two, on either side of its channel, the trees were barked and splintered up to their tops, the birches bent over, twisted, and sometimes finely split, like a stable-broom; some, a foot in diameter, snapped off, and whole clumps of trees bent over with the weight of rocks piled on them. In one place we noticed a rock, two or three feet in diameter, lodged nearly twenty feet high in the crotch of a tree. For the whole four miles we saw but one rill emptying in, and the volume of water did not seem to be increased from the first. We traveled thus very rapidly with a downward impetus, and grew remarkably expert at leaping from rock to rock, for leap we must, and leap we did, whether there was any rock at the right distance or not. It was a pleasant picture when the foremost turned about and looked up the winding ravine, walled in with rocks and the green forest, to see, at intervals of a rod or two, a red-shirted or green-jacketed mountaineer against the white torrent, leaping down the channel with his pack on his back, or pausing upon a convenient rock in the midst of the torrent to mend a rent in his clothes, or unstrap the dipper at his belt to take a draught of the water. At one place we were startled by seeing, on a little sandy shelf by the side of the stream, the fresh print of a man's foot, and for a moment realized how Robinson Crusoe felt in a similar case; but at last we remembered that we had struck this stream on our way up, though we could not have told where, and one had descended into the ravine for a drink. The cool air above and the continual bathing of our bodies in mountain water, alternate foot, sitz, douche, and plunge baths, made this walk exceedingly refreshing, and we had traveled only a mile or two, after leaving the torrent, before every thread of our clothes was as dry as usual, owing perhaps to a peculiar qual ity in the atmosphere.

After leaving the torrent, being in doubt about our course, Tom threw down his pack at the foot of the loftiest spruce tree at hand, and shinned up the bare trunk some twenty feet, and then climbed through the green tower, lost to our sight, until he held the topmost spray in his hand.[1] McCauslin, in his younger days, had marched through the wilderness with a body of troops, under General Somebody, and with one other man did all the scouting and spying service. The General's word was, "Throw down the top of that tree," and there was no tree in the Maine woods so high that it did not lose its top in such a case. I have heard a story of two men being lost once in these woods, nearer to the settlements than this, who climbed the loftiest pine they could find, some six feet in diameter at the ground, from whose top they discovered a solitary clearing and its smoke. When at this height, some two hundred feet from the ground, one of them became dizzy, and fainted in his companion's arms, and the latter had to accomplish the descent with him, alternately fainting and reviving, as best he could. To Tom we cried, "Where away does the summit bear? where the burnt lands?" The last he could only conjecture; he descried, however, a little meadow and pond, lying probably in our course, which we concluded to steer for. On reaching this secluded meadow, we found fresh tracks of moose on the shore of the pond, and the water was still unsettled as if they had fled before us.

[1] "The spruce tree," says Springer in '51, "is generally selected, principally for the superior facilities which its numerous limbs afford the climber. To gain the first limbs of this tree, which are from twenty to forty feet from the ground, a smaller tree is undercut and lodged against it, clambering up which the top of the spruce is reached. In some cases, when a very elevated position is desired, the spruce tree is lodged against the trunk of some lofty pine, up which we ascend to a height twice that of the surrounding forest."

To indicate the direction of pines, one throws down a branch, and a man on the ground takes the bearing.

A little farther, in a dense thicket, we seemed to be still on their trail. It was a small meadow, of a few acres, on the mountain-side, concealed by the forest, and perhaps never seen by a white man before, where one would think that the moose might browse and bathe, and rest in peace. Pursuing this course, we soon reached the open land, which went sloping down some miles toward the Penobscot.

Perhaps I most fully realized that this was primeval, untamed, and forever untamable *Nature*, or whatever else men call it, while coming down this part of the mountain. We were passing over "Burnt Lands," burnt by lightning, perchance, though they showed no recent marks of fire, hardly so much as a charred stump, but looked rather like a natural pasture for the moose and deer, exceedingly wild and desolate, with occasional strips of timber crossing them, and low poplars springing up, and patches of blueberries here and there. I found myself traversing them familiarly, like some pasture run to waste, or partially reclaimed by man; but when I reflected what man, what brother or sister or kinsman of our race made it and claimed it, I expected the proprietor to rise up and dispute my passage. It is difficult to conceive of a region uninhabited by man. We habitually presume his presence and influence everywhere. And yet we have not seen pure Nature, unless we have seen her thus vast and drear and inhuman, though in the midst of cities. Nature was here something savage and awful, though beautiful. I looked with awe at the ground I trod on, to see what the Powers had made there, the form and

fashion and material of their work. This was that
Earth of which we have heard, made out of Chaos and
Old Night. Here was no man's garden, but the un-
handseled globe. It was not lawn, nor pasture, nor
mead, nor woodland, nor lea, nor arable, nor waste
land. It was the fresh and natural surface of the planet
Earth, as it was made forever and ever, — to be the
dwelling of man, we say, — so Nature made it, and
man may use it if he can. Man was not to be associated with it. It was Matter, vast, terrific, — not
his Mother Earth that we have heard of, not for him
to tread on, or be buried in, — no, it were being too
familiar even to let his bones lie there, — the home,
this, of Necessity and Fate. There was clearly felt the
presence of a force not bound to be kind to man. It
was a place for heathenism and superstitious rites, —
to be inhabited by men nearer of kin to the rocks and
to wild animals than we. We walked over it with a
certain awe, stopping, from time to time, to pick the
blueberries which grew there, and had a smart and
spicy taste. Perchance where *our* wild pines stand,
and leaves lie on their forest floor, in Concord, there
were once reapers, and husbandmen planted grain; but
here not even the surface had been scarred by man,
but it was a specimen of what God saw fit to make this
world. What is it to be admitted to a museum, to
see a myriad of particular things, compared with being
shown some star's surface, some hard matter in its
home! I stand in awe of my body, this matter to which
I am bound has become so strange to me. I fear not
spirits, ghosts, of which I am one, — *that* my body

might, — but I fear bodies, I tremble to meet them.
What is this Titan that has possession of me? Talk
of mysteries! Think of our life in nature, — daily to
be shown matter, to come in contact with it, — rocks,
trees, wind on our cheeks! the *solid* earth! the *actual*
world! the *common sense! Contact! Contact! Who*
are we? *where* are we?

Erelong we recognized some rocks and other features
in the landscape which we had purposely impressed on
our memories, and, quickening our pace, by two o'clock
we reached the batteau.[1] Here we had expected to
dine on trout, but in this glaring sunlight they were
slow to take the bait, so we were compelled to make
the most of the crumbs of our hard-bread and our
pork, which were both nearly exhausted. Meanwhile
we deliberated whether we should go up the river a mile
farther, to Gibson's clearing, on the Sowadnehunk,
where there was a deserted log hut, in order to get a
half-inch auger, to mend one of our spike-poles with.
There were young spruce trees enough around us, and
we had a spare spike, but nothing to make a hole with.
But as it was uncertain whether we should find any
tools left there, we patched up the broken pole, as well
as we could, for the downward voyage, in which there
would be but little use for it. Moreover, we were unwilling to lose any time in this expedition, lest the wind
should rise before we reached the larger lakes, and detain us; for a moderate wind produces quite a sea on

[1] The bears had not touched things on our possessions. They sometimes tear a batteau to pieces for the sake of the tar with which it is
besmeared.

these waters, in which a batteau will not live for a moment; and on one occasion McCauslin had been delayed a week at the head of the North Twin, which is only four miles across. We were nearly out of provisions, and ill prepared in this respect for what might possibly prove a week's journey round by the shore, fording innumerable streams, and threading a trackless forest, should any accident happen to our boat.

It was with regret that we turned our backs on Chesuncook, which McCauslin had formerly logged on, and the Allegash lakes. There were still longer rapids and portages above; among the last the Ripogenus Portage, which he described as the most difficult on the river, and three miles long. The whole length of the Penobscot is two hundred and seventy-five miles, and we are still nearly one hundred miles from its source. Hodge, the Assistant State Geologist, passed up this river in 1837, and by a portage of only one mile and three quarters crossed over into the Allegash, and so went down that into the St. John, and up the Madawaska to the Grand Portage across to the St. Lawrence. His is the only account that I know of an expedition through to Canada in this direction. He thus describes his first sight of the latter river, which, to compare small things with great, is like Balboa's first sight of the Pacific from the mountains of the Isthmus of Darien. " When we first came in sight of the St. Lawrence," he says, " from the top of a high hill, the view was most striking, and much more interesting to me from having been shut up in the woods for the two previous months.

Directly before us lay the broad river, extending across nine or ten miles, its surface broken by a few islands and reefs, and two ships riding at anchor near the shore. Beyond, extended ranges of uncultivated hills, parallel with the river. The sun was just going down behind them, and gilding the whole scene with its parting rays."

About four o'clock, the same afternoon, we commenced our return voyage, which would require but little if any poling. In shooting rapids the boatmen use large and broad paddles, instead of poles, to guide the boat with. Though we glided so swiftly, and often smoothly, down, where it had cost us no slight effort to get up, our present voyage was attended with far more danger; for if we once fairly struck one of the thousand rocks by which we were surrounded, the boat would be swamped in an instant. When a boat is swamped under these circumstances, the boatmen commonly find no difficulty in keeping afloat at first, for the current keeps both them and their cargo up for a long way down the stream; and if they can swim, they have only to work their way gradually to the shore. The greatest danger is of being caught in an eddy behind some larger rock, where the water rushes up stream faster than elsewhere it does down, and being carried round and round under the surface till they are drowned. McCauslin pointed out some rocks which had been the scene of a fatal accident of this kind. Sometimes the body is not thrown out for several hours. He himself had performed such a circuit once, only his legs being visible to his companions; but he was fortunately thrown out in season to recover his breath.[1] In shooting the rapids, the boatman has this problem to solve: to choose a circuitous and safe course amid a thousand sunken rocks, scattered over a quarter or half a mile, at the same time that he is moving steadily on at the rate of fifteen miles an hour. Stop he cannot; the only question is, where will he go? The bowman chooses the course with all his eyes about him, striking broad off with his paddle, and drawing the boat by main force into her course. The sternman faithfully follows the bow.

We were soon at the Aboljacarmegus Falls. Anxious to avoid the delay, as well as the labor, of the portage here, our boatmen went forward first to reconnoitre, and concluded to let the batteau down the falls, carrying the baggage only over the portage. Jumping from rock to rock until nearly in the middle of the stream, we were ready to receive the boat and let her down over the first fall, some six or seven feet perpendicular. The boatmen stand upon the edge of a shelf of rock, where the fall is perhaps nine or ten feet perpendicular, in from one to two feet of rapid water, one on each side of the boat, and let it slide gently over, till the bow is run out ten or twelve feet in the air; then, letting it drop squarely, while one holds the painter, the other leaps in, and his companion following, they are whirled

---

[1] I cut this from a newspaper: "On the 11th (instant?) [May, '49], on Rappogenes Falls, Mr. John Delantee, of Orono, Me., was drowned while running logs. He was a citizen of Orono, and was twenty-six years of age. His companions found his body, enclosed it in bark, and buried it in the solemn woods."

down the rapids to a new fall or to smooth water. In a very few minutes they had accomplished a passage in safety, which would be as foolhardy for the unskillful to attempt as the descent of Niagara itself. It seemed as if it needed only a little familiarity, and a little more skill, to navigate down such falls as Niagara itself with safety. At any rate, I should not despair of such men in the rapids above Table Rock, until I saw them actually go over the falls, so cool, so collected, so fertile in resources are they. One might have thought that these were falls, and that falls were not to be waded through with impunity, like a mud-puddle. There was really danger of their losing their sublimity in losing their power to harm us. Familiarity breeds contempt. The boatman pauses, perchance, on some shelf beneath a table-rock under the fall, standing in some cove of backwater two feet deep, and you hear his rough voice come up through the spray, coolly giving directions how to launch the boat this time.

Having carried round Pockwockomus Falls, our oars soon brought us to the Katepskonegan, or Oak Hall carry, where we decided to camp half-way over, leaving our batteau to be carried over in the morning on fresh shoulders. One shoulder of each of the boatmen showed a red spot as large as one's hand, worn by the batteau on this expedition; and this shoulder, as it did all the work, was perceptibly lower than its fellow, from long service. Such toil soon wears out the strongest constitution. The drivers are accustomed to work in the cold water in the spring, rarely ever dry; and if one falls in all over he rarely changes his clothes till night, if then, even.

One who takes this precaution is called by a particular nickname, or is turned off. None can lead this life who are not almost amphibious. McCauslin said soberly, what is at any rate a good story to tell, that he had seen where six men were wholly under water at once, at a jam, with their shoulders to handspikes. If the log did not start, then they had to put out their heads to breathe. The driver works as long as he can see, from dark to dark, and at night has not time to eat his supper and dry his clothes fairly, before he is asleep on his cedar bed. We lay that night on the very bed made by such a party, stretching our tent over the poles which were still standing, but re-shingling the damp and faded bed with fresh leaves.

In the morning we carried our boat over and launched it, making haste lest the wind should rise. The boatmen ran down Passamagamet, and soon after Ambejijis Falls, while we walked round with the baggage. We made a hasty breakfast at the head of Ambejijis Lake on the remainder of our pork, and were soon rowing across its smooth surface again, under a pleasant sky, the mountain being now clear of clouds in the northeast. Taking turns at the oars, we shot rapidly across Deep Cove, the foot of Pamadumcook, and the North Twin, at the rate of six miles an hour, the wind not being high enough to disturb us, and reached the Dam at noon. The boatmen went through one of the log sluices in the batteau, where the fall was ten feet at the bottom, and took us in below. Here was the longest rapid in our voyage, and perhaps the running this was as dangerous and arduous a task as any. Shooting down sometimes

at the rate, as we judged, of fifteen miles an hour, if
we struck a rock we were split from end to end in an
instant. Now like a bait bobbing for some river monster, amid the eddies, now darting to this side of the
stream, now to that, gliding swift and smooth near to
our destruction, or striking broad off with the paddle
and drawing the boat to right or left with all our might,
in order to avoid a rock. I suppose that it was like
running the rapids of the Sault Sainte Marie, at the
outlet of Lake Superior, and our boatmen probably
displayed no less dexterity than the Indians there do.
We soon ran through this mile, and floated in Quakish
Lake.

After such a voyage, the troubled and angry waters,
which once had seemed terrible and not to be trifled
with, appeared tamed and subdued; they had been
bearded and worried in their channels, pricked and
whipped into submission with the spike-pole and paddle, gone through and through with impunity, and all
their spirit and their danger taken out of them, and the
most swollen and impetuous rivers seemed but playthings
henceforth. I began, at length, to understand the boatman's familiarity with, and contempt for, the rapids.
" Those Fowler boys," said Mrs. McCauslin, " are perfect ducks for the water." They had run down to
Lincoln, according to her, thirty or forty miles, in a
batteau, in the night, for a doctor, when it was so dark
that they could not see a rod before them, and the river
was swollen so as to be almost a continuous rapid, so
that the doctor *cried*, when they brought him up by daylight, " Why, Tom, how did you see to steer ? " " We

did n't steer much, — only kept her straight." And yet
they met with no accident. It is true, the more difficult
rapids are higher up than this.

When we reached the Millinocket opposite to Tom's
house, and were waiting for his folks to set us over, —
for we had left our batteau above the Grand Falls, —
we discovered two canoes, with two men in each, turning up this stream from Shad Pond, one keeping the
opposite side of a small island before us, while the other
approached the side where we were standing, examining the banks carefully for muskrats as they came along.
The last proved to be Louis Neptune and his companion, now, at last, on their way up to Chesuncook after
moose, but they were so disguised that we hardly knew
them. At a little distance they might have been taken
for Quakers, with their broad-brimmed hats and over-
coats with broad capes, the spoils of Bangor, seeking a
settlement in this Sylvania, — or, nearer at hand, for
fashionable gentlemen the morning after a spree. Met
face to face, these Indians in their native woods looked
like the sinister and slouching fellows whom you meet
picking up strings and paper in the streets of a city.
There is, in fact, a remarkable and unexpected resem-
blance between the degraded savage and the lowest
classes in a great city. The one is no more a child of
nature than the other. In the progress of degradation
the distinction of races is soon lost. Neptune at first
was only anxious to know what we " kill," seeing some
partridges in the hands of one of the party, but we
had assumed too much anger to permit of a reply. We
thought Indians had some honor before. But — " Me

been sick. Oh, me unwell now. You make bargain, then me go." They had in fact been delayed so long by a drunken frolic at the Five Islands, and they had not yet recovered from its effects. They had some young musquash in their canoes, which they dug out of the banks with a hoe, for food, not for their skins, for musquash are their principal food on these expeditions. So they went on up the Millinocket, and we kept down the bank of the Penobscot, after recruiting ourselves with a draught of Tom's beer, leaving Tom at his home.

Thus a man shall lead his life away here on the edge of the wilderness, on Indian Millinocket Stream, in a new world, far in the dark of a continent, and have a flute to play at evening here, while his strains echo to the stars, amid the howling of wolves; shall live, as it were, in the primitive age of the world, a primitive man. Yet he shall spend a sunny day, and in this century be my contemporary; perchance shall read some scattered leaves of literature, and sometimes talk with me. Why read history, then, if the ages and the generations are now? He lives three thousand years deep into time, an age not yet described by poets. Can you well go further back in history than this? Ay! ay! — for there turns up but now into the mouth of Millinocket Stream a still more ancient and primitive man, whose history is not brought down even to the former. In a bark vessel sewn with the roots of the spruce, with horn-beam paddles, he dips his way along. He is but dim and misty to me, obscured by the æons that lie between the bark canoe and the batteau. He builds no house of logs, but a wigwam of skins. He eats no hot bread and sweet cake, but musquash and moose meat and the fat of bears. He glides up the Millinocket and is lost to my sight, as a more distant and misty cloud is seen flitting by behind a nearer, and is lost in space. So he goes about his destiny, the red face of man.

After having passed the night, and buttered our boots for the last time, at Uncle George's, whose dogs almost devoured him for joy at his return, we kept on down the river the next day, about eight miles on foot, and then took a batteau, with a man to pole it, to Matta-wamkeag, ten more. At the middle of that very night, to make a swift conclusion to a long story, we dropped our buggy over the half-finished bridge at Oldtown, where we heard the confused din and clink of a hun-dred saws, which never rest, and at six o'clock the next morning one of the party was steaming his way to Massachusetts.

What is most striking in the Maine wilderness is the continuousness of the forest, with fewer open inter-vals or glades than you had imagined. Except the few burnt lands, the narrow intervals on the rivers, the bare tops of the high mountains, and the lakes and streams, the forest is uninterrupted. It is even more grim and wild than you had anticipated, a damp and intricate wilderness, in the spring everywhere wet and miry. The aspect of the country, indeed, is universally stern and savage, excepting the distant views of the forest from hills, and the lake prospects, which are mild and civilizing in a degree. The lakes are something which you are unprepared for; they lie up so high, exposed to the light, and the forest is diminished to a fine fringe on their edges, with here and there a blue mountain, like amethyst jewels set around some jewel of the first water, — so anterior, so superior, to all the changes that are to take place on their shores, even now civil and refined, and fair as they can ever be. These are not the artificial forests of an English king, — a royal preserve merely. Here prevail no forest laws but those of nature. The aborigines have never been dispossessed, nor nature disforested.

It is a country full of evergreen trees, of mossy silver birches and watery maples, the ground dotted with insipid small, red berries, and strewn with damp and moss-grown rocks, — a country diversified with innumerable lakes and rapid streams, peopled with trout and various species of *leucisci*, with salmon, shad, and pickerel, and other fishes; the forest resounding at rare intervals with the note of the chickadee, the blue jay, and the woodpecker, the scream of the fish hawk and the eagle, the laugh of the loon, and the whistle of ducks along the solitary streams; at night, with the hooting of owls and howling of wolves; in summer, swarming with myriads of black flies and mosquitoes, more formidable than wolves to the white man. Such is the home of the moose, the bear, the caribou, the wolf, the beaver, and the Indian. Who shall describe the inexpressible tenderness and immortal life of the grim forest, where Nature, though it be midwinter, is ever in her spring, where the moss-grown and decaying trees are not old, but seem to enjoy a perpetual youth;

and blissful, innocent Nature, like a serene infant, is too happy to make a noise, except by a few tinkling, lisping birds and trickling rills?

What a place to live, what a place to die and be buried in! There certainly men would live forever, and laugh at death and the grave. There they could have no such thoughts as are associated with the village graveyard, — that make a grave out of one of those moist evergreen hummocks!

> Die and be buried who will,
> I mean to live here still;
> My nature grows ever more young
> The primitive pines among.

I am reminded by my journey how exceedingly new this country still is. You have only to travel for a few days into the interior and back parts even of many of the old States, to come to that very America which the Northmen, and Cabot, and Gosnold, and Smith, and Raleigh visited. If Columbus was the first to discover the islands, Americus Vespucius and Cabot, and the Puritans, and we their descendants, have discovered only the shores of America. While the Republic has already acquired a history world-wide, America is still unsettled and unexplored. Like the English in New Holland, we live only on the shores of a continent even yet, and hardly know where the rivers come from which float our navy. The very timber and boards and shingles of which our houses are made grew but yesterday in a wilderness where the Indian still hunts and the moose runs wild. New York has her wilderness within her own borders; and though the sailors of

Europe are familiar with the soundings of her Hudson,
and Fulton long since invented the steamboat on its
waters, an Indian is still necessary to guide her scientific
men to its headwaters in the Adirondack country.

Have we even so much as discovered and settled
the shores? Let a man travel on foot along the coast,
from the Passamaquoddy to the Sabine, or to the Rio
Bravo, or to wherever the end is now, if he is swift
enough to overtake it, faithfully following the windings
of every inlet and of every cape, and stepping to the
music of the surf, — with a desolate fishing town once
a week, and a city's port once a month to cheer him,
and putting up at the lighthouses, when there are any,
— and tell me if it looks like a discovered and settled
country, and not rather, for the most part, like a desolate island, and No-Man's Land.

We have advanced by leaps to the Pacific, and left
many a lesser Oregon and California unexplored behind
us. Though the railroad and the telegraph have been
established on the shores of Maine, the Indian still looks
out from her interior mountains over all these to the
sea. There stands the city of Bangor, fifty miles up
the Penobscot, at the head of navigation for vessels of
the largest class, the principal lumber depot on this continent, with a population of twelve thousand, like a star
on the edge of night, still hewing at the forests of which
it is built, already overflowing with the luxuries and
refinement of Europe, and sending its vessels to Spain,
to England, and to the West Indies for its groceries, —
and yet only a few axemen have gone " up river," into
the howling wilderness which feeds it. The bear and

deer are still found within its limits; and the moose, as
he swims the Penobscot, is entangled amid its shipping,
and taken by foreign sailors in its harbor. Twelve miles
in the rear, twelve miles of railroad, are Orono and the
Indian Island, the home of the Penobscot tribe, and
then commence the batteau and the canoe, and the military road; and sixty miles above, the country is virtually unmapped and unexplored, and there still waves
the virgin forest of the New World.

WILD APPLES

WILD APPLES

THE HISTORY OF THE APPLE TREE

IT is remarkable how closely the history of the apple tree is connected with that of man. The geologist tells us that the order of the *Rosaceae*, which includes the apple, also the true grasses, and the *Labiatae*, or mints, were introduced only a short time previous to the appearance of man on the globe.

It appears that apples made a part of the food of that unknown primitive people whose traces have lately been found at the bottom of the Swiss lakes, supposed to be older than the foundation of Rome, so old that they had no metallic implements. An entire black and shriveled crab-apple has been recovered from their stores.

Tacitus says of the ancient Germans that they satisfied their hunger with wild apples (*agrestia poma*), among other things.

Niebuhr observes that "the words for a house, a field, a plow, plowing, wine, oil, milk, sheep, apples, and others relating to agriculture and the gentler way of life, agree in Latin and Greek, while the Latin words for all objects pertaining to war or the chase are utterly alien from the Greek." Thus the apple tree may be considered a symbol of peace no less than the olive.

The apple was early so important, and generally distributed, that its name traced to its root in many languages signifies fruit in general. Μῆλον, in Greek, means an apple, also the fruit of other trees, also a sheep and any cattle, and finally riches in general.

The apple tree has been celebrated by the Hebrews, Greeks, Romans, and Scandinavians. Some have thought that the first human pair were tempted by its fruit. Goddesses are fabled to have contended for it, dragons were set to watch it, and heroes were employed to pluck it.

The tree is mentioned in at least three places in the Old Testament, and its fruit in two or three more. Solomon sings, "As the apple-tree among the trees of the wood, so is my beloved among the sons." And again, "Stay me with flagons, comfort me with apples." The noblest part of man's noblest feature is named from this fruit, "the apple of the eye."

The apple tree is also mentioned by Homer and Herodotus. Ulysses saw in the glorious garden of Alcinoüs "pears and pomegranates, and apple trees bearing beautiful fruit" (καὶ μηλέαι ἀγλαόκαρποι). And according to Homer, apples were among the fruits which Tantalus could not pluck, the wind ever blowing their boughs away from him. Theophrastus knew and described the apple tree as a botanist.

According to the Prose Edda, "Iduna keeps in a box the apples which the gods, when they feel old age approaching, have only to taste of to become young again. It is in this manner that they will be kept in renovated youth until Ragnarök" (or the destruction of the gods).

I learn from Loudon that "the ancient Welsh bards were rewarded for excelling in song by the token of the apple-spray;" and "in the Highlands of Scotland the apple-tree is the badge of the clan Lamont."

The apple tree (*Pyrus malus*) belongs chiefly to the northern temperate zone. Loudon says that "it grows spontaneously in every part of Europe except the frigid zone, and throughout Western Asia, China, and Japan." We have also two or three varieties of the apple indigenous in North America. The cultivated apple tree was first introduced into this country by the earliest settlers, and is thought to do as well or better here than anywhere else. Probably some of the varieties which are now cultivated were first introduced into Britain by the Romans.

Pliny, adopting the distinction of Theophrastus, says, "Of trees there are some which are altogether wild (*sylvestres*), some more civilized (*urbaniores*)." Theophrastus includes the apple among the last; and, indeed, it is in this sense the most civilized of all trees. It is as harmless as a dove, as beautiful as a rose, and as valuable as flocks and herds. It has been longer cultivated than any other, and so is more humanized; and who knows but, like the dog, it will at length be no longer traceable to its wild original? It migrates with man, like the dog and horse and cow: first, perchance, from Greece to Italy, thence to England, thence to America; and our Western emigrant is still marching steadily toward the setting sun with the seeds of the apple in his pocket, or perhaps a few young trees strapped to his load. At least a million apple trees are thus set farther westward this year than any cultivated ones grew last year. Consider how the Blossom Week, like the Sabbath, is thus annually spreading over the prairies; for when man migrates, he carries with him not only his birds, quadrupeds, insects, vegetables, and his very sward, but his orchard also.

The leaves and tender twigs are an agreeable food to many domestic animals, as the cow, horse, sheep, and goat; and the fruit is sought after by the first, as well as by the hog. Thus there appears to have existed a natural alliance between these animals and this tree from the first. "The fruit of the crab in the forests of France" is said to be "a great resource for the wild boar."

Not only the Indian, but many indigenous insects, birds, and quadrupeds, welcomed the apple tree to these shores. The tent caterpillar saddled her eggs on the very first twig that was formed, and it has since shared her affections with the wild cherry; and the canker-worm also in a measure abandoned the elm to feed on it. As it grew apace, the bluebird, robin, cherry-bird, kingbird, and many more came with haste and built their nests and warbled in its boughs, and so became orchard-birds, and multiplied more than ever. It was an era in the history of their race. The downy woodpecker found such a savory morsel under its bark that he perforated it in a ring quite round the tree, before he left it, — a thing which he had never done before, to my knowledge. It did not take the partridge long to find out how sweet its buds were, and every winter eve she flew, and still flies, from the wood, to pluck them, much to the farmer's sorrow. The rabbit, too, was not slow to learn the taste of its twigs and bark;

and when the fruit was ripe, the squirrel half rolled, half carried it to his hole; and even the musquash crept up the bank from the brook at evening, and greedily devoured it, until he had worn a path in the grass there; and when it was frozen and thawed, the crow and the jay were glad to taste it occasionally. The owl crept into the first apple tree that became hollow, and fairly hooted with delight, finding it just the place for him; so, settling down into it, he has remained there ever since.

My theme being the Wild Apple, I will merely glance at some of the seasons in the annual growth of the cultivated apple, and pass on to my special province.

The flowers of the apple are perhaps the most beautiful of any tree's, so copious and so delicious to both sight and scent. The walker is frequently tempted to turn and linger near some more than usually handsome one, whose blossoms are two-thirds expanded. How superior it is in these respects to the pear, whose blossoms are neither colored nor fragrant!

By the middle of July, green apples are so large as to remind us of coddling, and of the autumn. The sward is commonly strewed with little ones which fall stillborn, as it were, — Nature thus thinning them for us. The Roman writer Palladius said, "If apples are inclined to fall before their time, a stone placed in a split root will retain them." Some such notion, still surviving, may account for some of the stones which we see placed, to be overgrown, in the forks of trees. They have a saying in Suffolk, England, —

"At Michaelmas time, or a little before,
Half an apple goes to the core."

Early apples begin to be ripe about the first of August; but I think that none of them are so good to eat as some to smell. One is worth more to scent your handkerchief with than any perfume which they sell in the shops. The fragrance of some fruits is not to be forgotten, along with that of flowers. Some gnarly apple which I pick up in the road reminds me by its fragrance of all the wealth of Pomona, — carrying me forward to those days when they will be collected in golden and ruddy heaps in the orchards and about the cider-mills.

A week or two later, as you are going by orchards or gardens, especially in the evenings, you pass through a little region possessed by the fragrance of ripe apples, and thus enjoy them without price, and without robbing anybody.

There is thus about all natural products a certain volatile and ethereal quality which represents their highest value, and which cannot be vulgarized, or bought and sold. No mortal has ever enjoyed the perfect flavor of any fruit, and only the godlike among men begin to taste its ambrosial qualities. For nectar and ambrosia are only those fine flavors of every earthly fruit which our coarse palates fail to perceive, — just as we occupy the heaven of the gods without knowing it. When I see a particularly mean man carrying a load of fair and fragrant early apples to market, I seem to see a contest going on between him and his horse, on the one side, and the apples on the other, and, to my mind, the apples always gain it. Pliny says that apples are the heaviest of all things, and that the oxen begin to sweat at the mere sight of a load of them. Our driver begins to lose his load the moment he tries to transport them to where they do not belong, that is, to any but the most beautiful. Though he gets out from time to time, and feels of them, and thinks they are all there, I see the stream of their evanescent and celestial qualities going to heaven from his cart, while the pulp and skin and core only are going to market. They are not apples, but pomace. Are not these still Iduna's apples, the taste of which keeps the gods forever young? and think you that they will let Loki or Thjassi carry them off to Jötunheim, while they grow wrinkled and gray? No, for Ragnarök, or the destruction of the gods, is not yet.

There is another thinning of the fruit, commonly near the end of August or in September, when the ground is strewn with windfalls; and this happens especially when high winds occur after rain. In some orchards you may see fully three quarters of the whole crop on the ground, lying in a circular form beneath the trees, yet hard and green, or, if it is a hillside, rolled far down the hill. However, it is an ill wind that blows nobody any good. All the country over, people are busy picking up the windfalls, and this will make them cheap for early apple pies.

In October, the leaves falling, the apples are more distinct on the trees. I saw one year in a neighboring town some trees fuller of fruit than I remember to have ever seen before, small yellow apples hanging over the road. The branches were gracefully drooping with their weight, like a barberry bush, so that the whole tree acquired a new character. Even the topmost branches,

instead of standing erect, spread and drooped in all directions; and there were so many poles supporting the
lower ones that they looked like pictures of banyan
trees. As an old English manuscript says, "The mo
appelen the tree bereth the more sche boweth to the
folk."

Surely the apple is the noblest of fruits. Let the most
beautiful or the swiftest have it. That should be the
"going" price of apples.

Between the 5th and 20th of October I see the barrels
lie under the trees. And perhaps I talk with one who
is selecting some choice barrels to fulfill an order. He
turns a specked one over many times before he leaves it
out. If I were to tell what is passing in my mind, I
should say that every one was specked which he had
handled; for he rubs off all the bloom, and those fu-
gacious ethereal qualities leave it. Cool evenings prompt
the farmers to make haste, and at length I see only the
ladders here and there left leaning against the trees.

It would be well, if we accepted these gifts with more
joy and gratitude, and did not think it enough simply
to put a fresh load of compost about the tree. Some
old English customs are suggestive at least. I find them
described chiefly in Brand's "Popular Antiquities."
It appears that "on Christmas Eve the farmers and
their men in Devonshire take a large bowl of cider,
with a toast in it, and carrying it in state to the orchard,
they salute the apple-trees with much ceremony, in
order to make them bear well the next season." This
salutation consists in "throwing some of the cider
about the roots of the tree, placing bits of the toast on

the branches," and then, "encircling one of the best bearing trees in the orchard, they drink the following toast three several times: —

> 'Here's to thee, old apple tree,
> Whence thou mayst bud, and whence thou mayst blow,
> And whence thou mayst bear apples enow!
> Hats-full! caps-full!
> Bushel, bushel, sacks-full!
> And my pockets full, too! Hurra!'"

Also what was called "apple-howling" used to be practiced in various counties of England on New Year's Eve. A troop of boys visited the different orchards, and, encircling the apple trees, repeated the following words: —

> "Stand fast, root! bear well, top!
> Pray God send us a good howling crop:
> Every twig, apples big;
> Every bough, apples enow!"

"They then shout in chorus, one of the boys accompanying them on a cow's horn. During this ceremony they rap the trees with their sticks." This is called "wassailing" the trees, and is thought by some to be "a relic of the heathen sacrifice to Pomona."

Herrick sings, —

> "Wassaile the trees that they may beare
> You many a plum and many a peare;
> For more or less fruits they will bring
> As you so give them wassailing."

Our poets have as yet a better right to sing of cider than of wine; but it behooves them to sing better than English Phillips did, else they will do no credit to their Muse.

THE WILD APPLE

So much for the more civilized apple trees (*urbani-ores*, as Pliny calls them). I love better to go through the old orchards of ungrafted appletrees, at what ever season of the year, — so irregularly planted: sometimes two trees standing close together; and the rows so devious that you would think that they not only had grown while the owner was sleeping, but had been set out by him in a somnambulic state. The rows of grafted fruit will never tempt me to wander amid them like these. But I now, alas, speak rather from memory than from any recent experience, such ravages have been made!

Some soils, like a rocky tract called the Easterbrooks Country in my neighborhood, are so suited to the apple, that it will grow faster in them without any care, or if only the ground is broken up once a year, than it will in many places with any amount of care. The owners of this tract allow that the soil is excellent for fruit, but they say that it is so rocky that they have not patience to plow it, and that, together with the distance, is the reason why it is not cultivated. There are, or were recently, extensive orchards there standing without order. Nay, they spring up wild and bear well there in the midst of pines, birches, maples, and oaks. I am often surprised to see rising amid these trees the rounded tops of apple trees glowing with red or yellow fruit, in harmony with the autumnal tints of the forest.

Going up the side of a cliff about the first of November, I saw a vigorous young apple tree, which, planted by birds or cows, had shot up amid the rocks and open woods there, and had now much fruit on it, uninjured by the frosts, when all cultivated apples were gathered. It was a rank, wild growth, with many green leaves on it still, and made an impression of thorniness. The fruit was hard and green, but looked as if it would be palatable in the winter. Some was dangling on the twigs, but more half buried in the wet leaves under the tree, or rolled far down the hill amid the rocks. The owner knows nothing of it. The day was not observed when it first blossomed, nor when it first bore fruit, unless by the chickadee. There was no dancing on the green beneath it in its honor, and now there is no hand to pluck its fruit, — which is only gnawed by squirrels, as I perceive. It has done double duty, — not only borne this crop, but each twig has grown a foot into the air. And this is *such* fruit! bigger than many berries, we must admit, and carried home will be sound and palatable next spring. What care I for Iduna's apples so long as I can get these?

When I go by this shrub thus late and hardy, and see its dangling fruit, I respect the tree, and I am grateful for Nature's bounty, even though I cannot eat it. Here on this rugged and woody hillside has grown an apple tree, not planted by man, no relic of a former orchard, but a natural growth, like the pines and oaks. Most fruits which we prize and use depend entirely on our care. Corn and grain, potatoes, peaches, melons, etc., depend altogether on our planting; but the apple emulates man's independence and enterprise. It is not simply carried, as I have said, but, like him, to some extent, it has migrated to this New World, and is even, here and there, making its way amid the aboriginal trees; just as the ox and dog and horse sometimes run wild and maintain themselves.

Even the sourest and crabbedest apple, growing in the most unfavorable position, suggests such thoughts as these, it is so noble a fruit.

THE CRAB

Nevertheless, *our* wild apple is wild only like myself, perchance, who belong not to the aboriginal race here, but have strayed into the woods from the cultivated stock. Wilder still, as I have said, there grows elsewhere in this country a native and aboriginal crab-apple, *Malus coronaria*, "whose nature has not yet been modified by cultivation." It is found from western New York to Minnesota, and southward. Michaux says that its ordinary height "is fifteen or eighteen feet, but it is sometimes found twenty-five or thirty feet high," and that the large ones "exactly resemble the common apple tree." "The flowers are white mingled with rose color, and are collected in corymbs." They are remarkable for their delicious odor. The fruit, according to him, is about an inch and a half in diameter, and is intensely acid. Yet they make fine sweetmeats and also cider of them. He concludes that "if, on being cultivated, it does not yield new and palatable varieties, it will at least be celebrated for the beauty of its flowers, and for the sweetness of its perfume."

I never saw the crab-apple till May, 1861. I had heard of it through Michaux, but more modern botanists, so far as I know, have not treated it as of any peculiar importance. Thus it was a half-fabulous tree to me. I contemplated a pilgrimage to the "Glades," a portion of Pennsylvania where it was said to grow to perfection. I thought of sending to a nursery for it, but doubted if they had it, or would distinguish it from European varieties. At last I had occasion to go to Minnesota, and on entering Michigan I began to notice from the cars a tree with handsome rose-colored flowers. At first I thought it some variety of thorn; but it was not long before the truth flashed on me, that this was my long-sought crab-apple. It was the prevailing flowering shrub or tree to be seen from the cars at that season of the year, — about the middle of May. But the cars never stopped before one, and so I was launched on the bosom of the Mississippi without having touched one, experiencing the fate of Tantalus. On arriving at St. Anthony's Falls, I was sorry to be told that I was too far north for the crab-apple. Nevertheless I succeeded in finding it about eight miles west of the Falls; touched it and smelled it, and secured a lingering corymb of flowers for my herbarium. This must have been near its northern limit.

HOW THE WILD APPLE GROWS

But though these are indigenous, like the Indians, I doubt whether they are any hardier than those back-woodsmen among the apple trees, which, though descended from cultivated stocks, plant themselves in distant fields and forests, where the soil is favorable to them. I know of no trees which have more difficulties

to contend with, and which more sturdily resist their
foes. These are the ones whose story we have to tell. It
oftentimes reads thus: —

Near the beginning of May, we notice little thickets
of apple trees just springing up in the pastures where
cattle have been, — as the rocky ones of our Easterbrooks Country, or the top of Nobscot Hill, in Sudbury. One or two of these, perhaps, survive the drought
and other accidents, — their very birthplace defending
them against the encroaching grass and some other dangers, at first.

> In two years' time 't had thus
> Reached the level of the rocks,
> Admired the stretching world,
> Nor feared the wandering flocks.
>
> But at this tender age
> Its sufferings began:
> There came a browsing ox
> And cut it down a span.

This time, perhaps, the ox does not notice it amid the
grass; but the next year, when it has grown more stout,
he recognizes it for a fellow-emigrant from the old
country, the flavor of whose leaves and twigs he well
knows; and though at first he pauses to welcome it,
and express his surprise, and gets for answer, "The
same cause that brought you here brought me," he
nevertheless browses it again, reflecting, it may be, that
he has some title to it.

Thus cut down annually, it does not despair; but,
putting forth two short twigs for every one cut off, it
spreads out low along the ground in the hollows or

between the rocks, growing more stout and scrubby, until it forms, not a tree as yet, but a little pyramidal, stiff, twiggy mass, almost as solid and impenetrable as a rock. Some of the densest and most impenetrable clumps of bushes that I have ever seen, as well on account of the closeness and stubbornness of their branches as of their thorns, have been these wild apple scrubs. They are more like the scrubby fir and black spruce on which you stand, and sometimes walk, on the tops of mountains, where cold is the demon they contend with, than anything else. No wonder they are prompted to grow thorns at last, to defend themselves against such foes. In their thorniness, however, there is no malice, only some malic acid.

The rocky pastures of the tract I have referred to — for they maintain their ground best in a rocky field — are thickly sprinkled with these little tufts, reminding you often of some rigid gray mosses or lichens, and you see thousands of little trees just springing up between them, with the seed still attached to them.

Being regularly clipped all around each year by the cows, as a hedge with shears, they are often of a perfect conical or pyramidal form, from one to four feet high, and more or less sharp, as if trimmed by the gardener's art. In the pastures on Nobscot Hill and its spurs, they make fine dark shadows when the sun is low. They are also an excellent covert from hawks for many small birds that roost and build in them. Whole flocks perch in them at night, and I have seen three robins' nests in one which was six feet in diameter.

No doubt many of these are already old trees, if you

Wild apple tree

Cows in Emerson's pasture

reckon from the day they were planted, but infants still when you consider their development and the long life before them. I counted the annual rings of some which were just one foot high, and as wide as high, and found that they were about twelve years old, but quite sound and thrifty! They were so low that they were unnoticed by the walker, while many of their contemporaries from the nurseries were already bearing considerable crops. But what you gain in time is perhaps in this case, too, lost in power, — that is, in the vigor of the tree. This is their pyramidal state.

The cows continue to browse them thus for twenty years or more, keeping them down and compelling them to spread, until at last they are so broad that they become their own fence, when some interior shoot, which their foes cannot reach, darts upward with joy: for it has not forgotten its high calling, and bears its own peculiar fruit in triumph.

Such are the tactics by which it finally defeats its bovine foes. Now, if you have watched the progress of a particular shrub, you will see that it is no longer a simple pyramid or cone, but that out of its apex there rises a sprig or two, growing more lustily perchance than an orchard-tree, since the plant now devotes the whole of its repressed energy to these upright parts. In a short time these become a small tree, an inverted pyramid resting on the apex of the other, so that the whole has now the form of a vast hour-glass. The spreading bottom, having served its purpose, finally disappears, and the generous tree permits the now harmless cows to come in and stand in its shade, and rub against and redden its trunk, which has grown in spite of them, and even to taste a part of its fruit, and so disperse the seed.

Thus the cows create their own shade and food; and the tree, its hour-glass being inverted, lives a second life, as it were.

It is an important question with some nowadays, whether you should trim young apple trees as high as your nose or as high as your eyes. The ox trims them up as high as he can reach, and that is about the right height, I think.

In spite of wandering kine, and other adverse circumstances, that despised shrub, valued only by small birds as a covert and shelter from hawks, has its blossom week at last, and in course of time its harvest, sincere, though small.

By the end of some October, when its leaves have fallen, I frequently see such a central sprig, whose progress I have watched, when I thought it had forgotten its destiny, as I had, bearing its first crop of small green or yellow or rosy fruit, which the cows cannot get at over the bushy and thorny hedge which surrounds it, and I make haste to taste the new and undescribed variety. We have all heard of the numerous varieties of fruit invented by Van Mons and Knight. This is the system of Van Cow, and she has invented far more and more memorable varieties than both of them.

Through what hardships it may attain to bear a sweet fruit! Though somewhat small, it may prove equal, if not superior, in flavor to that which has grown in a garden, — will perchance be all the sweeter and more palatable for the very difficulties it has had to contend with. Who knows but this chance wild fruit, planted by a cow or a bird on some remote and rocky hillside, where it is as yet unobserved by man, may be the choicest of all its kind, and foreign potentates shall hear of it, and royal societies seek to propagate it, though the virtues of the perhaps truly crabbed owner of the soil may never be heard of, — at least, beyond the limits of his village? It was thus the Porter and the Baldwin grew.

Every wild apple shrub excites our expectation thus, somewhat as every wild child. It is, perhaps, a prince in disguise. What a lesson to man! So are human beings, referred to the highest standard, the celestial fruit which they suggest and aspire to bear, browsed on by fate; and only the most persistent and strongest genius defends itself and prevails, sends a tender scion upward at last, and drops its perfect fruit on the ungrateful earth. Poets and philosophers and statesmen thus spring up in the country pastures, and outlast the hosts of unoriginal men.

Such is always the pursuit of knowledge. The celestial fruits, the golden apples of the Hesperides, are ever guarded by a hundred-headed dragon which never sleeps, so that it is an Herculean labor to pluck them.

This is one, and the most remarkable way in which the wild apple is propagated; but commonly it springs up at wide intervals in woods and swamp, and by the sides of roads, as the soil may suit it, and grows with comparative rapidity. Those which grow in dense woods are very tall and slender. I frequently pluck from these trees a perfectly mild and tamed fruit. As Palladius says, "*Et injussu consternitur ubere mali:*" And the ground is strewn with the fruit of an unbidden apple tree.

It is an old notion that, if these wild trees do not bear a valuable fruit of their own, they are the best stocks by which to transmit to posterity the most highly prized qualities of others. However, I am not in search of stocks, but the wild fruit itself, whose fierce gust has suffered no "inteneration." It is not my

> "highest plot
> To plant the Bergamot."

THE FRUIT, AND ITS FLAVOR

The time for wild apples is the last of October and the first of November. They then get to be palatable, for they ripen late, and they are still perhaps as beautiful as ever. I make a great account of these fruits, which the farmers do not think it worth the while to gather, — wild flavors of the Muse, vivacious and inspiriting. The farmer thinks that he has better in his barrels, but he is mistaken, unless he has a walker's appetite and imagination, neither of which can he have.

Such as grow quite wild, and are left out till the first of November, I presume that the owner does not mean to gather. They belong to children as wild as themselves, — to certain active boys that I know, — to the wild-eyed woman of the fields, to whom nothing comes amiss, who gleans after all the world, and, moreover, to us walkers. We have met with them, and they are ours. These rights, long enough insisted upon, have come to be an institution in some old countries, where they have learned how to live. I hear that "the custom of grippling, which may be called apple-gleaning, is, or was formerly, practiced in Herefordshire. It consists in leaving a few apples, which are called the gripples, on every tree, after the general gathering, for the boys, who go with climbing-poles and bags to collect them."

As for those I speak of, I pluck them as a wild fruit, native to this quarter of the earth, — fruit of old trees that have been dying ever since I was a boy and are not yet dead, frequented only by the woodpecker and the squirrel, deserted now by the owner, who has not faith enough to look under their boughs. From the appearance of the tree-top, at a little distance, you would expect nothing but lichens to drop from it, but your faith is rewarded by finding the ground strewn with spirited fruit, — some of it, perhaps, collected at squirrel-holes, with the marks of their teeth by which they carried them, — some containing a cricket or two silently feeding within, and some, especially in damp days, a shell-less snail. The very sticks and stones lodged in the tree-top might have convinced you of the savoriness of the fruit which has been so eagerly sought after in past years.

I have seen no account of these among the "Fruits and Fruit-Trees of America," though they are more memorable to my taste than the grafted kinds; more racy and wild American flavors do they possess when October and November, when December and January, and perhaps February and March even, have assuaged them somewhat. An old farmer in my neighborhood, who always selects the right word, says that "they have a kind of bow-arrow tang."

Apples for grafting appear to have been selected commonly, not so much for their spirited flavor, as for their mildness, their size, and bearing qualities, — not so much for their beauty, as for their fairness and soundness. Indeed, I have no faith in the selected lists of pomological gentlemen. Their "Favorites" and "None-suches" and "Seek-no-farthers," when I have fruited them, commonly turn out very tame and forgettable. They are eaten with comparatively little zest, and have no real *tang* nor *smack* to them.

What if some of these wildings are acrid and puckery, genuine *verjuice*, do they not still belong to the *Pomaceæ*, which are uniformly innocent and kind to our race? I still begrudge them to the cider-mill. Perhaps they are not fairly ripe yet.

No wonder that these small and high-colored apples are thought to make the best cider. Loudon quotes from the "Herefordshire Report," that "apples of a small size are always, if equal in quality, to be preferred to those of a larger size, in order that the rind and kernel may bear the greatest proportion to the pulp, which affords the weakest and most watery juice." And he says that, "to prove this, Dr. Symonds, of Hereford, about the year 1800, made one hogshead of cider entirely from the rinds and cores of apples, and another from the pulp only, when the first was found of extraordinary strength and flavor, while the latter was sweet and insipid."

Evelyn says that the "Red-strake" was the favorite cider-apple in his day; and he quotes one Dr. Newburg as saying, "In Jersey 't is a general observation, as I hear, that the more of red any apple has in its rind, the more proper it is for this use. Pale-faced apples they exclude as much as may be from their cider-vat." This opinion still prevails.

All apples are good in November. Those which the farmer leaves out as unsalable and unpalatable to those who frequent the markets are choicest fruit to the walker. But it is remarkable that the wild apple, which I praise as so spirited and racy when eaten in the fields or woods, being brought into the house has frequently a harsh and crabbed taste. The Saunterer's Apple not even the saunterer can eat in the house. The palate rejects it there, as it does haws and acorns, and demands a tamed one; for there you miss the November air, which is the sauce it is to be eaten with. Accordingly, when Tityrus, seeing the lengthening shadows, invites Melibœus to go home and pass the night with him, he promises him *mild* apples and soft chestnuts, — *mitia poma, castaneæ molles.* I frequently pluck wild apples of so rich and spicy a flavor that I wonder all orchardists do not get a scion from that tree, and I fail not to bring home my pockets full. But perchance, when I take one out of my desk and taste it in my chamber, I find it unexpectedly crude, — sour enough to set a squirrel's teeth on edge and make a jay scream.

These apples have hung in the wind and frost and rain till they have absorbed the qualities of the weather or season, and thus are highly *seasoned,* and they *pierce* and *sting* and *permeate* us with their spirit. They must be eaten in *season,* accordingly, — that is, out-of-doors.

To appreciate the wild and sharp flavors of these October fruits, it is necessary that you be breathing the sharp October or November air. The outdoor air and exercise which the walker gets give a different tone to his palate, and he craves a fruit which the sedentary would call harsh and crabbed. They must be eaten in the fields, when your system is all aglow with exercise, when the frosty weather nips your fingers, the wind rattles the bare boughs or rustles the few remaining leaves, and the jay is heard screaming around. What is sour in the house a bracing walk makes sweet. Some of these apples might be labeled, "To be eaten in the wind."

Of course no flavors are thrown away; they are intended for the taste that is up to them. Some apples have two distinct flavors, and perhaps one half of them must be eaten in the house, the other outdoors. One Peter Whitney wrote from Northborough in 1782, for the Proceedings of the Boston Academy, describing an apple tree in that town " producing fruit of opposite qualities, part of the same apple being frequently sour and the other sweet;" also some all sour, and others all sweet, and this diversity on all parts of the tree.

There is a wild apple on Nawshawtuct Hill in my town which has to me a peculiarly pleasant bitter tang, not perceived till it is three-quarters tasted. It remains on the tongue. As you eat it, it smells exactly like a squash-bug. It is a sort of triumph to eat and relish it.

I hear that the fruit of a kind of plum tree in Provence is "called *Prunes sibarelles*, because it is impossible to whistle after having eaten them, from their sourness."

But perhaps they were only eaten in the house and in summer, and if tried out-of-doors in a stinging atmosphere, who knows but you could whistle an octave higher and clearer?

In the fields only are the sours and bitters of Nature appreciated; just as the woodchopper eats his meal in a sunny glade, in the middle of a winter day, with content, basks in a sunny ray there, and dreams of summer in a degree of cold which, experienced in a chamber, would make a student miserable. They who are at work abroad are not cold, but rather it is they who sit shivering in houses. As with temperatures, so with flavors; as with cold and heat, so with sour and sweet. This natural raciness, the sours and bitters which the diseased palate refuses, are the true condiments.

Let your condiments be in the condition of your senses. To appreciate the flavor of these wild apples requires vigorous and healthy senses, *papillæ* firm and erect on the tongue and palate, not easily flattened and tamed.

From my experience with wild apples, I can understand that there may be reason for a savage's preferring many kinds of food which the civilized man rejects. The former has the palate of an outdoor man. It takes a savage or wild taste to appreciate a wild fruit.

What a healthy out-of-door appetite it takes to relish the apple of life, the apple of the world, then!

"Nor is it every apple I desire,
    Nor that which pleases every palate best;
'T is not the lasting Deuxan I require,
    Nor yet the red-cheeked Greening I request,

Nor that which first beshrewed the name of wife,
Nor that whose beauty caused the golden strife:
No, no! bring me an apple from the tree of life."

So there is one *thought* for the field, another for the
house. I would have my thoughts, like wild apples, to
be food for walkers, and will not warrant them to be
palatable if tasted in the house.

THEIR BEAUTY

Almost all wild apples are handsome. They cannot
be too gnarly and crabbed and rusty to look at. The
gnarliest will have some redeeming traits even to the
eye. You will discover some evening redness dashed or
sprinkled on some protuberance or in some cavity. It is
rare that the summer lets an apple go without streaking
or spotting it on some part of its sphere. It will have
some red stains, commemorating the mornings and
evenings it has witnessed; some dark and rusty blotches,
in memory of the clouds and foggy, mildewy days that
have passed over it; and a spacious field of green reflecting the general face of nature, — green even as the
fields; or a yellow ground, which implies a milder flavor,
— yellow as the harvest, or russet as the hills.

Apples, these I mean, unspeakably fair, — apples not
of Discord, but of Concord! Yet not so rare but that the
homeliest may have a share. Painted by the frosts, some
a uniform clear bright yellow, or red, or crimson, as if
their spheres had regularly revolved, and enjoyed the
influence of the sun on all sides alike, — some with the
faintest pink blush imaginable, — some brindled with
deep red streaks like a cow, or with hundreds of fine

blood-red rays running regularly from the stem-dimple to the blossom end, like meridional lines, on a straw-colored ground, — some touched with a greenish rust, like a fine lichen, here and there, with crimson blotches or eyes more or less confluent and fiery when wet, — and others gnarly, and freckled or peppered all over on the stem side with fine crimson spots on a white ground, as if accidentally sprinkled from the brush of Him who paints the autumn leaves. Others, again, are sometimes red inside, perfused with a beautiful blush, fairy food, too beautiful to eat, — apple of the Hesperides, apple of the evening sky! But like shells and pebbles on the sea-shore, they must be seen as they sparkle amid the withering leaves in some dell in the woods, in the autumnal air, or as they lie in the wet grass, and not when they have wilted and faded in the house.

THE NAMING OF THEM

It would be a pleasant pastime to find suitable names for the hundred varieties which go to a single heap at the cider-mill. Would it not tax a man's invention, — no one to be named after a man, and all in the *lingua vernacula?* Who shall stand godfather at the christening of the wild apples? It would exhaust the Latin and Greek languages, if they were used, and make the *lingua vernacula* flag. We should have to call in the sunrise and the sunset, the rainbow and the autumn woods and the wild-flowers, and the woodpecker and the purple finch and the squirrel and the jay and the butterfly, the November traveler and the truant boy, to our aid.

In 1836 there were in the garden of the London Horticultural Society more than fourteen hundred distinct sorts. But here are species which they have not in their catalogue, not to mention the varieties which our crab might yield to cultivation.

Let us enumerate a few of these. I find myself compelled, after all, to give the Latin names of some for the benefit of those who live where English is not spoken, — for they are likely to have a world-wide reputation.

There is, first of all, the Wood Apple (*Malus sylvatica*); the Blue-Jay Apple; the Apple which grows in Dells in the Woods (*sylvestrivallis*), also in Hollows in Pastures (*campestrivallis*); the Apple that grows in an old Cellar-Hole (*Malus cellaris*); the Meadow Apple; the Partridge Apple; the Truant's Apple (*cessatoris*), which no boy will ever go by without knocking off some, however *late* it may be; the Saunterer's Apple, — you must lose yourself before you can find the way to that; the Beauty of the Air (*decus aëris*); December-Eating; the Frozen-Thawed (*gelato-soluta*), good only in that state; the Concord Apple, possibly the same with the *Musketaquidensis;* the Assabet Apple; the Brindled Apple; Wine of New England; the Chickaree Apple; the Green Apple (*Malus viridis*), — this has many synonyms: in an imperfect state, it is the *choleramorbifera aut dysenterifera, puerulis dilectissima;* the Apple which Atalanta stopped to pick up; the Hedge Apple (*Malus sepium*); the Slug Apple (*limacea*); the Railroad Apple, which perhaps came from a core thrown out of the cars; the Apple whose Fruit we tasted in our Youth; our Particular Apple, not to be found in any catalogue; *pedestrium solatium;* also the Apple where hangs the Forgotten Scythe; Iduna's Apples, and the Apples which Loki found in the Wood; and a great many more I have on my list, too numerous to mention, — all of them good. As Bodæus exclaims, referring to the cultivated kinds, and adapting Virgil to his case, so I, adapting Bodæus, —

> "Not if I had a hundred tongues, a hundred mouths,
> An iron voice, could I describe all the forms
> And reckon up all the names of these *wild apples.*"

THE LAST GLEANING

By the middle of November the wild apples have lost some of their brilliancy, and have chiefly fallen. A great part are decayed on the ground, and the sound ones are more palatable than before. The note of the chickadee sounds now more distinct, as you wander amid the old trees, and the autumnal dandelion is half closed and tearful. But still, if you are a skillful gleaner, you may get many a pocketful even of grafted fruit, long after apples are supposed to be gone out-of-doors. I know a Blue Pearmain tree, growing within the edge of a swamp, almost as good as wild. You would not suppose that there was any fruit left there, on the first survey, but you must look according to system. Those which lie exposed are quite brown and rotten now, or perchance a few still show one blooming cheek here and there amid the wet leaves. Nevertheless, with experienced eyes, I explore amid the bare alders and the huckleberry bushes and the withered sedge, and in the crevices of the rocks, which are full of leaves, and pry under the fallen and decaying ferns, which, with apple and alder leaves, thickly strew the ground. For I know that they lie concealed, fallen into hollows long since and covered up by the leaves of the tree itself, — a proper kind of packing. From these lurking-places, anywhere within the circumference of the tree, I draw forth the fruit, all wet and glossy, maybe nibbled by rabbits and hollowed out by crickets, and perhaps with a leaf or two cemented to it (as Curzon an old manuscript from a monastery's mouldy cellar), but still with a rich bloom on it, and at least as ripe and well-kept, if not better than those in barrels, more crisp and lively than they. If these resources fail to yield anything, I have learned to look between the bases of the suckers which spring thickly from some horizontal limb, for now and then one lodges there, or in the very midst of an alder-clump, where they are covered by leaves, safe from cows which may have smelled them out. If I am sharp-set, for I do not refuse the Blue Pearmain, I fill my pockets on each side; and as I retrace my steps in the frosty eve, being perhaps four or five miles from home, I eat one first from this side, and then from that, to keep my balance.

I learn from Topsell's Gesner, whose authority appears to be Albertus, that the following is the way in which the hedgehog collects and carries home his apples. He says, — "His meat is apples, worms, or grapes: when he findeth apples or grapes on the earth, he rolleth himself upon them, until he have filled all his prickles, and then carrieth them home to his den, never bearing above one in his mouth; and if it fortune that one of them fall off by the way, he likewise shaketh off all the residue, and walloweth upon them afresh, until they be all settled upon his back again. So, forth he goeth, making a noise like a cart-wheel; and if he have any young ones in his nest, they pull off his load wherewithal he is loaded, eating thereof what they please, and laying up the residue for the time to come."

THE "FROZEN-THAWED" APPLE

Toward the end of November, though some of the sound ones are yet more mellow and perhaps more edible, they have generally, like the leaves, lost their beauty, and are beginning to freeze. It is finger-cold, and prudent farmers get in their barreled apples, and bring you the apples and cider which they have engaged; for it is time to put them into the cellar. Perhaps a few on the ground show their red cheeks above the early snow, and occasionally some even preserve their color and soundness under the snow throughout the winter. But generally at the beginning of the winter they freeze hard, and soon, though undecayed, acquire the color of a baked apple.

Before the end of December, generally, they experience their first thawing. Those which a month ago were sour, crabbed, and quite unpalatable to the civilized taste, such at least as were frozen while sound, let a warmer sun come to thaw them, — for they are extremely sensitive to its rays, — are found to be filled with a rich, sweet cider, better than any bottled cider that I know of, and with which I am better acquainted than with wine. All apples are good in this state, and your jaws are the cider-press. Others, which have more substance, are a sweet and luscious food, — in my opinion of more worth than the pineapples which are imported from the West Indies. Those which lately even I tasted only to repent of it, — for I am semicivilized, — which the farmer willingly left on the tree, I am now glad to find have the property of hanging on like the leaves of the young oaks. It is a way to keep cider sweet without boiling. Let the frost come to freeze them first, solid as stones, and then the rain or a warm winter day to thaw them, and they will seem to have borrowed a flavor from heaven through the medium of the air in which they hang. Or perchance you find, when you get home, that those which rattled in your pocket have thawed, and the ice is turned to cider. But after the third or fourth freezing and thawing they will not be found so good.

What are the imported half-ripe fruits of the torrid south, to this fruit matured by the cold of the frigid north? These are those crabbed apples with which I cheated my companion, and kept a smooth face that I might tempt him to eat. Now we both greedily fill our pockets with them, — bending to drink the cup and save our lappets from the overflowing juice, — and grow more social with their wine. Was there one that hung so high and sheltered by the tangled branches that our sticks could not dislodge it?

It is a fruit never carried to market, that I am aware of, — quite distinct from the apple of the markets, as from dried apple and cider, — and it is not every winter that produces it in perfection.

The era of the Wild Apple will soon be past. It is a fruit which will probably become extinct in New England. You may still wander through old orchards of native fruit of great extent, which for the most part went to the cider-mill, now all gone to decay. I have heard of an orchard in a distant town, on the side of a hill, where the apples rolled down and lay four feet deep against a wall on the lower side, and this the owner cut down for fear they should be made into cider. Since the temperance reform and the general introduction of grafted fruit, no native apple trees, such as I see everywhere in deserted pastures, and where the woods have grown up around them, are set out. I fear that he who walks over these fields a century hence will not know the pleasure of knocking off wild apples. Ah, poor man, there are many pleasures which he will not know! Notwithstanding the prevalence of the Baldwin and the Porter, I doubt if so extensive orchards are set out today in my town as there were a century ago, when those vast straggling cider-orchards were planted, when men both ate and drank apples, when the pomace-heap was the only nursery, and trees cost nothing but the trouble of setting them out. Men could afford then to stick a tree by every wall-side and let it take its chance. I see nobody planting trees to-day in such out of the way places, along the lonely roads and lanes, and at the bottom of dells in the wood. Now that they have grafted trees, and pay a price for them, they collect them into a plat by their houses, and fence them in, — and the end of it all will be that we shall be compelled to look for our apples in a barrel.

This is "The word of the Lord that came to Joel the son of Pethuel.

"Hear this, ye old men, and give ear, all ye inhabitants of the land! Hath this been in your days, or even in the days of your fathers? . . .

"That which the palmerworm hath left hath the locust eaten; and that which the locust hath left hath the cankerworm eaten; and that which the cankerworm hath left hath the caterpillar eaten.

"Awake, ye drunkards, and weep; and howl, all ye drinkers of wine, because of the new wine; for it is cut off from your mouth.

"For a nation is come up upon my land, strong, and without number, whose teeth are the teeth of a lion, and he hath the cheek teeth of a great lion.

"He hath laid my vine waste, and barked my fig tree: he hath made it clean bare, and cast it away; the branches thereof are made white. . . .

"Be ye ashamed, O ye husbandmen; howl, O ye vinedressers. . . .

"The vine is dried up, and the fig tree languisheth; the pomegranate tree, the palm tree also, and the apple tree, even all the trees of the field, are withered: because joy is withered away from the sons of men."

LIFE WITHOUT PRINCIPLE

From the Moxham daguerreotype, 1856

LIFE WITHOUT PRINCIPLE

At a lyceum, not long since, I felt that the lecturer had chosen a theme too foreign to himself, and so failed to interest me as much as he might have done. He described things not in or near to his heart, but toward his extremities and superficies. There was, in this sense, no truly central or centralizing thought in the lecture. I would have had him deal with his privatest experience, as the poet does. The greatest compliment that was ever paid me was when one asked me what I *thought*, and attended to my answer. I am surprised, as well as delighted, when this happens, it is such a rare use he would make of me, as if he were acquainted with the tool. Commonly, if men want anything of me, it is only to know how many acres I make of their land, — since I am a surveyor, — or, at most, what trivial news I have burdened myself with. They never will go to law for my meat; they prefer the shell. A man once came a considerable distance to ask me to lecture on Slavery; but on conversing with him, I found that he and his clique expected seven eighths of the lecture to be theirs, and only one eighth mine; so I declined. I take it for granted, when I am invited to lecture anywhere, — for I have had a little experience in that business, — that there is a desire to hear what I *think* on some subject, though I may be the greatest fool in the country, — and not that I should say pleasant things merely, or such as the audience will assent to; and I resolve, accordingly, that I will give them a strong dose of myself. They have sent for me, and engaged to pay for me, and I am determined that they shall have me, though I bore them beyond all precedent.

So now I would say something similar to you, my readers. Since *you* are my readers, and I have not been much of a traveler, I will not talk about people a thousand miles off, but come as near home as I can. As the time is short, I will leave out all the flattery, and retain all the criticism.

Let us consider the way in which we spend our lives.

This world is a place of business. What an infinite bustle! I am awaked almost every night by the panting of the locomotive. It interrupts my dreams. There is no sabbath. It would be glorious to see mankind at leisure for once. It is nothing but work, work, work. I cannot easily buy a blank-book to write thoughts in; they are commonly ruled for dollars and cents. An Irishman, seeing me making a minute in the fields, took it for granted that I was calculating my wages. If a man was tossed out of a window when an infant, and so made a cripple for life, or scared out of his wits by the Indians, it is regretted chiefly because he was thus incapacitated for — business! I think that there is nothing, not even crime, more opposed to poetry, to philosophy, ay, to life itself, than this incessant business.

There is a coarse and boisterous money-making fellow in the outskirts of our town, who is going to build a bank-wall under the hill along the edge of his meadow. The powers have put this into his head to keep him out of mischief, and he wishes me to spend

three weeks digging there with him. The result will be
that he will perhaps get some more money to hoard,
and leave for his heirs to spend foolishly. If I do this,
most will commend me as an industrious and hard-
working man; but if I choose to devote myself to certain
labors which yield more real profit, though but little
money, they may be inclined to look on me as an idler.
Nevertheless, as I do not need the police of meaningless labor to regulate me, and do not see anything absolutely praiseworthy in this fellow's undertaking any more
than in many an enterprise of our own or foreign governments, however amusing it may be to him or them,
I prefer to finish my education at a different school.

If a man walk in the woods for love of them half of
each day, he is in danger of being regarded as a loafer;
but if he spends his whole day as a speculator, shearing
off those woods and making earth bald before her time,
he is esteemed an industrious and enterprising citizen.
As if a town had no interest in its forests but to cut
them down!

Most men would feel insulted if it were proposed to
employ them in throwing stones over a wall, and then
in throwing them back, merely that they might earn
their wages. But many are no more worthily employed
now. For instance: just after sunrise, one summer
morning, I noticed one of my neighbors walking beside
his team, which was slowly drawing a heavy hewn
stone swung under the axle, surrounded by an atmosphere of industry, — his day's work begun, — his brow
commenced to sweat, — a reproach to all sluggards and
idlers, — pausing abreast the shoulders of his oxen,

and half turning round with a flourish of his merciful whip, while they gained their length on him. And I thought, Such is the labor which the American Congress exists to protect, — honest, manly toil, — honest as the day is long, — that makes his bread taste sweet, and keeps society sweet, — which all men respect and have consecrated; one of the sacred band, doing the needful but irksome drudgery. Indeed, I felt a slight reproach, because I observed this from a window, and was not abroad and stirring about a similar business. The day went by, and at evening I passed the yard of another neighbor, who keeps many servants, and spends much money foolishly, while he adds nothing to the common stock, and there I saw the stone of the morning lying beside a whimsical structure intended to adorn this Lord Timothy Dexter's premises, and the dignity forthwith departed from the teamster's labor, in my eyes. In my opinion, the sun was made to light worthier toil than this. I may add that his employer has since run off, in debt to a good part of the town, and, after passing through Chancery, has settled somewhere else, there to become once more a patron of the arts.

The ways by which you may get money almost without exception lead downward. To have done anything by which you earned money *merely* is to have been truly idle or worse. If the laborer gets no more than the wages which his employer pays him, he is cheated, he cheats himself. If you would get money as a writer or lecturer, you must be popular, which is to go down perpendicularly. Those services which the community will most readily pay for, it is most disagreeable to render. You are paid for being something less than a man. The state does not commonly reward a genius any more wisely. Even the poet laureate would rather not have to celebrate the accidents of royalty. He must be bribed with a pipe of wine; and perhaps another poet is called away from his muse to gauge that very pipe. As for my own business, even that kind of surveying which I could do with most satisfaction my employers do not want. They would prefer that I should do my work coarsely and not too well, ay, not well enough. When I observe that there are different ways of surveying, my employer commonly asks which will give him the most land, not which is most correct. I once invented a rule for measuring cord-wood, and tried to introduce it in Boston; but the measurer there told me that the sellers did not wish to have their wood measured correctly, — that he was already too accurate for them, and therefore they commonly got their wood measured in Charlestown before crossing the bridge.

The aim of the laborer should be, not to get his living, to get " a good job," but to perform well a certain work; and, even in a pecuniary sense, it would be economy for a town to pay its laborers so well that they would not feel that they were working for low ends, as for a livelihood merely, but for scientific, or even moral ends. Do not hire a man who does your work for money, but him who does it for love of it.

It is remarkable that there are few men so well employed, so much to their minds, but that a little money or fame would commonly buy them off from their pre-

sent pursuit. I see advertisements for *active* young men,
as if activity were the whole of a young man's capital.
Yet I have been surprised when one has with confidence proposed to me, a grown man, to embark in
some enterprise of his, as if I had absolutely nothing
to do, my life having been a complete failure hitherto.
What a doubtful compliment this to pay me! As if he
had met me half-way across the ocean beating up against
the wind, but bound nowhere, and proposed to me to
go along with him! If I did, what do you think the
underwriters would say? No, no! I am not without
employment at this stage of the voyage. To tell the
truth, I saw an advertisement for able-bodied seamen,
when I was a boy, sauntering in my native port, and as
soon as I came of age I embarked.

The community has no bribe that will tempt a wise
man. You may raise money enough to tunnel a mountain, but you cannot raise money enough to hire a man
who is minding *his own* business. An efficient and valuable man does what he can, whether the community
pay him for it or not. The inefficient offer their inefficiency to the highest bidder, and are forever expecting
to be put into office. One would suppose that they were
rarely disappointed.

Perhaps I am more than usually jealous with respect
to my freedom. I feel that my connection with and
obligation to society are still very slight and transient.
Those slight labors which afford me a livelihood, and
by which it is allowed that I am to some extent ser-
viceable to my contemporaries, are as yet commonly a
pleasure to me, and I am not often reminded that they

are a necessity. So far I am successful. But I foresee
that if my wants should be much increased, the labor
required to supply them would become a drudgery. If
I should sell both my forenoons and afternoons to society, as most appear to do, I am sure that for me there
would be nothing left worth living for. I trust that I
shall never thus sell my birthright for a mess of pot-
tage. I wish to suggest that a man may be very industrious, and yet not spend his time well. There is no
more fatal blunderer than he who consumes the greater
part of his life getting his living. All great enterprises
are self-supporting. The poet, for instance, must sustain his body by his poetry, as a steam planing-mill
feeds its boilers with the shavings it makes. You must
get your living by loving. But as it is said of the merchants that ninety-seven in a hundred fail, so the life
of men generally, tried by this standard, is a failure,
and bankruptcy may be surely prophesied.

Merely to come into the world the heir of a fortune
is not to be born, but to be still-born, rather. To be
supported by the charity of friends, or a government
pension, — provided you continue to breathe, — by
whatever fine synonyms you describe these relations, is
to go into the almshouse. On Sundays the poor debtor
goes to church to take an account of stock, and finds,
of course, that his outgoes have been greater than his
income. In the Catholic Church, especially, they go
into chancery, make a clean confession, give up all,
and think to start again. Thus men will lie on their
backs, talking about the fall of man, and never make
an effort to get up.

As for the comparative demand which men make on life, it is an important difference between two, that the one is satisfied with a level success, that his marks can all be hit by point-blank shots, but the other, however low and unsuccessful his life may be, constantly elevates his aim, though at a very slight angle to the horizon. I should much rather be the last man, — though, as the Orientals say, " Greatness doth not approach him who is forever looking down; and all those who are looking high are growing poor."

It is remarkable that there is little or nothing to be remembered written on the subject of getting a living; how to make getting a living not merely honest and honorable, but altogether inviting and glorious; for if *getting* a living is not so, then living is not. One would think, from looking at literature, that this question had never disturbed a solitary individual's musings. Is it that men are too much disgusted with their experience to speak of it? The lesson of value which money teaches, which the Author of the Universe has taken so much pains to teach us, we are inclined to skip altogether. As for the means of living, it is wonderful how indifferent men of all classes are about it, even reformers, so called, — whether they inherit, or earn, or steal it. I think that Society has done nothing for us in this respect, or at least has undone what she has done. Cold and hunger seem more friendly to my nature than those methods which men have adopted and advise to ward them off.

The title *wise* is, for the most part, falsely applied. How can one be a wise man, if he does not know any better how to live than other men? — if he is only more cunning and intellectually subtle? Does Wisdom work in a tread-mill? or does she teach how to succeed *by her example?* Is there any such thing as wisdom not applied to life? Is she merely the miller who grinds the finest logic? It is pertinent to ask if Plato got his *living* in a better way or more successfully than his contemporaries, — or did he succumb to the difficulties of life like other men? Did he seem to prevail over some of them merely by indifference, or by assuming grand airs? or find it easier to live, because his aunt remembered him in her will? The ways in which most men get their living, that is, live, are mere makeshifts, and a shirking of the real business of life, — chiefly because they do not know, but partly because they do not mean, any better.

The rush to California, for instance, and the attitude, not merely of merchants, but of philosophers and prophets, so called, in relation to it, reflect the greatest disgrace on mankind. That so many are ready to live by luck, and so get the means of commanding the labor of others less lucky, without contributing any value to society! And that is called enterprise! I know of no more startling development of the immorality of trade, and all the common modes of getting a living. The philosophy and poetry and religion of such a mankind are not worth the dust of a puffball. The hog that gets his living by rooting, stirring up the soil so, would be ashamed of such company. If I could command the wealth of all the worlds by lifting my finger, I would not pay *such* a price for it. Even Mahomet knew that

God did not make this world in jest. It makes God to be a moneyed gentleman who scatters a handful of pennies in order to see mankind scramble for them. The world's raffle! A subsistence in the domains of Nature a thing to be raffled for! What a comment, what a satire, on our institutions! The conclusion will be, that mankind will hang itself upon a tree. And have all the precepts in all the Bibles taught men only this? and is the last and most admirable invention of the human race only an improved muck-rake? Is this the ground on which Orientals and Occidentals meet? Did God direct us so to get our living, digging where we never planted, — and He would, perchance, reward us with lumps of gold?

God gave the righteous man a certificate entitling him to food and raiment, but the unrighteous man found a facsimile of the same in God's coffers, and appropriated it, and obtained food and raiment like the former. It is one of the most extensive systems of counterfeiting that the world has seen. I did not know that mankind was suffering for want of gold. I have seen a little of it. I know that it is very malleable, but not so malleable as wit. A grain of gold will gild a great surface, but not so much as a grain of wisdom.

The gold-digger in the ravines of the mountains is as much a gambler as his fellow in the saloons of San Francisco. What difference does it make whether you shake dirt or shake dice? If you win, society is the loser. The gold-digger is the enemy of the honest laborer, whatever checks and compensations there may be. It is not enough to tell me that you worked hard to get your gold. So does the Devil work hard. The way of transgressors may be hard in many respects. The humblest observer who goes to the mines sees and says that gold-digging is of the character of a lottery; the gold thus obtained is not the same thing with the wages of honest toil. But, practically, he forgets what he has seen, for he has seen only the fact, not the principle, and goes into trade there, that is, buys a ticket in what commonly proves another lottery, where the fact is not so obvious.

After reading Howitt's account of the Australian gold-diggings one evening, I had in my mind's eye, all night, the numerous valleys, with their streams, all cut up with foul pits, from ten to one hundred feet deep, and half a dozen feet across, as close as they can be dug, and partly filled with water, — the locality to which men furiously rush to probe for their fortunes, — uncertain where they shall break ground, — not knowing but the gold is under their camp itself, — sometimes digging one hundred and sixty feet before they strike the vein, or then missing it by a foot, — turned into demons, and regardless of each others' rights, in their thirst for riches, — whole valleys, for thirty miles, suddenly honeycombed by the pits of the miners, so that even hundreds are drowned in them, — standing in water, and covered with mud and clay, they work night and day, dying of exposure and disease. Having read this, and partly forgotten it, I was thinking, accidentally, of my own unsatisfactory life, doing as others do; and with that vision of the diggings still before me, I asked myself why *I* might not be washing some gold daily, though it were only the finest particles, — why *I* might not sink a shaft down to the gold within me, and work that mine. *There* is a Ballarat, a Bendigo for you, — what though it were a sulky-gully? At any rate, I might pursue some path, however solitary and narrow and crooked, in which I could walk with love and reverence. Wherever a man separates from the multitude, and goes his own way in this mood, there indeed is a fork in the road, though ordinary travelers may see only a gap in the paling. His solitary path across lots will turn out the *higher way* of the two.

Men rush to California and Australia as if the true gold were to be found in that direction; but that is to go to the very opposite extreme to where it lies. They go prospecting farther and farther away from the true lead, and are most unfortunate when they think themselves most successful. Is not our *native* soil auriferous? Does not a stream from the golden mountains flow through our native valley? and has not this for more than geologic ages been bringing down the shining particles and forming the nuggets for us? Yet, strange to tell, if a digger steal away, prospecting for this true gold, into the unexplored solitudes around us, there is no danger that any will dog his steps, and endeavor to supplant him. He may claim and undermine the whole valley even, both the cultivated and the uncultivated portions, his whole life long in peace, for no one will ever dispute his claim. They will not mind his cradles or his toms. He is not confined to a claim twelve feet square, as at Ballarat, but may mine anywhere, and wash the whole wide world in his tom.

Howitt says of the man who found the great nugget which weighed twenty-eight pounds, at the Bendigo diggings in Australia: "He soon began to drink; got a horse, and rode all about, generally at full gallop, and, when he met people, called out to inquire if they knew who he was, and then kindly informed them that he was 'the bloody wretch that had found the nugget.' At last he rode full speed against a tree, and nearly knocked his brains out." I think, however, there was no danger of that, for he had already knocked his brains out against the nugget. Howitt adds, "He is a hopelessly ruined man." But he is a type of the class. They are all fast men. Hear some of the names of the places where they dig: "Jackass Flat," — "Sheep's-Head Gully," — "Murderer's Bar," etc. Is there no satire in these names? Let them carry their ill-gotten wealth where they will, I am thinking it will still be "Jackass Flat," if not "Murderer's Bar," where they live.

The last resource of our energy has been the robbing of graveyards on the Isthmus of Darien, an enterprise which appears to be but in its infancy; for, according to late accounts, an act has passed its second reading in the legislature of New Granada, regulating this kind of mining; and a correspondent of the "Tribune" writes: "In the dry season, when the weather will permit of the country being properly prospected, no doubt other rich *guacas* [that is, graveyards] will be found." To emigrants he says: "Do not come before December; take the Isthmus route in preference to the Boca del Toro one; bring no useless baggage, and do not cumber yourself with a tent; but a good pair of blankets will be necessary; a pick, shovel, and axe of good material will be almost all that is required:" advice which might have been taken from the " Burker's Guide." And he concludes with this line in Italics and small capitals: " *If you are doing well at home*, STAY THERE," which may fairly be interpreted to mean, " If you are getting a good living by robbing graveyards at home, stay there."

But why go to California for a text? She is the child of New England, bred at her own school and church.

It is remarkable that among all the preachers there are so few moral teachers. The prophets are employed in excusing the ways of men. Most reverend seniors, the *illuminati* of the age, tell me, with a gracious, reminiscent smile, betwixt an aspiration and a shudder, not to be too tender about these things, — to lump all that, that is, make a lump of gold of it. The highest advice I have heard on these subjects was groveling. The burden of it was, — It is not worth your while to undertake to reform the world in this particular. Do not ask how your bread is buttered; it will make you sick, if you do, — and the like. A man had better starve at once than lose his innocence in the process of getting his bread. If within the sophisticated man there is not an unsophisticated one, then he is but one of the devil's angels. As we grow old, we live more coarsely, we relax a little in our disciplines, and, to some extent, cease to obey our finest instincts. But we should be fastidious to the extreme of sanity, disregarding the gibes of those who are more unfortunate than ourselves.

In our science and philosophy, even, there is commonly no true and absolute account of things. The spirit of sect and bigotry has planted its hoof amid the stars. You have only to discuss the problem, whether the stars are inhabited or not, in order to discover it. Why must we daub the heavens as well as the earth? It was an unfortunate discovery that Dr. Kane was a Mason, and that Sir John Franklin was another. But it was a more cruel suggestion that possibly that was the reason why the former went in search of the latter. There is not a popular magazine in this country that would dare to print a child's thought on important subjects without comment. It must be submitted to the D.D.'s. I would it were the chickadee-dees.

You come from attending the funeral of mankind to attend to a natural phenomenon. A little thought is sexton to all the world.

I hardly know an *intellectual* man, even, who is so broad and truly liberal that you can think aloud in his society. Most with whom you endeavor to talk soon come to a stand against some institution in which they appear to hold stock, — that is, some particular, not universal, way of viewing things. They will continually thrust their own low roof, with its narrow skylight, between you and the sky, when it is the unobstructed heavens you would view. Get out of the way with your cobwebs; wash your windows, I say! In some lyceums they tell me that they have voted to exclude the subject of religion. But how do I know what their religion is, and when I am near to or far from it? I have walked into such an arena and done my best to make a clean breast of what religion I have experienced, and the audience never suspected what I was about. The lecture was as harmless as moonshine to them. Whereas, if I had read to them the biography of the greatest scamps in history, they might have thought that I had written the lives of the deacons of their church. Ordinarily, the inquiry is, Where did you come from? or, Where are you going? That was a more pertinent question which I overheard one of my auditors put to another once, — "What does he lecture for?" It made me quake in my shoes.

To speak impartially, the best men that I know are not serene, a world in themselves. For the most part, they dwell in forms, and flatter and study effect only more finely than the rest. We select granite for the underpinning of our houses and barns; we build fences of stone; but we do not ourselves rest on an underpinning of granitic truth, the lowest primitive rock. Our sills are rotten. What stuff is the man made of who is not coexistent in our thought with the purest and subtilest truth? I often accuse my finest acquaintances of an immense frivolity; for, while there are manners and compliments we do not meet, we do not teach one another the lessons of honesty and sincerity that the brutes do, or of steadiness and solidity that the rocks do. The fault is commonly mutual, however; for we do not habitually demand any more of each other.

That excitement about Kossuth, consider how characteristic, but superficial, it was! — only another kind of politics or dancing. Men were making speeches to him all over the country, but each expressed only the thought, or the want of thought, of the multitude. No man stood on truth. They were merely banded together, as usual one leaning on another, and all together on nothing; as the Hindoos made the world rest on an elephant, the elephant on a tortoise, and the tortoise on a serpent, and had nothing to put under the serpent. For all fruit of that stir we have the Kossuth hat.

Just so hollow and ineffectual, for the most part, is our ordinary conversation. Surface meets surface. When our life ceases to be inward and private, conversation degenerates into mere gossip. We rarely meet a man who can tell us any news which he has not read in a newspaper, or been told by his neighbor; and, for the most part, the only difference between us and our fellow is that he has seen the newspaper, or been out to tea, and we have not. In proportion as our inward life fails, we go more constantly and desperately to the post-office. You may depend on it, that the poor fellow who walks away with the greatest number of letters, proud of his extensive correspondence, has not heard from himself this long while.

I do not know but it is too much to read one newspaper a week. I have tried it recently, and for so long it seems to me that I have not dwelt in my native region. The sun, the clouds, the snow, the trees say not so much to me. You cannot serve two masters. It requires more than a day's devotion to know and to possess the wealth of a day.

We may well be ashamed to tell what things we have read or heard in our day. I do not know why my news should be so trivial, — considering what one's dreams and expectations are, why the developments should be so paltry. The news we hear, for the most part, is not news to our genius. It is the stalest repetition. You are often tempted to ask why such stress is laid on a particular experience which you have had, — that, after twenty-five years, you should meet Hobbins, Registrar of Deeds, again on the sidewalk. Have you not budged an inch, then? Such is the daily news. Its facts appear to float in the atmosphere, insignificant as the sporules of fungi, and impinge on some neglected *thallus*, or surface of our minds, which affords a basis for them, and hence a parasitic growth. We should wash ourselves clean of such news. Of what consequence, though our planet explode, if there is no character involved in the explosion? In health we have not the least curiosity about such events. We do not live for idle amusement. I would not run round a corner to see the world blow up.

All summer, and far into the autumn, perchance, you unconsciously went by the newspapers and the news, and now you find it was because the morning and the evening were full of news to you. Your walks were full of incidents. You attended, not to the affairs of Europe, but to your own affairs in Massachusetts fields. If you chance to live and move and have your being in that thin stratum in which the events that make the news transpire, — thinner than the paper on which it is printed, — then these things will fill the world for you; but if you soar above or dive below that plane, you cannot remember nor be reminded of them. Really to see the sun rise or go down every day, so to relate our-

selves to a universal fact, would preserve us sane forever. Nations! What are nations? Tartars, and Huns,
and Chinamen! Like insects, they swarm. The histo-
rian strives in vain to make them memorable. It is for
want of a man that there are so many men. It is individuals that populate the world. Any man thinking
may say with the Spirit of Lodin, —

> "I look down from my height on nations,
> And they become ashes before me ; —
> Calm is my dwelling in the clouds ;
> Pleasant are the great fields of my rest."

Pray, let us live without being drawn by dogs,
Esquimaux-fashion, tearing over hill and dale, and
biting each other's ears.

Not without a slight shudder at the danger, I often
perceive how near I had come to admitting into my
mind the details of some trivial affair, — the news of
the street; and I am astonished to observe how willing
men are to lumber their minds with such rubbish, — to
permit idle rumors and incidents of the most insignificant kind to intrude on ground which should be sacred
to thought. Shall the mind be a public arena, where
the affairs of the street and the gossip of the tea-table
chiefly are discussed ? Or shall it be a quarter of heaven
itself, — an hypæthral temple, consecrated to the service
of the gods ? I find it so difficult to dispose of the few
facts which to me are significant, that I hesitate to
burden my attention with those which are insignificant,
which only a divine mind could illustrate. Such is, for
the most part, the news in newspapers and conversation. It is important to preserve the mind's chastity in

this respect. Think of admitting the details of a single case of the criminal court into our thoughts, to stalk profanely through their very *sanctum sanctorum* for an hour, ay, for many hours! to make a very barroom of the mind's inmost apartment, as if for so long the dust of the street had occupied us, — the very street itself, with all its travel, its bustle, and filth, had passed through our thoughts' shrine! Would it not be an intellectual and moral suicide? When I have been compelled to sit spectator and auditor in a court-room for some hours, and have seen my neighbors, who were not compelled, stealing in from time to time, and tiptoeing about with washed hands and faces, it has appeared to my mind's eye, that, when they took off their hats, their ears suddenly expanded into vast hoppers for sound, between which even their narrow heads were crowded. Like the vanes of windmills, they caught the broad but shallow stream of sound, which, after a few titillating gyrations in their coggy brains, passed out the other side. I wondered if, when they got home, they were as careful to wash their ears as before their hands and faces. It has seemed to me, at such a time, that the auditors and the witnesses, the jury and the counsel, the judge and the criminal at the bar, — if I may presume him guilty before he is convicted, — were all equally criminal, and a thunderbolt might be expected to descend and consume them all together.

By all kinds of traps and signboards, threatening the extreme penalty of the divine law, exclude such trespassers from the only ground which can be sacred to you. It is so hard to forget what it is worse than use-

less to remember! If I am to be a thoroughfare, I prefer
that it be of the mountain brooks, the Parnassian
streams, and not the town sewers. There is inspiration,
that gossip which comes to the ear of the attentive mind
from the courts of heaven. There is the profane and
stale revelation of the barroom and the police court.
The same ear is fitted to receive both communications.
Only the character of the hearer determines to which
it shall be open, and to which closed. I believe that
the mind can be permanently profaned by the habit of
attending to trivial things, so that all our thoughts shall
be tinged with triviality. Our very intellect shall be
macadamized, as it were, — its foundation broken into
fragments for the wheels of travel to roll over; and if
you would know what will make the most durable
pavement, surpassing rolled stones, spruce blocks, and
asphaltum, you have only to look into some of our
minds which have been subjected to this treatment so
long.

If we have thus desecrated ourselves, — as who has
not? — the remedy will be by wariness and devotion to
reconsecrate ourselves, and make once more a fane of
the mind. We should treat our minds, that is, ourselves,
as innocent and ingenuous children, whose guardians
we are, and be careful what objects and what subjects
we thrust on their attention. Read not the Times.
Read the Eternities. Conventionalities are at length as
bad as impurities. Even the facts of science may dust
the mind by their dryness, unless they are in a sense
effaced each morning, or rather rendered fertile by the
dews of fresh and living truth. Knowledge does not

come to us by details, but in flashes of light from
heaven. Yes, every thought that passes through the
mind helps to wear and tear it, and to deepen the ruts,
which, as in the streets of Pompeii, evince how much it
has been used. How many things there are concerning
which we might well deliberate whether we had better
know them, — had better let their peddling-carts be
driven, even at the slowest trot or walk, over that
bridge of glorious span by which we trust to pass at
last from the farthest brink of time to the nearest
shore of eternity! Have we no culture, no refinement,
— but skill only to live coarsely and serve the Devil? —
to acquire a little worldly wealth, or fame, or liberty,
and make a false show with it, as if we were all husk
and shell, with no tender and living kernel to us? Shall
our institutions be like those chestnut burs which contain abortive nuts, perfect only to prick the fingers?

America is said to be the arena on which the battle
of freedom is to be fought; but surely it cannot be freedom in a merely political sense that is meant. Even if
we grant that the American has freed himself from a
political tyrant, he is still the slave of an economical and
moral tyrant. Now that the republic — the *res-publica*
— has been settled, it is time to look after the *res-
privata*, — the private state, — to see, as the Roman
senate charged its consuls, "*ne quid res*-PRIVATA *detri-
menti caperet*," that the *private* state receive no detriment.

Do we call this the land of the free? What is it to be
free from King George and continue the slaves of King
Prejudice? What is it to be born free and not to live

free? What is the value of any political freedom, but as a means to moral freedom? Is it a freedom to be slaves, or a freedom to be free, of which we boast? We are a nation of politicians, concerned about the outmost defenses only of freedom. It is our children's children who may perchance be really free. We tax ourselves unjustly. There is a part of us which is not represented. It is taxation without representation. We quarter troops, we quarter fools and cattle of all sorts upon ourselves. We quarter our gross bodies on our poor souls, till the former eat up all the latter's substance.

With respect to a true culture and manhood, we are essentially provincial still, not metropolitan,—mere Jonathans. We are provincial, because we do not find at home our standards; because we do not worship truth, but the reflection of truth; because we are warped and narrowed by an exclusive devotion to trade and commerce and manufactures and agriculture and the like, which are but means, and not the end.

So is the English Parliament provincial. Mere country bumpkins, they betray themselves, when any more important question arises for them to settle, the Irish question, for instance,—the English question why did I not say? Their natures are subdued to what they work in. Their "good breeding" respects only secondary objects. The finest manners in the world are awkwardness and fatuity when contrasted with a finer intelligence. They appear but as the fashions of past days,—mere courtliness, knee-buckles and small-clothes, out of date. It is the vice, but not the excellence of manners, that they are continually being deserted by the character; they are cast-off clothes or shells, claiming the respect which belonged to the living creature. You are presented with the shells instead of the meat, and it is no excuse generally, that, in the case of some fishes, the shells are of more worth than the meat. The man who thrusts his manners upon me does as if he were to insist on introducing me to his cabinet of curiosities, when I wished to see himself. It was not in this sense that the poet Decker called Christ "the first true gentleman that ever breathed." I repeat that in this sense the most splendid court in Christendom is provincial, having authority to consult about Transalpine interests only, and not the affairs of Rome. A prætor or proconsul would suffice to settle the questions which absorb the attention of the English Parliament and the American Congress.

Government and legislation! these I thought were respectable professions. We have heard of heaven-born Numas, Lycurguses, and Solons, in the history of the world, whose *names* at least may stand for ideal legislators; but think of legislating to *regulate* the breeding of slaves, or the exportation of tobacco! What have divine legislators to do with the exportation or the importation of tobacco? what humane ones with the breeding of slaves? Suppose you were to submit the question to any son of God, — and has He no children in the Nineteenth Century? is it a family which is extinct? — in what condition would you get it again? What shall a State like Virginia say for itself at the last day, in which these have been the principal, the staple productions? What ground is there for patriotism in such a State? I derive my facts from statistical tables which the States themselves have published.

A commerce that whitens every sea in quest of nuts and raisins, and makes slaves of its sailors for this purpose! I saw, the other day, a vessel which had been wrecked, and many lives lost, and her cargo of rags, juniper berries, and bitter almonds were strewn along the shore. It seemed hardly worth the while to tempt the dangers of the sea between Leghorn and New York for the sake of a cargo of juniper berries and bitter almonds. America sending to the Old World for her bitters! Is not the sea-brine, is not shipwreck, bitter enough to make the cup of life go down here? Yet such, to a great extent, is our boasted commerce; and there are those who style themselves statesmen and philosophers who are so blind as to think that progress and civilization depend on precisely this kind of interchange and activity, — the activity of flies about a molasses-hogshead. Very well, observes one, if men were oysters. And very well, answer I, if men were mosquitoes.

Lieutenant Herndon, whom our government sent to explore the Amazon, and, it is said, to extend the area of slavery, observed that there was wanting there " an industrious and active population, who know what the comforts of life are, and who have artificial wants to draw out the great resources of the country." But what are the " artificial wants " to be encouraged? Not the love of luxuries, like the tobacco and slaves of, I believe, his native Virginia, nor the ice and granite and other material wealth of our native New England; nor are " the great resources of a country " that fertility or barrenness of soil which produces these. The chief want, in every State that I have been into, was a high and earnest purpose in its inhabitants. This alone draws out " the great resources " of Nature, and at last taxes her beyond her resources; for man naturally dies out of her. When we want culture more than potatoes, and illumination more than sugar-plums, then the great resources of a world are taxed and drawn out, and the result, or staple production, is, not slaves, nor operatives, but men, — those rare fruits called heroes, saints, poets, philosophers, and redeemers.

In short, as a snow-drift is formed where there is a lull in the wind, so, one would say, where there is a lull of truth, an institution springs up. But the truth blows right on over it, nevertheless, and at length blows it down.

What is called politics is comparatively something so superficial and inhuman, that practically I have never fairly recognized that it concerns me at all. The newspapers, I perceive, devote some of their columns specially to politics or government without charge; and this, one would say, is all that saves it; but as I love literature and to some extent the truth also, I never read those columns at any rate. I do not wish to blunt my sense of right so much. I have not got to answer for having read a single President's Message. A strange age of the world this, when empires, kingdoms, and republics come a-begging to a private man's door, and utter their complaints at his elbow! I cannot take up a

newspaper but I find that some wretched government
or other, hard pushed and on its last legs, is interced-
ing with me, the reader, to vote for it, — more impor-
tunate than an Italian beggar; and if I have a mind
to look at its certificate, made, perchance, by some
benevolent merchant's clerk, or the skipper that brought
it over, for it cannot speak a word of English itself, I
shall probably read of the eruption of some Vesuvius,
or the overflowing of some Po, true or forged, which
brought it into this condition. I do not hesitate, in such
a case, to suggest work, or the almshouse; or why not
keep its castle in silence, as I do commonly? The
poor President, what with preserving his popularity and
doing his duty, is completely bewildered. The newspapers are the ruling power. Any other government
is reduced to a few marines at Fort Independence. If
a man neglects to read the Daily Times, government
will go down on its knees to him, for this is the only
treason in these days.

Those things which now most engage the attention
of men, as politics and the daily routine, are, it is true,
vital functions of human society, but should be unconsciously performed, like the corresponding functions of
the physical body. They are *infra*-human, a kind of
vegetation. I sometimes awake to a half-consciousness
of them going on about me, as a man may become
conscious of some of the processes of digestion in a
morbid state, and so have the dyspepsia, as it is called.
It is as if a thinker submitted himself to be rasped by
the great gizzard of creation. Politics is, as it were, the
gizzard of society, full of grit and gravel, and the two

political parties are its two opposite halves, — sometimes split into quarters, it may be, which grind on each other. Not only individuals, but states, have thus a confirmed dyspepsia, which expresses itself, you can imagine by what sort of eloquence. Thus our life is not altogether a forgetting, but also, alas! to a great extent, a remembering, of that which we should never have been conscious of, certainly not in our waking hours. Why should we not meet, not always as dyspeptics, to tell our bad dreams, but sometimes as *eu*peptics, to congratulate each other on the ever-glorious morning? I do not make an exorbitant demand, surely.

AUTUMNAL TINTS

November woods

AUTUMNAL TINTS

EUROPEANS coming to America are surprised by the brilliancy of our autumnal foliage. There is no account of such a phenomenon in English poetry, because the trees acquire but few bright colors there. The most that Thomson says on this subject in his "Autumn" is contained in the lines, —

> "But see the fading many-colored woods
> Shade deepening over shade, the country round
> Imbrown; a crowded umbrage, dusk and dun,
> Of every hue, from wan declining green
> To sooty dark;"

and in the line in which he speaks of

> "Autumn beaming o'er the yellow woods."

The autumnal change of our woods has not made a deep impression on our own literature yet. October has hardly tinged our poetry.

A great many, who have spent their lives in cities, and have never chanced to come into the country at this season, have never seen this, the flower, or rather the ripe fruit, of the year. I remember riding with one such citizen, who, though a fortnight too late for the most brilliant tints, was taken by surprise, and would not believe that there had been any brighter. He had never heard of this phenomenon before. Not only many in our towns have never witnessed it, but it is scarcely remembered by the majority from year to year.

Most appear to confound changed leaves with withered ones, as if they were to confound ripe apples with rotten ones. I think that the change to some higher color in a leaf is an evidence that it has arrived at a late and perfect maturity, answering to the maturity of fruits. It is generally the lowest and oldest leaves which change first. But as the perfect-winged and usually bright-colored insect is short-lived, so the leaves ripen but to fall.

Generally, every fruit, on ripening, and just before it falls, when it commences a more independent and individual existence, requiring less nourishment from any source, and that not so much from the earth through its stem as from the sun and air, acquires a bright tint. So do leaves. The physiologist says it is "due to an increased absorption of oxygen." That is the scientific account of the matter, — only a reassertion of the fact. But I am more interested in the rosy cheek than I am to know what particular diet the maiden fed on. The very forest and herbage, the pellicle of the earth, must acquire a bright color, an evidence of its ripeness, — as if the globe itself were a fruit on its stem, with ever a cheek toward the sun.

Flowers are but colored leaves, fruits but ripe ones. The edible part of most fruits is, as the physiologist says, "the parenchyma or fleshy tissue of the leaf," of which they are formed.

Our appetites have commonly confined our views of ripeness and its phenomena, color, mellowness, and perfectness, to the fruits which we eat, and we are wont to forget that an immense harvest which we do not eat, hardly use at all, is annually ripened by Nature. At our annual cattle-shows and horticultural exhibitions, we make, as we think, a great show of fair fruits, destined, however, to a rather ignoble end, fruits not valued for their beauty chiefly. But round about and within our towns there is annually another show of fruits, on an infinitely grander scale, fruits which address our taste for beauty alone.

October is the month for painted leaves. Their rich glow now flashes round the world. As fruits and leaves and the day itself acquire a bright tint just before they fall, so the year near its setting. October is its sunset sky; November the later twilight.

I formerly thought that it would be worth the while to get a specimen leaf from each changing tree, shrub, and herbaceous plant, when it had acquired its brightest characteristic color, in its transition from the green to the brown state, outline it, and copy its color exactly, with paint, in a book, which should be entitled "October, or Autumnal Tints," — beginning with the earliest reddening woodbine and the lake of radical leaves, and coming down through the maples, hickories, and sumachs, and many beautifully freckled leaves less generally known, to the latest oaks and aspens. What a memento such a book would be! You would need only to turn over its leaves to take a ramble through the autumn woods whenever you pleased. Or if I could preserve the leaves themselves, unfaded, it would be better still. I have made but little progress toward such a book, but I have endeavored, instead, to describe all these bright tints in the order in which they present themselves. The following are some extracts from my notes.

THE PURPLE GRASSES

By the twentieth of August, everywhere in woods and swamps we are reminded of the fall, both by the richly spotted sarsaparilla leaves and brakes, and the withering and blackened skunk-cabbage and hellebore, and, by the riverside, the already blackening pontederia.

The purple grass (*Eragrostis pectinacea*) is now in the height of its beauty. I remember still when I first noticed this grass particularly. Standing on a hillside near our river, I saw, thirty or forty rods off, a stripe of purple half a dozen rods long, under the edge of a wood, where the ground sloped toward a meadow. It was as high-colored and interesting, though not quite so bright, as the patches of rhexia, being a darker purple, like a berry's stain laid on close and thick. On going to and examining it, I found it to be a kind of grass in bloom, hardly a foot high, with but few green blades, and a fine spreading panicle of purple flowers, a shallow, purplish mist trembling around me. Close at hand it appeared but a dull purple, and made little impression on the eye; it was even difficult to detect; and if you plucked a single plant, you were surprised to find how thin it was, and how little color it had. But viewed at a distance in a favorable light, it was of a fine lively purple, flower-like, enriching the earth. Such puny causes combine to produce these decided effects. I was the more surprised and charmed because grass is commonly of a sober and humble color.

With its beautiful purple blush it reminds me, and

supplies the place, of the rhexia, which is now leaving off, and it is one of the most interesting phenomena of August. The finest patches of it grow on waste strips or selvages of land at the base of dry hills, just above the edge of the meadows, where the greedy mower does not deign to swing his scythe; for this is a thin and poor grass, beneath his notice. Or, it may be, because it is so beautiful he does not know that it exists; for the same eye does not see this and timothy. He carefully gets the meadow-hay and the more nutritious grasses which grow next to that, but he leaves this fine purple mist for the walker's harvest, — fodder for his fancy stock. Higher up the hill, perchance, grow also blackberries, John's-wort, and neglected, withered, and wiry June-grass. How fortunate that it grows in such places, and not in the midst of the rank grasses which are annually cut! Nature thus keeps use and beauty distinct. I know many such localities, where it does not fail to present itself annually, and paint the earth with its blush. It grows on the gentle slopes, either in a continuous patch or in scattered and rounded tufts a foot in diameter, and it lasts till it is killed by the first smart frosts.

In most plants the corolla or calyx is the part which attains the highest color, and is the most attractive; in many it is the seed-vessel or fruit; in others, as the red maple, the leaves; and in others still it is the very culm itself which is the principal flower or blooming part.

The last is especially the case with the poke or garget (*Phytolacca decandra*). Some which stand under our cliffs quite dazzle me with their purple stems now and early in September. They are as interesting to me as most flowers, and one of the most important fruits of our autumn. Every part is flower (or fruit), such is its superfluity of color, — stem, branch, peduncle, pedicel, petiole, and even the at length yellowish, purple-veined leaves. Its cylindrical racemes of berries of various hues, from green to dark purple, six or seven inches long, are gracefully drooping on all sides, offering repasts to the birds; and even the sepals from which the birds have picked the berries are a brilliant lake red, with crimson flame-like reflections, equal to anything of the kind, — all on fire with ripeness. Hence the *lacca*, from *lac*, lake. There are at the same time flower-buds, flowers, green berries, dark-purple or ripe ones, and these flower-like sepals, all on the same plant.

We love to see any redness in the vegetation of the temperate zone. It is the color of colors. This plant speaks to our blood. It asks a bright sun on it to make it show to best advantage, and it must be seen at this season of the year. On warm hillsides its stems are ripe by the twenty-third of August. At that date I walked through a beautiful grove of them, six or seven feet high, on the side of one of our cliffs, where they ripen early. Quite to the ground they were a deep, brilliant purple, with a bloom contrasting with the still clear green leaves. It appears a rare triumph of Nature to have produced and perfected such a plant, as if this were enough for a summer. What a perfect maturity it arrives at! It is the emblem of a successful life concluded by a death not premature, which is an ornament

to Nature. What if we were to mature as perfectly, root
and branch, glowing in the midst of our decay, like the
poke! I confess that it excites me to behold them. I cut
one for a cane, for I would fain handle and lean on it.
I love to press the berries between my fingers, and see
their juice staining my hand. To walk amid these upright, branching casks of purple wine, which retain and
diffuse a sunset glow, tasting each one with your eye,
instead of counting the pipes on a London dock, what
a privilege! For Nature's vintage is not confined to
the vine. Our poets have sung of wine, the product of
a foreign plant which commonly they never saw, as if
our own plants had no juice in them more than the
singers. Indeed, this has been called by some the American grape, and, though a native of America, its juices
are used in some foreign countries to improve the color
of the wine; so that the poetaster may be celebrating
the virtues of the poke without knowing it. Here are
berries enough to paint afresh the western sky, and
play the bacchanal with, if you will. And what flutes
its ensanguined stems would make, to be used in such a
dance! It is truly a royal plant. I could spend the evening of the year musing amid the poke stems. And perchance amid these groves might arise at last a new school
of philosophy or poetry. It lasts all through September.

At the same time with this, or near the end of August,
a to me very interesting genus of grasses, andropogons,
or beard-grasses, is in its prime: *Andropogon furcatus*,
forked beard-grass, or call it purple-fingered grass;
Andropogon scoparius, purple wood-grass; and *Andropogon* (now called *Sorghum*) *nutans*, Indian-grass.

The first is a very tall and slender-culmed grass, three to seven feet high, with four or five purple finger-like spikes raying upward from the top. The second is also quite slender, growing in tufts two feet high by one wide, with culms often somewhat curving, which, as the spikes go out of bloom, have a whitish, fuzzy look. These two are prevailing grasses at this season on dry and sandy fields and hillsides. The culms of both, not to mention their pretty flowers, reflect a purple tinge, and help to declare the ripeness of the year. Perhaps I have the more sympathy with them because they are despised by the farmer, and occupy sterile and neglected soil. They are high-colored, like ripe grapes, and express a maturity which the spring did not suggest. Only the August sun could have thus burnished these culms and leaves. The farmer has long since done his upland haying, and he will not condescend to bring his scythe to where these slender wild grasses have at length flowered thinly; you often see spaces of bare sand amid them. But I walk encouraged between the tufts of purple wood-grass over the sandy fields, and along the edge of the shrub oaks, glad to recognize these simple contemporaries. With thoughts cutting a broad swathe I "get" them, with horse-raking thoughts I gather them into windrows. The fine-eared poet may hear the whetting of my scythe. These two were almost the first grasses that I learned to distinguish, for I had not known by how many friends I was surrounded; I had seen them simply as grasses standing. The purple of their culms also excites me like that of the poke-weed stems.

Think what refuge there is for one, before August is over, from college commencements and society that isolates! I can skulk amid the tufts of purple wood-grass on the borders of the "Great Fields." Wherever I walk these afternoons, the purple-fingered grass also stands like a guide-board, and points my thoughts to more poetic paths than they have lately traveled.

A man shall perhaps rush by and trample down plants as high as his head, and cannot be said to know that they exist, though he may have cut many tons of them, littered his stables with them, and fed them to his cattle for years. Yet, if he ever favorably attends to them, he may be overcome by their beauty. Each humblest plant, or weed, as we call it, stands there to express some thought or mood of ours; and yet how long it stands in vain! I had walked over those Great Fields so many Augusts, and never yet distinctly recognized these purple companions that I had there. I had brushed against them and trodden on them, forsooth; and now, at last, they, as it were, rose up and blessed me. Beauty and true wealth are always thus cheap and despised. Heaven might be defined as the place which men avoid. Who can doubt that these grasses, which the farmer says are of no account to him, find some compensation in your appreciation of them? I may say that I never saw them before; though, when I came to look them face to face, there did come down to me a purple gleam from previous years; and now, wherever I go, I see hardly anything else. It is the reign and presidency of the andropogons.

Almost the very sands confess the ripening influence

of the August sun, and methinks, together with the slender grasses waving over them, reflect a purple tinge. The impurpled sands! Such is the consequence of all this sunshine absorbed into the pores of plants and of the earth. All sap or blood is now wine-colored. At last we have not only the purple sea, but the purple land.

The chestnut beard-grass, Indian-grass, or wood-grass, growing here and there in waste places, but more rare than the former (from two to four or five feet high), is still handsomer and of more vivid colors than its congeners, and might well have caught the Indian's eye. It has a long, narrow, one-sided, and slightly nodding panicle of bright purple and yellow flowers, like a banner raised above its reedy leaves. These bright standards are now advanced on the distant hillsides, not in large armies, but in scattered troops or single file, like the red men. They stand thus fair and bright, representative of the race which they are named after, but for the most part unobserved as they. The expression of this grass haunted me for a week, after I first passed and noticed it, like the glance of an eye. It stands like an Indian chief taking a last look at his favorite hunting-grounds.

THE RED MAPLE

By the twenty-fifth of September, the red maples generally are beginning to be ripe. Some large ones have been conspicuously changing for a week, and some single trees are now very brilliant. I notice a small one, half a mile off across a meadow, against the green woodside there, a far brighter red than the blos-

soms of any tree in summer, and more conspicuous.
I have observed this tree for several autumns invariably
changing earlier than its fellows, just as one tree ripens
its fruit earlier than another. It might serve to mark
the season, perhaps. I should be sorry if it were cut
down. I know of two or three such trees in different
parts of our town, which might, perhaps, be propagated
from, as early ripeners or September trees, and their
seed be advertised in the market, as well as that of
radishes, if we cared as much about them.

At present these burning bushes stand chiefly along
the edge of the meadows, or I distinguish them afar on
the hillsides here and there. Sometimes you will see
many small ones in a swamp turned quite crimson when
all other trees around are still perfectly green, and the
former appear so much the brighter for it. They take
you by surprise, as you are going by on one side, across
the fields, thus early in the season, as if it were some
gay encampment of the red men, or other foresters, of
whose arrival you had not heard.

Some single trees, wholly bright scarlet, seen against
others of their kind still freshly green, or against evergreens, are more memorable than whole groves will be
by and by. How beautiful, when a whole tree is like
one great scarlet fruit full of ripe juices, every leaf,
from lowest limb to topmost spire, all aglow, especially
if you look toward the sun! What more remarkable
object can there be in the landscape? Visible for miles,
too fair to be believed. If such a phenomenon occurred
but once, it would be handed down by tradition to
posterity, and get into the mythology at last.

The whole tree thus ripening in advance of its fellows attains a singular preëminence, and sometimes maintains it for a week or two. I am thrilled at the sight of it, bearing aloft its scarlet standard for the regiment of green-clad foresters around, and I go half a mile out of my way to examine it. A single tree becomes thus the crowning beauty of some meadowy vale, and the expression of the whole surrounding forest is at once more spirited for it.

A small red maple has grown, perchance, far away at the head of some retired valley, a mile from any road, unobserved. It has faithfully discharged the duties of a maple there, all winter and summer, neglected none of its economies, but added to its stature in the virtue which belongs to a maple, by a steady growth for so many months, never having gone gadding abroad, and is nearer heaven than it was in the spring. It has faithfully husbanded its sap, and afforded a shelter to the wandering bird, has long since ripened its seeds and committed them to the winds, and has the satisfaction of knowing, perhaps, that a thousand little well-behaved maples are already settled in life somewhere. It deserves well of Mapledom. Its leaves have been asking it from time to time, in a whisper, "When shall we redden?" And now, in this month of September, this month of traveling, when men are hastening to the seaside, or the mountains, or the lakes, this modest maple, still without budging an inch, travels in its reputation, — runs up its scarlet flag on that hillside, which shows that it has finished its summer's work before all other trees, and withdraws from the

contest. At the eleventh hour of the year, the tree which
no scrutiny could have detected here when it was most
industrious is thus, by the tint of its maturity, by its
very blushes, revealed at last to the careless and distant traveler, and leads his thoughts away from the
dusty road into those brave solitudes which it inhabits. It flashes out conspicuous with all the virtue and
beauty of a maple, — *Acer rubrum*. We may now read
its title, or *rubric*, clear. Its *virtues*, not its sins, are as
scarlet.

Notwithstanding the red maple is the most intense
scarlet of any of our trees, the sugar maple has been
the most celebrated, and Michaux in his "Sylva" does
not speak of the autumnal color of the former. About
the second of October, these trees, both large and small,
are most brilliant, though many are still green. In
"sprout-lands" they seem to vie with one another,
and ever some particular one in the midst of the crowd
will be of a peculiarly pure scarlet, and by its more
intense color attract our eye even at a distance, and
carry off the palm. A large red maple swamp, when
at the height of its change, is the most obviously brilliant of all tangible things, where I dwell, so abundant
is this tree with us. It varies much both in form and
color. A great many are merely yellow; more, scarlet;
others, scarlet deepening into crimson, more red than
common. Look at yonder swamp of maples mixed
with pines, at the base of a pine-clad hill, a quarter
of a mile off, so that you get the full effect of the bright
colors, without detecting the imperfections of the leaves,
and see their yellow, scarlet, and crimson fires, of all

tints, mingled and contrasted with the green. Some maples are yet green, only yellow or crimson-tipped on the edges of their flakes, like the edges of a hazelnut bur; some are wholly brilliant scarlet, raying out regularly and finely every way, bilaterally, like the veins of a leaf; others, of more irregular form, when I turn my head slightly, emptying out some of its earthiness and concealing the trunk of the tree, seem to rest heavily flake on flake, like yellow and scarlet clouds, wreath upon wreath, or like snow-drifts driving through the air, stratified by the wind. It adds greatly to the beauty of such a swamp at this season, that, even though there may be no other trees interspersed, it is not seen as a simple mass of color, but, different trees being of different colors and hues, the outline of each crescent treetop is distinct, and where one laps on to another. Yet a painter would hardly venture to make them thus distinct a quarter of a mile off.

As I go across a meadow directly toward a low rising ground this bright afternoon, I see, some fifty rods off toward the sun, the top of a maple swamp just appearing over the sheeny russet edge of the hill, a stripe apparently twenty rods long by ten feet deep, of the most intensely brilliant scarlet, orange, and yellow, equal to any flowers or fruits, or any tints ever painted. As I advance, lowering the edge of the hill which makes the firm foreground or lower frame of the picture, the depth of the brilliant grove revealed steadily increases, suggesting that the whole of the inclosed valley is filled with such color. One wonders that the tithing-men and fathers of the town are not out to see what the trees

mean by their high colors and exuberance of spirits,
fearing that some mischief is brewing. I do not see what
the Puritans did at this season, when the maples blaze
out in scarlet. They certainly could not have worshiped
in groves then. Perhaps that is what they built meeting-
houses and fenced them round with horse-sheds for.

THE ELM

Now too, the first of October, or later, the elms are
at the height of their autumnal beauty, — great brown-
ish-yellow masses, warm from their September oven,
hanging over the highway. Their leaves are perfectly
ripe. I wonder if there is any answering ripeness in the
lives of the men who live beneath them. As I look down
our street, which is lined with them, they remind me
both by their form and color of yellowing sheaves of
grain, as if the harvest had indeed come to the village
itself, and we might expect to find some maturity and
flavor in the thoughts of the villagers at last. Under
those bright rustling yellow piles just ready to fall on
the heads of the walkers, how can any crudity or greenness of thought or act prevail? When I stand where
half a dozen large elms droop over a house, it is as if
I stood within a ripe pumpkin-rind, and I feel as mellow as if I were the pulp, though I may be somewhat
stringy and seedy withal. What is the late greenness
of the English elm, like a cucumber out of season,
which does not know when to have done, compared
with the early and golden maturity of the American
tree? The street is the scene of a great harvest-home.
It would be worth the while to set out these trees, if only

for their autumnal value. Think of these great yellow
canopies or parasols held over our heads and houses
by the mile together, making the village all one and
compact, — an *ulmarium*, which is at the same time a
nursery of men! And then how gently and unobserved
they drop their burden and let in the sun when it is
wanted, their leaves not heard when they fall on our
roofs and in our streets; and thus the village parasol
is shut up and put away! I see the market-man driving into the village, and disappearing under its canopy
of elm-tops, with *his* crop, as into a great granary or
barn-yard. I am tempted to go thither as to a husking
of thoughts, now dry and ripe, and ready to be separated from their integuments; but, alas! I foresee that
it will be chiefly husks and little thought, blasted pig-
corn, fit only for cob-meal, — for, as you sow, so shall
you reap.

FALLEN LEAVES

By the sixth of October the leaves generally begin
to fall, in successive showers, after frost or rain; but
the principal leaf-harvest, the acme of the *Fall*, is commonly about the sixteenth. Some morning at that date
there is perhaps a harder frost than we have seen, and
ice formed under the pump, and now, when the morning
wind rises, the leaves come down in denser showers than
ever. They suddenly form thick beds or carpets on the
ground, in this gentle air, or even without wind, just
the size and form of the tree above. Some trees, as
small hickories, appear to have dropped their leaves
instantaneously, as a soldier grounds arms at a signal;

and those of the hickory, being bright yellow still, though withered, reflect a blaze of light from the ground where they lie. Down they have come on all sides, at the first earnest touch of autumn's wand, making a sound like rain.

Or else it is after moist and rainy weather that we notice how great a fall of leaves there has been in the night, though it may not yet be the touch that loosens the rock maple leaf. The streets are thickly strewn with the trophies, and fallen elm leaves make a dark brown pavement under our feet. After some remarkably warm Indian-summer day or days, I perceive that it is the unusual heat which, more than anything, causes the leaves to fall, there having been, perhaps, no frost nor rain for some time. The intense heat suddenly ripens and wilts them, just as it softens and ripens peaches and other fruits, and causes them to drop.

The leaves of late red maples, still bright, strew the earth, often crimson-spotted on a yellow ground, like some wild apples, — though they preserve these bright colors on the ground but a day or two, especially if it rains. On causeways I go by trees here and there all bare and smoke-like, having lost their brilliant clothing; but there it lies, nearly as bright as ever, on the ground on one side, and making nearly as regular a figure as lately on the tree. I would rather say that I first observe the trees thus flat on the ground like a permanent colored shadow, and they suggest to look for the boughs that bore them. A queen might be proud to walk where these gallant trees have spread their bright cloaks in the mud. I see wagons roll over them as a shadow or a reflection, and the drivers heed them just as little as they did their shadows before.

Birds' nests, in the huckleberry and other shrubs, and in trees, are already being filled with the withered leaves. So many have fallen in the woods that a squirrel cannot run after a falling nut without being heard. Boys are raking them in the streets, if only for the pleasure of dealing with such clean, crisp substances. Some sweep the paths scrupulously neat, and then stand to see the next breath strew them with new trophies. The swamp floor is thickly covered, and the *Lycopodium lucidulum* looks suddenly greener amid them. In dense woods they half cover pools that are three or four rods long. The other day I could hardly find a well-known spring, and even suspected that it had dried up, for it was completely concealed by freshly fallen leaves; and when I swept them aside and revealed it, it was like striking the earth, with Aaron's rod, for a new spring. Wet grounds about the edges of swamps look dry with them. At one swamp, where I was surveying, thinking to step on a leafy shore from a rail, I got into the water more than a foot deep.

When I go to the river the day after the principal fall of leaves, the sixteenth, I find my boat all covered, bottom and seats, with the leaves of the golden willow under which it is moored, and I set sail with a cargo of them rustling under my feet. If I empty it, it will be full again to-morrow. I do not regard them as litter, to be swept out, but accept them as suitable straw or matting for the bottom of my carriage. When I turn up into the mouth of the Assabet, which is wooded, large fleets of leaves are floating on its surface, as it were getting out to sea, with room to tack; but next the shore, a little farther up, they are thicker than foam, quite concealing the water for a rod in width, under and amid the alders, button-bushes, and maples, still perfectly light and dry, with fibre unrelaxed; and at a rocky bend where they are met and stopped by the morning wind, they sometimes form a broad and dense crescent quite across the river. When I turn my prow that way, and the wave which it makes strikes them, list what a pleasant rustling from these dry substances getting on one another! Often it is their undulation only which reveals the water beneath them. Also every motion of the wood turtle on the shore is betrayed by their rustling there. Or even in mid-channel, when the wind rises, I hear them blown with a rustling sound. Higher up they are slowly moving round and round in some great eddy which the river makes, as that at the "Leaning Hemlocks," where the water is deep, and the current is wearing into the bank.

Perchance, in the afternoon of such a day, when the water is perfectly calm and full of reflections, I paddle gently down the main stream, and, turning up the Assabet, reach a quiet cove, where I unexpectedly find myself surrounded by myriads of leaves, like fellow-voyagers, which seem to have the same purpose, or want of purpose, with myself. See this great fleet of scattered leaf-boats which we paddle amid, in this smooth river-bay, each one curled up on every side by the sun's skill, each nerve a stiff spruce knee, — like boats of hide, and of all patterns, — Charon's boat probably among the rest, — and some with lofty prows and poops, like the stately vessels of the ancients, scarcely moving in the sluggish current, — like the great fleets, the dense Chinese cities of boats, with which you mingle on entering some great mart, some New York or Canton, which we are all steadily approaching together. How gently each has been deposited on the water! No violence has been used towards them yet, though, perchance, palpitating hearts were present at the launching. And painted ducks, too, the splendid wood duck among the rest, often come to sail and float amid the painted leaves, — barks of a nobler model still!

What wholesome herb drinks are to be had in the swamps now! What strong medicinal but rich scents from the decaying leaves! The rain falling on the freshly dried herbs and leaves, and filling the pools and ditches into which they have dropped thus clean and rigid, will soon convert them into tea, — green, black, brown, and yellow teas, of all degrees of strength, enough to set all Nature a-gossiping. Whether we drink them or not, as yet, before their strength is drawn, these leaves, dried on great Nature's coppers, are of such various pure and delicate tints as might make the fame of Oriental teas.

How they are mixed up, of all species, oak and maple and chestnut and birch! But Nature is not cluttered with them; she is a perfect husbandman; she stores them all. Consider what a vast crop is thus annually shed on the earth! This, more than any mere grain or seed, is the great harvest of the year. The trees are now repaying the earth with interest what they have

taken from it. They are discounting. They are about
to add a leaf's thickness to the depth of the soil. This
is the beautiful way in which Nature gets her muck,
while I chaffer with this man and that, who talks to
me about sulphur and the cost of carting. We are all
the richer for their decay. I am more interested in this
crop than in the English grass alone or in the corn. It
prepares the virgin mould for future corn-fields and
forests, on which the earth fattens. It keeps our homestead in good heart.

For beautiful variety no crop can be compared with
this. Here is not merely the plain yellow of the grains,
but nearly all the colors that we know, the brightest
blue not excepted: the early blushing maple, the poison
sumach blazing its sins as scarlet, the mulberry ash,
the rich chrome yellow of the poplars, the brilliant red
huckleberry, with which the hills' backs are painted,
like those of sheep. The frost touches them, and, with
the slightest breath of returning day or jarring of earth's
axle, see in what showers they come floating down!
The ground is all parti-colored with them. But they
still live in the soil, whose fertility and bulk they increase, and in the forests that spring from it. They
stoop to rise, to mount higher in coming years, by
subtle chemistry, climbing by the sap in the trees; and
the sapling's first fruits thus shed, transmuted at last,
may adorn its crown, when, in after years, it has become the monarch of the forest.

It is pleasant to walk over the beds of these fresh,
crisp, and rustling leaves. How beautifully they go
to their graves! how gently lay themselves down and

turn to mould! — painted of a thousand hues, and fit
to make the beds of us living. So they troop to their last
resting-place, light and frisky. They put on no weeds,
but merrily they go scampering over the earth, selecting
the spot, choosing a lot, ordering no iron fence, whis-
pering all through the woods about it, — some choosing
the spot where the bodies of men are mouldering beneath, and meeting them half-way. How many flutter-
ings before they rest quietly in their graves! They that
soared so loftily, how contentedly they return to dust
again, and are laid low, resigned to lie and decay at the
foot of the tree, and afford nourishment to new generations of their kind, as well as to flutter on high! They
teach us how to die. One wonders if the time will ever
come when men, with their boasted faith in immortality, will lie down as gracefully and as ripe, — with
such an Indian-summer serenity will shed their bodies,
as they do their hair and nails.

When the leaves fall, the whole earth is a cemetery
pleasant to walk in. I love to wander and muse over
them in their graves. Here are no lying nor vain epi-
taphs. What though you own no lot at Mount Auburn?
Your lot is surely cast somewhere in this vast cemetery,
which has been consecrated from of old. You need
attend no auction to secure a place. There is room
enough here. The loosestrife shall bloom and the
huckleberry-bird sing over your bones. The woodman and hunter shall be your sextons, and the children
shall tread upon the borders as much as they will. Let
us walk in the cemetery of the leaves; this is your true
Greenwood Cemetery.

THE SUGAR MAPLE

But think not that the splendor of the year is over; for as one leaf does not make a summer, neither does one falling leaf make an autumn. The smallest sugar maples in our streets make a great show as early as the fifth of October, more than any other trees there. As I look up the main street, they appear like painted screens standing before the houses; yet many are green. But now, or generally by the seventeenth of October, when almost all red maples and some white maples are bare, the large sugar maples also are in their glory, glowing with yellow and red, and show unexpectedly bright and delicate tints. They are remarkable for the contrast they often afford of deep blushing red on one half and green on the other. They, become at length dense masses of rich yellow with a deep scarlet blush, or more than blush, on the exposed surfaces. They are the brightest trees now in the street.

The large ones on our Common are particularly beautiful. A delicate but warmer than golden yellow is now the prevailing color, with scarlet cheeks. Yet, standing on the east side of the Common just before sundown, when the western light is transmitted through them, I see that their yellow even, compared with the pale lemon yellow of an elm close by, amounts to a scarlet, without noticing the bright scarlet portions. Generally, they are great regular oval masses of yellow and scarlet. All the sunny warmth of the season, the Indian summer, seems to be absorbed in their leaves. The lowest and inmost leaves next the bole are, as usual, of the most delicate yellow and green, like the complexion of young men brought up in the house. There is an auction on the Common to-day, but its red flag is hard to be discerned amid this blaze of color.

Little did the fathers of the town anticipate this brilliant success, when they caused to be imported from farther in the country some straight poles with their tops cut off, which they called sugar maples; and, as I remember, after they were set out, a neighboring merchant's clerk, by way of jest, planted beans about them. Those which were then jestingly called bean-poles are to-day far the most beautiful objects noticeable in our streets. They are worth all and more than they have cost, — though one of the selectmen, while setting them out, took the cold which occasioned his death, — if only because they, have filled the open eyes of children with their rich color unstintedly so many Octobers. We will not ask them to yield us sugar in the spring, while they afford us so fair a prospect in the autumn. Wealth indoors may be the inheritance of few, but it is equally distributed on the Common. All children alike can revel in this golden harvest.

Surely trees should be set in our streets with a view to their October splendor, though I doubt whether this is ever considered by the "Tree Society." Do you not think it will make some odds to these children that they were brought up under the maples? Hundreds of eyes are steadily drinking in this color, and by these teachers even the truants are caught and educated the moment they step abroad. Indeed, neither the truant nor the studious is at present taught color in the schools.

These are instead of the bright colors in apothecaries'
shops and city windows. It is a pity that we have no
more *red* maples, and some hickories, in our streets as
well. Our paint-box is very imperfectly filled. Instead
of, or beside, supplying such paint-boxes as we do, we
might supply these natural colors to the young. Where
else will they study color under greater advantages?
What School of Design can vie with this? Think how
much the eyes of painters of all kinds, and of manufacturers of cloth and paper, and paper-stainers, and
countless others, are to be educated by these autumnal colors. The stationer's envelopes may be of very
various tints, yet not so various as those of the leaves
of a single tree. If you want a different shade or tint of
a particular color, you have only to look farther within
or without the tree or the wood. These leaves are not
many dipped in one dye, as at the dye-house, but they
are dyed in light of infinitely various degrees of strength
and left to set and dry there.

Shall the names of so many of our colors continue
to be derived from those of obscure foreign localities, as
Naples yellow, Prussian blue, raw Sienna, burnt Um-
ber, Gamboge? (surely the Tyrian purple must have
faded by this time), or from comparatively trivial articles of commerce, — chocolate, lemon, coffee, cinnamon,
claret? (shall we compare our hickory to a lemon,
or a lemon to a hickory?) or from ores and oxides
which few ever see? Shall we so often, when describing
to our neighbors the color of something we have seen,
refer them, not to some natural object in our neighborhood, but perchance to a bit of earth fetched from the

other side of the planet, which possibly they may find
at the apothecary's, but which probably neither they
nor we ever saw? Have we not an *earth* under our feet,
— aye, and a sky over our heads? Or is the last *all*
ultramarine? What do we know of sapphire, amethyst, emerald, ruby, amber, and the like, — most of us
who take these names in vain? Leave these precious
words to cabinet-keepers, virtuosos, and maids-of-honor,
— to the Nabobs, Begums, and Chobdars of Hindostan,
or wherever else. I do not see why, since America and
her autumn woods have been discovered, our leaves
should not compete with the precious stones in giving
names to colors; and, indeed, I believe that in course
of time the names of some of our trees and shrubs, as
well as flowers, will get into our popular chromatic
nomenclature.

But of much more importance than a knowledge of
the names and distinctions of color is the joy and ex-
hilaration which these colored leaves excite. Already
these brilliant trees throughout the street, without any
more variety, are at least equal to an annual festival
and holiday, or a week of such. These are cheap and
innocent gala-days, celebrated by one and all without
the aid of committees or marshals, such a show as may
safely be licensed, not attracting gamblers or rum-
sellers, not requiring any special police to keep the peace.
And poor indeed must be that New England village's
October which has not the maple in its streets. This
October festival costs no powder, nor ringing of bells,
but every tree is a living liberty-pole on which a thousand bright flags are waving.

No wonder that we must have our annual cattle-show, and fall training, and perhaps cornwallis, our September courts, and the like. Nature herself holds her annual fair in October, not only in the streets, but in every hollow and on every hillside. When lately we looked into that red maple swamp all ablaze, where the trees were clothed in their vestures of most dazzling tints, did it not suggest a thousand gypsies beneath, — a race capable of wild delight, — or even the fabled fauns, satyrs, and wood-nymphs come back to earth? Or was it only a congregation of wearied woodchoppers, or of proprietors come to inspect their lots, that we thought of? Or, earlier still, when we paddled on the river through that fine-grained September air, did there not appear to be something new going on under the sparkling surface of the stream, a shaking of props, at least, so that we made haste in order to be up in time? Did not the rows of yellowing willows and button-bushes on each side seem like rows of booths, under which, perhaps, some fluviatile egg-pop equally yellow was effervescing? Did not all these suggest that man's spirits should rise as high as Nature's, — should hang out their flag, and the routine of his life be interrupted by an analogous expression of joy and hilarity?

No annual training or muster of soldiery, no celebration with its scarfs and banners, could import into the town a hundredth part of the annual splendor of our October. We have only to set the trees, or let them stand, and Nature will find the colored drapery, — flags of all her nations, some of whose private signals hardly the botanist can read, — while we walk under the triumphal arches of the elms. Leave it to Nature to appoint the days, whether the same as in neighboring States or not, and let the clergy read her proclamations, if they can understand them. Behold what a brilliant drapery is her woodbine flag! What public-spirited merchant, think you, has contributed this part of the show? There is no handsomer shingling and paint than this vine, at present covering a whole side of some houses. I do not believe that the ivy *never sere* is comparable to it. No wonder it has been extensively introduced into London. Let us have a good many maples and hickories and scarlet oaks, then, I say. Blaze away! Shall that dirty roll of bunting in the gun-house be all the colors a village can display? A village is not complete, unless it have these trees to mark the season in it. They are important, like the town clock. A village that has them not will not be found to work well. It has a screw loose, an essential part is wanting. Let us have willows for spring, elms for summer, maples and walnuts and tupeloes for autumn, evergreens for winter, and oaks for all seasons. What is a gallery in a house to a gallery in the streets, which every market-man rides through, whether he will or not? Of course, there is not a picture-gallery in the country which would be worth so much to us as is the western view at sunset under the elms of our main street. They are the frame to a picture which is daily painted behind them. An avenue of elms as large as our largest and three miles long would seem to lead to some admirable place, though only C—— were at the end of it.

A village needs these innocent stimulants of bright

and cheering prospects to keep off melancholy and superstition. Show me two villages, one embowered in trees and blazing with all the glories of October, the other a merely trivial and treeless waste, or with only a single tree or two for suicides, and I shall be sure that in the latter will be found the most starved and bigoted religionists and the most desperate drinkers. Every wash-tub and milk-can and gravestone will be exposed. The inhabitants will disappear abruptly behind their barns and houses, like desert Arabs amid their rocks, and I shall look to see spears in their hands. They will be ready to accept the most barren and forlorn doctrine, — as that the world is speedily coming to an end, or has already got to it, or that they themselves are turned wrong side outward. They will perchance crack their dry joints at one another and call it a spiritual communication.

But to confine ourselves to the maples. What if we were to take half as much pains in protecting them as we do in setting them out, — not stupidly tie our horses to our dahlia stems?

What meant the fathers by establishing this *perfectly living* institution before the church, — this institution which needs no repairing nor repainting, which is continually enlarged and repaired by its growth? Surely they

> "Wrought in a sad sincerity;
> Themselves from God they could not free;
> They *planted* better than they knew; —
> The conscious *trees* to beauty grew."

Verily these maples are cheap preachers, permanently

settled, which preach their half-century, and century, aye, and century-and-a-half sermons, with constantly increasing unction and influence, ministering to many generations of men; and the least we can do is to supply them with suitable colleagues as they grow infirm.

THE SCARLET OAK

Belonging to a genus which is remarkable for the beautiful form of its leaves, I suspect that some scarlet oak leaves surpass those of all other oaks in the rich and wild beauty of their outlines. I judge from an acquaintance with twelve species, and from drawings which I have seen of many others.

Stand under this tree and see how finely its leaves are cut against the sky, — as it were, only a few sharp points extending from a midrib. They look like double, treble, or quadruple crosses. They are far more ethereal than the less deeply scalloped oak leaves. They have so little leafy *terra firma* that they appear melting away in the light, and scarcely obstruct our view. The leaves of very young plants are, like those of full-grown oaks of other species, more entire, simple, and lumpish in their outlines, but these, raised high on old trees, have solved the leafy problem. Lifted higher and higher, and sublimated more and more, putting off some earthiness and cultivating more intimacy with the light each year, they have at length the least possible amount of earthy matter, and the greatest spread and grasp of skyey influences. There they dance, arm in arm with the light, — tripping it on fantastic points, fit partners in those aerial halls. So intimately mingled are they with it,

that, what with their slenderness and their glossy surfaces, you can hardly tell at last what in the dance is
leaf and what is light. And when no zephyr stirs, they
are at most but a rich tracery to the forest windows.

I am again struck with their beauty, when, a month
later, they thickly strew the ground in the woods, piled
one upon another under my feet. They are then brown
above, but purple beneath. With their narrow lobes
and their bold, deep scallops reaching almost to the
middle, they suggest that the material must be cheap, or
else there has been a lavish expense in their creation,
as if so much had been cut out. Or else they seem to us
the remnants of the stuff out of which leaves have been
cut with a die. Indeed, when they lie thus one upon
another, they remind me of a pile of scrap-tin.

Or bring one home, and study it closely at your leisure,
by the fireside. It is a type, not from any Oxford font,
not in the Basque nor the arrow-headed character, not
found on the Rosetta Stone, but destined to be copied
in sculpture one day, if they ever get to whittling stone
here. What a wild and pleasing outline, a combination
of graceful curves and angles! The eye rests with equal
delight on what is not leaf and on what is leaf, — on
the broad, free, open sinuses, and on the long, sharp,
bristle-pointed lobes. A simple oval outline would in-
clude it all, if you connected the points of the leaf; but
how much richer is it than that, with its half-dozen deep
scallops, in which the eye and thought of the beholder
are embayed! If I were a drawing-master, I would set
my pupils to copying these leaves, that they might
learn to draw firmly and gracefully.

Regarded as water, it is like a pond with half a dozen broad rounded promontories extending nearly to its middle, half from each side, while its watery bays extend far inland, like sharp friths, at each of whose heads several fine streams empty in, — almost a leafy archipelago.

But it oftener suggests land, and, as Dionysius and Pliny compared the form of the Morea to that of the leaf of the Oriental plane tree, so this leaf reminds me of some fair wild island in the ocean, whose extensive coast, alternate rounded bays with smooth strands, and sharp-pointed rocky capes, mark it as fitted for the habitation of man, and destined to become a centre of civilization at last. To the sailor's eye, it is a much indented shore. Is it not, in fact, a shore to the aerial ocean, on which the windy surf beats? At sight of this leaf we are all mariners, — if not vikings, buccaneers, and filibusters. Both our love of repose and our spirit of adventure are addressed. In our most casual glance, perchance, we think that if we succeed in doubling those sharp capes we shall find deep, smooth, and secure havens in the ample bays. How different from the white oak leaf, with its rounded headlands, on which no lighthouse need be placed! That is an England, with its long civil history, that may be read. This is some still unsettled New-found Island or Celebes. Shall we go and be rajahs there?

By the twenty-sixth of October the large scarlet oaks are in their prime, when other oaks are usually withered. They have been kindling their fires for a week past, and now generally burst into a blaze. This alone of *our* indigenous deciduous trees (excepting the dog-wood, of which I do not know half a dozen, and they are but large bushes) is now in its glory. The two aspens and the sugar maple come nearest to it in date, but they have lost the greater part of their leaves. Of evergreens, only the pitch pine is still commonly bright.

But it requires a particular alertness, if not devotion to these phenomena, to appreciate the wide-spread, but late and unexpected glory of the scarlet oaks. I do not speak here of the small trees and shrubs, which are commonly observed, and which are now withered, but of the large trees. Most go in and shut their doors, thinking that bleak and colorless November has already come, when some of the most brilliant and memorable colors are not yet lit.

This very perfect and vigorous one, about forty feet high, standing in an open pasture, which was quite glossy green on the twelfth, is now, the twenty-sixth, completely changed to bright dark-scarlet, — every leaf, between you and the sun, as if it had been dipped into a scarlet dye. The whole tree is much like a heart in form, as well as color. Was not this worth waiting for? Little did you think, ten days ago, that that cold green tree would assume such color as this. Its leaves are still firmly attached, while those of other trees are falling around it. It seems to say : "I am the last to blush, but I blush deeper than any of ye. I bring up the rear in my red coat. We scarlet ones, alone of oaks, have not given up the fight."

The sap is now, and even far into November, fre-quently flowing fast in these trees, as in maples in the spring; and apparently their bright tints, now that most other oaks are withered, are connected with this phenomenon. They are full of life. It has a pleasantly astringent, acorn-like taste, this strong oak wine, as I find on tapping them with my knife.

Looking across this woodland valley, a quarter of a mile wide, how rich those scarlet oaks embosomed in pines, their bright red branches intimately intermingled with them! They have their full effect there. The pine boughs are the green calyx to their red petals. Or, as we go along a road in the woods, the sun striking endwise through it, and lighting up the red tents of the oaks, which on each side are mingled with the liquid green of the pines, makes a very gorgeous scene. Indeed, without the evergreens for contrast, the autumnal tints would lose much of their effect.

The scarlet oak asks a clear sky and the brightness of late October days. These bring out its colors. If the sun goes into a cloud they become comparatively indistinct. As I sit on a cliff in the southwest part of our town, the sun is now getting low, and the woods in Lincoln, south and east of me, are lit up by its more level rays; and in the scarlet oaks, scattered so equally over the forest, there is brought out a more brilliant redness than I had believed was in them. Every tree of this species which is visible in those directions, even to the horizon, now stands out distinctly red. Some great ones lift their red backs high above the woods, in the next town, like huge roses with a myriad of fine petals; and some more slender ones, in a small grove of white pines on Pine Hill in the east, on the very verge of the horizon, alter-

nating with the pines on the edge of the grove, and
shouldering them with their red coats, look like soldiers
in red amid hunters in green. This time it is Lincoln
green, too. Till the sun got low, I did not believe that
there were so many redcoats in the forest army. Theirs
is an intense, burning red, which would lose some of
its strength, methinks, with every step you might take
toward them; for the shade that lurks amid their foliage
does not report itself at this distance, and they are unani-
mously red. The focus of their reflected color is in the
atmosphere far on this side. Every such tree becomes a
nucleus of red, as it were, where, with the declining sun,
that color grows and glows. It is partly borrowed fire,
gathering strength from the sun on its way to your eye.
It has only some comparatively dull red leaves for a
rallying-point, or kindling-stuff, to start it, and it becomes an intense scarlet or red mist, or fire, which finds
fuel for itself in the very atmosphere. So vivacious is
redness. The very rails reflect a rosy light at this hour
and season. You see a redder tree than exists.

If you wish to count the scarlet oaks, do it now.
In a clear day stand thus on a hilltop in the woods,
when the sun is an hour high, and every one within range
of your vision, excepting in the west, will be revealed.
You might live to the age of Methuselah and never find
a tithe of them, otherwise. Yet sometimes even in a dark
day I have thought them as bright as I ever saw them.
Looking westward, their colors are lost in a blaze of
light; but in other directions the whole forest is a flower-
garden, in which these late roses burn, alternating with
green, while the so-called "gardeners," walking here

and there, perchance, beneath, with spade and water-pot, see only a few little asters amid withered leaves.

These are *my* China-asters, *my* late garden-flowers. It costs me nothing for a gardener. The falling leaves, all over the forest, are protecting the roots of my plants. Only look at what is to be seen, and you will have garden enough, without deepening the soil in your yard. We have only to elevate our view a little, to see the whole forest as a garden. The blossoming of the scarlet oak, — the forest-flower, surpassing all in splendor (at least since the maple)! I do not know but they interest me more than the maples, they are so widely and equally dispersed throughout the forest; they are so hardy, a nobler tree on the whole; our chief November flower, abiding the approach of winter with us, imparting warmth to early November prospects. It is remarkable that the latest bright color that is general should be this deep, dark scarlet and red, the intensest of colors. The ripest fruit of the year; like the cheek of a hard, glossy red apple, from the cold Isle of Orleans, which will not be mellow for eating till next spring! When I rise to a hilltop, a thousand of these great oak roses, distributed on every side, as far as the horizon! I admire them four or five miles off! This my unfailing prospect for a fort-night past! This late forest-flower surpasses all that spring or summer could do. Their colors were but rare and dainty specks comparatively (created for the near-sighted, who walk amid the humblest herbs and under-woods), and made no impression on a distant eye. Now it is an extended forest or a mountain-side, through or along which we journey from day to day, that bursts into bloom. Comparatively, our gardening is on a petty scale, — the gardener still nursing a few asters amid dead weeds, ignorant of the gigantic asters and roses which, as it were, overshadow him, and ask for none of his care. It is like a little red paint ground on a saucer, and held up against the sunset sky. Why not take more elevated and broader views, walk in the great garden; not skulk in a little "debauched" nook of it? consider the beauty of the forest, and not merely of a few impounded herbs?

Let your walks now be a little more adventurous; ascend the hills. If, about the last of October, you ascend any hill in the outskirts of our town, and probably of yours, and look over the forest, you may see — well, what I have endeavored to describe. All this you surely *will* see, and much more, if you are prepared to see it, — if you *look* for it. Otherwise, regular and universal as this phenomenon is, whether you stand on the hilltop or in the hollow, you will think for threescore years and ten that all the wood is, at this season, sere and brown. Objects are concealed from our view, not so much because they are out of the course of our visual ray as because we do not bring our minds and eyes to bear on them; for there is no power to see in the eye itself, any more than in any other jelly. We do not realize how far and widely, or how near and narrowly, we are to look. The greater part of the phenomena of Nature are for this reason concealed from us all our lives. The gardener sees only the gardener's garden. Here, too, as in political economy, the supply answers to the demand. Nature does not cast pearls before

swine. There is just as much beauty visible to us in the
landscape as we are prepared to appreciate, — not a
grain more. The actual objects which one man will see
from a particular hilltop are just as different from those
which another will see as the beholders are different.
The scarlet oak must, in a sense, be in your eye when
you go forth. We cannot see anything until we are possessed with the idea of it, take it into our heads, — and
then we can hardly see anything else. In my botanical
rambles I find that, first, the idea, or image, of a plant
occupies my thoughts, though it may seem very foreign
to this locality, — no nearer than Hudson's Bay, —
and for some weeks or months I go thinking of it, and
expecting it, unconsciously, and at length I surely see it.
This is the history of my finding a score or more of rare
plants which I could name. A man sees only what concerns him. A botanist absorbed in the study of grasses
does not distinguish the grandest pasture oaks. He, as
it were, tramples down oaks unwittingly in his walk,
or at most sees only their shadows. I have found that
it required a different intention of the eye, in the same
locality, to see different plants, even when they were
closely allied, as *Juncaceae* and *Gramineae:* when I was
looking for the former, I did not see the latter in the
midst of them. How much more, then, it requires different intentions of the eye and of the mind to attend to
different departments of knowledge! How differently
the poet and the naturalist look at objects!

Take a New England selectman, and set him on the
highest of our hills, and tell him to look, — sharpening
his sight to the utmost, and putting on the glasses that

suit him best (aye, using a spy-glass, if he likes), —
and make a full report. What, probably, will he *spy?* —
what will he *select* to look at? Of course, he will see a
Brocken spectre of himself. He will see several meeting-
houses, at least, and, perhaps, that somebody ought to
be assessed higher than he is, since he has so handsome
a wood-lot. Now take Julius Cæsar, or Emanuel Swe-
denborg, or a Fiji-Islander, and set him up there. Or
suppose all together, and let them compare notes afterward. Will it appear that they have enjoyed the same
prospect? What they will see will be as different as
Rome was from heaven or hell, or the last from the
Fiji Islands. For aught we know, as strange a man as
any of these is always at our elbow.

Why, it takes a sharpshooter to bring down even
such trivial game as snipes and woodcocks; he must
take very particular aim, and know what he is aiming
at. He would stand a very small chance, if he fired at
random into the sky, being told that snipes were flying
there. And so is it with him that shoots at beauty;
though he wait till the sky falls, he will not bag any, if
he does not already know its seasons and haunts, and
the color of its wing, — if he has not dreamed of it, so
that he can *anticipate* it; then, indeed, he flushes it at
every step, shoots double and on the wing, with both
barrels, even in corn-fields. The sportsman trains himself, dresses, and watches unweariedly, and loads and
primes for his particular game. He prays for it, and
offers sacrifices, and so he gets it. After due and long
preparation, schooling his eye and hand, dreaming
awake and asleep, with gun and paddle and boat, he

goes out after meadow-hens, which most of his towns-men never saw nor dreamed of, and paddles for miles against a head wind, and wades in water up to his knees, being out all day without his dinner, and *therefore* he gets them. He had them half-way into his bag when he started, and has only to shove them down. The true sportsman can shoot you almost any of his game from his windows: what else has he windows or eyes for? It comes and perches at last on the barrel of his gun; but the rest of the world never see it *with the feathers on.* The geese fly exactly under his zenith, and honk when they get there, and he will keep himself supplied by firing up his chimney; twenty musquash have the refusal of each one of his traps before it is empty. If he lives, and his game spirit increases, heaven and earth shall fail him sooner than game; and when he dies, he will go to more extensive and, perchance, happier hunting-grounds. The fisherman, too, dreams of fish, sees a bobbing cork in his dreams, till he can almost catch them in his sink-spout. I knew a girl who, being sent to pick huckleberries, picked wild goose-berries by the quart, where no one else knew that there were any, because she was accustomed to pick them up-country where she came from. The astronomer knows where to go star-gathering, and sees one clearly in his mind before any have seen it with a glass. The hen scratches and finds her food right under where she stands; but such is not the way with the hawk.

These bright leaves which I have mentioned are not the exception, but the rule; for I believe that all leaves, even grasses and mosses, acquire brighter colors just before their fall. When you come to observe faithfully the changes of each humblest plant, you find that each has, sooner or later, its peculiar autumnal tint; and if you undertake to make a complete list of the bright tints, it will be nearly as long as a catalogue of the plants in your vicinity.

Fallen leaves

A WINTER WALK

Snow-laden pitch pines

A WINTER WALK

THE wind has gently murmured through the blinds, or puffed with feathery softness against the windows, and occasionally sighed like a summer zephyr lifting the leaves along, the livelong night. The meadow mouse has slept in his snug gallery in the sod, the owl has sat in a hollow tree in the depth of the swamp, the rabbit, the squirrel, and the fox have all been housed. The watch-dog has lain quiet on the hearth, and the cattle have stood silent in their stalls. The earth itself has slept, as it were its first, not its last sleep, save when some street-sign or wood-house door has faintly creaked upon its hinge, cheering forlorn nature at her midnight work, — the only sound awake 'twixt Venus and Mars, — advertising us of a remote inward warmth, a divine cheer and fellowship, where gods are met together, but where it is very bleak for men to stand. But while the earth has slumbered, all the air has been alive with feathery flakes descending, as if some northern Ceres reigned, showering her silvery grain over all the fields.

We sleep, and at length awake to the still reality of a winter morning. The snow lies warm as cotton or down upon the window-sill; the broadened sash and frosted panes admit a dim and private light, which enhances the snug cheer within. The stillness of the morning is impressive. The floor creaks under our feet as we move toward the window to look abroad through some clear

space over the fields. We see the roofs stand under their
snow burden. From the eaves and fences hang stalactites of snow, and in the yard stand stalagmites covering
some concealed core. The trees and shrubs rear white
arms to the sky on every side; and where were walls and
fences, we see fantastic forms stretching in frolic gambols
across the dusky landscape, as if Nature had strewn her
fresh designs over the fields by night as models for man's
art.

Silently we unlatch the door, letting the drift fall in,
and step abroad to face the cutting air. Already the
stars have lost some of their sparkle, and a dull, leaden
mist skirts the horizon. A lurid brazen light in the east
proclaims the approach of day, while the western landscape is dim and spectral still, and clothed in a sombre
Tartarean light, like the shadowy realms. They are
Infernal sounds only that you hear, — the crowing of
cocks, the barking of dogs, the chopping of wood, the
lowing of kine, all seem to come from Pluto's barnyard
and beyond the Styx, — not for any melancholy they
suggest, but their twilight bustle is too solemn and mysterious for earth. The recent tracks of the fox or otter,
in the yard, remind us that each hour of the night is
crowded with events, and the primeval nature is still
working and making tracks in the snow. Opening the
gate, we tread briskly along the lone country road,
crunching the dry and crisped snow under our feet, or
aroused by the sharp, clear creak of the wood-sled, just
starting for the distant market, from the early farmer's
door, where it has lain the summer long, dreaming amid
the chips and stubble; while far through the drifts and

powdered windows we see the farmer's early candle, like
a paled star, emitting a lonely beam, as if some severe
virtue were at its matins there. And one by one the
smokes begin to ascend from the chimneys amid the
trees and snows.

> The sluggish smoke curls up from some deep dell,
> The stiffened air exploring in the dawn,
> And making slow acquaintance with the day
> Delaying now upon its heavenward course,
> In wreathèd loiterings dallying with itself,
> With as uncertain purpose and slow deed
> As its half-wakened master by the hearth,
> Whose mind still slumbering and sluggish thoughts
> Have not yet swept into the onward current
> Of the new day; — and now it streams afar,
> The while the chopper goes with step direct,
> And mind intent to swing the early axe.
> First in the dusky dawn he sends abroad
> His early scout, his emissary, smoke,
> The earliest, latest pilgrim from the roof,
> To feel the frosty air, inform the day;
> And while he crouches still beside the hearth,
> Nor musters courage to unbar the door,
> It has gone down the glen with the light wind,
> And o'er the plain unfurled its venturous wreath,
> Draped the tree-tops, loitered upon the hill,
> And warmed the piniòns of the early bird;
> And now, perchance, high in the crispy air,
> Has caught sight of the day o'er the earth's edge,
> And greets its master's eye at his low door,
> As some refulgent cloud in the upper sky.

We hear the sound of wood-chopping at the farmers'
doors, far over the frozen earth, the baying of the house-
dog, and the distant clarion of the cock, — though the
thin and frosty air conveys only the finer particles of

sound to our ears, with short and sweet vibrations, as the waves subside soonest on the purest and lightest liquids, in which gross substances sink to the bottom. They come clear and bell-like, and from a greater distance in the horizon, as if there were fewer impediments than in summer to make them faint and ragged. The ground is sonorous, like seasoned wood, and even the ordinary rural sounds are melodious, and the jingling of the ice on the trees is sweet and liquid. There is the least possible moisture in the atmosphere, all being dried up or congealed, and it is of such extreme tenuity and elasticity that it becomes a source of delight. The withdrawn and tense sky seems groined like the aisles of a cathedral, and the polished air sparkles as if there were crystals of ice floating in it. As they who have resided in Greenland tell us that when it freezes " the sea smokes like burning turf-land, and a fog or mist arises, called frost-smoke," which " cutting smoke frequently raises blisters on the face and hands, and is very pernicious to the health." But this pure, stinging cold is an elixir to the lungs, and not so much a frozen mist as a crystallized midsummer haze, refined and purified by cold.

The sun at length rises through the distant woods, as if with the faint clashing, swinging sound of cymbals, melting the air with his beams, and with such rapid steps the morning travels, that already his rays are gilding the distant western mountains. Meanwhile we step hastily along through the powdery snow, warmed by an inward heat, enjoying an Indian summer still, in the increased glow of thought and feeling. Probably if our lives were more conformed to nature, we should not need to defend ourselves against her heats and colds, but find her our constant nurse and friend, as do plants and quadrupeds. If our bodies were fed with pure and simple elements, and not with a stimulating and heating diet, they would afford no more pasture for cold than a leafless twig, but thrive like the trees, which find even winter genial to their expansion.

The wonderful purity of nature at this season is a most pleasing fact. Every decayed stump and moss-grown stone and rail, and the dead leaves of autumn, are concealed by a clean napkin of snow. In the bare fields and tinkling woods, see what virtue survives. In the coldest and bleakest places, the warmest charities still maintain a foothold. A cold and searching wind drives away all contagion, and nothing can withstand it but what has a virtue in it, and accordingly, whatever we meet with in cold and bleak places, as the tops of mountains, we respect for a sort of sturdy innocence, a Puritan toughness. All things beside seem to be called in for shelter, and what stays out must be part of the original frame of the universe, and of such valor as God himself. It is invigorating to breathe the cleansed air. Its greater fineness and purity are visible to the eye, and we would fain stay out long and late, that the gales may sigh through us, too, as through the leafless trees, and fit us for the winter, — as if we hoped so to borrow some pure and steadfast virtue, which will stead us in all seasons.

There is a slumbering subterranean fire in nature which never goes out, and which no cold can chill. It

finally melts the great snow, and in January or July
is only buried under a thicker or thinner covering. In
the coldest day it flows somewhere, and the snow melts
around every tree. This field of winter rye, which
sprouted late in the fall, and now speedily dissolves
the snow, is where the fire is very thinly covered. We
feel warmed by it. In the winter, warmth stands for all
virtue, and we resort in thought to a trickling rill, with
its bare stones shining in the sun, and to warm springs
in the woods, with as much eagerness as rabbits and
robins. The steam which rises from swamps and pools
is as dear and domestic as that of our own kettle. What
fire could ever equal the sunshine of a winter's day,
when the meadow mice come out by the wall-sides,
and the chickadee lisps in the defiles of the wood? The
warmth comes directly from the sun, and is not radiated
from the earth, as in summer; and when we feel his
beams on our backs as we are treading some snowy
dell, we are grateful as for a special kindness, and bless
the sun which has followed us into that by-place.

This subterranean fire has its altar in each man's
breast; for in the coldest day, and on the bleakest hill,
the traveler cherishes a warmer fire within the folds of
his cloak than is kindled on any hearth. A healthy man,
indeed, is the complement of the seasons, and in winter,
summer is in his heart. There is the south. Thither
have all birds and insects migrated, and around the
warm springs in his breast are gathered the robin and
the lark.

At length, having reached the edge of the woods,
and shut out the gadding town, we enter within their

covert as we go under the roof of a cottage, and cross
its threshold, all ceiled and banked up with snow. They
are glad and warm still, and as genial and cheery in
winter as in summer. As we stand in the midst of the
pines in the flickering and checkered light which strag-
gles but little way into their maze, we wonder if the
towns have ever heard their simple story. It seems to
us that no traveler has ever explored them, and notwithstanding the wonders which science is elsewhere
revealing every day, who would not like to hear their
annals? Our humble villages in the plain are their
contribution. We borrow from the forest the boards
which shelter and the sticks which warm us. How
important is their evergreen to the winter, that portion
of the summer which does not fade, the permanent
year, the unwithered grass! Thus simply, and with
little expense of altitude, is the surface of the earth diversified. What would human life be without forests,
those natural cities? From the tops of mountains they
appear like smooth-shaven lawns, yet whither shall we
walk but in this taller grass?

In this glade covered with bushes of a year's growth,
see how the silvery dust lies on every seared leaf and
twig, deposited in such infinite and luxurious forms
as by their very variety atone for the absence of color.
Observe the tiny tracks of mice around every stem,
and the triangular tracks of the rabbit. A pure elastic
heaven hangs over all, as if the impurities of the summer sky, refined and shrunk by the chaste winter's
cold, had been winnowed from the heavens upon the
earth.

Nature confounds her summer distinctions at this season. The heavens seem to be nearer the earth. The elements are less reserved and distinct. Water turns to ice, rain to snow. The day is but a Scandinavian night. The winter is an arctic summer.

How much more living is the life that is in nature, the furred life which still survives the stinging nights, and, from amidst fields and woods covered with frost and snow, sees the sun rise!

"The foodless wilds
Pour forth their brown inhabitants."

The gray squirrel and rabbit are brisk and playful in the remote glens, even on the morning of the cold Friday. Here is our Lapland and Labrador, and for our Esquimaux and Knistenaux, Dog-ribbed Indians, Novazemblaites, and Spitzbergeners, are there not the ice-cutter and woodchopper, the fox, muskrat, and mink?

Still, in the midst of the arctic day, we may trace the summer to its retreats, and sympathize with some contemporary life. Stretched over the brooks, in the midst of the frost-bound meadows, we may observe the submarine cottages of the caddis-worms, the larvæ of the Plicipennes; their small cylindrical cases built around themselves, composed of flags, sticks, grass, and withered leaves, shells, and pebbles, in form and color like the wrecks which strew the bottom, — now drifting along over the pebbly bottom, now whirling in tiny eddies and dashing down steep falls, or sweeping rapidly along with the current, or else swaying to and fro at the end of some grass-blade or root. Anon they will leave their sunken habitations, and, crawling up the stems of plants, or to the surface, like gnats, as perfect insects henceforth, flutter over the surface of the water, or sacrifice their short lives in the flame of our candles at evening. Down yonder little glen the shrubs are drooping under their burden, and the red alderberries contrast with the white ground. Here are the marks of a myriad feet which have already been abroad. The sun rises as proudly over such a glen as over the valley of the Seine or the Tiber, and it seems the residence of a pure and self-subsistent valor, such as they never witnessed, — which never knew defeat nor fear. Here reign the simplicity and purity of a primitive age, and a health and hope far remote from towns and cities. Standing quite alone, far in the forest, while the wind is shaking down snow from the trees, and leaving the only human tracks behind us, we find our reflections of a richer variety than the life of cities. The chickadee and nuthatch are more inspiring society than statesmen and philosophers, and we shall return to these last as to more vulgar companions. In this lonely glen, with its brook draining the slopes, its creased ice and crystals of all hues, where the spruces and hemlocks stand up on either side, and the rush and sere wild oats in the rivulet itself, our lives are more serene and worthy to contemplate.

As the day advances, the heat of the sun is reflected by the hillsides, and we hear a faint but sweet music, where flows the rill released from its fetters, and the icicles are melting on the trees; and the nuthatch and partridge are heard and seen. The south wind melts the snow at noon, and the bare ground appears with its withered grass and leaves, and we are invigorated by the perfume which exhales from it, as by the scent of strong meats.

Let us go into this deserted woodman's hut, and see how he has passed the long winter nights and the short and stormy days. For here man has lived under this south hillside, and it seems a civilized and public spot. We have such associations as when the traveler stands by the ruins of Palmyra or Hecatompolis. Singing birds and flowers perchance have begun to appear here, for flowers as well as weeds follow in the footsteps of man. These hemlocks whispered over his head, these hickory logs were his fuel, and these pitch pine roots kindled his fire; yonder fuming rill in the hollow, whose thin and airy vapor still ascends as busily as ever, though he is far off now, was his well. These hemlock boughs, and the straw upon this raised platform, were his bed, and this broken dish held his drink. But he has not been here this season, for the phœbes built their nest upon this shelf last summer. I find some embers left as if he had but just gone out, where he baked his pot of beans; and while at evening he smoked his pipe, whose stemless bowl lies in the ashes, chatted with his only companion, if perchance he had any, about the depth of the snow on the morrow, already falling fast and thick without, or disputed whether the last sound was the screech of an owl, or the creak of a bough, or imagination only; and through his broad chimney-throat, in the late winter evening, ere he stretched himself upon the straw, he looked up to learn the progress of the storm, and, seeing the bright stars of Cassiopeia's Chair shining brightly down upon him, fell contentedly asleep.

See how many traces from which we may learn the chopper's history! From this stump we may guess the sharpness of his axe, and from the slope of the stroke, on which side he stood, and whether he cut down the tree without going round it or changing hands; and, from the flexure of the splinters, we may know which way it fell. This one chip contains inscribed on it the whole history of the woodchopper and of the world. On this scrap of paper, which held his sugar or salt, perchance, or was the wadding of his gun, sitting on a log in the forest, with what interest we read the tattle of cities, of those larger huts, empty and to let, like this, in High Streets and Broadways. The eaves are dripping on the south side of this simple roof, while the titmouse lisps in the pine and the genial warmth of the sun around the door is somewhat kind and human.

After two seasons, this rude dwelling does not deform the scene. Already the birds resort to it, to build their nests, and you may track to its door the feet of many quadrupeds. Thus, for a long time, nature overlooks the encroachment and profanity of man. The wood still cheerfully and unsuspiciously echoes the strokes of the axe that fells it, and while they are few and seldom, they enhance its wildness, and all the elements strive to naturalize the sound.

Now our path begins to ascend gradually to the top of this high hill, from whose precipitous south side we can look over the broad country of forest and field and river, to the distant snowy mountains. See yonder thin column of smoke curling up through the woods from some invisible farmhouse, the standard raised over some rural homestead. There must be a warmer and more genial spot there below, as where we detect the vapor from a spring forming a cloud above the trees. What fine relations are established between the traveler who discovers this airy column from some eminence in the forest and him who sits below! Up goes the smoke as silently and naturally as the vapor exhales from the leaves, and as busy disposing itself in wreaths as the housewife on the hearth below. It is a hieroglyphic of man's life, and suggests more intimate and important things than the boiling of a pot. Where its fine column rises above the forest, like an ensign, some human life has planted itself, — and such is the beginning of Rome, the establishment of the arts, and the foundation of empires, whether on the prairies of America or the steppes of Asia.

And now we descend again, to the brink of this woodland lake, which lies in a hollow of the hills, as if it were their expressed juice, and that of the leaves which are annually steeped in it. Without outlet or inlet to the eye, it has still its history, in the lapse of its waves, in the rounded pebbles on its shore, and in the pines which grow down to its brink. It has not been idle, though sedentary, but, like Abu Musa, teaches that "sitting still at home is the heavenly way; the going out is the way of the world." Yet in its evaporation it travels as far as any. In summer it is the earth's liquid eye, a mirror in the breast of nature. The sins of the

wood are washed out in it. See how the woods form
an amphitheatre about it, and it is an arena for all the
genialness of nature. All trees direct the traveler to its
brink, all paths seek it out, birds fly to it, quadrupeds
flee to it, and the very ground inclines toward it. It is
nature's saloon, where she has sat down to her toilet.
Consider her silent economy and tidiness; how the
sun comes with his evaporation to sweep the dust
from its surface each morning, and a fresh surface is
constantly welling up; and annually, after whatever
impurities have accumulated herein, its liquid transparency appears again in the spring. In summer a
hushed music seems to sweep across its surface. But now
a plain sheet of snow conceals it from our eyes, except
where the wind has swept the ice bare, and the sere
leaves are gliding from side to side, tacking and veering
on their tiny voyages. Here is one just keeled up against
a pebble on shore, a dry beech leaf, rocking still, as if
it would start again. A skillful engineer, methinks,
might project its course since it fell from the parent
stem. Here are all the elements for such a calculation.
Its present position, the direction of the wind, the level
of the pond, and how much more is given. In its
scarred edges and veins is its log rolled up.

We fancy ourselves in the interior of a larger house.
The surface of the pond is our deal table or sanded floor,
and the woods rise abruptly from its edge, like the walls
of a cottage. The lines set to catch pickerel through
the ice look like a larger culinary preparation, and the
men stand about on the white ground like pieces of
forest furniture. The actions of these men, at the dis-

tance of half a mile over the ice and snow, impress us as when we read the exploits of Alexander in history. They seem not unworthy of the scenery, and as momentous as the conquest of kingdoms.

Again we have wandered through the arches of the wood, until from its skirts we hear the distant booming of ice from yonder bay of the river, as if it were moved by some other and subtler tide than oceans know. To me it has a strange sound of home, thrilling as the voice of one's distant and noble kindred. A mild summer sun shines over forest and lake, and though there is but one green leaf for many rods, yet nature enjoys a serene health. Every sound is fraught with the same mysterious assurance of health, as well now the creaking of the boughs in January, as the soft sough of the wind in July.

> When Winter fringes every bough
> 　With his fantastic wreath,
> And puts the seal of silence now
> 　Upon the leaves beneath;
>
> When every stream in its penthouse
> 　Goes gurgling on its way,
> And in his gallery the mouse
> 　Nibbleth the meadow hay;
>
> Methinks the summer still is nigh,
> 　And lurketh underneath,
> As that same meadow mouse doth lie
> 　Snug in that last year's heath.
>
> And if perchance the chickadee
> 　Lisp a faint note anon,
> The snow is summer's canopy,
> 　Which she herself put on.

Fair blossoms deck the cheerful trees,
   And dazzling fruits depend;
The north wind sighs a summer breeze,
   The nipping frosts to fend,

Bringing glad tidings unto me,
   The while I stand all ear,
Of a serene eternity,
   Which need not winter fear.

Out on the silent pond straightway
   The restless ice doth crack,
And pond sprites merry gambols play
   Amid the deafening rack.

Eager I hasten to the vale,
   As if I heard brave news,
How nature held high festival,
   Which it were hard to lose.

I gambol with my neighbor ice,
   And sympathizing quake,
As each new crack darts in a trice
   Across the gladsome lake.

One with the cricket in the ground,
   And fagot on the hearth,
Resounds the rare domestic sound
   Along the forest path.

Before night we will take a journey on skates along
the course of this meandering river, as full of novelty
to one who sits by the cottage fire all the winter's day,
as if it were over the polar ice, with Captain Parry or
Franklin; following the winding of the stream, now
flowing amid hills, now spreading out into fair meadows,
and forming a myriad coves and bays where the pine

and hemlock overarch. The river flows in the rear of the towns, and we see all things from a new and wilder side. The fields and gardens come down to it with a frankness, and freedom from pretension, which they do not wear on the highway. It is the outside and edge of the earth. Our eyes are not offended by violent contrasts. The last rail of the farmer's fence is some swaying willow bough, which still preserves its freshness, and here at length all fences stop, and we no longer cross any road. We may go far up within the country now by the most retired and level road, never climbing a hill, but by broad levels ascending to the upland meadows. It is a beautiful illustration of the law of obedience, the flow of a river; the path for a sick man, a highway down which an acorn cup may float secure with its freight. Its slight occasional falls, whose precipices would not diversify the landscape, are celebrated by mist and spray, and attract the traveler from far and near. From the remote interior, its current conducts him by broad and easy steps, or by one gentler inclined plane, to the sea. Thus by an early and constant yielding to the inequalities of the ground it secures itself the easiest passage.

No domain of nature is quite closed to man at all times, and now we draw near to the empire of the fishes. Our feet glide swiftly over unfathomed depths, where in summer our line tempted the pout and perch, and where the stately pickerel lurked in the long corridors formed by the bulrushes. The deep, impenetrable marsh, where the heron waded and bittern squatted, is made pervious to our swift shoes, as if a thousand railroads had been made into it. With one impulse we are carried to the cabin of the muskrat, that earliest settler, and see him dart away under the transparent ice, like a furred fish, to his hole in the bank; and we glide rapidly over meadows where lately "the mower whet his scythe," through beds of frozen cranberries mixed with meadow-grass. We skate near to where the blackbird, the pewee, and the kingbird hung their nests over the water, and the hornets builded from the maple in the swamp. How many gay warblers, following the sun, have radiated from this nest of silver birch and thistle-down! On the swamp's outer edge was hung the supermarine village, where no foot penetrated. In this hollow tree the wood duck reared her brood, and slid away each day to forage in yonder fen.

In winter, nature is a cabinet of curiosities, full of dried specimens, in their natural order and position. The meadows and forests are a *hortus siccus*. The leaves and grasses stand perfectly pressed by the air without screw or gum, and the birds' nests are not hung on an artificial twig, but where they builded them. We go about dry-shod to inspect the summer's work in the rank swamp, and see what a growth have got the alders, the willows, and the maples; testifying to how many warm suns, and fertilizing dews and showers. See what strides their boughs took in the luxuriant summer, — and anon these dormant buds will carry them onward and upward another span into the heavens.

Occasionally we wade through fields of snow, under whose depths the river is lost for many rods, to appear again to the right or left, where we least expected; still holding on its way underneath, with a faint, stertorous, rumbling sound, as if, like the bear and marmot, it too had hibernated, and we had followed its faint summer trail to where it earthed itself in snow and ice. At first we should have thought that rivers would be empty and dry in midwinter, or else frozen solid till the spring thawed them; but their volume is not diminished even, for only a superficial cold bridges their surfaces. The thousand springs which feed the lakes and streams are flowing still. The issues of a few surface springs only are closed, and they go to swell the deep reservoirs. Nature's wells are below the frost. The summer brooks are not filled with snow-water, nor does the mower quench his thirst with that alone. The streams are swollen when the snow melts in the spring, because nature's work has been delayed, the water being turned into ice and snow, whose particles are less smooth and round, and do not find their level so soon.

Far over the ice, between the hemlock woods and snow-clad hills, stands the pickerel-fisher, his lines set in some retired cove, like a Finlander, with his arms thrust into the pouches of his dreadnaught; with dull, snowy, fishy thoughts, himself a finless fish, separated a few inches from his race; dumb, erect, and made to be enveloped in clouds and snows, like the pines on shore. In these wild scenes, men stand about in the scenery, or move deliberately and heavily, having sacrificed the sprightliness and vivacity of towns to the dumb sobriety of nature. He does not make the scenery less wild, more than the jays and muskrats, but stands there as a part of it, as the natives are represented in the voyages of early navigators, at Nootka Sound, and on the Northwest coast, with their furs about them, before they were tempted to loquacity by a scrap of iron. He belongs to the natural family of man, and is planted deeper in nature and has more root than the inhabitants of towns. Go to him, ask what luck, and you will learn that he too is a worshiper of the unseen. Hear with what sincere deference and waving gesture in his tone he speaks of the lake pickerel, which he has never seen, his primitive and ideal race of pickerel. He is connected with the shore still, as by a fish-line, and yet remembers the season when he took fish through the ice on the pond, while the peas were up in his garden at home.

But now, while we have loitered, the clouds have gathered again, and a few straggling snowflakes are beginning to descend. Faster and faster they fall, shutting out the distant objects from sight. The snow falls on every wood and field, and no crevice is forgotten; by the river and the pond, on the hill and in the valley. Quadrupeds are confined to their coverts and the birds sit upon their perches this peaceful hour. There is not so much sound as in fair weather, but silently and gradually every slope, and the gray walls and fences, and the polished ice, and the sere leaves, which were not buried before, are concealed, and the tracks of men and beasts are lost. With so little effort does nature reassert her rule and blot out the traces of men. Hear how Homer has described the same: "The snowflakes fall thick and fast on a winter's day. The winds are lulled, and the snow falls incessant, covering the tops of the mountains, and the hills, and the plains where the lotus-tree grows, and the cultivated fields, and they are falling

by the inlets and shores of the foaming sea, but are
silently dissolved by the waves." The snow levels all
things, and infolds them deeper in the bosom of nature,
as, in the slow summer, vegetation creeps up to the
entablature of the temple, and the turrets of the castle,
and helps her to prevail over art.

The surly night-wind rustles through the wood, and
warns us to retrace our steps, while the sun goes down
behind the thickening storm, and birds seek their roosts,
and cattle their stalls.

> "Drooping the lab'rer ox
> Stands covered o'er with snow, and *now* demands
> The fruit of all his toil."

Though winter is represented in the almanac as an old
man, facing the wind and sleet, and drawing his cloak
about him, we rather think of him as a merry woodchopper, and warm-blooded youth, as blithe as summer.
The unexplored grandeur of the storm keeps up the
spirits of the traveler. It does not trifle with us, but has
a sweet earnestness. In winter we lead a more inward
life. Our hearts are warm and cheery, like cottages
under drifts, whose windows and doors are half concealed, but from whose chimneys the smoke cheerfully
ascends. The imprisoning drifts increase the sense of
comfort which the house affords, and in the coldest days
we are content to sit over the hearth and see the sky
through the chimney-top, enjoying the quiet and serene
life that may be had in a warm corner by the chimney-
side, or feeling our pulse by listening to the low of cattle
in the street, or the sound of the flail in distant barns all
the long afternoon. No doubt a skillful physician could

determine our health by observing how these simple and natural sounds affected us. We enjoy now, not an Oriental, but a Boreal leisure, around warm stoves and fireplaces, and watch the shadow of motes in the sunbeams.

Sometimes our fate grows too homely and familiarly serious ever to be cruel. Consider how for three months the human destiny is wrapped in furs. The good Hebrew Revelation takes no cognizance of all this cheerful snow. Is there no religion for the temperate and frigid zones? We know of no scripture which records the pure benignity of the gods on a New England winter night. Their praises have never been sung, only their wrath deprecated. The best scripture, after all, records but a meagre faith. Its saints live reserved and austere. Let a brave, devout man spend the year in the woods of Maine or Labrador, and see if the Hebrew Scriptures speak adequately to his condition and experience, from the setting in of winter to the breaking up of the ice.

Now commences the long winter evening around the farmer's hearth, when the thoughts of the indwellers travel far abroad, and men are by nature and necessity charitable and liberal to all creatures. Now is the happy resistance to cold, when the farmer reaps his reward, and thinks of his preparedness for winter, and, through the glittering panes, sees with equanimity "the mansion of the northern bear," for now the storm is over, —

"The full ethereal round,
Infinite worlds disclosing to the view,
Shines out intensely keen; and all one cope
Of starry glitter glows from pole to pole."